COMPILATION OF SELECTED
UNITED STATES COAST GUARD AND
MARITIME TRANSPORTATION RELATED
LAWS
VOLUME 4

Updated through the 118th Congress.

Prepared By M. TWINCHEK

2025

Forward

T his Compilation of Selected United States Coast Guard and Maritime Transportation Related Laws is a resource for those interested in U.S. laws governing the Coast Guard. This compilation includes laws governing United States Coast Guard and its establishment; the Coast Guard Academy; water pollution; lifesaving; ports and waterways; merchant marines; and other aspects of the United States Coast Guard.

The materials included comes from publicly available, open source information, prepared for the public by the Office of the Legislative Counsel of the U.S. House of Representatives and the Office of the Law Revision Counsel.

Items listed as a Statute Compilation do not appear in the U.S. Code or that have been classified to a title of the U.S. Code that has not been enacted into positive law. Each Statute Compilation incorporates the amendments made to the underlying statute since it was originally enacted and are current as of the date noted.

This compilation is not an official document and should not be cited as evidence of any law. The official version of Federal law is found in the United States Statutes at Large and in the U.S. Code, the legal effect of which is established in sections 112 and 204, respectively, of title 1, United States Code.

A special thanks is extended to the Office of Law Revision Counsel and the House Office of the Legislative Counsel for providing the U.S. Code and statute compilations; and to the Government Publications Office for hosting and making these available for use to the public. An additional thank you is offered to the staff of the House and Senate Committees who were gracious in responding to inquiries and providing background information on the legislation included.

Questions and comments may be directed to:
M. Twinchek
Email: mtwinchek@outlook.com

Contents

SECURITY AND ACCOUNTABILITY FOR EVERY PORT ACT OF 2006 - SEC. 232

PUBLIC LAW 109-347
AS AMENDED THROUGH P.L. 115-254

Security and Accountability For Every Port Act of 2006

[(Public Law 109–347; Approved October 13, 2006)]

[As Amended Through P.L. 115–254, Enacted October 5, 2018]

AN ACT To improve maritime and cargo security through enhanced layered defenses, and for other purposes.

Be it enacted by the Senate and House of Representatives of the United States of America in Congress assembled,

SECTION 1. SHORT TITLE; TABLE OF CONTENTS.

(a) [6 U.S.C. 901 note] SHORT TITLE.—This Act may be cited as the "Security and Accountability For Every Port Act of 2006" or the "SAFE Port Act".

(b) TABLE OF CONTENTS.—The table of contents for this Act is as follows:

TITLE II—SECURITY OF THE INTERNATIONAL SUPPLY CHAIN

* * * * * * *

Subtitle C—Miscellaneous Provisions

* * * * * * *

SEC. 232. [6 U.S.C. 982] SCREENING AND SCANNING OF CARGO CONTAINERS.

(a) ONE HUNDRED PERCENT SCREENING OF CARGO CONTAINERS AND 100 PERCENT SCANNING OF HIGH-RISK CONTAINERS.—

(1) SCREENING OF CARGO CONTAINERS.—The Secretary shall ensure that 100 percent of the cargo containers originating outside the United States and unloaded at a United States seaport undergo a screening to identify high-risk containers.

(2) SCANNING OF HIGH-RISK CONTAINERS.—The Secretary shall ensure that 100 percent of the containers that have been identified as high-risk under paragraph (1), or through other means, are scanned or searched before such containers leave a United States seaport facility.

(b) FULL-SCALE IMPLEMENTATION.—The Secretary, in coordination with the Secretary of Energy and foreign partners, as appropriate, shall ensure integrated scanning systems are fully deployed to scan, using nonintrusive imaging equipment and radiation detection equipment, all containers entering the United States before such containers arrive in the United States as soon as possible, but not before the Secretary determines that the integrated scanning system—

(1) meets the requirements set forth in section 231(c);

(2) has a sufficiently low false alarm rate for use in the supply chain;

(3) is capable of being deployed and operated at ports overseas;

(4) is capable of integrating, as necessary, with existing systems;

(5) does not significantly impact trade capacity and flow of cargo at foreign or United States ports; and

(6) provides an automated notification of questionable or high-risk cargo as a trigger for further inspection by appropriately trained personnel.

(c) REPORT.—Not later than 6 months after the submission of a report under section 231(d), and every 6 months thereafter, the Secretary shall submit a report to the appropriate congressional committees describing the status of full-scale deployment under subsection (b) and the cost of deploying the system at each foreign port at which the integrated scanning systems are deployed.

* * * * * * *

SEC. 233. [6 U.S.C. 983] INSPECTION TECHNOLOGY AND TRAINING.

(a) IN GENERAL.—The Secretary, in coordination with the Secretary of State, the Secretary of Energy, and appropriate representatives of other Federal agencies, may provide technical assistance, equipment, and training to facilitate the implementation of supply chain security measures at ports designated under the Container Security Initiative.

(b) ACQUISITION AND TRAINING.—Unless otherwise prohibited by law, the Secretary may—

(1) lease, loan, provide, or otherwise assist in the deployment of nonintrusive inspection and radiation detection equipment at foreign land and sea ports under such terms and conditions as the Secretary prescribes, including nonreimbursable loans or the transfer of ownership of equipment; and

(2) provide training and technical assistance for domestic or foreign personnel responsible for operating or maintaining such equipment.

SEC. 234. FOREIGN PORT ASSESSMENTS.

Section 70108 of title 46, United States Code, is amended by adding at the end the following:

"(d) PERIODIC REASSESSMENT.—The Secretary, acting through the Commandant of the Coast Guard, shall reassess the effectiveness of antiterrorism measures maintained at ports as described under subsection (a) and of procedures described in subsection (b) not less than once every 3 years."

[Section 235 was repealed by section 1816(f) of division J of Public Law 115–254.]

SEC. 236. [6 U.S.C. 985] INFORMATION SHARING RELATING TO

SUPPLY CHAIN SECURITY COOPERATION.

(a) PURPOSES.—The purposes of this section are—

(1) to establish continuing liaison and to provide for supply chain security cooperation between Department and the private sector; and

(2) to provide for regular and timely interchange of information between the private sector and the Department concerning developments and security risks in the supply chain environment.

(b) SYSTEM.—The Secretary shall develop a system to collect from and share appropriate risk information related to the supply chain with the private sector entities determined appropriate by the Secretary.

(c) CONSULTATION.—In developing the system under subsection (b), the Secretary shall consult with the Commercial Operations Advisory Committee and a broad range of public and private sector entities likely to utilize the system, including importers, exporters, carriers, customs brokers, and freight forwarders, among other parties.

(d) INDEPENDENTLY OBTAINED INFORMATION.—Nothing in this section shall be construed to limit or otherwise affect the ability of a Federal, State, or local government entity, under applicable law, to obtain supply chain security information, including any information lawfully and properly disclosed generally or broadly to the public and to use such information in any manner permitted by law.

(e) AUTHORITY TO ISSUE WARNINGS.—The Secretary may provide advisories, alerts, and warnings to relevant companies, targeted sectors, other governmental entities, or the general public regarding potential risks to the supply chain as appropriate. In issuing a warning, the Secretary shall take appropriate actions to protect from disclosure—

(1) the source of any voluntarily submitted supply chain security information that forms the basis for the warning; and

(2) information that is proprietary, business sensitive, relates specifically to the submitting person or entity, or is otherwise not appropriately in the public domain.

* * * * * * *

NONINDIGENOUS AQUATIC NUISANCE PREVENTION AND CONTROL ACT OF 1990

PUBLIC LAW 101-646
AS AMENDED THROUGH P.L. 117-328

NONINDIGENOUS AQUATIC NUISANCE PREVENTION
AND CONTROL ACT OF 1990

[Public Law 101–646; Approved November 29, 1990]

[As Amended Through P.L. 117–328, Enacted December 29, 2022]

AN ACT To prevent and control infestations of the coastal inland waters of the United States by the zebra mussel and other nonindigenous aquatic nuisance species, to reauthorize the National Sea Grant College Program, and for other purposes.

Be it enacted by the Senate and House of Representatives of the United States of America in Congress assembled,

TITLE I—AQUATIC NUISANCE PREVENTION AND CONTROL

Subtitle A—General Provisions

SECTION 1001. SHORT TITLE.
This title may be cited as the "Nonindigenous Aquatic Nuisance Prevention and Control Act of 1990".
[16 U.S.C. 4701 nt]

SEC. 1002. FINDINGS AND PURPOSES.
(a) FINDINGS.—The Congress finds that—

(1) the discharge of untreated water in the ballast tanks of vessels and through other means results in unintentional introductions of nonindigenous species to fresh, brackish, and saltwater environments;

(2) when environmental conditions are favorable, nonindigenous species become established, may compete with

or prey upon native species of plants, fish, and wildlife, may carry diseases or parasites that affect native species, and may disrupt the aquatic environment and economy of affected nearshore areas;

(3) the zebra mussel was unintentionally introduced into the Great Lakes and has infested—

(A) waters south of the Great Lakes, into a good portion of the Mississippi River drainage;

(B) waters west of the Great Lakes, into the Arkansas River in Oklahoma; and

(C) waters east of the Great Lakes, into the Hudson River and Lake Champlain;

(4) the potential economic disruption to communities affected by the zebra mussel due to its colonization of water pipes, boat hulls and other hard surfaces has been estimated at $5,000,000,000 by the year 2000, and the potential disruption to the diversity and abundance of native fish and other species by the zebra mussel and ruffe, round goby, and other nonindigenous species could be severe;

(5) the zebra mussel was discovered on Lake Champlain during 1993 and the opportunity exists to act quickly to establish zebra mussel controls before Lake Champlain is further infested and management costs escalate;

(6) in 1992, the zebra mussel was discovered at the northernmost reaches of the Chesapeake Bay watershed;

(7) the zebra mussel poses an imminent risk of invasion in the main waters of the Chesapeake Bay;

(8) since the Chesapeake Bay is the largest recipient of foreign ballast water on the East Coast, there is a risk of further invasions of other nonindigenous species;

(9) the zebra mussel is only one example of thousands of nonindigenous species that have become established in waters of the United States and may be causing economic and ecological degradation with respect to the natural resources of waters of the United States;

(10) since their introduction in the early 1980's in ballast water discharges, ruffe—

(A) have caused severe declines in populations of other

species of fish in Duluth Harbor (in Minnesota and Wisconsin);

(B) have spread to Lake Huron; and

(C) are likely to spread quickly to most other waters in North America if action is not taken promptly to control their spread;

(11) examples of nonindigenous species that, as of the date of enactment of the National Invasive Species Act of 1996, infest coastal waters of the United States and that have the potential for causing adverse economic and ecological effects include—

(A) the mitten crab (Eriocher sinensis) that has become established on the Pacific Coast;

(B) the green crab (Carcinus maenas) that has become established in the coastal waters of the Atlantic Ocean;

(C) the brown mussel (Perna perna) that has become established along the Gulf of Mexico; and

(D) certain shellfish pathogens;

(12) many aquatic nuisance vegetation species, such as Eurasian watermilfoil, hydrilla, water hyacinth, and water chestnut, have been introduced to waters of the United States from other parts of the world causing or having a potential to cause adverse environmental, ecological, and economic effects;

(13) if preventive management measures are not taken nationwide to prevent and control unintentionally introduced nonindigenous aquatic species in a timely manner, further introductions and infestations of species that are as destructive as, or more destructive than, the zebra mussel or the ruffe infestations may occur;

(14) once introduced into waters of the United States, aquatic nuisance species are unintentionally transported and introduced into inland lakes and rivers by recreational boaters, commercial barge traffic, and a variety of other pathways; and

(15) resolving the problems associated with aquatic nuisance species will require the participation and cooperation of the Federal Government and State governments, and investment in the development of prevention technologies.

(b) PURPOSES.—The purposes of this Act are—

(1) to prevent unintentional introduction and dispersal of nonindigenous species into waters of the United States through ballast water management and other requirements;

(2) to coordinate federally conducted, funded, or authorized research, prevention control, information dissemination and other activities regarding the zebra mussel and other aquatic nuisance species;

(3) to develop and carry out environmentally sound control methods to prevent, monitor and control unintentional introductions of nonindigenous species from pathways other than ballast water exchange;

(4) to understand and minimize economic and ecological impacts of nonindigenous aquatic nuisance species that become established, including the zebra mussel; and

(5) to establish a program of research and technology development and assistance to States in the management and removal of zebra mussels.

[16 U.S.C. 4701]

SEC. 1003. DEFINITIONS.

As used in this Act, the term—

(1) "aquatic nuisance species" means a nonindigenous species that threatens the diversity or abundance of native species or the ecological stability of infested waters, or commercial, agricultural, aquacultural or recreational activities dependent on such waters;

(2) "Assistant Secretary" means the Assistant Secretary of the Army (Civil Works);

(3) "ballast water" means any water and associated sediments used to manipulate the trim and stability of a vessel;

(4) "Director" means the Director of the United States Fish and Wildlife Service;

(5) "exclusive economic zone" means the Exclusive Economic Zone of the United States established by Proclamation Number 5030, dated March 10, 1983, and the equivalent zone of Canada;

(6) "environmentally sound" methods, efforts, actions or programs means methods, efforts, actions or programs to

prevent introductions or control infestations of aquatic nuisance species that minimize adverse impacts to the structure and function of an ecosystem and adverse effects on non-target organisms and ecosystems and emphasize integrated pest management techniques and nonchemical measures;

(7) "Great Lakes" means Lake Ontario, Lake Erie, Lake Huron (including Lake St. Clair), Lake Michigan, Lake Superior, and the connecting channels (Saint Mary's River, Saint Clair River, Detroit River, Niagara River, and Saint Lawrence River to the Canadian Border), and includes all other bodies of water within the drainage basin of such lakes and connecting channels.

(8) "Great Lakes region" means the 8 States that border on the Great Lakes;

(9) "Indian tribe" means any Indian tribe, band, nation, or other organized group or community, including any Alaska Native village or regional corporation (as defined in or established pursuant to the Alaska Native Claims Settlement Act (43 U.S.C. 1601 et seq.)) that is recognized as eligible for the special programs and services provided by the United States to Indians because of their status as Indians;

(10) "interstate organization" means an entity—

(A) established by—

(i) an interstate compact that is approved by Congress;

(ii) a Federal statute; or

(iii) a treaty or other international agreement with respect to which the United States is a party; and

(B)(i) that represents 2 or more—

(I) States or political subdivisions thereof; or

(II) Indian tribes; or

(ii) that represents—

(I) 1 or more States or political subdivisions thereof; and

(II) 1 or more Indian tribes; or

(iii) that represents the Federal Government and

1 or more foreign governments; and

(C) has jurisdiction over, serves as forum for coordinating, or otherwise has a role or responsibility for the management of, any land or other natural resource;

(11) "nonindigenous species" means any species or other viable biological material that enters an ecosystem beyond its historic range, including any such organism transferred from one country into another;

(12) "Secretary" means the Secretary of the department in which the Coast Guard is operating;

(13) "State" means each of the several States, the District of Columbia, American Samoa, Guam, Puerto Rico, the Northern Mariana Islands, and the Virgin Islands of the United States;

(14) "recreational vessel" has the meaning given that term in section 502 of the Federal Water Pollution Control Act (33 U.S.C. 1362);

(15) "Task Force" means the Aquatic Nuisance Species Task Force established under section 1201 of this Act;

(16) "territorial sea" means the belt of the sea measured from the baseline of the United States determined in accordance with international law, as set forth in Presidential Proclamation Number 5928, dated December 27, 1988;

(17) "Under Secretary" means the Under Secretary of Commerce for Oceans and Atmosphere;

(18) "waters of the United States" means the navigable waters and the territorial sea of the United States; and

(19) "unintentional introduction" means an introduction of nonindigenous species that occurs as the result of activities other than the purposeful or intentional introduction of the species involved, such as the transport of nonindigenous species in ballast or in water used to transport fish, mollusks or crustaceans for aquaculture or other purposes.

[16 U.S.C. 4702]

Subtitle B—Prevention of Unintentional Introductions of Nonindigenous Aquatic Species [Section

1101 was repealed by section 903(a)(2)(A)(i) of P.L. 115-282.]

SEC. 1102. NATIONAL BALLAST WATER MANAGEMENT INFORMATION.

(a) STUDIES ON INTRODUCTION OF AQUATIC NUISANCE SPECIES BY VESSELS.—

(1) BALLAST EXCHANGE STUDY.—The Task Force, in cooperation with the Secretary, shall conduct a study—

(A) to assess the environmental effects of ballast water exchange on the diversity and abundance of native species in receiving estuarine, marine, and fresh waters of the United States; and

(B) to identify areas within the waters of the United States and the exclusive economic zone, if any, where the exchange of ballast water does not pose a threat of infestation or spread of aquatic nuisance species in the Great Lakes and other waters of the United States.

(2) BIOLOGICAL STUDY.—The Task Force, in cooperation with the Secretary, shall conduct a study to determine whether aquatic nuisance species threaten the ecological characteristics and economic uses of Lake Champlain and other waters of the United States other than the Great Lakes.

(3) SHIPPING STUDY.—The Secretary shall conduct a study to determine the need for controls on vessels entering waters of the United States, other than the Great Lakes, to minimize the risk of unintentional introduction and dispersal of aquatic nuisance species in those waters. The study shall include an examination of—

(A) the degree to which shipping may be a major pathway of transmission of aquatic nuisance species in those waters;

(B) possible alternatives for controlling introduction of those species through shipping; and

(C) the feasibility of implementing regional versus national control measures.

(b) ECOLOGICAL AND BALLAST WATER DISCHARGE SURVEYS.—

(1) ECOLOGICAL SURVEYS.—

(A) IN GENERAL.—The Task Force, in cooperation with

the Secretary, shall conduct ecological surveys of the Chesapeake Bay, San Francisco Bay, and Honolulu Harbor and, as necessary, of other estuaries of national significance and other waters that the Task Force determines—

(i) to be highly susceptible to invasion by aquatic nuisance species resulting from ballast water operations and other operations of vessels; and

(ii) to require further study.

(B) REQUIREMENTS FOR SURVEYS.—In conducting the surveys under this paragraph, the Task Force shall, with respect to each such survey—

(i) examine the attributes and patterns of invasions of aquatic nuisance species; and

(ii) provide an estimate of the effectiveness of ballast water management and other vessel management guidelines issued and regulations promulgated under this subtitle in abating invasions of aquatic nuisance species in the waters that are the subject of the survey.

(2) BALLAST WATER DISCHARGE SURVEYS.—

(A) IN GENERAL.—The Secretary, in cooperation with the Task Force, shall conduct surveys of ballast water discharge rates and practices in the waters referred to in paragraph (1)(A) on the basis of the criteria under clauses (i) and (ii) of such paragraph.

(B) REQUIREMENTS FOR SURVEYS.—In conducting the surveys under this paragraph, the Secretary shall—

(i) examine the rate of, and trends in, ballast water discharge in the waters that are the subject of the survey; and

(ii) assess the effectiveness of voluntary guidelines issued, and regulations promulgated, under this subtitle in altering ballast water discharge practices to reduce the probability of accidental introductions of aquatic nuisance species.

(3) COLUMBIA RIVER.—The Secretary, in cooperation with the Task Force and academic institutions in each of the States

affected, shall conduct an ecological and ballast water discharge survey of the Columbia River system consistent with the requirements of paragraphs (1) and (2).

(c) REPORTS.—

(1) BALLAST EXCHANGE.—Not later than 18 months after the date of enactment of this Act and prior to the effective date of the regulations issued under section 1101(b) (as in effect on the day before the date of enactment of the Vessel Incidental Discharge Act of 2018), the Task Force shall submit a report to the Congress that presents the results of the study required under subsection (a)(1) and makes recommendations with respect to such regulations.

(2) BIOLOGICAL AND SHIPPING STUDIES.—Not later than 18 months after the date of enactment of this Act, the Secretary and the Task Force shall each submit to the Congress a report on the results of their respective studies under paragraphs (2) and (3) of subsection (a).

(d) NEGOTIATIONS.—The Secretary, working through the International Maritime Organization, is encouraged to enter into negotiations with the governments of foreign countries concerning the planning and implementation of measures aimed at the prevention and control of unintentional introductions of aquatic nuisance species in coastal waters.

(e) REGIONAL RESEARCH GRANTS.—Out of amounts appropriated to carry out this subsection for a fiscal year, the Under Secretary may—

(1) make available not to exceed $750,000 to fund research on aquatic nuisance species prevention and control in the Chesapeake Bay through grants, to be competitively awarded and subject to peer review, to universities and research institutions;

(2) make available not to exceed $500,000 to fund research on aquatic nuisance species prevention and control in the Gulf of Mexico through grants, to be competitively awarded and subject to peer review, to universities and research institutions;

(3) make available not to exceed $500,000 to fund research on aquatic nuisance species prevention and control for the Pacific Coast through grants, to be competitively awarded and subject to peer review, to universities and research institutions;

(4) make available not to exceed $500,000 to fund research on aquatic nuisance species prevention and control for the Atlantic Coast through grants, to be competitively awarded and subject to peer review, to universities and research institutions; and

(5) make available not to exceed $750,000 to fund research on aquatic nuisance species prevention and control in the San Francisco Bay-Delta Estuary through grants, to be competitively awarded and subject to peer review, to universities and research institutions.

(f) NATIONAL BALLAST INFORMATION CLEARINGHOUSE.—

(1) IN GENERAL.—The Secretary shall develop and maintain, in consultation and cooperation with the Task Force and the Smithsonian Institution (acting through the Smithsonian Environmental Research Center), a clearinghouse of national data concerning—

(A) ballasting practices;

(B) compliance with the guidelines issued pursuant to section 1101(c) (as in effect on the day before the date of enactment of the Vessel Incidental Discharge Act of 2018); and

(C) any other information obtained by the Task Force under subsection (b).

(2) BALLAST WATER REPORTING REQUIREMENTS.—

(A) IN GENERAL.—The owner or operator of a vessel subject to this title shall submit to the National Ballast Information Clearinghouse, by not later than 6 hours after the arrival of the vessel at a United States port or place of destination, the ballast water management report form approved by the Office of Management and Budget numbered OMB 1625–0069 (or a successor form), unless the vessel is operating exclusively on a voyage between ports or places within contiguous portions of a single Captain of the Port Zone.

(B) MULTIPLE DISCHARGES.—The owner or operator of a vessel subject to this title may submit a single report under subparagraph (A) for multiple ballast water discharges within a single port or place of destination during the same voyage.

(C) ADVANCE REPORT TO STATES.—A State may require the owner or operator of a vessel subject to this title to submit directly to the State, or to an appropriate regional forum, a ballast water management report form—

(i) not later than 24 hours prior to arrival at a United States port or place of destination in the State, if the voyage of the vessel is anticipated to exceed 24 hours; or

(ii) before departing the port or place of departure, if the voyage of the vessel to the United States port or place of destination is not anticipated to exceed 24 hours.

(3) VESSEL REPORTING DATA.—

(A) DISSEMINATION TO STATES.—On receipt of a ballast water management report under paragraph (2), the National Ballast Information Clearinghouse shall—

(i) in the case of a form submitted electronically, immediately disseminate the report to interested States; or

(ii) in the case of a form submitted by means other than electronically, disseminate the report to interested States as soon as practicable.

(B) AVAILABILITY TO PUBLIC.—Not later than 30 days after the date of receipt of a ballast water management report under paragraph (2), the National Ballast Information Clearinghouse shall make the data in the report fully and readily available to the public in a searchable and fully retrievable electronic format.

(4) REPORT.—

(A) IN GENERAL.—Not later than July 1, 2019, and annually thereafter, the Secretary shall prepare and submit a report in accordance with this paragraph.

(B) CONTENTS.—Each report under this paragraph shall synthesize and analyze the data described in paragraph (1) for the preceding 2-year period to evaluate nationwide status and trends relating to—

(i) ballast water delivery and management; and

(ii) invasions of aquatic nuisance species resulting

from ballast water.

(C) DEVELOPMENT.—The Secretary shall prepare each report under this paragraph in consultation and cooperation with—

(i) the Task Force; and

(ii) the Smithsonian Institution (acting through the Smithsonian Environmental Research Center).

(D) SUBMISSION.—The Secretary shall—

(i) submit each report under this paragraph to—

(I) the Task Force;

(II) the Committee on Commerce, Science, and Transportation of the Senate; and

(III) the Committee on Transportation and Infrastructure of the House of Representatives; and

(ii) make each report available to the public.

(5) WORKING GROUP.—Not later than 1 year after the date of enactment of this paragraph, the Secretary shall establish a working group, including members from the National Ballast Information Clearinghouse and States with ballast water management programs, to establish a process for compiling and readily sharing Federal and State commercial vessel reporting and enforcement data regarding compliance with this Act.

[16 U.S.C. 4712]

SEC. 1103. ARMED SERVICES BALLAST WATER PROGRAMS.

(a) DEPARTMENT OF DEFENSE VESSELS.—Subject to operational conditions, the Secretary of Defense, in consultation with the Secretary, the Task Force, and the International Maritime Organization, shall implement a ballast water management program for seagoing vessels of the Department of Defense to minimize the risk of introduction of nonindigenous species from releases of ballast water.

(b) COAST GUARD VESSELS.—Subject to operational conditions, the Secretary, in consultation with the Task Force and the International Maritime Organization, shall implement a ballast water management program for seagoing vessels of the Coast Guard to minimize the risk of introduction of nonindigenous species from releases of ballast water.

[16 U.S.C. 4713]

SEC. 1104. BALLAST WATER MANAGEMENT DEMONSTRATION PROGRAM.

(a) TECHNOLOGIES AND PRACTICES DEFINED.—For purposes of this section, the term "technologies and practices" means those technologies and practices that—

(1) may be retrofitted—

(A) on existing vessels or incorporated in new vessel designs; and

(B) on existing land-based ballast water treatment facilities;

(2) may be designed into new water treatment facilities;

(3) are operationally practical;

(4) are safe for a vessel and crew;

(5) are environmentally sound;

(6) are cost-effective;

(7) a vessel operator is capable of monitoring; and

(8) are effective against a broad range of aquatic nuisance species.

(b) DEMONSTRATION PROGRAM.—

(1) IN GENERAL.—During the 18-month period beginning on the date that funds are made available by appropriations pursuant to section 1301(e), the Secretary of the Interior and the Secretary of Commerce, with the concurrence of and in cooperation with the Secretary, shall conduct a ballast water management demonstration program to demonstrate technologies and practices to prevent aquatic nonindigenous species from being introduced into and spread through ballast water in the Great Lakes and other waters of the United States.

(2) LOCATION.—The installation and construction of the technologies and practices used in the demonstration program conducted under this subsection shall be performed in the United States.

(3) VESSEL SELECTION.—In demonstrating technologies and practices on vessels under this subsection, the Secretary of the

Interior and the Secretary of Commerce, shall—

(A) use only vessels that—

(i) are approved by the Secretary;

(ii) have ballast water systems conducive to testing aboard-vessel or land-based technologies and practices applicable to a significant number of merchant vessels; and

(iii) are—

(I) publicly or privately owned; and

(II) in active use for trade or other cargo shipment purposes during the demonstration;

(B) select vessels for participation in the program by giving priority consideration—

(i) first, to vessels documented under chapter 121 of title 46, United States Code;

(ii) second, to vessels that are a majority owned by citizens of the United States, as determined by the Secretary; and

(iii) third, to any other vessels that regularly call on ports in the United States; and

(C) seek to use a variety of vessel types, including vessels that—

(i) call on ports in the United States and on the Great Lakes; and

(ii) are operated along major coasts of the United States and inland waterways, including the San Francisco Bay and Chesapeake Bay.

(4) SELECTION OF TECHNOLOGIES AND PRACTICES.—In selecting technologies and practices for demonstration under this subsection, the Secretary of the Interior and the Secretary of Commerce shall give priority consideration to technologies and practices identified as promising by the National Research Council Marine Board of the National Academy of Sciences in its report on ships' ballast water operations issued in July 1996.

(5) REPORT.—Not later than 3 years after the date of enactment of the National Invasive Species Act of 1996, the Secretary of the Interior and the Secretary of Commerce shall

prepare and submit a report to the Congress on the demonstration program conducted pursuant to this section. The report shall include findings and recommendations of the Secretary of the Interior and the Secretary of Commerce concerning technologies and practices.

(c) AUTHORITIES; CONSULTATION AND COOPERATION WITH INTERNATIONAL MARITIME ORGANIZATION AND TASK FORCE.—

(1) AUTHORITIES.—In conducting the demonstration program under subsection (b), the Secretary of the Interior may—

(A) enter into cooperative agreements with appropriate officials of other agencies of the Federal Government, agencies of States and political subdivisions thereof, and private entities;

(B) accept funds, facilities, equipment, or personnel from other Federal agencies; and

(C) accept donations of property and services.

(2) CONSULTATION AND COOPERATION.—The Secretary of the Interior shall consult and cooperate with the International Maritime Organization and the Task Force in carrying out this section.

[16 U.S.C. 4714]

Subtitle C—Prevention and Control of Aquatic Nuisance Species Dispersal

SEC. 1201. ESTABLISHMENT OF TASK FORCE.

(a) TASK FORCE.—There is hereby established an "Aquatic Nuisance Species Task Force".

(b) MEMBERSHIP.—Membership of the Task Force shall consist of—

(1) the Director;

(2) the Under Secretary;

(3) the Administrator of the Environmental Protection Agency;

(4) the Commandant of the United States Coast Guard;

(5) the Assistant Secretary;

(6) the Secretary of Agriculture;

(7) the Director of the National Park Service;

(8) the Director of the Bureau of Land Management;

(9) the Commissioner of Reclamation; and

(10) the head of any other Federal agency that the chairpersons designated under subsection (d) deem appropriate.

(c) EX OFFICIO MEMBERS.—The chairpersons designated under subsection (d) shall invite representatives of the Great Lakes Commission, the Patrick Leahy Lake Champlain Basin Program, the Chesapeake Bay Program, the San Francisco Bay-Delta Estuary Program,and State agencies and other governmental entities to participate as ex officio members of the Task Force.

(d) CHAIRPERSONS.—The Director and the Under Secretary shall serve as co-chairpersons of the Task Force and shall be jointly responsible, and are authorized to undertake such activities as may be necessary, for carrying out this subtitle in consultation and cooperation with the other members of the Task Force.

(e) MEMORANDUM OF UNDERSTANDING.—Within six months of the date of enactment of this Act, the Director and the Under Secretary shall develop a memorandum of understanding that describes the role of each in jointly carrying out this subtitle.

(f) COORDINATION.—Each Task Force member shall coordinate any action to carry out this subtitle with any such action by other members of the Task Force, and regional, State and local entities.

(g) OBSERVERS.—The chairpersons designated under subsection (d) may invite representatives of nongovernmental entities to participate as observers of the Task Force.

[16 U.S.C. 4721]

SEC. 1202. AQUATIC NUISANCE SPECIES PROGRAM.

(a) IN GENERAL.—The Task Force shall develop and implement a program for waters of the United States to prevent introduction and dispersal of aquatic nuisance species; to monitor, control and study such species; and to disseminate related information.

(b) CONTENT.—The program developed under subsection (a) shall—

(1) identify the goals, priorities, and approaches for aquatic

nuisance species prevention, monitoring, control, education and research to be conducted or funded by the Federal Government;

(2) describe the specific prevention, monitoring, control, education and research activities to be conducted by each Task Force member;

(3) coordinate aquatic nuisance species programs and activities of Task Force members and affected State agencies;

(4) describe the role of each Task Force member in implementing the elements of the program as set forth in this subtitle;

(5) include recommendations for funding to implement elements of the program; and

(6) develop a demonstration program of prevention, monitoring, control, education and research for the zebra mussel, to be implemented in the Great Lakes and any other waters infested, or likely to become infested in the near future, by the zebra mussel.

(c) PREVENTION.—

(1) IN GENERAL.—The Task Force shall establish and implement measures, within the program developed under subsection (a), to minimize the risk of introduction of aquatic nuisance species to waters of the United States, including—

(A) identification of pathways by which aquatic organisms are introduced to waters of the United States;

(B) assessment of the risk that an aquatic organism carried by an identified pathway may become an aquatic nuisance species; and

(C) evaluation of whether measures to prevent introductions of aquatic nuisance species are effective and environmentally sound.

(2) IMPLEMENTATION.—Whenever the Task Force determines that there is a substantial risk of unintentional introduction of an aquatic nuisance species by an identified pathway and that the adverse consequences of such an introduction are likely to be substantial, the Task Force shall, acting through the appropriate Federal agency, and after an opportunity for public comment, carry out cooperative, environmentally sound efforts with regional, State and local

entities to minimize the risk of such an introduction.

(d) MONITORING.—The Task Force shall establish and implement monitoring measures, within the program developed under subsection (a), to—

(1) detect unintentional introductions of aquatic nuisance species;

(2) determine the dispersal of aquatic nuisance species after introduction; and

(3) provide for the early detection and prevention of infestations of aquatic nuisance species in unaffected drainage basins.

(e) CONTROL.—

(1) IN GENERAL.—The Task Force may develop cooperative efforts, within the program established under subsection (a), to control established aquatic nuisance species to minimize the risk of harm to the environment and the public health and welfare. For purposes of this Act, control efforts include eradication of infestations, reductions of populations, development of means of adapting human activities and public facilities to accommodate infestations, and prevention of the spread of aquatic nuisance species from infested areas. Such control efforts shall be developed in consultation with affected Federal agencies, States, Indian Tribes, local governments, interjurisdictional organizations, and other appropriate entities. Control actions authorized by this section shall be based on the best available scientific information and shall be conducted in an environmentally sound manner.

(2) DECISIONS.—The Task Force or any other affected agency or entity may recommend that the Task Force initiate a control effort. In determining whether a control program is warranted, the Task Force shall evaluate the need for control (including the projected consequences of no control and less than full control); the technical and biological feasibility and cost-effectiveness of alternative control strategies and actions; whether the benefits of control, including costs avoided, exceed the costs of the program; the risk of harm to non-target organisms and ecosystems, public health and welfare; and such other considerations the Task Force determines appropriate. The Task Force shall also determine the nature and extent of

control of target aquatic nuisance species that is feasible and desirable.

(3) PROGRAMS.—If the Task Force determines in accordance with paragraph (2) that control of an aquatic nuisance species is warranted, the Task Force shall develop a proposed control program to achieve the target level of control. A notice summarizing the proposed action and soliciting comments shall be published in the Federal Register, in major newspapers in the region affected, and in principal trade publications of the industries affected. Within 180 days of proposing a control program, and after consultation with affected governmental and other appropriate entities and taking into consideration other comments received, the Task Force shall complete development of the proposed control program.

(4) TECHNICAL ASSISTANCE AND RECOMMENDATIONS.—The Task Force may provide technical assistance and recommendations for best practices to an agency or entity engaged in vessel inspections or decontaminations for the purpose of—

(A) effectively managing and controlling the movement of aquatic nuisance species into, within, or out of water of the United States; and

(B) inspecting recreational vessels in a manner that minimizes disruptions to public access for boating and recreation in non-contaminated vessels.

(5) CONSULTATION AND INPUT.—In carrying out paragraph (4), including the development of recommendations, the Task Force may consult with Indian Tribes and solicit input from—

(A) State and Tribal fish and wildlife management agencies;

(B) other State and Tribal agencies that manage fishery resources of the State or sustain fishery habitat; and

(C) relevant nongovernmental entities.

(f) RESEARCH.—

(1) PRIORITIES.—The Task Force shall, within the program developed under subsection (a), conduct research concerning—

(A) the environmental and economic risks and impacts associated with the introduction of aquatic nuisance species into the waters of the United States;

(B) the principal pathways by which aquatic nuisance species are introduced and dispersed;

(C) possible methods for the prevention, monitoring and control of aquatic nuisance species; and

(D) the assessment of the effectiveness of prevention, monitoring and control methods.

(2) PROTOCOL.—Within 90 days of the date of enactment of this Act, the Task Force shall establish and follow a protocol to ensure that research activities carried out under this subtitle do not result in the introduction of aquatic nuisance species to waters of the United States.

(3) GRANTS FOR RESEARCH.—The Task Force shall allocate funds authorized under this Act for competitive research grants to study all aspects of aquatic nuisance species, which shall be administered through the National Sea Grant College Program and the Cooperative Fishery and Wildlife Research Units. Grants shall be conditioned to ensure that any recipient of funds follows the protocol established under paragraph (2) of this subsection.

(g) TECHNICAL ASSISTANCE.—The Task Force shall, within the program developed under subsection (a), provide technical assistance to State and local governments and persons to minimize the environmental, public health, and safety risks associated with aquatic nuisance species, including an early warning system for advance notice of possible infestations and appropriate responses.

(h) EDUCATION.—The Task Force shall, with the program developed under subsection (a), establish and implement educational programs through Sea Grant Marine Advisory Services and any other available resources that it determines to be appropriate to inform the general public, State governments, governments of political subdivisions of States, and industrial and recreational users of aquatic resources in connection with matters concerning the identification of aquatic nuisance species, and control methods for such species, including the prevention of the further distribution of such species.

(i) ZEBRA MUSSEL DEMONSTRATION PROGRAM.—

(1) ZEBRA MUSSEL.—

(A) IN GENERAL.—The Task Force shall, within the program developed under subsection (a), undertake a program of prevention, monitoring, control, education and research for the zebra mussel to be implemented in the Great Lakes and any other waters of the United States infested or likely to become infested by the zebra mussel, including—

(i) research and development concerning the species life history, environmental tolerances and impacts on fisheries and other ecosystem components, and the efficacy of control mechanisms and means of avoiding or minimizing impacts;

(ii) tracking the dispersal of the species and establishment of an early warning system to alert likely areas of future infestations;

(iii) development of control plans in coordination with regional, State and local entities; and

(iv) provision of technical assistance to regional, State and local entities to carry out this section.

(B) PUBLIC FACILITY RESEARCH AND DEVELOPMENT.—The Assistant Secretary, in consultation with the Task Force, shall develop a program of research, technology development, and demonstration for the environmentally sound control of zebra mussels in and around public facilities. The Assistant Secretary shall collect and make available, through publications and other appropriate means, information pertaining to such control methods.

(C) VOLUNTARY GUIDELINES.—Not later than 1 year after the date of enactment of this subparagraph, the Task Force shall develop and submit to the Secretary voluntary guidelines for controlling the spread of the zebra mussel and, if appropriate, other aquatic nuisance species through recreational activities, including boating and fishing. Not later than 4 months after the date of such submission, and after providing notice and an opportunity for public comment, the Secretary shall issue voluntary guidelines that are based on the guidelines developed by the Task

Force under this subparagraph.

(2) DISPERSAL CONTAINMENT ANALYSIS.—

(A) RESEARCH.—The Administrator of the Environmental Protection Agency, in cooperation with the National Science Foundation and the Task Force, shall provide research grants on a competitive basis for projects that—

(i) identify environmentally sound methods for controlling the dispersal of aquatic nuisance species, such as the zebra mussel; and

(ii) adhere to research protocols developed pursuant to subsection (f)(2).

(B) AUTHORIZATION OF APPROPRIATIONS.—There are authorized to be appropriated to the Environmental Protection Agency to carry out this paragraph, $500,000.

(3) DISPERSAL BARRIER DEMONSTRATION.—

(A) IN GENERAL.—The Assistant Secretary, in consultation with the Task Force, shall investigate and identify environmentally sound methods for preventing and reducing the dispersal of aquatic nuisance species between the Great Lakes-Saint Lawrence drainage and the Mississippi River drainage through the Chicago River Ship and Sanitary Canal, including any of those methods that could be incorporated into the operation or construction of the lock system of the Chicago River Ship and Sanitary Canal.

(B) REPORT.—Not later than 18 months after the date of enactment of this paragraph, the Assistant Secretary shall issue a report to the Congress that includes recommendations concerning—

(i) which of the methods that are identified under the study conducted under this paragraph are most promising with respect to preventing and reducing the dispersal of aquatic nuisance species; and

(ii) ways to incorporate those methods into ongoing operations of the United States Army Corps of Engineers that are conducted at the Chicago River Ship and Sanitary Canal.

(C) AUTHORIZATION OF APPROPRIATIONS.—There are authorized to be appropriated to the Department of the Army such sums as are necessary to carry out the dispersal barrier demonstration project directed by this paragraph.

(4) CONTRIBUTIONS.—To the extent allowable by law, in carrying out the studies under paragraphs (2) and (3), the Administrator of the Environmental Protection Agency and the Secretary of the Army may enter into an agreement with an interested party under which that party provides in kind or monetary contributions for the study.

(5) TECHNICAL ASSISTANCE.—The Great Lakes Environmental Research Laboratory of the National Oceanic and Atmospheric Administration shall provide technical assistance to appropriate entities to assist in the research conducted pursuant to this subsection.

(j) IMPLEMENTATION.—

(1) REGULATIONS.—The Director, the Secretary, and the Under Secretary may issue such rules and regulations as may be necessary to implement this section.

(2) PARTICIPATION OF OTHERS.—The Task Force shall provide opportunities for affected Federal agencies which are not part of the Task Force, State and local government agencies, and regional and other entities with the necessary expertise to participate in control programs. If these other agencies or entities have sufficient authority or jurisdiction and expertise and where this will be more efficient or effective, responsibility for implementing all or a portion of a control program may be delegated to such agencies or entities.

(k) REPORTS.—

(1) Not later than 12 months after the date of enactment of this Act, the Task Force shall submit a report describing the program developed under subsection (a), including the research protocol required under subsection (f)(2), to the Congress.

(2) On an annual basis after the submission of the report under paragraph (1), the Task Force shall submit a report to the Congress detailing progress in carrying out this section.

(3) Not later than 90 days after the date of enactment of the Don Young Coast Guard Authorization Act of 2022, the Task Force shall submit a report to Congress recommending

legislative, programmatic, or regulatory changes to eliminate remaining gaps in authorities between members of the Task Force to effectively manage and control the movement of aquatic nuisance species.

[16 U.S.C. 4722]

SEC. 1203. REGIONAL COORDINATION.

(a) GREAT LAKES PANEL.—

(1) IN GENERAL.—Not later than 30 days following the date of enactment of this Act, the Task Force shall request that the Great Lakes Commission (established under Article IV of the Great Lakes Compact to which the Congress granted consent in the Act of July 24, 1968, P.L. 90–419) convene a panel of Great Lakes region representatives from Federal, State and local agencies and from private environmental and commercial interests to—

(A) identify priorities for the Great Lakes region with respect to aquatic nuisance species;

(B) make recommendations to the Task Force regarding programs to carry out section 1202(i) of this Act;

(C) assist the Task Force in coordinating Federal aquatic nuisance species program activities in the Great Lakes region;

(D) coordinate, where possible, aquatic nuisance species program activities in the Great Lakes region that are not conducted pursuant to this Act;

(E) provide advice to public and private individuals and entities concerning methods of controlling aquatic nuisance species; and

(F) submit annually a report to the Task Force describing activities within the Great Lakes region related to aquatic nuisance species prevention, research, and control.

(2) CONSULTATION.—The Task Force shall request that the Great Lakes Fishery Commission provide information to the panel convened under this subsection on technical and policy matters related to the international fishery resources of the Great Lakes.

(3) CANADIAN PARTICIPATION.—The panel convened under

this subsection is encouraged to invite representatives from the Federal, provincial or territorial governments of Canada to participate as observers.

(b) WESTERN REGIONAL PANEL.—Not later than 30 days after the date of enactment of the National Invasive Species Act of 1996, the Task Force shall request a Western regional panel, comprised of Western region representatives from Federal, State, and local agencies and from private environmental and commercial interests, to—

(1) identify priorities for the Western region with respect to aquatic nuisance species;

(2) make recommendations to the Task Force regarding an education, monitoring (including inspection), prevention, and control program to prevent the spread of the zebra mussel west of the 100th Meridian pursuant to section 1202(i) of this Act;

(3) coordinate, where possible, other aquatic nuisance species program activities in the Western region that are not conducted pursuant to this Act;

(4) develop an emergency response strategy for Federal, State, and local entities for stemming new invasions of aquatic nuisance species in the region;

(5) provide advice to public and private individuals and entities concerning methods of preventing and controlling aquatic nuisance species infestations; and

(6) submit annually a report to the Task Force describing activities within the Western region related to aquatic nuisance species prevention, research, and control.

(c) ADDITIONAL REGIONAL PANELS.—The Task Force shall—

(1) encourage the development and use of regional panels and other similar entities in regions in addition to the Great Lakes and Western regions (including providing financial assistance for the development and use of such entities) to carry out, with respect to those regions, activities that are similar to the activities described in subsections (a) and (b); and

(2) cooperate with regional panels and similar entities that carry out the activities described in paragraph (1).

[16 U.S.C. 4723]

SEC. 1204. STATE AQUATIC NUISANCE SPECIES MANAGEMENT

PLANS.

(a) STATE OR INTERSTATE INVASIVE SPECIES MANAGEMENT PLANS.—

(1) IN GENERAL.—After providing notice and opportunity for public comment, the Governor of each State may prepare and submit, or the Governors of the States and the governments of the Indian tribes involved in an interstate organization, may jointly prepare and submit—

(A) a comprehensive management plan to the Task Force for approval which identifies those areas or activities within the State or within the interstate region involved, other than those related to public facilities, for which technical, enforcement, or financial assistance (or any combination thereof) is needed to eliminate or reduce the environmental, public health, and safety risks associated with aquatic nuisance species, particularly the zebra mussel; and

(B) a public facility management plan to the Assistant Secretary for approval which is limited solely to identifying those public facilities within the State or within the interstate region involved for which technical and financial assistance is needed to reduce infestations of zebra mussels.

(2) CONTENT.—Each plan shall, to the extent possible, identify the management practices and measures that will be undertaken to reduce infestations of aquatic nuisance species. Each plan shall—

(A) identify and describe State and local programs for environmentally sound prevention and control of the target aquatic nuisance species;

(B) identify Federal activities that may be needed for environmentally sound prevention and control of aquatic nuisance species and a description of the manner in which those activities should be coordinated with State and local government activities;

(C) identify any authority that the State (or any State or Indian tribe involved in the interstate organization) does not have at the time of the development of the plan that may be necessary for the State (or any State or Indian tribe involved in the interstate organization) to protect public health, property, and the environment from harm by aquatic nuisance species; and

(D) a schedule of implementing the plan, including a schedule of annual objectives, and enabling legislation.

(3) CONSULTATION.—

(A) In developing and implementing a management plan, the State or interstate organization should, to the maximum extent practicable, involve local governments and regional entities, Indian tribes, and public and private organizations that have expertise in the control of aquatic nuisance species.

(B) Upon the request of a State or the appropriate official of an interstate organization, the Task Force or the Assistant Secretary, as appropriate under paragraph (1), may provide technical assistance in developing and implementing a management plan.

(4) PLAN APPROVAL.—Within 90 days after the submission of a management plan, the Task Force or the Assistant Secretary in consultation with the Task Force, as appropriate under paragraph (1), shall review the proposed plan and approve it if it meets the requirements of this subsection or return the plan to the Governor or the interstate organization with recommended modifications.

(b) GRANT PROGRAM.—

(1) STATE GRANTS.—The Director may, at the recommendation of the Task Force, make grants to States with management plans approved under subsection (a) for the implementation of those plans.

(2) APPLICATION.—An application for a grant under this subsection shall include an identification and description of the best management practices and measures which the State proposes to utilize in implementing an approved management plan with any Federal assistance to be provided under the grant.

(3) FEDERAL SHARE.—

(A) The Federal share of the cost of each comprehensive management plan implemented with Federal assistance under this section in any fiscal year shall not exceed 75 percent of the cost incurred by the State in implementing such management program and the non-Federal share of such costs shall be provided from non-Federal sources.

(B) The Federal share of the cost of each public facility management plan implemented with Federal assistance under this section in any fiscal year shall not exceed 50 percent of the cost incurred by the State in implementing such management program and the non-Federal share of such costs shall be provided from non-Federal sources.

(4) ADMINISTRATIVE COSTS.—For the purposes of this section, administrative costs for activities and programs carried out with a grant in any fiscal year shall not exceed 5 percent of the amount of the grant in that year.

(5) IN-KIND CONTRIBUTIONS.—In addition to cash outlays and payments, in-kind contributions of property or personnel services by non-Federal interests for activities under this section may be used for the non-Federal share of the cost of those activities.

(c) ENFORCEMENT ASSISTANCE.—Upon request of a State or Indian tribe, the Director or the Under Secretary, to the extent allowable by law and in a manner consistent with section 141 of title 14, United States Code, may provide assistance to a State or Indian tribe in enforcing an approved State or interstate invasive species management plan.

[16 U.S.C. 4724]

SEC. 1205. RELATIONSHIP TO OTHER LAWS.

(a) CONSISTENCY WITH ENVIRONMENTAL LAWS.—All actions taken by Federal agencies in implementing the provisions of section 1202 shall be consistent with all applicable Federal, State, and local environmental laws.

(b) EFFECT OF TITLE.—

(1) IN GENERAL.—Except as provided in paragraph (2), nothing in this title shall affect the authority of any State or political subdivision thereof to adopt or enforce control measures for aquatic nuisance species, or diminish or affect the jurisdiction of any State over species of fish and wildlife.

(2) EXCEPTION.—Any discharge incidental to the normal

operation of a vessel, including any discharge of ballast water (as those terms are defined in subsections (a) and (p)(1) of section 312 of the Federal Water Pollution Control Act (33 U.S.C. 1322)), shall be regulated in accordance with that section.

(c) EFFECT OF COMPLIANCE.—Compliance with the control and eradication measures of any State or political subdivision thereof regarding aquatic nuisance species shall not relieve any person of the obligation to comply with the provisions of this subtitle.

[16 U.S.C. 4725]

SEC. 1206. INTERNATIONAL COOPERATION.

(a) ADVICE.—The Task Force shall provide timely advice to the Secretary of State concerning aquatic nuisance species that infest waters shared with other countries.

(b) NEGOTIATIONS.—The Secretary of State, in consultation with the Task Force, is encouraged to initiate negotiations with the governments of foreign countries concerning the planning and implementation of prevention, monitoring, research, education, and control programs related to aquatic nuisance species infesting shared water resources.

[16 U.S.C. 4726]

SEC. 1207. INTENTIONAL INTRODUCTIONS POLICY REVIEW.

Within one year of the date of enactment of this Act, the Task Force shall, in consultation with State fish and wildlife agencies, other regional, State and local entities, potentially affected industries and other interested parties, identify and evaluate approaches for reducing the risk of adverse consequences associated with intentional introduction of aquatic organisms and submit a report of their findings, conclusions and recommendations to the Congress.

[16 U.S.C. 4727]

SEC. 1208. INJURIOUS SPECIES.

Section 42(a) of title 18, United States Code is amended by inserting "of the zebra mussel of the species Dreissena polymorpha;" after "Pteropus;".

SEC. 1209. BROWN TREE SNAKE CONTROL PROGRAM.

The Task Force shall, within the program developed under

section 1202(a), undertake a comprehensive, environmentally sound program in coordination with regional, territorial, State and local entities to control the brown tree snake (Boiga irregularis) in Guam and other areas where the species is established outside of its historic range.
[16 U.S.C. 4728]

Subtitle D—Authorizations of Appropriation

SEC. 1301. AUTHORIZATIONS.

(a) PREVENTION OF UNINTENTIONAL INTRODUCTIONS.—There are authorized to be appropriated to develop and implement the provisions of subtitle B—

(1) $500,000 until the end of fiscal year 1992 to the Secretary to carry out sections 1101 and 1102(a)(3);

(2) $2,000,000 until the end of fiscal year 1992 to the Director and Under Secretary to carry out the studies under sections 1102(a)(1) and 1102(a)(2);

(3) to the Secretary to carry out section 1101—

(A) $2,000,000 for each of fiscal years 1997 and 1998; and

(B) $3,000,000 for each of fiscal years 1999 through 2002;

(4) for each of fiscal years 1997 through 2002, to carry out paragraphs (1) and (2) of section 1102(b)—

(A) $1,000,000 to the Department of the Interior, to be used by the Director; and

(B) $1,000,000 to the Secretary; and

(5) for each of fiscal years 1997 through 2002—

(A) $3,000,000, which shall be made available from funds otherwise authorized to be appropriated if such funds are so authorized, to the Under Secretary to carry out section 1102(e); and

(B) $500,000 to the Secretary to carry out section 1102(f).

(b) TASK FORCE AND AQUATIC NUISANCE SPECIES

PROGRAM.—There are authorized to be appropriated for each of fiscal years 1997 through 2002 to develop and implement the provisions of subtitle C—

(1) $6,000,000 to the Department of the Interior, to be used by the Director to carry out sections 1202 and 1209;

(2) $1,000,000 to the Department of Commerce, to be used by the Under Secretary to carry out section 1202;

(3) $1,625,000, which shall be made available from funds otherwise authorized to be appropriated if such funds are so authorized, to fund aquatic nuisance species prevention and control research under section 1202(i) at the Great Lakes Environmental Research Laboratory of the National Oceanic and Atmospheric Administration, of which $500,000 shall be made available for grants, to be competitively awarded and subject to peer review, for research relating to Lake Champlain;

(4) $5,000,000 for competitive grants for university research on aquatic nuisance species under section 1202(f)(3) as follows:

(A) $2,800,000, which shall be made available from funds otherwise authorized to be appropriated if such funds are so authorized, to fund grants under section 205 of the National Sea Grant College Program Act (33 U.S.C. 1124);

(B) $1,200,000 to fund grants to colleges for the benefit of agriculture and the mechanic arts referred to in the first section of the Act of August 30, 1890 (26 Stat. 417, chapter 841; 7 U.S.C. 322); and

(C) $1,000,000 to fund grants through the Cooperative Fisheries and Wildlife Research Unit Program of the United States Fish and Wildlife Service;

(5) $3,000,000 to the Department of the Army, to be used by the Assistant Secretary to carry out section 1202(i)(1)(B); and

(6) $300,000 to the Department of the Interior, to be used by the Director to fund regional panels and similar entities under section 1203, of which $100,000 shall be used to fund activities of the Great Lakes Commission.

(c) GRANTS FOR STATE MANAGEMENT PROGRAMS.—There are authorized to be appropriated for each of fiscal years 1997 through 2002 $4,000,000 to the Department of the Interior, to be used by the

Director for making grants under section 1204, of which $1,500,000 shall be used by the Director, in consultation with the Assistant Secretary, for management of aquatic nuisance vegetation species.

(d) INTENTIONAL INTRODUCTIONS POLICY REVIEW.—There are authorized to be appropriated for fiscal year 1991, $500,000 to the Director and the Under Secretary to conduct the intentional introduction policy review under section 1207.

(e) BALLAST WATER MANAGEMENT DEMONSTRATION PROGRAM.—There are authorized to be appropriated $2,500,000 to carry out section 1104.

(f) RESEARCH.—There are authorized to be appropriated to the Director $1,000,000 to carry out research on the prevention, monitoring, and control of aquatic nuisance species in Narragansett Bay, Rhode Island. The funds shall be made available for use by the Department of Environmental Management of the State of Rhode Island.

[16 U.S.C. 4741]

Subtitle E—Cooperative Environmental Analyses

SEC. 1401. ENVIRONMENTAL IMPACT ANALYSES.

The Secretary of State, in consultation with the Council on Environmental Quality, is encouraged to enter into negotiations with the governments of Canada and Mexico to provide for reciprocal cooperative environmental impact analysis of major Federal actions which have significant transboundary effects on the quality of the human environment in the United States, Canada, and Mexico.

[16 U.S.C. 4751]

TITLE III—WETLANDS[1]

SEC. 301. SHORT TITLE.

This title may be cited as the "Coastal Wetlands Planning, Protection and Restoration Act".

---

[1] Title II was repealed by the amendment made by section 3(b) of the Great Lakes Fish and Wildlife Restoration Act of 1998 (Public Law 105–265; 112 Stat. 2358).

[16 U.S.C. 3951 nt]

SEC. 302. DEFINITIONS.

As used in this title, the term—

(1) "Secretary" means the Secretary of the Army;

(2) "Administrator" means the Administrator of the Environmental Protection Agency;

(3) "development activities" means any activity, including the discharge of dredged or fill material, which results directly in a more than de minimus change in the hydrologic regime, bottom contour, or the type, distribution or diversity of hydrophytic vegetation, or which impairs the flow, reach, or circulation of surface water within wetlands or other waters;

(4) "State" means the State of Louisiana;

(5) "coastal State" means a State of the United States in, or bordering on, the Atlantic, Pacific, or Arctic Ocean, the Gulf of Mexico, Long Island Sound, or one or more of the Great Lakes; for the purposes of this title, the term also includes Puerto Rico, the Virgin Islands, Guam, the Commonwealth of the Northern Mariana Islands, and the Trust Territories of the Pacific Islands, and American Samoa;

(6) "coastal wetlands restoration project" means any technically feasible activity to create, restore, protect, or enhance coastal wetlands through sediment and freshwater diversion, water management, or other measures that the Task Force finds will significantly contribute to the long-term restoration or protection of the physical, chemical and biological integrity of coastal wetlands in the State of Louisiana, and includes any such activity authorized under this title or under any other provision of law, including, but not limited to, new projects, completion or expansion of existing or on-going projects, individual phases, portions, or components of projects and operation, maintanence and rehabilitation of completed projects; the primary purpose of a "coastal wetlands restoration project" shall not be to provide navigation, irrigation or flood control benefits;

(7) "coastal wetlands conservation project" means—

(A) the obtaining of a real property interest in coastal lands or waters, if the obtaining of such interest is subject to terms and conditions that will ensure that the real property will be administered for the long-term conservation of such lands and waters and the hydrology, water quality and fish and wildlife dependent thereon; and

(B) the restoration, management, or enhancement of coastal wetlands ecosystems if such restoration, management, or enhancement is conducted on coastal lands and waters that are administered for the long-term conservation of such lands and waters and the hydrology, water quality and fish and wildlife dependent thereon;

(8) "Governor" means the Governor of Louisiana;

(9) "Task Force" means the Louisiana Coastal Wetlands Conservation and Restoration Task Force which shall consist of the Secretary, who shall serve as chairman, the Administrator, the Governor, the Secretary of the Interior, the Secretary of Agriculture and the Secretary of Commerce; and

(10) "Director" means the Director of the United States Fish and Wildlife Service.

[16 U.S.C. 3951]

SEC. 303. PRIORITY LOUISIANA COASTAL WETLANDS RESTORATION PROJECTS.

(a) PRIORITY PROJECT LIST.—

(1) PREPARATION OF LIST.—Within forty-five days after the date of enactment of this title, the Secretary shall convene the Task Force to initiate a process to identify and prepare a list of coastal wetlands restoration projects in Louisiana to provide for the long-term conservation of such wetlands and dependent fish and wildlife populations in order of priority, based on the cost-effectiveness of such projects in creating, restoring, protecting, or enhancing coastal wetlands, taking into account the quality of such coastal wetlands, with due allowance for small-scale projects necessary to demonstrate the use of new techniques or materials for coastal wetlands restoration.

(2) TASK FORCE PROCEDURES.—The Secretary shall convene meetings of the Task Force as appropriate to ensure that the list is produced and transmitted annually to the Congress as required by this subsection. If necessary to ensure transmittal of the list on a timely basis, the Task Force shall produce the

list by a majority vote of those Task Force members who are present and voting; except that no coastal wetlands restoration project shall be placed on the list without the concurrence of the lead Task Force member that the project is cost effective and sound from an engineering perspective. Those projects which potentially impact navigation or flood control on the lower Mississippi River System shall be constructed consistent with section 304 of this Act.

(3) TRANSMITTAL OF LIST.—No later than one year after the date of enactment of this title, the Secretary shall transmit to the Congress the list of priority coastal wetlands restoration projects required by paragraph (1) of this subsection. Thereafter, the list shall be updated annually by the Task Force members and transmitted by the Secretary to the Congress as part of the President's annual budget submission. Annual transmittals of the list to the Congress shall include a status report on each project and a statement from the Secretary of the Treasury indicating the amounts available for expenditure to carry out this title.

(4) LIST OF CONTENTS.—

(A) AREA IDENTIFICATION; PROJECT DESCRIPTION.—The list of priority coastal wetlands restoration projects shall include, but not be limited to—

(i) identification, by map or other means, of the coastal area to be covered by the coastal wetlands restoration project; and

(ii) a detailed description of each proposed coastal wetlands restoration project including a justification for including such project on the list, the proposed activities to be carried out pursuant to each coastal wetlands restoration project, the benefits to be realized by such project, the identification of the lead Task Force member to undertake each proposed coastal wetlands restoration project and the responsibilities of each other participating Task Force member, an estimated timetable for the completion of each coastal wetlands restoration project, and the estimated cost of each project.

(B) PRE-PLAN.—Prior to the date on which the plan required by subsection (b) of this section becomes effective, such list shall include only those coastal wetlands restoration projects that can be substantially completed during a five-year period commencing on the date the project is placed on the list.

(C) Subsequent to the date on which the plan required by subsection (b) of this section becomes effective, such list shall include only those coastal wetlands restoration projects that have been identified in such plan.

(5) FUNDING.—The Secretary shall, with the funds made available in accordance with section 306 of this title, allocate funds among the members of the Task Force based on the need for such funds and such other factors as the Task Force deems appropriate to carry out the purposes of this subsection.

(b) FEDERAL AND STATE PROJECT PLANNING.—

(1) PLAN PREPARATION.—The Task Force shall prepare a plan to identify coastal wetlands restoration projects, in order of priority, based on the cost-effectiveness of such projects in creating, restoring, protecting, or enhancing the long-term conservation of coastal wetlands, taking into account the quality of such coastal wetlands, with due allowance for small-scale projects necessary to demonstrate the use of new techniques or materials for coastal wetlands restoration. Such restoration plan shall be completed within three years from the date of enactment of this title.

(2) PURPOSE OF THE PLAN.—The purpose of the restoration plan is to develop a comprehensive approach to restore and prevent the loss of, coastal wetlands in Louisiana. Such plan shall coordinate and integrate coastal wetlands restoration projects in a manner that will ensure the long-term conservation of the coastal wetlands of Louisiana.

(3) INTEGRATION OF EXISTING PLANS.—In developing the restoration plan, the Task Force shall seek to integrate the "Louisiana Comprehensive Coastal Wetlands Feasibility Study" conducted by the Secretary of the Army and the "Coastal Wetlands Conservation and Restoration Plan" prepared by the State of Louisiana's Wetlands Conservation and Restoration Task Force.

(4) ELEMENTS OF THE PLAN.—The restoration plan developed pursuant to this subsection shall include—

(A) identification of the entire area in the State that contains coastal wetlands;

(B) identification, by map or other means, of coastal areas in Louisiana in need of coastal wetlands restoration projects;

(C) identification of high priority coastal wetlands restoration projects in Louisiana needed to address the areas identified in subparagraph (B) and that would provide for the long-term conservation of restored wetlands and dependent fish and wildlife populations;

(D) a listing of such coastal wetlands restoration projects, in order of priority, to be submitted annually, incorporating any project identified previously in lists produced and submitted under subsection (a) of this section;

(E) a detailed description of each proposed coastal wetlands restoration project, including a justification for including such project on the list;

(F) the proposed activities to be carried out pursuant to each coastal wetlands restoration project;

(G) the benefits to be realized by each such project;

(H) an estimated timetable for completion of each coastal wetlands restoration project;

(I) an estimate of the cost of each coastal wetlands restoration project;

(J) identification of a lead Task Force member to undertake each proposed coastal wetlands restoration project listed in the plan;

(K) consultation with the public and provision for public review during development of the plan; and

(L) evaluation of the effectiveness of each coastal wetlands restoration project in achieving long-term solutions to arresting coastal wetlands loss in Louisiana.

(5) PLAN MODIFICATION.—The Task Force may modify the restoration plan from time to time as necessary to carry out the purposes of this section.

(6) PLAN SUBMISSION.—Upon completion of the restoration plan, the Secretary shall submit the plan to the Congress. The

restoration plan shall become effective ninety days after the date of its submission to the Congress.

(7) PLAN EVALUATION.—Not less than three years after the completion and submission of the restoration plan required by this subsection and at least every three years thereafter, the Task Force shall provide a report to the Congress containing a scientific evaluation of the effectiveness of the coastal wetlands restoration projects carried out under the plan in creating, restoring, protecting and enhancing coastal wetlands in Louisiana.

(c) COASTAL WETLANDS RESTORATION PROJECT BENEFITS.—Where such a determination is required under applicable law, the net ecological, aesthetic, and cultural benefits, together with the economic benefits, shall be deemed to exceed the costs of any coastal wetlands restoration project within the State which the Task Force finds to contribute significantly to wetlands restoration.

(d) CONSISTENCY.—(1) In implementing, maintaining, modifying, or rehabilitating navigation, flood control or irrigation projects, other than emergency actions, under other authorities, the Secretary, in consultation with the Director and the Administrator, shall ensure that such actions are consistent with the purposes of the restoration plan submitted pursuant to this section.

(2) At the request of the Governor of the State of Louisiana, the Secretary of Commerce shall approve the plan as an amendment to the State's coastal zone management program approved under section 306 of the Coastal Zone Management Act of 1972 (16 U.S.C. 1455).

(e) FUNDING OF WETLANDS RESTORATION PROJECTS.—The Secretary shall, with the funds made available in accordance with this title, allocate such funds among the members of the Task Force to carry out coastal wetlands restoration projects in accordance with the priorities set forth in the list transmitted in accordance with this section. The Secretary shall not fund a coastal wetlands restoration project unless that project is subject to such terms and conditions as necessary to ensure that wetlands restored, enhanced or managed through that project will be administered for the long-term conservation of such lands and waters and dependent fish and wildlife populations.

(f) COST-SHARING.—

(1) FEDERAL SHARE.—Amounts made available in accordance with section 306 of this title to carry out coastal wetlands restoration projects under this title shall provide 75 percent of the cost of such projects.

(2) FEDERAL SHARE UPON CONSERVATION PLAN APPROVAL.—Notwithstanding the previous paragraph, if the State develops a Coastal Wetlands Conservation Plan pursuant to this title, and such conservation plan is approved pursuant to section 304 of this title, amounts made available in accordance with section 306 of this title for any coastal wetlands restoration project under this section shall be 85 percent of the cost of the project. In the event that the Secretary, the Director, and the Administrator jointly determine that the State is not taking reasonable steps to implement and administer a conservation plan developed and approved pursuant to this title, amounts made available in accordance with section 306 of this title for any coastal wetlands restoration project shall revert to 75 percent of the cost of the project: *Provided, however,* that such reversion to the lower cost share level shall not occur until the Governor has been provided notice of, and opportunity for hearing on, any such determination by the Secretary, the Director, and Administrator, and the State has been given ninety days from such notice or hearing to take corrective action.

(3) FORM OF STATE SHARE.—The share of the cost required of the State shall be from a non-Federal source. Such State share shall consist of a cash contribution of not less than 5 percent of the cost of the project. The balance of such State share may take the form of lands, easements, or right-of-way, or any other form of in-kind contribution determined to be appropriate by the lead Task Force member.

(4) Paragraphs (1), (2), and (3) of this subsection shall not affect the existing cost-sharing agreements for the following projects: Caernarvon Freshwater Diversion, Davis Pond Freshwater Diversion, and Bonnet Carre Freshwater Diversion.

[16 U.S.C. 3952]

SEC. 304. LOUISIANA COASTAL WETLANDS CONSERVATION PLANNING.

(a) DEVELOPMENT OF CONSERVATION PLAN.—

(1) AGREEMENT.—The Secretary, the Director, and the Administrator are directed to enter into an agreement with the Governor, as set forth in paragraph (2) of this subsection, upon notification of the Governor's willingness to enter into such agreement.

(2) TERMS OF AGREEMENT.—

(A) Upon receiving notification pursuant to paragraph (1) of this subsection, the Secretary, the Director, and the Administrator shall promptly enter into an agreement (hereafter in this section referred to as the "agreement") with the State under the terms set forth in subparagraph (B) of this paragraph.

(B) The agreement shall—

(i) set forth a process by which the State agrees to develop, in accordance with this section, a coastal wetlands conservation plan (hereafter in this section referred to as the "conservation plan");

(ii) designate a single agency of the State to develop the conservation plan;

(iii) assure an opportunity for participation in the development of the conservation plan, during the planning period, by the public and by Federal and State agencies;

(iv) obligate the State, not later than three years after the date of signing the agreement, unless extended by the parties thereto, to submit the conservation plan to the Secretary, the Director, and the Administrator for their approval; and

(v) upon approval of the conservation plan, obligate the State to implement the conservation plan.

(3) GRANTS AND ASSISTANCE.—Upon the date of signing the agreement—

(A) the Administrator shall, in consultation with the Director, with the funds made available in accordance with section 306 of this title, make grants during the development of the conservation plan to assist the designated State agency in developing such plan. Such grants shall not exceed 75 percent of the cost of developing the plan; and

(B) the Secretary, the Director, and the Administrator shall provide technical assistance to the State to assist it in the development of the plan.

(b) CONSERVATION PLAN GOAL.—If a conservation plan is developed pursuant to this section, it shall have a goal of achieving no net loss of wetlands in the coastal areas of Louisiana as a result of development activities initiated subsequent to approval of the plan, exclusive of any wetlands gains achieved through implementation of the preceding section of this title.

(c) ELEMENTS OF CONSERVATION PLAN.—The conservation plan authorized by this section shall include—

(1) identification of the entire coastal area in the State that contains coastal wetlands;

(2) designation of a single State agency with the responsibility for implementing and enforcing the plan;

(3) identification of measures that the State shall take in addition to existing Federal authority to achieve a goal of no net loss of wetlands as a result of development activities, exclusive of any wetlands gains achieved through implementation of the preceding section of this title;

(4) a system that the State shall implement to account for gains and losses of coastal wetlands within coastal areas for purposes of evaluating the degree to which the goal of no net loss of wetlands as a result of development activities in such wetlands or other waters has been attained;

(5) satisfactory assurances that the State will have adequate personnel, funding, and authority to implement the plan;

(6) a program to be carried out by the State for the purpose of educating the public concerning the necessity to conserve wetlands;

(7) a program to encourage the use of technology by persons engaged in development activities that will result in negligible impact on wetlands; and

(8) a program for the review, evaluation, and identification of regulatory and nonregulatory options that will be adopted by

the State to encourage and assist private owners of wetlands to continue to maintain those lands as wetlands.

(d) APPROVAL OF CONSERVATION PLAN.—

(1) IN GENERAL.—If the Governor submits a conservation plan to the Secretary, the Director, and the Administrator for their approval, the Secretary, the Director, and the Administrator shall, within one hundred and eighty days following receipt of such plan, approve or disapprove it.

(2) APPROVAL CRITERIA.—The Secretary, the Director, and the Administrator shall approve a conservation plan submitted by the Governor, if they determine that—

(A) the State has adequate authority to fully implement all provisions of such a plan;

(B) such a plan is adequate to attain the goal of no net loss of coastal wetlands as a result of development activities and complies with the other requirements of this section; and

(C) the plan was developed in accordance with terms of the agreement set forth in subsection (a) of this section.

(e) MODIFICATION OF CONSERVATION PLAN.—

(1) NONCOMPLIANCE.—If the Secretary, the Director, and the Administrator determine that a conservation plan submitted by the Governor does not comply with the requirements of subsection (d) of this section, they shall submit to the Governor a statement explaining why the plan is not in compliance and how the plan should be changed to be in compliance.

(2) RECONSIDERATION.—If the Governor submits a modified conservation plan to the Secretary, the Director, and the Administrator for their reconsideration, the Secretary, the Director, and Administrator shall have ninety days to determine whether the modifications are sufficient to bring the plan into compliance with requirements of subsection (d) of this section.

(3) APPROVAL OF MODIFIED PLAN.—If the Secretary, the Director, and the Administrator fail to approve or disapprove the conservation plan, as modified, within the ninety-day period following the date on which it was submitted to them by the Governor, such plan, as modified, shall be deemed to

be approved effective upon the expiration of such ninety-day period.

(f) AMENDMENTS TO CONSERVATION PLAN.—If the Governor amends the conservation plan approved under this section, any such amended plan shall be considered a new plan and shall be subject to the requirements of this section; except that minor changes to such plan shall not be subject to the requirements of this section.

(g) IMPLEMENTATION OF CONSERVATION PLAN.—A conservation plan approved under this section shall be implemented as provided therein.

(h) FEDERAL OVERSIGHT.—

(1) INITIAL REPORT TO CONGRESS.—Within one hundred and eighty days after entering into the agreement required under subsection (a) of this section, the Secretary, the Director, and the Administrator shall report to the Congress as to the status of a conservation plan approved under this section and the progress of the State in carrying out such a plan, including and accounting, as required under subsection (c) of this section, of the gains and losses of coastal wetlands as a result of development activities.

(2) REPORT TO CONGRESS.—Twenty-four months after the initial one hundred and eighty day period set forth in paragraph (1), and at the end of each twenty-four-month period thereafter, the Secretary, the Director, and the Administrator shall, report to the Congress on the status of the conservation plan and provide an evaluation of the effectiveness of the plan in meeting the goal of this section.

[16 U.S.C. 3953]

SEC. 305 NATIONAL COASTAL WETLANDS CONSERVATION GRANTS.

(a) MATCHING GRANTS.—The Director shall, with the funds made available in accordance with the next following section of this title, make matching grants to any coastal State to carry out coastal wetlands conservation projects from funds made available for that purpose.

(b) PRIORITY.—Subject to the cost-sharing requirements of this section, the Director may grant or otherwise provide any matching moneys to any coastal State which submits a proposal substantial in character and design to carry out a coastal wetlands conservation project. In awarding such matching grants, the Director shall give priority to coastal wetlands conservation projects that are—

(1) consistent with the National Wetlands Priority Conservation Plan developed under section 301 of the Emergency Wetlands Resources Act (16 U.S.C. 3921); and

(2) in coastal States that have established dedicated funding for programs to acquire coastal wetlands, natural areas and open spaces. In addition, priority consideration shall be given to coastal wetlands conservation projects in maritime forests on coastal barrier islands.

(c) CONDITIONS.—The Director may only grant or otherwise provide matching moneys to a coastal State for purposes of carrying out a coastal wetlands conservation project if the grant or provision is subject to terms and conditions that will ensure that any real property interest acquired in whole or in part, or enhanced, managed, or restored with such moneys will be administered for the long-term conservation of such lands and waters and the fish and wildlife dependent thereon.

(d) COST-SHARING.—

(1) FEDERAL SHARE.—Grants to coastal States of matching moneys by the Director for any fiscal year to carry out coastal wetlands conservation projects shall be used for the payment of not to exceed 50 percent of the total costs of such projects: except that such matching moneys may be used for payment of not to exceed 75 percent of the costs of such projects if a coastal State has established and is using one of the following for the purpose of acquiring coastal wetlands, other natural areas or open spaces:

(A) a trust fund from which the principal is not spent; or

(B) a fund derived from a dedicated recurring source of monies including, but not limited to, real estate transfer fees or taxes, cigarette taxes, tax check-offs, or motor vehicle license plate fees.

(2) FORM OF STATE SHARE.—The matching moneys required of a coastal State to carry out a coastal wetlands conservation project shall be derived from a non-Federal source.

(3) IN-KIND CONTRIBUTIONS.—In addition to cash outlays

and payments, in-kind contributions of property or personnel services by non-Federal interests for activities under this section may be used for the non-Federal share of the cost of those activities.

(e) PARTIAL PAYMENTS.—

(1) The Director may from time to time make matching payments to carry out coastal wetlands conservation projects as such projects progress, but such payments, including previous payments, if any, shall not be more than the Federal pro rata share of any such project in conformity with subsection (d) of this section.

(2) The Director may enter into agreements to make matching payments on an initial portion of a coastal wetlands conservation project and to agree to make payments on the remaining Federal share of the costs of such project from subsequent moneys if and when they become available. The liability of the United States under such an agreement is contingent upon the continued availability of funds for the purpose of this section.

(f) WETLANDS ASSESSMENT.—The Director shall, with the funds made available in accordance with the next following section of this title, direct the U.S. Fish and Wildlife Service's National Wetland Inventory to update and digitize wetlands maps in the State of Texas and to conduct an assessment of the status, condition, and trends of wetlands in that State.

[16 U.S.C. 3954]

SEC. 306. DISTRIBUTION OF APPROPRIATIONS.

(a) PRIORITY PROJECT AND CONSERVATION PLANNING EXPENDITURES.—Of the total amount appropriated during a given fiscal year to carry out this title, 70 percent shall be available, and shall remain available until expended, for the purposes of making expenditures—

(1) not to exceed the aggregate amount of $5,000,000 annually to assist the Task Force in the preparation of the list required under this title and the plan required under this title, including preparation of—

(A) preliminary assessments;

(B) general or site-specific inventories;

(C) reconnaissance, engineering or other studies;

(D) preliminary design work; and

(E) such other studies as may be necessary to identify and evaluate the feasibility of coastal wetland restoration projects;

(2) to carry out coastal wetlands restoration projects in accordance with the priorities set forth on the list prepared under this title;

(3) to carry out wetlands restoration projects in accordance with the priorities set forth in the restoration plan prepared under this title;

(4) to make grants not to exceed $2,500,000 annually or $10,000,000 in total, to assist the agency designated by the State in development of the Coastal Wetlands Conservation Plan pursuant to this title.

(b) COASTAL WETLANDS CONSERVATION GRANTS.—Of the total amount appropriated during a given fiscal year to carry out this title, 15 percent shall be available, and shall remain available to the Director, for purposes of making grants—

(1) to any coastal State, except States eligible to receive funding under section 306(a), to carry out coastal wetlands conservation projects in accordance with section 305 of this title; and

(2) in the amount of $2,500,000 in total for an assessment of the status, condition, and trends of wetlands in the State of Texas.

(c) NORTH AMERICAN WETLANDS CONSERVATION.—Of the total amount appropriated during a given fiscal year to carry out this title, 15 percent shall be available to, and shall remain available until expended by, the Secretary of the Interior for allocation to carry out wetlands conservation projects in coastal wetlands ecosystems in any coastal State under section 8 of the North American Wetlands Conservation Act (Public Law 101–233, 103 Stat. 1968, December 13, 1989).

[16 U.S.C. 3955]

SEC. 307. GENERAL PROVISIONS.

(a) ADDITIONAL AUTHORITY FOR THE CORPS OF ENGINEERS.—The Secretary is authorized to carry out projects for the protection, restoration, or enhancement of aquatic and associated ecosystems, including projects for the protection, restoration, or creation of wetlands and coastal ecosystems. In carrying out such projects, the Secretary shall give such projects equal consideration with projects relating to irrigation, navigation, or flood control.

(b) STUDY.—The Secretary is hereby authorized and directed to study the feasibility of modifying the operation of existing navigation and flood control projects to allow for an increase in the share of the Mississippi River flows and sediment sent down the Atchafalaya River for purposes of land building and wetlands nourishment.

[16 U.S.C. 3956]

SEC. 308. CONFORMING AMENDMENT.

16 U.S.C. 777c is amended by adding the following after the first sentence: "The Secretary shall distribute 18 per centum of each annual appropriation made in accordance with the provisions of section 777b of this title as provided in the Coastal Wetlands Planning, Protection and Restoration Act: *Provided,* That, notwithstanding the provisions of section 777b, such sums shall remain available to carry out such Act through fiscal year 1999.".

SEC. 309. ENVIRONMENTAL BANKS.

(a) GUIDELINES.—Not later than 1 year after the date of enactment of the Water Resources Development Act of 2016, the Task Force shall, after public notice and opportunity for comment, issue guidelines for the use, maintenance, and oversight of environmental banks in Louisiana.

(b) REQUIREMENTS.—The guidelines issued pursuant to subsection (a) shall—

(1) set forth procedures for establishment and approval of environmental banks subject to the approval of the heads of the appropriate Federal agencies responsible for implementation of Federal environmental laws for which mitigation credits may be used;

(2) establish criteria for siting of environmental banks that enhance the resilience of coastal resources to inundation and coastal erosion in high priority areas, as identified within Federal or State restoration plans, including the restoration

of resources within the scope of a project authorized for construction;

(3) establish criteria that ensure environmental banks secure adequate financial assurances and legally enforceable protection for the land or resources that generate the credits from environmental banks;

(4) stipulate that credits from environmental banks may not be used for mitigation of impacts required under section 404 of the Federal Water Pollution Control Act (33 U.S.C. 1342) or the Endangered Species Act (16 U.S.C. 1531 et seq.) in an area where an existing mitigation bank approved pursuant to such laws within 5 years of enactment of the Water Resources Development Act of 2016 has credits available;

(5) establish performance criteria for environmental banks; and

(6) establish criteria and financial assurance for the operation and monitoring of environmental banks.

(c) ENVIRONMENTAL BANK.—

(1) DEFINITION OF ENVIRONMENTAL BANK.—In this section, the term "environmental bank" means a project, project increment, or projects for purposes of restoring, creating, or enhancing natural resources at a designated site to establish mitigation credits.

(2) CREDITS.—Mitigation credits created from environmental banks approved pursuant to this section may be used to satisfy existing liability under Federal environmental laws.

(d) SAVINGS CLAUSE.—

(1) APPLICATION OF FEDERAL LAW.—Guidelines developed under this section and mitigation carried out through an environmental bank established pursuant to such guidelines shall comply with all applicable requirements of Federal law (including regulations), including—

(A) the Federal Water Pollution Control Act (33 U.S.C. 1251 et seq.);

(B) the Endangered Species Act (16 U.S.C. 1531 et seq.);

(C) the Oil Pollution Act of 1990 (33 U.S.C. 2701 et

seq.);

(D) the National Environmental Policy Act of 1969 (42 U.S.C. 4321 et seq.); and

(E) section 906 of the Water Resources Development Act of 1986 (33 U.S.C. 2283).

(2) STATUTORY CONSTRUCTION.—Nothing in this section may be construed to affect—

(A) any authority, regulatory determination, or legal obligation in effect the day before the date of enactment of the Water Resources Development Act of 2016; or

(B) the obligations or requirements of any Federal environmental law.

(e) SUNSET.—No new environmental bank may be created or approved pursuant to this section after the date that is 12 years after the date of enactment of this section.

[16 U.S.C. 3957]

TITLE IV—GREAT LAKES OIL POLLUTION RESEARCH AND DEVELOPMENT

SEC. 4001. SHORT TITLE.

This title may be cited as the "Great Lakes Oil Pollution Research and Development Act".

SEC. 4002. GREAT LAKES OIL POLLUTION RESEARCH AND DEVELOPMENT.

Section 7001 of the Oil Pollution Act of 1990 (Public Law 101–380) is amended as follows:

(1) GREAT LAKES DEMONSTRATION PROJECT.—In subsection (c)(6), strike "3" and insert "4", strike "and" after "California,", and insert "and (D) ports on the Great Lakes," after "Louisiana,".

(2) FUNDING.—In subsection (f) strike "21,250,000" and insert "22,000,000" and in subsection (f)(2) strike "2,250,000" and insert "3,000,000".

TITLE IV—GREAT LAKES OIL POLLUTION RESEARCH AND DEVELOPMENT

18 U.S.C. CHPT. 50 – GAMBLING SHIPS

18 U.S.C. CHAPTER 50

TITLE 18—CRIMES AND CRIMINAL PROCEDURE

This title was enacted by act June 25, 1948, ch. 645, §1, 62 Stat. 683

Part		Sec.
I.	Crimes	1

* * * * * * *

PART I—CRIMES

Chap.		Sec.

* * * * * * *

50.	Gambling	1081

* * * * * * *

CHAPTER 50—GAMBLING

§1081. DEFINITIONS

As used in this chapter:

The term "gambling ship" means a vessel used principally for the operation of one or more gambling establishments. Such term does not include a vessel with respect to gambling aboard such vessel beyond the territorial waters of the United States during a covered voyage (as defined in section 4472 of the Internal Revenue Code of 1986 as in effect on January 1, 1994).

The term "gambling establishment" means any common gaming or gambling establishment operated for the purpose of gaming or gambling, including accepting, recording, or registering bets, or carrying on a policy game or any other lottery, or playing any game of chance, for money or other thing of value.

The term "vessel" includes every kind of water and air craft or other contrivance used or capable of being used as a means of transportation on water, or on water and in the air, as well as any ship, boat, barge, or other water craft or any structure capable of floating on the water.

The term "American vessel" means any vessel documented or numbered under the laws of the United States; and includes any vessel which is neither documented or numbered under the laws of the United States nor documented under the laws of any foreign country, if such vessel is owned by, chartered to, or otherwise controlled by one or more citizens or residents of the United States or corporations organized under the laws of the United States or of any State.

The term "wire communication facility" means any and all instrumentalities, personnel, and services (among other things, the receipt, forwarding, or delivery of communications) used or useful in the transmission of writings, signs, pictures, and sounds of all kinds by aid of wire, cable, or other like connection between the points of origin and reception of such transmission.

(Added May 24, 1949, ch. 139, §23, 63 Stat. 92; amended Pub. L. 87–216, §1, Sept. 13, 1961, 75 Stat. 491; Pub. L. 103–322, title XXXII, §320501, Sept. 13, 1994, 108 Stat. 2114.)

§1082. GAMBLING SHIPS

(a) It shall be unlawful for any citizen or resident of the United States, or any other person who is on an American vessel or is otherwise under or within the jurisdiction of the United States, directly or indirectly—

(1) to set up, operate, or own or hold any interest in any gambling ship or any gambling establishment on any gambling ship; or

(2) in pursuance of the operation of any gambling establishment on any gambling ship, to conduct or deal any gambling game, or to conduct or operate any gambling device, or to induce, entice, solicit, or permit any person to bet or play at any such establishment,

if such gambling ship is on the high seas, or is an American vessel or otherwise under or within the jurisdiction of the United States, and is not within the jurisdiction of any State.

(b) Whoever violates the provisions of subsection (a) of this section shall be fined under this title or imprisoned not more than two years, or both.

(c) Whoever, being (1) the owner of an American vessel, or (2) the owner of any vessel under or within the jurisdiction of the United States, or (3) the owner of any vessel and being an American citizen, shall use, or knowingly permit the use of, such vessel in violation of any provision of this section shall, in addition to any other penalties provided by this chapter, forfeit such vessel, together with her tackle, apparel, and furniture, to the United States.

(Added May 24, 1949, ch. 139, §23, 63 Stat. 92; amended Pub. L. 103–322, title XXXIII, §330016(1)(L), Sept. 13, 1994, 108 Stat. 2147.)

§1083. TRANSPORTATION BETWEEN SHORE AND SHIP; PENALTIES

(a) It shall be unlawful to operate or use, or to permit the operation or use of, a vessel for the carriage or transportation, or for any part of the carriage or transportation, either directly or indirectly, of any passengers, for hire or otherwise, between a point or place within the United States and a gambling ship which is not within the jurisdiction of any State. This section does not apply to any carriage or transportation to or from a vessel in case of emergency involving the safety or protection of life or property.

(b) The Secretary of the Treasury shall prescribe necessary and reasonable rules and regulations to enforce this section and to prevent violations of its provisions.

For the operation or use of any vessel in violation of this section or of any rule or regulation issued hereunder, the owner or charterer of such vessel shall be subject to a civil penalty of $200 for each passenger carried or transported in violation of such provisions, and the master or other person in charge of such vessel shall be subject to a civil penalty of $300. Such penalty shall constitute a lien on such vessel, and proceedings to enforce such lien may be brought summarily by way of libel in any court of the United States having jurisdiction thereof. The Secretary of the Treasury may mitigate or remit any of the penalties provided by this section on such terms as he deems proper.

(Added May 24, 1949, ch. 139, §23, 63 Stat. 92.)

§1084. TRANSMISSION OF WAGERING INFORMATION; PENALTIES

(a) Whoever being engaged in the business of betting or wagering knowingly uses a wire communication facility for the transmission in interstate or foreign commerce of bets or wagers or information assisting in the placing of bets or wagers on any sporting event or contest, or for the transmission of a wire communication which entitles the recipient to receive money or credit as a result of bets or wagers, or for information assisting in the placing of bets or wagers, shall be fined under this title or imprisoned not more than two years, or both.

(b) Nothing in this section shall be construed to prevent the transmission in interstate or foreign commerce of information for use in news reporting of sporting events or contests, or for the transmission of information assisting in the placing of bets or wagers on a sporting event or contest from a State or foreign country where betting on that sporting event or contest is legal into a State or foreign country in which such betting is legal.

(c) Nothing contained in this section shall create immunity from criminal prosecution under any laws of any State.

(d) When any common carrier, subject to the jurisdiction of the Federal Communications Commission, is notified in writing by a Federal, State, or local law enforcement agency, acting within its jurisdiction, that any facility furnished by it is being used or will be used for the purpose of transmitting or receiving gambling information in interstate or foreign commerce in violation of Federal, State or local law, it shall discontinue or refuse, the leasing, furnishing, or maintaining of such facility, after reasonable notice to the subscriber, but no damages, penalty or forfeiture, civil or criminal, shall be found against any common carrier for any act done in compliance with any notice received from a law enforcement agency. Nothing in this section shall be deemed to prejudice the right of any person affected thereby to secure an appropriate determination, as otherwise provided by law, in a Federal court or in a State or local tribunal or agency, that such facility should not be discontinued or removed, or should be restored.

(e) As used in this section, the term "State" means a State of the United States, the District of Columbia, the Commonwealth of Puerto Rico, or a commonwealth, territory or possession of the United States.

(Added Pub. L. 87–216, §2, Sept. 13, 1961, 75 Stat. 491; amended Pub. L. 100–690, title VII, §7024, Nov. 18, 1988, 102 Stat. 4397; Pub. L. 101–647, title XII, §1205(g), Nov. 29, 1990, 104 Stat. 4831; Pub. L. 103–322, title XXXIII, §330016(1)(L), Sept. 13, 1994, 108 Stat. 2147.)

FEDERAL WATER POLLUTION

CONTROL ACT
SECTIONS 311 AND 312

CHAPTER 758 OF THE 80TH CONGRESS
AS AMENDED THROUGH P.L. 118-198

Federal Water Pollution Control Act

[Chapter 758 of the 80th Congress]
[33 U.S.C. 1251 et seq.]

[As Amended Through P.L. 118–198, Enacted December 23, 2024]

AN ACT To provide for water pollution control activities in the Public Health Service of the Federal Security Agency and in the Federal Works Agency, and for other purposes.

Be it enacted by the Senate and House of Representatives of the United States of America in Congress assembled,

* * * * * * *

OIL AND HAZARDOUS SUBSTANCE LIABILITY

SEC. 311. (a) For the purpose of this section, the term—

(1) "oil" means oil of any kind or in any form, including, but not limited to, petroleum, fuel oil, sludge, oil refuse, and oil mixed with wastes other than dredged spoil;

(2) "discharge" includes, but is not limited to, any spilling, leaking, pumping, pouring, emitting, emptying or dumping, but excludes (A) discharges in compliance with a permit under section 402 of this Act, (B) discharges resulting from circumstances identified and reviewed and made a part of the public record with respect to a permit issued or modified under section 402 of this Act, and subject to a condition in such permit, ,(C)[13] continuous or anticipated intermittent discharges from a point source, identified in a permit or permit application under section 402 of this Act, which are caused by events occurring within the scope of relevant operating or treatment systems, and (D) discharges incidental to mechanical removal authorized by the President under subsection (c) of this

section;

---
[13] So in law.

---

(3) "vessel" means every description of watercraft or other artificial contrivance used, or capable of being used, as a means of transportation on water other than a public vessel;

(4) "public vessel" means a vessel owned or bareboat-chartered and operated by the United States, or by a State or political subdivision thereof, or by a foreign nation, except when such vessel is engaged in commerce;

(5) "United States" means the States, the District of Columbia, the Commonwealth of Puerto Rico, the Commonwealth of the Northern Mariana Islands, Guam, American Samoa, the Virgin Islands, and the Trust Territory of the Pacific Islands;

(6) "owner or operator" means (A) in the case of a vessel, any person owning, operating, or chartering by demise, such vessel, and (B) in the case of an onshore facility, and an offshore facility, any person owning or operating such onshore facility or offshore facility, and (C) in the case of any abandoned offshore facility, the person who owned or operated such facility immediately prior to such abandonment;

(7) "person" includes an individual, firm, corporation, association, and a partnership;

(8) "remove" or "removal" refers to containment and removal of the oil or hazardous substances from the water and shorelines or the taking of such other actions as may be necessary to prevent, minimize, or mitigate damage to the public health or welfare, including, but not limited to, fish, shellfish, wildlife, and public and private property, shorelines, and beaches;

(9) "contiguous zone" means the entire zone established or to be established by the United States under article 24 of the Convention on the Territorial Sea and the Contiguous Zone;

(10) "onshore facility" means any facility (including, but not limited to, motor vehicles and rolling stock) of any kind located in, on, or under, any land within the United States other than submerged land;

(11) "offshore facility" means any facility of any kind located in, on, or under, any of the navigable waters of the United States, any facility of any kind which is subject to the jurisdiction of the United States and is located in, on, or under any other waters, other than a vessel or a public vessel, and, for the purposes of applying subsections (b), (c), (e), and (o), any foreign offshore unit (as defined in section 1001 of the Oil Pollution Act) or any other facility located seaward of the exclusive economic zone;

(12) "act of God" means an act occasioned by an unanticipated grave natural disaster;

(13) "barrel" means 42 United States gallons at 60 degrees Fahrenheit;

(14) "hazardous substance" means any substance designated pursuant to subsection (b)(2) of this section;

(15) "inland oil barge" means a non-self-propelled vessel carrying oil in bulk as cargo and certificated to operate only in the inland waters of the United States, while operating in such waters;

(16) "inland waters of the United States" means those waters of the United States lying inside the baseline from which the territorial sea is measured and those waters outside such baseline which are a part of the Gulf Intracoastal Waterway;

(17) "otherwise subject to the jurisdiction of the United States" means subject to the jurisdiction of the United States by virtue of United States citizenship, United States vessel documentation or numbering, or as provided for by international agreement to which the United States is a party;

(18) "Area Committee" means an Area Committee established under subsection (j);

(19) "Area Contingency Plan" means an Area Contingency Plan prepared under subsection (j);

(20) "Coast Guard District Response Group" means a Coast Guard District Response Group established under subsection (j);

(21) "Federal On-Scene Coordinator" means a Federal On-Scene Coordinator designated in the National Contingency Plan;

(22) "National Contingency Plan" means the National Contingency Plan prepared and published under subsection (d);

(23) "National Response Unit" means the National Response Unit established under subsection (j);

(24) "worst case discharge" means—

(A) in the case of a vessel, a discharge in adverse weather conditions of its entire cargo; and

(B) in the case of an offshore facility or onshore facility, the largest foreseeable discharge in adverse weather conditions;

(25) "removal costs" means—

(A) the costs of removal of oil or a hazardous substance that are incurred after it is discharged; and

(B) in any case in which there is a substantial threat of a discharge of oil or a hazardous substance, the costs to prevent, minimize, or mitigate that threat;

(26) "nontank vessel" means a self-propelled vessel that—

(A) is at least 400 gross tons as measured under section 14302 of title 46, United States Code, or, for vessels not measured under that section, as measured under section 14502 of that title;

(B) is not a tank vessel;

(C) carries oil of any kind as fuel for main propulsion; and

(D) operates on the navigable waters of the United States, as defined in section 2101(23) of that title;

(27) the term "best available science" means science that—

(A) maximizes the quality, objectivity, and integrity of information, including statistical information;

(B) uses peer-reviewed and publicly available data; and

(C) clearly documents and communicates risks and uncertainties in the scientific basis for such projects;

(28) the term "Chairperson" means the Chairperson of the Council;

(29) the term "coastal political subdivision" means any local political jurisdiction that is immediately below the State level

of government, including a county, parish, or borough, with a coastline that is contiguous with any portion of the United States Gulf of Mexico;

(30) the term "Comprehensive Plan" means the comprehensive plan developed by the Council pursuant to subsection (t);

(31) the term "Council" means the Gulf Coast Ecosystem Restoration Council established pursuant to subsection (t);

(32) the term "Deepwater Horizon oil spill" means the blowout and explosion of the mobile offshore drilling unit *Deepwater Horizon* that occurred on April 20, 2010, and resulting hydrocarbon releases into the environment;

(33) the term "Gulf Coast region" means—

(A) in the Gulf Coast States, the coastal zones (as that term is defined in section 304 of the Coastal Zone Management Act of 1972 (16 U.S.C. 1453)), except that, in this section, the term "coastal zones" includes land within the coastal zones that is held in trust by, or the use of which is by law subject solely to the discretion of, the Federal Government or officers or agents of the Federal Government)) that border the Gulf of Mexico;

(B) any adjacent land, water, and watersheds, that are within 25 miles of the coastal zones described in subparagraph (A) of the Gulf Coast States; and

(C) all Federal waters in the Gulf of Mexico;

(34) the term "Gulf Coast State" means any of the States of Alabama, Florida, Louisiana, Mississippi, and Texas; and

(35) the term "Trust Fund" means the Gulf Coast Restoration Trust Fund established pursuant to section 1602 of the Resources and Ecosystems Sustainability, Tourist Opportunities, and Revived Economies of the Gulf Coast States Act of 2012.

(b) (1) The Congress hereby declares that it is the policy of the United States that there should be no discharges of oil or hazardous substances into or upon the navigable waters of the United States, adjoining shorelines, or into or upon the waters of the contiguous zone, or in connection with activities under the Outer Continental Shelf Lands Act or the Deepwater Port Act of 1974, or which may affect natural resources belonging to, appertaining to, or under the exclusive management authority of the United States (including resources under the Fishery Conservation and Management Act of 1976).

(2) (A) The Administrator shall develop, promulgate, and revise as may be appropriate, regulations designating as hazardous substances, other than oil as defined in this section, such elements and compounds which, when discharged in any quantity into or upon the navigable waters of the United States or adjoining shorelines or the waters of the contiguous zone or in connection with activities under the Outer Continental Shelf Lands Act or the Deepwater Port Act of 1974, or which may affect natural resources belonging to, appertaining to, or under the exclusive management authority of the United States (including resources under the Fishery Conservation and Management Act of 1976), present an imminent and substantial danger to the public health or welfare, including, but not limited to, fish, shellfish, wildlife, shorelines, and beaches.

(B) The Administrator shall within 18 months after the date of enactment of this paragraph, conduct a study and report to the Congress on methods, mechanisms, and procedures to create incentives to achieve a higher standard of care in all aspects of the management and movement of hazardous substances on the part of owners, operators, or persons in charge of onshore facilities, offshore facilities, or vessels. The Administrator shall include in such study (1) limits of liability, (2) liability for third party damages, (3) penalties and fees, (4) spill prevention plans, (5) current practices in the insurance and banking industries, and (6) whether the penalty enacted in subclause (bb) of clause (iii) of subparagraph (B) of subsection (b)(2) of section 311 of Public Law 92–500 should be enacted.

(3) The discharge of oil or hazardous substances (i) into or upon the navigable waters of the United States, adjoining shorelines, or into or upon the waters of the contiguous zone, or (ii) in connection with activities under the Outer Continental Shelf Lands Act or the Deepwater Port Act of 1974, or which may affect natural resources belonging to, appertaining to, or under the exclusive management authority of the United States

(including resources under the Fishery Conservation and Management Act of 1976), in such quantities as may be harmful as determined by the President under paragraph (4) of this subsection, is prohibited, except (A) in the case of such discharges into the waters of the contiguous zone or which may affect natural resources belonging to, appertaining to, or under the exclusive management authority of the United States (including resources under the Fishery Conservation and Management Act of 1976), where permitted under the Protocol of 1978 Relating to the International Convention for the Prevention of Pollution from Ships, 1973, and (B) where permitted in quantities and at times and locations or under such circumstances or conditions as the President may, by regulation, determine not to be harmful. Any regulations issued under this subsection shall be consistent with maritime safety and with marine and navigation laws and regulations and applicable water quality standards.

(4) The President shall by regulation determine for the purposes of this section those quantities of oil and any hazardous substances the discharge of which may be harmful to the public health or welfare or the environment of the United States, including but not limited to fish, shellfish, wildlife, and public and private property, shorelines, and beaches.

(5) Any person in charge of a vessel or of an onshore facility or an offshore facility shall, as soon as he has knowledge of any discharge of oil or a hazardous substance from such vessel or facility in violation of paragraph (3) of this subsection, immediately notify the appropriate agency of the United States Government of such discharge. The Federal agency shall immediately notify the appropriate State agency of any State which is, or may reasonably be expected to be, affected by the discharge of oil or a hazardous substance. Any such person (A) in charge of a vessel from which oil or a hazardous substance is discharged in violation of paragraph (3)(i) of this subsection, or (B) in charge of a vessel from which oil or a hazardous substance is discharged in violation of paragraph (3)(ii) of this subsection and who is otherwise subject to the jurisdiction of the United States at the time of the discharge, or (C) in charge of an onshore facility or an offshore facility, who fails to notify immediately such agency of such discharge shall, upon conviction, be fined in accordance with title 18, United States

Code, or imprisoned for not more than 5 years, or both. Notification received pursuant to this paragraph shall not be used against any such natural person in any criminal case, except a prosecution for perjury or for giving a false statement.

(6) ADMINISTRATIVE PENALTIES.—

(A) VIOLATIONS.— Any owner, operator, or person in charge of any vessel, onshore facility, or offshore facility—

(i) from which oil or a hazardous substance is discharged in violation of paragraph (3), or

(ii) who fails or refuses to comply with any regulation issued under subsection (j) to which that owner, operator, or person in charge is subject,

may be assessed a class I or class II civil penalty by the Secretary of the department in which the Coast Guard is operating, the Secretary of Transportation, or the Administrator.

(B) CLASSES OF PENALTIES.—

(i) CLASS I.— The amount of a class I civil penalty under subparagraph (A) may not exceed $10,000 per violation, except that the maximum amount of any class I civil penalty under this subparagraph shall not exceed $25,000. Before assessing a civil penalty under this clause, the Administrator or Secretary, as the case may be, shall give to the person to be assessed such penalty written notice of the Administrator's or Secretary's proposal to assess the penalty and the opportunity to request, within 30 days of the date the notice is received by such person, a hearing on the proposed penalty. Such hearing shall not be subject to section 554 or 556 of title 5, United States Code, but shall provide a reasonable opportunity to be heard and to present evidence.

(ii) CLASS II.— The amount of a class II civil penalty under subparagraph (A) may not exceed $10,000 per day for each day during which the violation continues; except that the maximum amount of any class II civil penalty under this subparagraph shall not exceed $125,000. Except as otherwise provided in this subsection, a class II civil penalty shall be assessed and collected in the same manner, and subject to the same provisions, as in the case of civil penalties assessed and collected after notice and opportunity for a hearing on the record in accordance with section 554 of title 5, United States Code. The Administrator and Secretary may issue rules for discovery procedures for hearings under this paragraph.

(C) RIGHTS OF INTERESTED PERSONS.—

(i) PUBLIC NOTICE.— Before issuing an order assessing a class II civil penalty under this paragraph the Administrator or Secretary, as the case may be, shall provide public notice of and reasonable opportunity to comment on the proposed issuance of such order.

(ii) PRESENTATION OF EVIDENCE.— Any person who comments on a proposed assessment of a class II civil penalty under this paragraph shall be given notice of any hearing held under this paragraph and of the order assessing such penalty. In any hearing held under this paragraph, such person shall have a reasonable opportunity to be heard and to present evidence.

(iii) RIGHTS OF INTERESTED PERSONS TO A HEARING.— If no hearing is held under subparagraph (B) before issuance of an order assessing a class II civil penalty under this paragraph, any person who commented on the proposed assessment may petition, within 30 days after the issuance of such order, the Administrator or Secretary, as the case may be, to set aside such order and to provide a hearing on the penalty. If the evidence presented by the petitioner in support of the petition is material and was not considered in the issuance of the order, the Administrator or Secretary shall immediately set aside such order and provide a hearing in accordance with subparagraph (B)(ii). If the Administrator or Secretary denies a hearing under this clause, the Administrator or Secretary shall provide to the petitioner, and publish in the Federal Register, notice of and the reasons for such denial.

(D) FINALITY OF ORDER.— An order assessing a class II civil penalty under this paragraph shall become final 30 days after its issuance unless a petition for judicial review is filed under subparagraph (G) or a hearing is requested under subparagraph (C)(iii). If such a hearing is denied, such order shall become final 30 days after such denial.

(E) EFFECT OF ORDER.— Action taken by the Administrator or Secretary, as the case may be, under this paragraph shall not affect or limit the Administrator's or Secretary's authority to enforce any provision of this Act; except that any violation—

    (i) with respect to which the Administrator or Secretary has commenced and is diligently prosecuting an action to assess a class II civil penalty under this paragraph, or

    (ii) for which the Administrator or Secretary has issued a final order assessing a class II civil penalty not subject to further judicial review and the violator has paid a penalty assessed under this paragraph,

shall not be the subject of a civil penalty action under section 309(d), 309(g), or 505 of this Act or under paragraph (7).

(F) EFFECT OF ACTION ON COMPLIANCE.— No action by the Administrator or Secretary under this paragraph shall affect any person's obligation to comply with any section of this Act.

(G) JUDICIAL REVIEW.— Any person against whom a civil penalty is assessed under this paragraph or who commented on the proposed assessment of such penalty in accordance with subparagraph (C) may obtain review of such assessment—

    (i) in the case of assessment of a class I civil penalty, in the United States District Court for the District of Columbia or in the district in which the violation is alleged to have occurred, or

    (ii) in the case of assessment of a class II civil penalty, in United States Court of Appeals for the District of Columbia Circuit or for any other circuit in which such person resides or transacts business,

by filing a notice of appeal in such court within the 30-day period beginning on the date the civil penalty order is issued and by simultaneously sending a copy of such notice by certified mail to the Administrator or Secretary, as the case may be, and the Attorney General. The Administrator or Secretary shall promptly file in such court a certified copy of the record on which the order was issued. Such court shall not set aside or remand such order unless there is not substantial evidence in the record, taken as a whole, to support the finding of a violation or unless the Administrator's or Secretary's assessment of the penalty constitutes an abuse of discretion and shall not impose additional civil penalties for the same violation unless the Administrator's or Secretary's assessment of the penalty constitutes an abuse of discretion.

(H) COLLECTION.— If any person fails to pay an assessment of a civil penalty—

(i) after the assessment has become final, or

(ii) after a court in an action brought under subparagraph (G) has entered a final judgment in favor of the Administrator or Secretary, as the case may be,

the Administrator or Secretary shall request the Attorney General to bring a civil action in an appropriate district court to recover the amount assessed (plus interest at currently prevailing rates from the date of the final order or the date of the final judgment, as the case may be). In such an action, the validity, amount, and appropriateness of such penalty shall not be subject to review. Any person who fails to pay on a timely basis the amount of an assessment of a civil penalty as described in the first sentence of this subparagraph shall be required to pay, in addition to such amount and interest, attorneys fees and costs for collection proceedings and a quarterly nonpayment penalty for each quarter during which such failure to pay persists. Such nonpayment penalty shall be in an amount equal to 20 percent of the aggregate amount of such person's penalties and nonpayment penalties which are unpaid as of the beginning of such quarter.

(I) SUBPOENAS.— The Administrator or Secretary, as the case may be, may issue subpoenas for the attendance and testimony of witnesses and the production of relevant papers, books, or documents in connection with hearings under this paragraph. In case of contumacy or refusal to obey a subpoena issued pursuant to this subparagraph and served upon any person, the district court of the United States for any district in which such person is found, resides, or transacts business, upon application by the United States and after notice to such person, shall have jurisdiction to issue an order requiring such person to appear and give testimony before the administrative law judge or to appear and produce documents before the administrative law judge, or both, and any failure to obey such order of the court may be punished by such court as a contempt thereof.

(7) CIVIL PENALTY ACTION.—

(A) DISCHARGE, GENERALLY.— Any person who is the owner, operator, or person in charge of any vessel, onshore facility, or offshore facility from which oil or a hazardous substance is discharged in violation of paragraph (3), shall be subject to a civil penalty in an amount up to $25,000 per day of violation or an amount up to $1,000 per barrel of oil or unit of reportable quantity of hazardous substances discharged.

(B) FAILURE TO REMOVE OR COMPLY.— Any person described in subparagraph (A) who, without sufficient cause—

(i) fails to properly carry out removal of the discharge under an order of the President pursuant to subsection (c); or

(ii) fails to comply with an order pursuant to subsection (e)(1)(B);

shall be subject to a civil penalty in an amount up to $25,000 per day of violation or an amount up to 3 times the costs incurred by the Oil Spill Liability Trust Fund as a result of such failure.

(C) FAILURE TO COMPLY WITH REGULATION.— Any person who fails or refuses to comply with any regulation issued under subsection (j) shall be subject to a civil penalty in an amount up to $25,000 per day of violation.

(D) GROSS NEGLIGENCE.— In any case in which a violation of paragraph (3) was the result of gross negligence or willful misconduct of a person described in subparagraph (A), the person shall be subject to a civil penalty of not less than $100,000, and not more than $3,000 per barrel of oil or unit of reportable quantity of hazardous substance discharged.

(E) JURISDICTION.— An action to impose a civil penalty under this paragraph may be brought in the district court of the United States for the district in which the defendant is located, resides, or is doing business, and such court shall have jurisdiction to assess such penalty.

(F) LIMITATION.— A person is not liable for a civil penalty under this paragraph for a discharge if the person has been assessed a civil penalty under paragraph (6) for the discharge.

(8) DETERMINATION OF AMOUNT.— In determining the amount of a civil penalty under paragraphs (6) and (7), the Administrator, Secretary, or the court, as the case may be, shall consider the seriousness of the violation or violations, the economic benefit to the violator, if any, resulting from the violation, the degree of culpability involved, any other penalty for the same incident, any history of prior violations, the nature, extent, and degree of success of any efforts of the violator to minimize or mitigate the effects of the discharge, the economic impact of the penalty on the violator, and any other matters as justice may require.

(9) MITIGATION OF DAMAGE.— In addition to establishing a penalty for the discharge of oil or a hazardous substance, the Administrator or the Secretary of the department in which the Coast Guard is operating may act to mitigate the damage to the public health or welfare caused by such discharge. The cost of such mitigation shall be deemed a cost incurred under subsection (c) of this section for the removal of such substance by the United States Government.

(10) RECOVERY OF REMOVAL COSTS.— Any costs of removal incurred in connection with a discharge excluded by subsection (a)(2)(C) of this section shall be recoverable from the owner or

operator of the source of the discharge in an action brought under section 309(b) of this Act.

(11) LIMITATION.— Civil penalties shall not be assessed under both this section and section 309 for the same discharge.

(12)[14] WITHHOLDING CLEARANCE.— If any owner, operator, or person in charge of a vessel is liable for a civil penalty under this subsection, or if reasonable cause exists to believe that the owner, operator, or person in charge may be subject to a civil penalty under this subsection, the Secretary of the Treasury, upon the request of the Secretary of the department in which the Coast Guard is operating or the Administrator, shall with respect to such vessel refuse or revoke—

---

[14]   Indentation so in law.

(A) the clearance required by section 4197 of the Revised Statutes of the United States (46 U.S.C. App. 91);

(B) a permit to proceed under section 4367 of the Revised Statutes of the United States (46 U.S.C. App. 313); and

(C) a permit to depart required under section 443 of the Tariff Act of 1930 (19 U.S.C. 1443);

as applicable. Clearance or a permit refused or revoked under this paragraph may be granted upon the filing of a bond or other surety satisfactory to the Secretary of the department in which the Coast Guard is operating or the Administrator.

(c) FEDERAL REMOVAL AUTHORITY.—

(1) GENERAL REMOVAL REQUIREMENT.— (A) The President shall, in accordance with the National Contingency Plan and any appropriate Area Contingency Plan, ensure effective and immediate removal of a discharge, and mitigation or prevention of a substantial threat of a discharge, of oil or a hazardous substance—

(i) into or on the navigable waters;

(ii) on the adjoining shorelines to the navigable waters;

(iii) into or on the waters of the exclusive economic zone; or

(iv) that may affect natural resources belonging to, appertaining to, or under the exclusive management authority of the United States.

(B) In carrying out this paragraph, the President may—

(i) remove or arrange for the removal of a discharge, and mitigate or prevent a substantial threat of a discharge, at any time;

(ii) direct or monitor all Federal, State, and private actions to remove a discharge; and

(iii) remove and, if necessary, destroy a vessel discharging, or threatening to discharge, by whatever means are available.

(2) DISCHARGE POSING SUBSTANTIAL THREAT TO PUBLIC HEALTH OR WELFARE.— (A) If a discharge, or a substantial threat of a discharge, of oil or a hazardous substance from a vessel, offshore facility, or onshore facility is of such a size or character as to be a substantial threat to the public health or welfare of the United States (including but not limited to fish, shellfish, wildlife, other natural resources, and the public and private beaches and shorelines of the United States), the President shall direct all Federal, State, and private actions to remove the discharge or to mitigate or prevent the threat of the discharge.

(B) In carrying out this paragraph, the President may, without regard to any other provision of law governing contracting procedures or employment of personnel by the Federal Government—

(i) remove or arrange for the removal of the discharge, or mitigate or prevent the substantial threat of the discharge; and

(ii) remove and, if necessary, destroy a vessel discharging, or threatening to discharge, by whatever means are available.

(3) ACTIONS IN ACCORDANCE WITH NATIONAL CONTINGENCY PLAN.— (A) Each Federal agency, State, owner or operator, or other person participating in efforts under this subsection shall act in accordance with the National Contingency Plan or as directed by the President.

(B) An owner or operator participating in efforts under this subsection shall act in accordance with the National

Contingency Plan and the applicable response plan required under subsection (j), or as directed by the President, except that the owner or operator may deviate from the applicable response plan if the President or the Federal On-Scene Coordinator determines that deviation from the response plan would provide for a more expeditious or effective response to the spill or mitigation of its environmental effects.

(C) In any case in which the President or the Federal On-Scene Coordinator authorizes a deviation from the salvor as part of a deviation under subparagraph (B) from the applicable response plan required under subsection (j), the Commandant of the Coast Guard shall submit to the Committee on Transportation and Infrastructure of the House of Representatives and the Committee on Commerce, Science, and Transportation of the Senate a report describing the deviation and the reasons for such deviation not less than 3 days after such deviation is authorized.

(4) EXEMPTION FROM LIABILITY.— (A) A person is not liable for removal costs or damages which result from actions taken or omitted to be taken in the course of rendering care, assistance, or advice consistent with the National Contingency Plan or as otherwise directed by the President relating to a discharge or a substantial threat of a discharge of oil or a hazardous substance.

(B) Subparagraph (A) does not apply—

(i) to a responsible party;

(ii) to a response under the Comprehensive Environmental Response, Compensation, and Liability Act of 1980 (42 U.S.C. 9601 et seq.);

(iii) with respect to personal injury or wrongful death; or

(iv) if the person is grossly negligent or engages in willful misconduct.

(C) A responsible party is liable for any removal costs and damages that another person is relieved of under subparagraph (A).

(5) OBLIGATION AND LIABILITY OF OWNER OR OPERATOR NOT

AFFECTED.— Nothing in this subsection affects—

(A) the obligation of an owner or operator to respond immediately to a discharge, or the threat of a discharge, of oil; or

(B) the liability of a responsible party under the Oil Pollution Act of 1990.

(6) RESPONSIBLE PARTY DEFINED.— For purposes of this subsection, the term "responsible party" has the meaning given that term under section 1001 of the Oil Pollution Act of 1990.

(d) NATIONAL CONTINGENCY PLAN.—

(1) PREPARATION BY PRESIDENT.— The President shall prepare and publish a National Contingency Plan for removal of oil and hazardous substances pursuant to this section.

(2) CONTENTS.— The National Contingency Plan shall provide for efficient, coordinated, and effective action to minimize damage from oil and hazardous substance discharges, including containment, dispersal, and removal of oil and hazardous substances, and shall include, but not be limited to, the following:

(A) Assignment of duties and responsibilities among Federal departments and agencies in coordination with State and local agencies and port authorities including, but not limited to, water pollution control and conservation and trusteeship of natural resources (including conservation of fish and wildlife).

(B) Identification, procurement, maintenance, and storage of equipment and supplies.

(C) Establishment or designation of Coast Guard strike teams, consisting of—

(i) personnel who shall be trained, prepared, and available to provide necessary services to carry out the National Contingency Plan;

(ii) adequate oil and hazardous substance pollution control equipment and material; and

(iii) a detailed oil and hazardous substance pollution and prevention plan, including measures to protect fisheries and wildlife.

(D) A system of surveillance and notice designed to

safeguard against as well as ensure earliest possible notice of discharges of oil and hazardous substances and imminent threats of such discharges to the appropriate State and Federal agencies.

(E) Establishment of a national center to provide coordination and direction for operations in carrying out the Plan.

(F) Procedures and techniques to be employed in identifying, containing, dispersing, and removing oil and hazardous substances.

(G) A schedule, prepared in cooperation with the States, identifying—

(i) dispersants, other chemicals, and other spill mitigating devices and substances, if any, that may be used in carrying out the Plan,

(ii) the waters in which such dispersants, other chemicals, and other spill mitigating devices and substances may be used, and

(iii) the quantities of such dispersant, other chemicals, or other spill mitigating device or substance which can be used safely in such waters,

which schedule shall provide in the case of any dispersant, chemical, spill mitigating device or substance, or waters not specifically identified in such schedule that the President, or his delegate, may, on a case-by-case basis, identify the dispersants, other chemicals, and other spill mitigating devices and substances which may be used, the waters in which they may be used, and the quantities which can be used safely in such waters.

(H) A system whereby the State or States affected by a discharge of oil or hazardous substance may act where necessary to remove such discharge and such State or States may be reimbursed in accordance with the Oil Pollution Act of 1990, in the case of any discharge of oil from a vessel or facility, for the reasonable costs incurred for that removal, from the Oil Spill Liability Trust Fund.

(I) Establishment of criteria and procedures to ensure immediate and effective Federal identification of, and response to, a discharge, or the threat of a discharge, that results in a substantial threat to the public health or welfare of the United States, as required under subsection (c)(2).

(J) Establishment of procedures and standards for removing a worst case discharge of oil, and for mitigating or preventing a substantial threat of such a discharge.

(K) Designation of the Federal official who shall be the Federal On-Scene Coordinator for each area for which an Area Contingency Plan is required to be prepared under subsection (j).

(L) Establishment of procedures for the coordination of activities of—

(i) Coast Guard strike teams established under subparagraph (C);

(ii) Federal On-Scene Coordinators designated under subparagraph (K);

(iii) District Response Groups established under subsection (j); and

(iv) Area Committees established under subsection (j).

(M) A fish and wildlife response plan, developed in consultation with the United States Fish and Wildlife Service, the National Oceanic and Atmospheric Administration, and other interested parties (including State fish and wildlife conservation officials), for the immediate and effective protection, rescue, and rehabilitation of, and the minimization of risk of damage to, fish and wildlife resources and their habitat that are harmed or that may be jeopardized by a discharge.

(3) REVISIONS AND AMENDMENTS.— The President may, from time to time, as the President deems advisable, revise or otherwise amend the National Contingency Plan.

(4) ACTIONS IN ACCORDANCE WITH NATIONAL CONTINGENCY PLAN.— After publication of the National Contingency Plan, the removal of oil and hazardous substances and actions to minimize damage from oil and hazardous substance discharges shall, to the greatest extent possible, be in accordance with the National Contingency Plan.

(e) CIVIL ENFORCEMENT.—

(1) ORDERS PROTECTING PUBLIC HEALTH.— In addition to any action taken by a State or local government, when the President determines that there may be an imminent and substantial threat to the public health or welfare of the United States, including fish, shellfish, and wildlife, public and private property, shorelines, beaches, habitat, and other living and nonliving natural resources under the jurisdiction or control of the United States, because of an actual or threatened discharge of oil or a hazardous substance from a vessel or facility in violation of subsection (b), the President may—

(A) require the Attorney General to secure any relief from any person, including the owner or operator of the vessel or facility, as may be necessary to abate such endangerment; or

(B) after notice to the affected State, take any other action under this section, including issuing administrative orders, that may be necessary to protect the public health and welfare.

(2) JURISDICTION OF DISTRICT COURTS.— The district courts of the United States shall have jurisdiction to grant any relief under this subsection that the public interest and the equities of the case may require.

(f) (1) Except where an owner or operator can prove that a discharge was caused solely by (A) an act of God, (B) an act of war, (C) negligence on the part of the United States Government, or (D) an act or omission of a third party without regard to whether any such act or omission was or was not negligent, or any combination of the foregoing clauses, such owner or operator of any vessel from which oil or a hazardous substance is discharged in violation of subsection (b)(3) of this section shall, notwithstanding any other provision of law, be liable to the United States Government for the actual costs incurred under subsection (c) for the removal of such oil or substance by the United States Government in an amount not to exceed, in the case of an inland oil barge $125 per gross ton of such barge, or $125,000, whichever is greater, and in the case of any other vessel, $150 per gross ton of such vessel (or, for a vessel carrying oil or hazardous substances as cargo, $250,000), whichever is greater, except that where the United States can show that such discharge was the result of willful negligence or willful misconduct within the privity and knowledge of the owner, such owner or operator shall be liable to the United States Government for the full amount of such costs. Such costs shall constitute a maritime lien on such vessel which may be recovered in an action in rem in the district court of the United States for any district within which any vessel may be found. The United States may also bring an action against the owner or operator of such vessel in any court of competent jurisdiction to recover such costs.

(2) Except where an owner or operator of an onshore facility can prove that a discharge was caused solely by (A) an act of God, (B) an act of war, (C) negligence on the part of the United States Government, or (D) an act or omission of a third party without regard to whether any such act or omission was or was not negligent, or any combination of the foregoing clauses, such owner or operator of any such facility from which oil or a hazardous substance is discharged in violation of subsection (b)(3) of this section shall be liable to the United States Government for the actual costs incurred under subsection (c) for the removal of such oil or substance by the United States Government in an amount not to exceed $50,000,000, except that where the United States can show that such discharge was the result of willful negligence or willful misconduct within the privity and knowledge of the owner, such owner or operator shall be liable to the United States Government for the full amount of such costs. The United States may bring an action against the owner or operator of such facility in any court of competent jurisdiction to recover such costs. The Administrator is authorized, by regulation, after consultation with the Secretary of Commerce and the Small Business Administration, to establish reasonable and equitable classifications, of those onshore facilities having a total fixed storage capacity of 1,000 barrels or less which he determines because of size, type, and location do not present a substantial risk of the discharge of oil or hazardous substance in violation of subsection (b)(3) of this section, and apply with respect to such classifications differing limits of liability which may be less than the amount contained in this paragraph.

(3) Except where an owner or operator of an offshore facility can prove that a discharge was caused solely by (A) an act of God, (B) an act of war, (C) negligence on the part of the United States Government, or (D) an act or omission of a

third party without regard to whether any such act or omission was or was not negligent, or any combination of the foregoing clauses, such owner or operator of any such facility from which oil or a hazardous substance is discharged in violation of subsection (b)(3) of this section shall, notwithstanding any other provision of law, be liable to the United States Government for the actual costs incurred under subsection (c) for the removal of such oil or substance by the United States Government in an amount not to exceed $50,000,000, except that where the United States can show that such discharge was the result of willful negligence or willful misconduct within the privity and knowledge of the owner, such owner or operator shall be liable to the United States Government for the full amount of such costs. The United States may bring an action against the owner or operator of such a facility in any court of competent jurisdiction to recover such costs.

(4) The costs of removal of oil or a hazardous substance for which the owner or operator of a vessel or onshore or offshore facility is liable under subsection (f) of this section shall include any costs or expenses incurred by the Federal Government or any State government in the restoration or replacement of natural resources damaged or destroyed as a result of a discharge of oil or a hazardous substance in violation of subsection (b) of this section.

(5) The President, or the authorized representative of any State, shall act on behalf of the public as trustee of the natural resources to recover for the costs of replacing or restoring such resources. Sums recovered shall be used to restore, rehabilitate, or acquire the equivalent of such natural resources by the appropriate agencies of the Federal Government, or the State government.

(g) Where the owner or operator of a vessel (other than an inland oil barge) carrying oil or hazardous substances as cargo or an onshore or offshore facility which handles or stores oil or hazardous substances in bulk, from which oil or a hazardous substance is discharged in violation of subsection (b) of this section, alleges that such discharge was caused solely by an act or omission of a third party, such owner or operator shall pay to the United States Government the actual costs incurred under subsection (c) for removal of such oil or substance and shall be entitled by subrogation to all rights of the United States Government to recover such costs from such third party under this subsection. In any case where an owner or operator of a vessel, of an onshore facility, or of an offshore facility, from which oil or a hazardous substance is discharged in violation of subsection (b)(3) of this section, proves that such discharge of oil or hazardous substance was caused solely by an act or omission of a third party, or was caused solely by such an act or omission in combination with an act of God, an act of war, or negligence on the part of the United States Government, such third party shall, not withstanding any other provision of law, be liable to the United States Government for the actual costs incurred under subsection (c) for removal of such oil or substance by the United States Government, except where such third party can prove that such discharge was caused solely by (A) an act of God, (B) an act of war, (C) negligence on the part of the United States Government, or (D) an act or omission of another party without regard to whether such act or omission was or was not negligent, or any combination of the foregoing clauses. If such third party was the owner or operator of a vessel which caused the discharge of oil or a hazardous substance in violation of subsection (b)(3) of this section, the liability of such third party under this subsection shall not exceed, in the case of an inland oil barge $125 per gross ton of such barge, $125,000, whichever is greater, and in the case of any other vessel, $150 per gross ton of such vessel (or, for a vessel carrying oil or hazardous substances as cargo, $250,000), whichever is greater. In any other case the liability of such third party shall not exceed the limitation which would have been applicable to the owner or operator of the vessel or the onshore or offshore facility from which the discharge actually occurred if such owner or operator were liable. If the United States can show that the discharge of oil or a hazardous substance in violation of subsection (b)(3) of this section was the result of willful negligence or willful misconduct within the privity and knowledge of such third party, such third party shall be liable to the United States Government for the full amount of such removal costs. The United States may bring an action against the third party in any court of competent jurisdiction to recover such removal costs.

(h) The liabilities established by this section shall in no way affect any rights which (1) the owner or operator of a vessel or of an onshore facility or an offshore facility may have against any third party whose acts may in any way have caused or contributed to such discharge, or (2) The[15] United States Government may have against any third party whose actions may in any way have caused or contributed to the discharge of oil or hazardous substance.

---

[15]   So in law. Should not be capitalized.

(i) In any case where an owner or operator of a vessel or an onshore facility or an offshore facility from which oil or a hazardous substance is discharged in violation of subsection (b)(3) of this section acts to remove such oil or substance in accordance with regulations promulgated pursuant to this section, such owner or operator shall be entitled to recover the reasonable costs incurred in such removal upon establishing, in a suit which may be brought against the United States Government in the United States Claims Court, that such discharge was caused solely by (A) an act of God, (B) an act of war, (C) negligence on the part of the United States Government, or (D) an act or omission of a third party without regard to whether such act or omission was or was not negligent, or of any combination of the foregoing clauses.

(j) NATIONAL RESPONSE SYSTEM.—

(1) IN GENERAL.— Consistent with the National Contingency Plan required by subsection (c)(2) of this section, as soon as practicable after the effective date of this section, and from time to time thereafter, the President shall issue regulations consistent with maritime safety and with marine and navigation laws (A) establishing methods and procedures for removal of discharged oil and hazardous substances, (B) establishing criteria for the development and implementation of local and regional oil and hazardous substance removal contingency plans, (C) establishing procedures, methods, and equipment and other requirements for equipment to prevent discharges of oil and hazardous substances from vessels and from onshore facilities and offshore facilities, and to contain such discharges, and (D) governing the inspection of vessels carrying cargoes of oil and hazardous substances and the inspection of such cargoes in order to reduce the likelihood of discharges of oil from vessels in violation of this section.

(2) NATIONAL RESPONSE UNIT.— The Secretary of the department in which the Coast Guard is operating shall establish a National Response Unit at Elizabeth City, North Carolina. The Secretary, acting through the National Response

Unit—

(A) shall compile and maintain a comprehensive computer list of spill removal resources, personnel, and equipment that is available worldwide and within the areas designated by the President pursuant to paragraph (4), and of information regarding previous spills, including data from universities, research institutions, State governments, and other nations, as appropriate, which shall be disseminated as appropriate to response groups and area committees, and which shall be available to Federal and State agencies and the public;

(B) shall provide technical assistance, equipment, and other resources requested by a Federal On-Scene Coordinator;

(C) shall coordinate use of private and public personnel and equipment to remove a worst case discharge, and to mitigate or prevent a substantial threat of such a discharge, from a vessel, offshore facility, or onshore facility operating in or near an area designated by the President pursuant to paragraph (4);

(D) may provide technical assistance in the preparation of Area Contingency Plans required under paragraph (4);

(E) shall administer Coast Guard strike teams established under the National Contingency Plan;

(F) shall maintain on file all Area Contingency Plans approved by the President under this subsection; and

(G) shall review each of those plans that affects its responsibilities under this subsection.

(3) COAST GUARD DISTRICT RESPONSE GROUPS.— (A) The Secretary of the department in which the Coast Guard is operating shall establish in each Coast Guard district a Coast Guard District Response Group.

(B) Each Coast Guard District Response Group shall consist of—

(i) the Coast Guard personnel and equipment, including firefighting equipment, of each port within the district;

(ii) additional prepositioned equipment; and

(iii) a district response advisory staff.

(C) Coast Guard district response groups—

(i) shall provide technical assistance, equipment, and other resources when required by a Federal On-Scene Coordinator;

(ii) shall maintain all Coast Guard response equipment within its district;

(iii) may provide technical assistance in the preparation of Area Contingency Plans required under paragraph (4); and

(iv) shall review each of those plans that affect its area of geographic responsibility.

(4) AREA COMMITTEES AND AREA CONTINGENCY PLANS.— (A) There is established for each area designated by the President an Area Committee comprised of members appointed by the President from qualified—

(i) personnel of Federal, State, and local agencies; and

(ii) members of federally recognized Indian tribes, where applicable.

(B) Each Area Committee, under the direction of the Federal On-Scene Coordinator for its area, shall—

(i) prepare for its area the Area Contingency Plan required under subparagraph (C);

(ii) work with State, local, and tribal officials to enhance the contingency planning of those officials and to assure preplanning of joint response efforts, including appropriate procedures for mechanical recovery, dispersal, shoreline cleanup, protection of sensitive environmental areas, and protection, rescue, and rehabilitation of fisheries and wildlife, including advance planning with respect to the closing and reopening of fishing areas following a discharge; and

(iii) work with State, local, and tribal officials to expedite decisions for the use of dispersants and other mitigating substances and devices.

(C) Each Area Committee shall prepare and submit to the President for approval an Area Contingency Plan for its area. The Area Contingency Plan shall—

(i) when implemented in conjunction with the National Contingency Plan, be adequate to remove a worst case discharge, and to mitigate or prevent a substantial threat of such a discharge, from a vessel, offshore facility, or onshore facility operating in or near the area;

(ii) describe the area covered by the plan, including the areas of special economic or environmental importance that might be damaged by a discharge;

(iii) describe in detail the responsibilities of an owner or operator and of Federal, State, and local agencies in removing a discharge, and in mitigating or preventing a substantial threat of a discharge;

(iv) list the equipment (including firefighting equipment), dispersants or other mitigating substances and devices, and personnel available to an owner or operator, Federal, State, and local agencies, and tribal governments, to ensure an effective and immediate removal of a discharge, and to ensure mitigation or prevention of a substantial threat of a discharge;

(v) compile a list of local scientists, both inside and outside Federal Government service, with expertise in the environmental effects of spills of the types of oil typically transported in the area, who may be contacted to provide information or, where appropriate, participate in meetings of the scientific support team convened in response to a spill, and describe the procedures to be followed for obtaining an expedited decision regarding the use of dispersants;

(vi) describe in detail how the plan is integrated into other Area Contingency Plans and vessel, offshore facility, and onshore facility response plans approved under this subsection, and into operating procedures of the National Response Unit;

(vii) include a framework for advance planning and decisionmaking with respect to the closing and reopening of fishing areas following a discharge, including protocols and standards for the closing and reopening of fishing areas;

(viii) include any other information the President requires; and

(ix) be updated periodically by the Area Committee.

(D) The President shall—

(i) review and approve Area Contingency Plans under this paragraph; and

(ii) periodically review Area Contingency Plans so approved.

(5) TANK VESSEL, NONTANK VESSEL, AND FACILITY RESPONSE PLANS.— (A) (i) The President shall issue regulations which require an owner or operator of a tank vessel or facility described in subparagraph (C) to prepare and submit to the President a plan for responding, to the maximum extent practicable, to a worst case discharge, and to a substantial threat of such a discharge, of oil or a hazardous substance.

(ii) The President shall also issue regulations which require an owner or operator of a nontank vessel to prepare and submit to the President a plan for responding, to the maximum extent practicable, to a worst case discharge, and to a substantial threat of such a discharge, of oil.

(B) The Secretary of the Department in which the Coast Guard is operating may issue regulations which require an owner or operator of a tank vessel, a nontank vessel, or a facility described in subparagraph (C) that transfers noxious liquid substances in bulk to or from a vessel to prepare and submit to the Secretary a plan for responding, to the maximum extent practicable, to a worst case discharge, and to a substantial threat of such a discharge, of a noxious liquid substance that is not designated as a hazardous substance or regulated as oil in any other law or regulation. For purposes of this paragraph, the term "noxious liquid substance" has the same meaning when that term is used in the MARPOL Protocol described in section 2(a)(3) of the Act to Prevent Pollution from Ships (33 U.S.C. 1901(a)(3)).

(C) The tank vessels, nontank vessels, and facilities referred to in subparagraphs (A) and (B) are the following:

(i) A tank vessel, as defined under section 2101 of title 46, United States Code.

(ii) A nontank vessel.

(iii) An offshore facility.

(iv) An onshore facility that, because of its location, could reasonably be expected to cause substantial harm to the environment by discharging into or on the navigable waters, adjoining shorelines, or the exclusive economic zone.

(D) A response plan required under this paragraph shall—

(i) be consistent with the requirements of the National Contingency Plan and Area Contingency Plans;

(ii) identify the qualified individual having full authority to implement removal actions, and require immediate communications between that individual and the appropriate Federal official and the persons providing personnel and equipment pursuant to clause (iii);

(iii) identify, and ensure by contract or other means approved by the President the availability of, private personnel and equipment necessary to remove to the maximum extent practicable a worst case discharge (including a discharge resulting from fire or explosion), and to mitigate or prevent a substantial threat of such a discharge;

(iv) describe the training, equipment testing, periodic unannounced drills, and response actions of persons on the vessel or at the facility, to be carried out under the plan to ensure the safety of the vessel or facility and to mitigate or prevent the discharge, or the substantial threat of a discharge;

(v) be updated periodically; and

(vi) be resubmitted for approval of each significant change.

(E) With respect to any response plan submitted under this paragraph for an onshore facility that, because of its location, could reasonably be expected to cause significant and substantial harm to the environment by discharging into or on the navigable waters or adjoining shorelines or the exclusive economic zone, and with respect to each response plan submitted under this paragraph for a tank vessel, nontank vessel, or offshore facility, the President shall—

(i) promptly review such response plan;

(ii) require amendments to any plan that does not meet the requirements of this paragraph;

(iii) approve any plan that meets the requirements of this paragraph;

(iv) review each plan periodically thereafter; and

(v) in the case of a plan for a nontank vessel, consider any applicable State-mandated response plan in effect on the date of the enactment of the Coast Guard and Maritime Transportation Act of 2004 and ensure consistency to the extent practicable.

(F)[16] A tank vessel, nontank vessel, offshore facility, or onshore facility required to prepare a response plan under this subsection may not handle, store, or transport oil unless—

---

[16]   Subparagraph (F) of section 311(j)(5) (as redesignated) shall take effect 36 months (August 18, 1993) after the date of the enactment of Public Law 101-380. See P.L. 101-380, sec. 4202(b)(4)(C), 104 Stat. 532.

(i) in the case of a tank vessel, nontank vessel, offshore facility, or onshore facility for which a response plan is reviewed by the President under subparagraph (E), the plan has been approved by the President; and

(ii) the vessel or facility is operating in compliance with the plan.

(G) Notwithstanding subparagraph (E), the President may authorize a tank vessel, nontank vessel, offshore facility, or onshore facility to operate without a response plan approved under this paragraph, until not later than 2 years after the date of the submission to the President of a plan for the tank vessel, nontank vessel, or facility, if the owner or operator certifies that the owner or operator has ensured by contract or other means approved by the President the availability of private personnel and equipment necessary to respond, to the maximum extent practicable, to a worst case discharge or a substantial threat of such a discharge.

(H) The owner or operator of a tank vessel, nontank vessel, offshore facility, or onshore facility may not claim as a defense to liability under title I of the Oil Pollution Act of 1990 that the owner or operator was acting in accordance with an approved response plan.

(I) The Secretary shall maintain, in the Vessel Identification System established under chapter 125 of title 46, United States Code, the dates of approval and review of a response plan under this paragraph for each tank vessel and nontank vessel that is a vessel of the United States.

(6) EQUIPMENT REQUIREMENTS AND INSPECTION.— The President may require—

(A) periodic inspection of containment booms, skimmers, vessels, and other major equipment used to remove discharges; and

(B) vessels operating on navigable waters and carrying oil or a hazardous substance in bulk as cargo, and nontank vessels carrying oil of any kind as fuel for main propulsion, to carry appropriate removal equipment that employs the best technology economically feasible and that is compatible with the safe operation of the vessel.

(7) AREA DRILLS.— The President shall periodically conduct drills of removal capability, without prior notice, in areas for which Area Contingency Plans are required under this subsection and under relevant tank vessel, nontank vessel, and facility response plans. The drills may include participation by Federal, State, and local agencies, the owners and operators of vessels and facilities in the area, and private industry. The President may publish annual reports on these drills, including assessments of the effectiveness of the plans and a list of amendments made to improve plans.

(8) UNITED STATES GOVERNMENT NOT LIABLE.— The United States Government is not liable for any damages arising from its actions or omissions relating to any response plan required by this section.

(9) WESTERN ALASKA OIL SPILL PLANNING CRITERIA PROGRAM.—

(A) DEFINITIONS.— In this paragraph:

(i) ALTERNATIVE PLANNING CRITERIA.— The term "alternative planning criteria" means criteria submitted under section 155.1065 or 155.5067 of title 33, Code of Federal Regulations (as in effect on the date of enactment of this paragraph), for vessel response plans.

(ii) PRINCE WILLIAM SOUND CAPTAIN OF THE PORT ZONE.— The term "Prince William Sound Captain of the Port Zone" means the area described in section 3.85–15(b) of title 33, Code of Federal Regulations (or successor regulations).

(iii) SECRETARY.— The term "Secretary" means the Secretary of the department in which the Coast Guard is operating.

(iv) VESSEL RESPONSE PLAN.— The term "vessel response plan" means a plan required to be submitted by the owner or operator of a tank vessel or a nontank vessel under regulations issued by the President under paragraph (5).

(v) WESTERN ALASKA CAPTAIN OF THE PORT ZONE.— The term "Western Alaska Captain of the Port Zone" means the area described in section 3.85–15(a) of title 33, Code of Federal Regulations (as in effect on the date of enactment of this paragraph).

(B) REQUIREMENT.— Except as provided in subparagraph (I), for any part of the area of responsibility of the Western Alaska Captain of the Port Zone or the Prince William Sound Captain of the Port Zone for which the Secretary has determined that the national planning criteria established pursuant to this subsection are inappropriate for a vessel operating in such area, a vessel response plan with respect to a discharge of oil for such a vessel shall comply with the Western Alaska oil spill planning criteria established under subparagraph (D)(i).

(C) RELATION TO NATIONAL PLANNING CRITERIA.— The Western Alaska oil spill planning criteria established under subparagraph (D)(i) shall, with respect to a discharge of oil from a vessel described in subparagraph (B), apply in lieu of any alternative planning criteria accepted for vessels operating, prior to the date on which the Western Alaska oil spill planning criteria are established, in any part of the area of responsibility of the Western Alaska Captain of the Port Zone or the Prince William Sound Captain of the Port Zone for which the Secretary has determined that the national planning criteria established pursuant to this subsection are inappropriate for a vessel operating in such area.

(D) ESTABLISHMENT OF WESTERN ALASKA OIL SPILL PLANNING CRITERIA.—

(i) IN GENERAL.— The President, acting through the Commandant, in consultation with the Western Alaska Oil Spill Criteria Program Manager selected under section 323 of title 14, United States Code, shall establish—

(I) Western Alaska oil spill planning criteria for a worst case discharge of oil, and a substantial threat of such a discharge, within any part of the area of responsibility of the Western Alaska Captain of the Port Zone or Prince William Sound Captain of the Port Zone for which the Secretary has determined that the national planning criteria established pursuant to this subsection are inappropriate for a vessel operating in such area; and

(II) standardized submission, review, approval, and compliance verification processes for the Western Alaska oil spill planning criteria established under this clause, including the quantity and frequency of drills and on-site verifications of vessel response plans approved pursuant to such planning criteria.

(ii) DEVELOPMENT OF SUBREGIONS.—

(I) DEVELOPMENT.— After establishing the Western Alaska oil spill planning criteria under clause (i), and if necessary to adequately reflect the needs and capabilities of various locations within the Western Alaska Captain of the Port Zone, the President, acting through the Commandant, and in consultation with the Western Alaska Oil Spill Criteria Program Manager selected under section 323 of title 14, United States Code, may develop subregions for which planning criteria may differ from planning criteria for other subregions in the Western Alaska Captain of the Port Zone.

(II) LIMITATION.— Any planning criteria for a subregion developed under this clause may not be less stringent than the Western Alaska oil spill planning criteria established under clause (i).

(iii) ASSESSMENT.—

(I) IN GENERAL.— Prior to developing a subregion, the President, acting through the Commandant, shall conduct an assessment on any potential impacts to the entire Western Alaska Captain of the Port Zone to include quantity and availability of response resources in the proposed subregion and in surrounding areas and any changes or impacts to surrounding areas resulting in the development of a subregion with different standards.

(II) CONSULTATION.— In conducting an assessment under this clause, the President, acting through the Commandant, shall consult with State and local governments, Tribes (as defined in section 323 of title 14, United States Code), the owners and operators that would operate under the proposed subregions, oil spill removal organizations, Alaska Native organizations, and environmental nongovernmental organizations, and shall take into account any experience with the prior use of subregions within the State of Alaska.

(III) SUBMISSION.— The President, acting through the Commandant, shall submit the results of an assessment conducted under this clause to the Committee on Transportation and Infrastructure of the House of Representatives and the Committee on Commerce, Science, and Transportation of the Senate.

(E) INCLUSIONS.—

(i) REQUIREMENTS.— The Western Alaska oil spill planning criteria established under subparagraph (D)(i) shall include planning criteria for the following:

(I) Mechanical oil spill response resources that are required to be located within any part of the area of responsibility of the Western Alaska Captain of the Port Zone or the Prince William Sound Captain of the Port Zone for which the Secretary has determined that the national planning criteria established pursuant to this subsection are inappropriate for a vessel operating in such area.

(II) Response times for mobilization of oil spill response resources and arrival on the scene of a worst case discharge of oil, or substantial threat of such a discharge, occurring within such part of such area.

(III) Pre-identified vessels for oil spill response that are capable of operating in the ocean environment.

(IV) Ensuring the availability of at least 1 oil spill removal organization that is classified by the Coast Guard and that—

(aa) is capable of responding in all operating environments in such part of such area;

(bb) controls oil spill response resources of dedicated and nondedicated resources within such part of such area, through ownership, contracts, agreements, or other means approved by the President, sufficient—

(AA) to mobilize and sustain a response to a worst case discharge of oil; and

(BB) to contain, recover, and temporarily store discharged oil;

(cc) has pre-positioned oil spill response resources in strategic locations throughout such part of such area in a manner that ensures the ability to support response personnel, marine operations, air cargo, or other related logistics infrastructure;

(dd) has temporary storage capability using both dedicated and non-dedicated assets located within such part of such area;

(ee) has non-mechanical oil spill response resources capable of responding to a discharge of persistent oil and a discharge of nonpersistent oil, whether the discharged oil was carried by a vessel as fuel or cargo; and

(ff) has wildlife response resources for primary, secondary, and tertiary responses to support carcass collection, sampling, deterrence, rescue, and rehabilitation of birds, sea turtles, marine mammals, fishery resources, and other wildlife.

(V) With respect to tank barges carrying nonpersistent oil in bulk as cargo, oil spill response resources that are required to be carried on board.

(VI) Specifying a minimum length of time that approval of a vessel response plan under this paragraph is valid.

(VII) Managing wildlife protection and rehabilitation, including identified wildlife protection and rehabilitation resources in that area.

(ii) ADDITIONAL CONSIDERATIONS.— The Western Alaska oil spill planning criteria established under subparagraph (D)(i) may include planning criteria for the following:

(I) Vessel routing measures consistent with international routing measure deviation protocols.

(II) Maintenance of real-time continuous vessel tracking, monitoring, and engagement protocols with the ability to detect and address vessel operation anomalies.

(F) REQUIREMENT FOR APPROVAL.— The President may approve a vessel response plan for a vessel under this paragraph only if the owner or operator of the vessel demonstrates the availability of the oil spill response resources required to be included in the vessel response plan under the Western Alaska oil spill planning criteria established under subparagraph (D)(i).

(G) PERIODIC AUDITS.— The Secretary shall conduct periodic audits to ensure compliance of vessel response plans and oil spill removal organizations within the Western Alaska Captain of the Port Zone and the Prince William Sound Captain of the Port Zone with the Western Alaska oil spill planning criteria established under subparagraph (D)(i).

(H) REVIEW OF DETERMINATION.— Not less frequently than once every 5 years, the Secretary shall review each determination of the Secretary under subparagraph (B) that the national planning criteria established pursuant to this subsection are inappropriate for a vessel operating in the area of responsibility of the Western Alaska Captain of the Port Zone and the Prince William Sound Captain of the Port Zone.

(I) VESSELS IN COOK INLET.— Unless otherwise authorized by the Secretary, a vessel may only operate in Cook Inlet, Alaska, under a vessel response plan approved under paragraph (5) that meets the requirements of the national planning criteria established pursuant to this subsection.

(J) SAVINGS PROVISIONS.— Nothing in this paragraph affects—

(i) the requirements under this subsection applicable to vessel response plans for vessels operating within the area of responsibility of the Western Alaska Captain of the Port Zone, within Cook Inlet, Alaska;

(ii) the requirements under this subsection applicable to vessel response plans for vessels operating within the area of responsibility of the Prince William Sound Captain of the Port Zone that are subject to section 5005 of the Oil Pollution Act of 1990 (33 U.S.C. 2735); or

(iii) the authority of a Federal On-Scene Coordinator to use any available resources when responding to an oil spill.

[Subsection (k) was repealed by sec. 2002(b)(2) of P.L. 101-380.]

(l) The President is authorized to delegate the administration of this section to the heads of those Federal departments, agencies, and instrumentalities which he determines to be appropriate. Each such department, agency, and instrumentality, in order to avoid duplication of effort, shall, whenever appropriate, utilize the personnel, services, and facilities of other Federal departments, agencies, and instrumentalities.

(m) ADMINISTRATIVE PROVISIONS.—

(1) FOR VESSELS.— Anyone authorized by the President to enforce the provisions of this section with respect to any vessel may, except as to public vessels—

(A) board and inspect any vessel upon the navigable waters of the United States or the waters of the contiguous zone,

(B) with or without a warrant, arrest any person who in the presence or view of the authorized person violates the provisions of this section or any regulation issued thereunder, and

(C) execute any warrant or other process issued by an officer or court of competent jurisdiction.

(2) FOR FACILITIES.—

(A) RECORDKEEPING.— Whenever required to carry out the purposes of this section, the Administrator, the Secretary of Transportation, or the Secretary of the Department in which the Coast Guard is operating shall require the owner or operator of a facility to which this section applies to establish and maintain such records, make such reports, install, use, and maintain such monitoring equipment and methods, and provide such other information as the Administrator, the Secretary of Transportation, or Secretary, as the case may be, may require to carry out the objectives of this section.

(B) ENTRY AND INSPECTION.— Whenever required to carry out the purposes of this section, the Administrator, the Secretary of Transportation, or the Secretary of the Department in which the Coast Guard is operating or an authorized representative of the Administrator, the Secretary of Transportation, or Secretary, upon presentation of appropriate credentials, may—

(i) enter and inspect any facility to which this section applies, including any facility at which any records are required to be maintained under subparagraph (A); and

(ii) at reasonable times, have access to and copy any records, take samples, and inspect any monitoring equipment or methods required under subparagraph (A).

(C) ARRESTS AND EXECUTION OF WARRANTS.— Anyone authorized by the Administrator or the Secretary of the department in which the Coast Guard is operating to enforce the provisions of this section with respect to any facility may—

(i) with or without a warrant, arrest any person who violates the provisions of this section or any regulation issued thereunder in the presence or view of the person so authorized; and

(ii) execute any warrant or process issued by an officer or court of competent jurisdiction.

(D) PUBLIC ACCESS.— Any records, reports, or information obtained under this paragraph shall be subject to the same public access and disclosure requirements which are applicable to records, reports, and information obtained pursuant to section 308.

(n) The several district courts of the United States are invested with jurisdiction for any actions, other than actions pursuant to subsection (i)(1), arising under this section. In the case of Guam and the Trust Territory of the Pacific Islands, such actions may be brought in the district court of Guam, and in the case of the Virgin Islands such actions may be brought in the district court of the Virgin Islands. In the case of American Samoa and the Trust Territory of the Pacific Islands, such actions may be brought in the District Court of the United States for the District of Hawaii and such court shall have jurisdiction of such actions. In the case of the Canal Zone, such actions may be brought in the United States District Court for the District of the Canal Zone.

(o) (1) Nothing in this section shall affect or modify in any way the obligations of any owner or operator of any vessel, or of any owner or operator of any onshore facility or offshore facility to any person or agency under any provision of law for damages to any publicly owned or privately owned property resulting from a discharge of any oil or hazardous substance or from the removal of any such oil or hazardous substance.

(2) Nothing in this section shall be construed as preempting any State or political subdivision thereof from imposing any requirement or liability with respect to the discharge of oil or hazardous substance into any waters within such State, or with respect to any removal activities related to such discharge.

(3) Nothing in this section shall be construed as affecting or modifying any other existing authority of any Federal department, agency, or instrumentality, relative to onshore or offshore facilities under this Act or any other provision of law, or to affect any State or local law not in conflict with this section.

[Subsection (p) was repealed by sec. 2002(b)(4) of Public Law 101-380, 104 Stat. 507.]

(q) The President is authorized to establish, with respect to any class or category of onshore or offshore facilities, a maximum limit of liability under subsections (f)(2) and (3) of this section of less than $50,000,000, but not less than, $8,000,000.

(r) Nothing in this section shall be construed to impose, or authorize the imposition of, any limitation on liability under the Outer Continental Shelf Lands Act or the Deepwater Port Act of 1974.

(s) The Oil Spill Liability Trust Fund established under section 9509 of the Internal Revenue Code of 1986 (26 U.S.C. 9509) shall be available to carry out subsections (b), (c), (d), (j), and (l) as those subsections apply to discharges, and substantial threats of discharges, of oil. Any amounts received by the United States under this section shall be deposited in the Oil Spill Liability Trust Fund except as provided in subsection (t).

(t) GULF COAST RESTORATION AND RECOVERY.—

(1) STATE ALLOCATION AND EXPENDITURES.—

(A) IN GENERAL.— Of the total amounts made available in any fiscal year from the Trust Fund, 35 percent shall be available, in accordance with the requirements of this section, to the Gulf Coast States in equal shares for expenditure for ecological and economic restoration of the Gulf Coast region in accordance with this subsection.

(B) USE OF FUNDS.—

(i) ELIGIBLE ACTIVITIES IN THE GULF COAST REGION.— Subject to clause (iii), amounts provided to the Gulf Coast States under this subsection may only be used to carry out 1 or more of the following activities in the Gulf Coast region:

(I) Restoration and protection of the natural resources, ecosystems, fisheries, marine and wildlife habitats, beaches, and coastal wetlands of the Gulf Coast region.

(II) Mitigation of damage to fish, wildlife, and natural resources.

(III) Implementation of a federally approved marine, coastal, or comprehensive conservation management plan, including fisheries monitoring.

(IV) Workforce development and job creation.

(V) Improvements to or on State parks located in coastal areas affected by the Deepwater Horizon oil spill.

(VI) Infrastructure projects benefitting the economy or ecological resources, including port infrastructure.

(VII) Coastal flood protection and related

infrastructure.

(VIII) Planning assistance.

(IX) Administrative costs of complying with this subsection.

(ii) ACTIVITIES TO PROMOTE TOURISM AND SEAFOOD IN THE GULF COAST REGION.— Amounts provided to the Gulf Coast States under this subsection may be used to carry out 1 or more of the following activities:

(I) Promotion of tourism in the Gulf Coast Region, including recreational fishing.

(II) Promotion of the consumption of seafood harvested from the Gulf Coast Region.

(iii) LIMITATION.—

(I) IN GENERAL.— Of the amounts received by a Gulf Coast State under this subsection, not more than 3 percent may be used for administrative costs eligible under clause (i)(IX).

(II) CLAIMS FOR COMPENSATION.— Activities funded under this subsection may not be included in any claim for compensation paid out by the Oil Spill Liability Trust Fund after the date of enactment of this subsection.

(C) COASTAL POLITICAL SUBDIVISIONS.—

(i) DISTRIBUTION.— In the case of a State where the coastal zone includes the entire State—

(I) 75 percent of funding shall be provided directly to the 8 disproportionately affected counties impacted by the Deepwater Horizon oil spill; and

(II) 25 percent shall be provided directly to nondisproportionately impacted counties within the State.

(ii) NONDISPROPORTIONATELY IMPACTED COUNTIES.— The total amounts made available to coastal political subdivisions in the State of Florida under clause (i)(II) shall be distributed according to the following weighted formula:

(I) 34 percent based on the weighted average

of the population of the county.

(II) 33 percent based on the weighted average of the county per capita sales tax collections estimated for fiscal year 2012.

(III) 33 percent based on the inverse proportion of the weighted average distance from the Deepwater Horizon oil rig to each of the nearest and farthest points of the shoreline.

(D) LOUISIANA.—

(i) IN GENERAL.— Of the total amounts made available to the State of Louisiana under this paragraph:

(I) 70 percent shall be provided directly to the State in accordance with this subsection.

(II) 30 percent shall be provided directly to parishes in the coastal zone (as defined in section 304 of the Coastal Zone Management Act of 1972 (16 U.S.C. 1453)) of the State of Louisiana according to the following weighted formula:

(aa) 40 percent based on the weighted average of miles of the parish shoreline oiled.

(bb) 40 percent based on the weighted average of the population of the parish.

(cc) 20 percent based on the weighted average of the land mass of the parish.

(ii) CONDITIONS.—

(I) LAND USE PLAN.— As a condition of receiving amounts allocated under this paragraph, the chief executive of the eligible parish shall certify to the Governor of the State that the parish has completed a comprehensive land use plan.

(II) OTHER CONDITIONS.— A coastal political subdivision receiving funding under this paragraph shall meet all of the conditions in subparagraph (E).

(E) CONDITIONS.— As a condition of receiving amounts from the Trust Fund, a Gulf Coast State, including the entities described in subparagraph (F), or a coastal political subdivision shall—

(i) agree to meet such conditions, including audit requirements, as the Secretary of the Treasury determines necessary to ensure that amounts disbursed from the Trust Fund will be used in accordance with this subsection;

(ii) certify in such form and in such manner as the Secretary of the Treasury determines necessary that the project or program for which the Gulf Coast State or coastal political subdivision is requesting amounts—

(I) is designed to restore and protect the natural resources, ecosystems, fisheries, marine and wildlife habitats, beaches, coastal wetlands, or economy of the Gulf Coast;

(II) carries out 1 or more of the activities described in clauses (i) and (ii) of subparagraph (B);

(III) was selected based on meaningful input from the public, including broad-based participation from individuals, businesses, and nonprofit organizations; and

(IV) in the case of a natural resource protection or restoration project, is based on the best available science;

(iii) certify that the project or program and the awarding of a contract for the expenditure of amounts received under this paragraph are consistent with the standard procurement rules and regulations governing a comparable project or program in that State, including all applicable competitive bidding and audit requirements; and

(iv) develop and submit a multiyear implementation plan for the use of such amounts, which may include milestones, projected completion of each activity, and a mechanism to evaluate the success of each activity in helping to restore and protect the Gulf Coast region impacted by the Deepwater Horizon oil spill.

(F) APPROVAL BY STATE ENTITY, TASK FORCE, OR
AGENCY.— The following Gulf Coast State entities, task
forces, or agencies shall carry out the duties of a Gulf Coast
State pursuant to this paragraph:

(i) ALABAMA.—

(I) IN GENERAL.— In the State of Alabama, the
Alabama Gulf Coast Recovery Council, which shall
be comprised of only the following:

(aa) The Governor of Alabama, who shall
also serve as Chairperson and preside over
the meetings of the Alabama Gulf Coast
Recovery Council.

(bb) The Director of the Alabama State
Port Authority, who shall also serve as Vice
Chairperson and preside over the meetings of
the Alabama Gulf Coast Recovery Council in
the absence of the Chairperson.

(cc) The Chairman of the Baldwin County
Commission.

(dd) The President of the Mobile County
Commission.

(ee) The Mayor of the city of Bayou La
Batre.

(ff) The Mayor of the town of Dauphin
Island.

(gg) The Mayor of the city of Fairhope.

(hh) The Mayor of the city of Gulf Shores.

(ii) The Mayor of the city of Mobile.

(jj) The Mayor of the city of Orange
Beach.

(II) VOTE.— Each member of the Alabama
Gulf Coast Recovery Council shall be entitled to 1
vote.

(III) MAJORITY VOTE.— All decisions of the
Alabama Gulf Coast Recovery Council shall be
made by majority vote.

(IV)   LIMITATION   ON   ADMINISTRATIVE

111

EXPENSES.— Administrative duties for the Alabama Gulf Coast Recovery Council may only be performed by public officials and employees that are subject to the ethics laws of the State of Alabama.

(ii) LOUISIANA.— In the State of Louisiana, the Coastal Protection and Restoration Authority of Louisiana.

(iii) MISSISSIPPI.— In the State of Mississippi, the Mississippi Department of Environmental Quality.

(iv) TEXAS.— In the State of Texas, the Office of the Governor or an appointee of the Office of the Governor.

(G) COMPLIANCE WITH ELIGIBLE ACTIVITIES.— If the Secretary of the Treasury determines that an expenditure by a Gulf Coast State or coastal political subdivision of amounts made available under this subsection does not meet one of the activities described in clauses (i) and (ii) of subparagraph (B), the Secretary shall make no additional amounts from the Trust Fund available to that Gulf Coast State or coastal political subdivision until such time as an amount equal to the amount expended for the unauthorized use—

(i) has been deposited by the Gulf Coast State or coastal political subdivision in the Trust Fund; or

(ii) has been authorized by the Secretary of the Treasury for expenditure by the Gulf Coast State or coastal political subdivision for a project or program that meets the requirements of this subsection.

(H) COMPLIANCE WITH CONDITIONS.— If the Secretary of the Treasury determines that a Gulf Coast State or coastal political subdivision does not meet the requirements of this paragraph, including the conditions of subparagraph (E), where applicable, the Secretary of the Treasury shall make no amounts from the Trust Fund available to that Gulf Coast State or coastal political subdivision until all conditions of this paragraph are met.

(I) PUBLIC INPUT.— In meeting any condition of this paragraph, a Gulf Coast State may use an appropriate procedure for public consultation in that Gulf Coast State, including consulting with one or more established task forces or other entities, to develop recommendations for proposed projects and programs that would restore and protect the natural resources, ecosystems, fisheries, marine and wildlife habitats, beaches, coastal wetlands, and economy of the Gulf Coast.

(J) PREVIOUSLY APPROVED PROJECTS AND PROGRAMS.— A Gulf Coast State or coastal political subdivision shall be considered to have met the conditions of subparagraph (E) for a specific project or program if, before the date of enactment of the Resources and Ecosystems Sustainability, Tourist Opportunities, and Revived Economies of the Gulf Coast States Act of 2012—

(i) the Gulf Coast State or coastal political subdivision has established conditions for carrying out projects and programs that are substantively the same as the conditions described in subparagraph (E); and

(ii) the applicable project or program carries out 1 or more of the activities described in clauses (i) and (ii) of subparagraph (B).

(K) LOCAL PREFERENCE.— In awarding contracts to carry out a project or program under this paragraph, a Gulf Coast State or coastal political subdivision may give a preference to individuals and companies that reside in, are headquartered in, or are principally engaged in business in the State of project execution.

(L) UNUSED FUNDS.— Funds allocated to a State or coastal political subdivision under this paragraph shall remain in the Trust Fund until such time as the State or coastal political subdivision develops and submits a plan identifying uses for those funds in accordance with subparagraph (E)(iv).

(M) JUDICIAL REVIEW.— If the Secretary of the Treasury determines that a Gulf Coast State or coastal political subdivision does not meet the requirements of this paragraph, including the conditions of subparagraph (E), the Gulf Coast State or coastal political subdivision may obtain expedited judicial review within 90 days after that decision in a district court of the United States, of appropriate jurisdiction and venue, that is located within the State seeking the review.

(N) COST-SHARING.—

(i) IN GENERAL.— A Gulf Coast State or coastal political subdivision may use, in whole or in part, amounts made available under this paragraph to that Gulf Coast State or coastal political subdivision to satisfy the non-Federal share of the cost of any project or program authorized by Federal law that is an eligible activity described in clauses (i) and (ii) of subparagraph (B).

(ii) EFFECT ON OTHER FUNDS.— The use of funds made available from the Trust Fund to satisfy the non-Federal share of the cost of a project or program that meets the requirements of clause (i) shall not affect the priority in which other Federal funds are allocated or awarded.

(2) COUNCIL ESTABLISHMENT AND ALLOCATION.—

(A) IN GENERAL.— Of the total amount made available in any fiscal year from the Trust Fund, 30 percent shall be disbursed to the Council to carry out the Comprehensive Plan.

(B) COUNCIL EXPENDITURES.—

(i) IN GENERAL.— In accordance with this paragraph, the Council shall expend funds made available from the Trust Fund to undertake projects and programs, using the best available science, that would restore and protect the natural resources, ecosystems, fisheries, marine and wildlife habitats, beaches, coastal wetlands, and economy of the Gulf Coast.

(ii) ALLOCATION AND EXPENDITURE PROCEDURES.— The Secretary of the Treasury shall develop such conditions, including audit requirements, as the Secretary of the Treasury determines necessary to ensure that amounts disbursed from the Trust Fund to the Council to implement the Comprehensive Plan will be used in accordance with this paragraph.

(iii) ADMINISTRATIVE EXPENSES.— Of the amounts

received by the Council under this paragraph, not more than 3 percent may be used for administrative expenses, including staff.

(C) GULF COAST ECOSYSTEM RESTORATION COUNCIL.—

(i) ESTABLISHMENT.— There is established as an independent entity in the Federal Government a council to be known as the "Gulf Coast Ecosystem Restoration Council".

(ii) MEMBERSHIP.— The Council shall consist of the following members, or in the case of a Federal agency, a designee at the level of the Assistant Secretary or the equivalent:

(I) The Secretary of the Interior.

(II) The Secretary of the Army.

(III) The Secretary of Commerce.

(IV) The Administrator of the Environmental Protection Agency.

(V) The Secretary of Agriculture.

(VI) The head of the department in which the Coast Guard is operating.

(VII) The Governor of the State of Alabama.

(VIII) The Governor of the State of Florida.

(IX) The Governor of the State of Louisiana.

(X) The Governor of the State of Mississippi.

(XI) The Governor of the State of Texas.

(iii) ALTERNATE.— A Governor appointed to the Council by the President may designate an alternate to represent the Governor on the Council and vote on behalf of the Governor.

(iv) CHAIRPERSON.— From among the Federal agency members of the Council, the representatives of States on the Council shall select, and the President shall appoint, 1 Federal member to serve as Chairperson of the Council.

(v) PRESIDENTIAL APPOINTMENT.— All Council members shall be appointed by the President.

(vi) COUNCIL ACTIONS.—

(I) IN GENERAL.— The following actions by the Council shall require the affirmative vote of the Chairperson and a majority of the State members to be effective:

(aa) Approval of a Comprehensive Plan and future revisions to a Comprehensive Plan.

(bb) Approval of State plans pursuant to paragraph (3)(B)(iv).

(cc) Approval of reports to Congress pursuant to clause (vii)(VII).

(dd) Approval of transfers pursuant to subparagraph (E)(ii)(I).

(ee) Other significant actions determined by the Council.

(II) QUORUM.— A majority of State members shall be required to be present for the Council to take any significant action.

(III) AFFIRMATIVE VOTE REQUIREMENT CONSIDERED MET.— For approval of State plans pursuant to paragraph (3)(B)(iv), the certification by a State member of the Council that the plan satisfies all requirements of clauses (i) and (ii) of paragraph (3)(B), when joined by an affirmative vote of the Federal Chairperson of the Council, shall be considered to satisfy the requirements for affirmative votes under subclause (I).

(IV) PUBLIC TRANSPARENCY.— Appropriate actions of the Council, including significant actions and associated deliberations, shall be made available to the public via electronic means prior to any vote.

(vii) DUTIES OF COUNCIL.— The Council shall—

(I) develop the Comprehensive Plan and future revisions to the Comprehensive Plan;

(II) identify as soon as practicable the projects that—

(aa) have been authorized prior to the date of enactment of this subsection but not yet commenced; and

(bb) if implemented quickly, would restore and protect the natural resources, ecosystems, fisheries, marine and wildlife habitats, beaches, barrier islands, dunes, and coastal wetlands of the Gulf Coast region;

(III) establish such other 1 or more advisory committees as may be necessary to assist the Council, including a scientific advisory committee and a committee to advise the Council on public policy issues;

(IV) collect and consider scientific and other research associated with restoration of the Gulf Coast ecosystem, including research, observation, and monitoring carried out pursuant to sections 1604 and 1605 of the Resources and Ecosystems Sustainability, Tourist Opportunities, and Revived Economies of the Gulf Coast States Act of 2012;

(V) develop standard terms to include in contracts for projects and programs awarded pursuant to the Comprehensive Plan that provide a preference to individuals and companies that reside in, are headquartered in, or are principally engaged in business in a Gulf Coast State;

(VI) prepare an integrated financial plan and recommendations for coordinated budget requests for the amounts proposed to be expended by the Federal agencies represented on the Council for projects and programs in the Gulf Coast States; and

(VII) submit to Congress an annual report that—

(aa) summarizes the policies, strategies, plans, and activities for addressing the restoration and protection of the Gulf Coast region;

(bb) describes the projects and programs being implemented to restore and protect the

Gulf Coast region, including—

(AA) a list of each project and program;

(BB) an identification of the funding provided to projects and programs identified in subitem (AA);

(CC) an identification of each recipient for funding identified in subitem (BB); and

(DD) a description of the length of time and funding needed to complete the objectives of each project and program identified in subitem (AA);

(cc) makes such recommendations to Congress for modifications of existing laws as the Council determines necessary to implement the Comprehensive Plan;

(dd) reports on the progress on implementation of each project or program—

(AA) after 3 years of ongoing activity of the project or program, if applicable; and

(BB) on completion of the project or program;

(ee) includes the information required to be submitted under section 1605(c)(4) of the Resources and Ecosystems Sustainability, Tourist Opportunities, and Revived Economies of the Gulf Coast States Act of 2012; and

(ff) submits the reports required under item (dd) to—

(AA) the Committee on Science, Space, and Technology, the Committee on Natural Resources, the Committee on Transportation and Infrastructure, and the Committee on Appropriations of the House of Representatives; and

(BB) the Committee on Environment
and Public Works, the Committee on
Commerce, Science, and Transportation,
the Committee on Energy and Natural
Resources, and the Committee on
Appropriations of the Senate.

(viii) APPLICATION OF CHAPTER 10 OF TITLE 5,
UNITED STATES CODE.— The Council, or any other
advisory committee established under this
subparagraph, shall not be considered an advisory
committee under chapter 10 of title 5, United States
Code.

(ix) SUNSET.— The authority for the Council, and
any other advisory committee established under this
subparagraph, shall terminate on the date all funds in
the Trust Fund have been expended.

(D) COMPREHENSIVE PLAN.—

(i) PROPOSED PLAN.—

(I) IN GENERAL.— Not later than 180 days
after the date of enactment of the Resources and
Ecosystems Sustainability, Tourist Opportunities,
and Revived Economies of the Gulf Coast States
Act of 2012, the Chairperson, on behalf of the
Council and after appropriate public input,
review, and comment, shall publish a proposed
plan to restore and protect the natural resources,
ecosystems, fisheries, marine and wildlife
habitats, beaches, and coastal wetlands of the Gulf
Coast region.

(II) INCLUSIONS.— The proposed plan
described in subclause (I) shall include and
incorporate the findings and information prepared
by the President's Gulf Coast Restoration Task
Force.

(ii) PUBLICATION.—

(I) INITIAL PLAN.— Not later than 1 year after
the date of enactment of the Resources and
Ecosystems Sustainability, Tourist Opportunities,
and Revived Economies of the Gulf Coast States

Act of 2012 and after notice and opportunity for public comment, the Chairperson, on behalf of the Council and after approval by the Council, shall publish in the Federal Register the initial Comprehensive Plan to restore and protect the natural resources, ecosystems, fisheries, marine and wildlife habitats, beaches, and coastal wetlands of the Gulf Coast region.

(II) COOPERATION WITH GULF COAST RESTORATION TASK FORCE.— The Council shall develop the initial Comprehensive Plan in close coordination with the President's Gulf Coast Restoration Task Force.

(III) CONSIDERATIONS.— In developing the initial Comprehensive Plan and subsequent updates, the Council shall consider all relevant findings, reports, or research prepared or funded under section 1604 or 1605 of the Resources and Ecosystems Sustainability, Tourist Opportunities, and Revived Economies of the Gulf Coast States Act of 2012.

(IV) CONTENTS.— The initial Comprehensive Plan shall include—

(aa) such provisions as are necessary to fully incorporate in the Comprehensive Plan the strategy, projects, and programs recommended by the President's Gulf Coast Restoration Task Force;

(bb) a list of any project or program authorized prior to the date of enactment of this subsection but not yet commenced, the completion of which would further the purposes and goals of this subsection and of the Resources and Ecosystems Sustainability, Tourist Opportunities, and Revived Economies of the Gulf Coast States Act of 2012;

(cc) a description of the manner in which amounts from the Trust Fund projected to be made available to the Council for the succeeding 10 years will be allocated; and

(dd) subject to available funding in accordance with clause (iii), a prioritized list of specific projects and programs to be funded and carried out during the 3-year period immediately following the date of publication of the initial Comprehensive Plan, including a table that illustrates the distribution of projects and programs by the Gulf Coast State.

(V) PLAN UPDATES.— The Council shall update—

(aa) the Comprehensive Plan every 5 years in a manner comparable to the manner established in this subparagraph for each 5-year period for which amounts are expected to be made available to the Gulf Coast States from the Trust Fund; and

(bb) the 3-year list of projects and programs described in subclause (IV)(dd) annually.

(iii) RESTORATION PRIORITIES.— Except for projects and programs described in clause (ii)(IV)(bb), in selecting projects and programs to include on the 3-year list described in clause (ii)(IV)(dd), based on the best available science, the Council shall give highest priority to projects that address 1 or more of the following criteria:

(I) Projects that are projected to make the greatest contribution to restoring and protecting the natural resources, ecosystems, fisheries, marine and wildlife habitats, beaches, and coastal wetlands of the Gulf Coast region, without regard to geographic location within the Gulf Coast region.

(II) Large-scale projects and programs that are projected to substantially contribute to restoring and protecting the natural resources, ecosystems, fisheries, marine and wildlife habitats, beaches, and coastal wetlands of the Gulf Coast ecosystem.

(III) Projects contained in existing Gulf Coast State comprehensive plans for the restoration and protection of natural resources, ecosystems, fisheries, marine and wildlife habitats, beaches, and coastal wetlands of the Gulf Coast region.

(IV) Projects that restore long-term resiliency of the natural resources, ecosystems, fisheries, marine and wildlife habitats, beaches, and coastal wetlands most impacted by the Deepwater Horizon oil spill.

(E) IMPLEMENTATION.—

(i) IN GENERAL.— The Council, acting through the Federal agencies represented on the Council and Gulf Coast States, shall expend funds made available from the Trust Fund to carry out projects and programs adopted in the Comprehensive Plan.

(ii) ADMINISTRATIVE RESPONSIBILITY.—

(I) IN GENERAL.— Primary authority and responsibility for each project and program included in the Comprehensive Plan shall be assigned by the Council to a Gulf Coast State represented on the Council or a Federal agency.

(II) TRANSFER OF AMOUNTS.— Amounts necessary to carry out each project or program included in the Comprehensive Plan shall be transferred by the Secretary of the Treasury from the Trust Fund to that Federal agency or Gulf Coast State as the project or program is implemented, subject to such conditions as the Secretary of the Treasury, in consultation with the Secretary of the Interior and the Secretary of Commerce, established pursuant to section 1602 of the Resources and Ecosystems Sustainability, Tourist Opportunities, and Revived Economies of the Gulf Coast States Act of 2012.

(III) LIMITATION ON TRANSFERS.—

(aa) GRANTS TO NONGOVERNMENTAL

ENTITIES.— In the case of funds transferred to a Federal or State agency under subclause (II), the agency shall not make 1 or more grants or cooperative agreements to a nongovernmental entity if the total amount provided to the entity would equal or exceed 10 percent of the total amount provided to the agency for that particular project or program, unless the 1 or more grants have been reported in accordance with item (bb).

(bb) REPORTING OF GRANTEES.— At least 30 days prior to making a grant or entering into a cooperative agreement described in item (aa), the name of each grantee, including the amount and purpose of each grant or cooperative agreement, shall be published in the Federal Register and delivered to the congressional committees listed in subparagraph (C)(vii)(VII)(ff).

(cc) ANNUAL REPORTING OF GRANTEES.— Annually, the name of each grantee, including the amount and purposes of each grant or cooperative agreement, shall be published in the Federal Register and delivered to Congress as part of the report submitted pursuant to subparagraph (C)(vii)(VII).

(IV) PROJECT AND PROGRAM LIMITATION.— The Council, a Federal agency, or a State may not carry out a project or program funded under this paragraph outside of the Gulf Coast region.

(F) COORDINATION.— The Council and the Federal members of the Council may develop memoranda of understanding establishing integrated funding and implementation plans among the member agencies and authorities.

(3) OIL SPILL RESTORATION IMPACT ALLOCATION.—

(A) IN GENERAL.—

(i) DISBURSEMENT.— Of the total amount made available from the Trust Fund, 30 percent shall be disbursed pursuant to the formula in clause (ii) to the Gulf Coast States on the approval of the plan described in subparagraph (B)(i).

(ii) FORMULA.— Subject to subparagraph (B), for each Gulf Coast State, the amount disbursed under this paragraph shall be based on a formula established by the Council by regulation that is based on a weighted average of the following criteria:

(I) 40 percent based on the proportionate number of miles of shoreline in each Gulf Coast State that experienced oiling on or before April 10, 2011, compared to the total number of miles of shoreline that experienced oiling as a result of the Deepwater Horizon oil spill.

(II) 40 percent based on the inverse proportion of the average distance from the mobile offshore drilling unit *Deepwater Horizon* at the time of the explosion to the nearest and farthest point of the shoreline that experienced oiling of each Gulf Coast State.

(III) 20 percent based on the average population in the 2010 decennial census of coastal counties bordering the Gulf of Mexico within each Gulf Coast State.

(iii) MINIMUM ALLOCATION.— The amount disbursed to a Gulf Coast State for each fiscal year under clause (ii) shall be at least 5 percent of the total amounts made available under this paragraph.

(B) DISBURSEMENT OF FUNDS.—

(i) IN GENERAL.— The Council shall disburse amounts to the respective Gulf Coast States in accordance with the formula developed under subparagraph (A) for projects, programs, and activities that will improve the ecosystems or economy of the Gulf Coast region, subject to the condition that each Gulf Coast State submits a plan for the expenditure of amounts disbursed under this paragraph that meets the following criteria:

(I) All projects, programs, and activities

included in the plan are eligible activities pursuant to clauses (i) and (ii) of paragraph (1)(B).

(II) The projects, programs, and activities included in the plan contribute to the overall economic and ecological recovery of the Gulf Coast.

(III) The plan takes into consideration the Comprehensive Plan and is consistent with the goals and objectives of the Plan, as described in paragraph (2)(B)(i).

(ii) FUNDING.—

(I) IN GENERAL.— Except as provided in subclause (II), the plan described in clause (i) may use not more than 25 percent of the funding made available for infrastructure projects eligible under subclauses (VI) and (VII) of paragraph (1)(B)(i).

(II) EXCEPTION.— The plan described in clause (i) may propose to use more than 25 percent of the funding made available for infrastructure projects eligible under subclauses (VI) and (VII) of paragraph (1)(B)(i) if the plan certifies that—

(aa) ecosystem restoration needs in the State will be addressed by the projects in the proposed plan; and

(bb) additional investment in infrastructure is required to mitigate the impacts of the Deepwater Horizon Oil Spill to the ecosystem or economy.

(iii) DEVELOPMENT.— The plan described in clause (i) shall be developed by—

(I) in the State of Alabama, the Alabama Gulf Coast Recovery Council established under paragraph (1)(F)(i);

(II) in the State of Florida, a consortia[17] of local political subdivisions that includes at a minimum 1 representative of each affected county;

---

[17]   So in law. Probably should read "consortium".

(III) in the State of Louisiana, the Coastal

Protection and Restoration Authority of Louisiana;

(IV) in the State of Mississippi, the Office of the Governor or an appointee of the Office of the Governor; and

(V) in the State of Texas, the Office of the Governor or an appointee of the Office of the Governor.

(iv) APPROVAL.— Not later than 60 days after the date on which a plan is submitted under clause (i), the Council shall approve or disapprove the plan based on the conditions of clause (i).

(C) DISAPPROVAL.— If the Council disapproves a plan pursuant to subparagraph (B)(iv), the Council shall—

(i) provide the reasons for disapproval in writing; and

(ii) consult with the State to address any identified deficiencies with the State plan.

(D) FAILURE TO SUBMIT ADEQUATE PLAN.— If a State fails to submit an adequate plan under this paragraph, any funds made available under this paragraph shall remain in the Trust Fund until such date as a plan is submitted and approved pursuant to this paragraph.

(E) JUDICIAL REVIEW.— If the Council fails to approve or take action within 60 days on a plan, as described in subparagraph (B)(iv), the State may obtain expedited judicial review within 90 days of that decision in a district court of the United States, of appropriate jurisdiction and venue, that is located within the State seeking the review.

(F) COST-SHARING.—

(i) IN GENERAL.— A Gulf Coast State or coastal political subdivision may use, in whole or in part, amounts made available to that Gulf Coast State or coastal political subdivision under this paragraph to satisfy the non-Federal share of any project or program that—

(I) is authorized by other Federal law; and

(II) is an eligible activity described in clause

(i) or (ii) of paragraph (1)(B).

(ii) EFFECT ON OTHER FUNDS.— The use of funds made available from the Trust Fund under this paragraph to satisfy the non-Federal share of the cost of a project or program described in clause (i) shall not affect the priority in which other Federal funds are allocated or awarded.

(4) AUTHORIZATION OF INTEREST TRANSFERS.— Of the total amount made available for any fiscal year from the Trust Fund that is equal to the interest earned by the Trust Fund and proceeds from investments made by the Trust Fund in the preceding fiscal year—

(A) 50 percent shall be divided equally between—

(i) the Gulf Coast Ecosystem Restoration Science, Observation, Monitoring, and Technology program authorized in section 1604 of the Resources and Ecosystems Sustainability, Tourist Opportunities, and Revived Economies of the Gulf Coast States Act of 2012; and

(ii) the centers of excellence research grants authorized in section 1605 of that Act; and

(B) 50 percent shall be made available to the Gulf Coast Ecosystem Restoration Council to carry out the Comprehensive Plan pursuant to paragraph (2).

[33 U.S.C. 1321]

SEC. 312. MARINE SANITATION DEVICES; DISCHARGES INCIDENTAL TO THE NORMAL OPERATION OF VESSELS.

(a) DEFINITIONS.— In this section, the term—

(1) "new vessel" includes every description of watercraft or other artificial contrivance used, or capable of being used, as a means of transportation on the navigable waters, the construction of which is initiated after promulgation of standards and regulations under this section;

(2) "existing vessel" includes every description of watercraft or other artificial contrivance used, or capable of being used, as a means of transportation on the navigable waters, the construction of which is initiated before promulgation of standards and regulations under this section;

(3) "public vessel" means a vessel owned or bareboat chartered and operated by the United States, by a State or political subdivision thereof, or by a foreign nation, except when such vessel is engaged in commerce;

(4) "United States" includes the States, the District of Columbia, the Commonwealth of Puerto Rico, the Virgin Islands, Guam, American Samoa, the Canal Zone, and the Trust Territory of the Pacific Islands;

(5) "marine sanitation device" includes any equipment for installation on board a vessel which is designed to receive, retain, treat, or discharge sewage, and any process to treat such sewage;

(6) "sewage" means human body wastes and the wastes from toilets and other receptacles intended to receive or retain body wastes except that, with respect to commercial vessels on the Great Lakes, such term shall include graywater;

(7) "manufacture" means any person engaged in the manufacturing, assembling, or importation of marine sanitation devices, marine pollution control device equipment, or vessels subject to standards and regulations promulgated under this section;

(8) "person" means an individual, partnership, firm, corporation, association, or agency of the United States, but does not include an individual on board a public vessel;

(9) "discharge" includes, but is not limited to, any spilling, leaking, pumping, pouring, emitting, emptying or dumping;

(10) "commercial vessels" means those vessels used in the business of transporting property for compensation or hire, or in transporting property in the business of the owner, lessee, or operator of the vessel;

(11) "graywater" means galley, bath, and shower water;

(12) "discharge incidental to the normal operation of a vessel"—

   (A) means a discharge, including—

      (i) graywater, bilge water, cooling water, weather deck runoff, ballast water, oil water separator effluent, and any other pollutant discharge from the operation of a marine propulsion system, shipboard maneuvering system, crew habitability system, or installed major equipment, such as an aircraft carrier elevator or a catapult, or from a protective, preservative, or absorptive application to the hull of the vessel; and

(ii) a discharge in connection with the testing, maintenance, and repair of a system described in clause (i) whenever the vessel is waterborne; and

(B) does not include—

(i) a discharge of rubbish, trash, garbage, or other such material discharged overboard;

(ii) an air emission resulting from the operation of a vessel propulsion system, motor driven equipment, or incinerator; or

(iii) a discharge that is not covered by part 122.3 of title 40, Code of Federal Regulations (as in effect on the date of the enactment of subsection (n));

(13) "marine pollution control device" means, except as provided in subsection (p), any equipment or management practice, for installation or use on board a vessel of the Armed Forces, that is—

(A) designed to receive, retain, treat, control, or discharge a discharge incidental to the normal operation of a vessel; and

(B) determined by the Administrator and the Secretary of Defense to be the most effective equipment or management practice to reduce the environmental impacts of the discharge consistent with the considerations set forth in subsection (n)(2)(B); and

(14) "vessel of the Armed Forces" means—

(A) any vessel owned or operated by the Department of Defense, other than a time or voyage chartered vessel; and

(B) any vessel owned or operated by the Department of Transportation that is designated by the Secretary of the department in which the Coast Guard is operating as a vessel equivalent to a vessel described in subparagraph (A).

(b) (1) As soon as possible, after the enactment of this section and subject to the provisions of section 104(j) of this Act, the

Administrator, after consultation with the Secretary of the department in which the Coast Guard is operating, after giving appropriate consideration to the economic costs involved, and within the limits of available technology, shall promulgate Federal standards of performance for marine sanitation devices (hereinafter in this section referred to as "standards") which shall be designed to prevent the discharge of untreated or inadequately treated sewage into or upon the navigable waters from new vessels and existing vessels, except vessels not equipped with installed toilet facilities. Such standards and standards established under subsection (c)(1)(B) of this section shall be consistent with maritime safety and the marine and navigation laws and regulations and shall be coordinated with the regulations issued under this subsection by the Secretary of the department in which the Coast Guard is operating. The Secretary of the department in which the Coast Guard is operating shall promulgate regulations, which are consistent with standards promulgated under this subsection and subsection (c) of this section and with maritime safety and the marine and navigation laws and regulations governing the design, construction, installation, and operation of any marine sanitation device on board such vessels.

(2) Any existing vessel equipped with a marine sanitation device on the date of promulgation of initial standards and regulations under this section, which device is in compliance with such initial standards and regulations, shall be deemed in compliance with this section until such time as the device is replaced or is found not to be in compliance with such initial standards and regulations.

(c) (1) (A) Initial standards and regulations under this section shall become effective for new vessels two years after promulgation; and for existing vessels five years after promulgation. Revisions of standards and regulations shall be effective upon promulgation, unless another effective date is specified, except that no revision shall take effect before the effective date of the standard or regulation being revised.

(B) The Administrator shall, with respect to commercial vessels on the Great Lakes, establish standards which require at a minimum the equivalent of secondary treatment as defined under section 304(d) of this Act. Such standards and regulations shall take effect for existing vessels after such time as the Administrator determines to be reasonable for the upgrading of marine sanitation devices to attain such standard.

(2) The Secretary of the department in which the Coast Guard is operating with regard to his regulatory authority established by this section, after consultation with the Administrator, may distinguish among classes, type[18], and sizes of vessels as well as between new and existing vessels, and may waive applicability of standards and regulations as necessary or appropriate for such classes, types, and sizes of vessels (including existing vessels equipped with marine sanitation devices on the date of promulgation of the initial standards required by this section), and, upon application, for individual vessels.

[18] So in law. Probably should read "types".

(d) The provisions of this section and the standards and regulations promulgated hereunder apply to vessels owned and operated by the United States unless the Secretary of Defense finds that compliance would not be in the interest of national security. With respect to vessels owned and operated by the Department of Defense, regulations under the last sentence of subsection (b)(1) of this section and certifications under subsection (g)(2) of this section shall be promulgated and issued by the Secretary of Defense.

(e) Before the standards and regulations under this section are promulgated, the Administrator and the Secretary of the department in which the Coast Guard is operating shall consult with the Secretary of State; the Secretary of Health, Education, and Welfare; the Secretary of Defense; the Secretary of the Treasury; the Secretary of Commerce; other interested Federal agencies; and the States and industries interested; and otherwise comply with the requirements of section 553 of title 5 of the United States Code.

(f) (1) (A) Except as provided in subparagraph (B), after the effective date of the initial standards and regulations promulgated under this section, no State or political subdivision thereof shall adopt or enforce any statute or regulation of such State or political subdivision with respect to the design, manufacture, or installation or use of any marine sanitation device on any vessel subject to the provisions of this section.

(B) A State may adopt and enforce a statute or regulation

with respect to the design, manufacture, or installation or use of any marine sanitation device on a houseboat, if such statute or regulation is more stringent than the standards and regulations promulgated under this section. For purposes of this paragraph, the term "houseboat" means a vessel which, for a period of time determined by the State in which the vessel is located, is used primarily as a residence and is not used primarily as a means of transportation.

(2) If, after promulgation of the initial standards and regulations and prior to their effective date, a vessel is equipped with a marine sanitation device in compliance with such standards and regulations and the installation and operation of such device is in accordance with such standards and regulations, such standards and regulations shall, for the purposes of paragraph (1) of this subsection, become effective with respect to such vessel on the date of such compliance.

(3) After the effective date of the initial standards and regulations promulgated under this section, if any State determines that the protection and enhancement of the quality of some or all of the waters within such State require greater environmental protection, such State may completely prohibit the discharge from all vessels of any sewage, whether treated or not, into such waters, except that no such prohibition shall apply until the Administrator determines that adequate facilities for the safe and sanitary removal and treatment of sewage from all vessels are reasonably available for such water to which such prohibition would apply. Upon application of the State, the Administrator shall make such determination within 90 days of the date of such application.

(4) (A) If the Administrator determines upon application by a State that the protection and enhancement of the quality of specified waters within such State requires such a prohibition, he shall by regulation completely prohibit the discharge from a vessel of any sewage (whether treated or not) into such waters.

(B) Upon application by a State, the Administrator shall, by regulation, establish a drinking water intake zone in any waters within such State and prohibit the discharge of sewage from vessels within that zone.

(g) (1) No manufacturer of a marine sanitation device or marine pollution control device equipment shall sell, offer for sale, or introduce or deliver for introduction in interstate commerce, or import into the United States for sale or resale any marine sanitation device or marine pollution control device equipment manufactured after the effective date of the standards and regulations promulgated under this section unless such device or equipment is in all material respects substantially the same as a test device or equipment certified under this subsection.

(2) Upon application of the manufacturer, the Secretary of the department in which the Coast Guard is operating shall so certify a marine sanitation device or marine pollution control device equipment if he determines, in accordance with the provisions of this paragraph, that it meets the appropriate standards and regulations promulgated under this section. The Secretary of the department in which the Coast Guard is operating shall test or require such testing of the device or equipment in accordance with procedures set forth by the Administrator as to standards of performance and for such other purposes as may be appropriate. If the Secretary of the department in which the Coast Guard is operating determines that the device or equipment is satisfactory from the standpoint of safety and any other requirements of maritime law or regulation, and after consideration of the design, installation, operation, material, or other appropriate factors, he shall certify the device or equipment. Any device or equipment manufactured by such manufacturer which is in all material respects substantially the same as the certified test device or equipment shall be deemed to be in conformity with the appropriate standards and regulations established under this section.

(3) Every manufacturer shall establish and maintain such records, make such reports, and provide such information as the Administrator or the Secretary of the department in which the Coast Guard is operating may reasonably require to enable him to determine whether such manufacturer has acted or is acting in compliance with this section and regulations issued thereunder and shall, upon request of an officer or employee duly designated by the Administrator or the Secretary of the department in which the Coast Guard is operating, permit such officer or employee at reasonable times to have access to and copy such records. All information reported to or otherwise obtained by the Administrator or the Secretary of the

department in which the Coast Guard is operating or their representatives pursuant to this subsection which contains or relates to a trade secret or other matter referred in section 1905 of title 18 of the United States Code shall be considered confidential for the purpose of that section, except that such information may be disclosed to other officers or employees concerned with carrying out this section. This paragraph shall not apply in the case of the construction of a vessel by an individual for his own use.

(h) SALE AND RESALE OF PROPERLY EQUIPPED VESSELS; OPERABILITY OF CERTIFIED MARINE SANITATION DEVICES.—

(1) IN GENERAL.— Subject to paragraph (2), after the effective date of standards and regulations promulgated under this section, it shall be unlawful—

(A) for the manufacturer of any vessel subject to such standards and regulations to manufacture for sale, to sell or offer for sale, or to distribute for sale or resale any such vessel unless it is equipped with a marine sanitation device and marine pollution control device equipment which is in all material respects substantially the same as the appropriate test device certified pursuant to this section;

(B) for any person, prior to the sale or delivery of a vessel subject to such standards and regulations to the ultimate purchaser, wrongfully to remove or render inoperative any certified marine sanitation device or element of design of such device or any certified marine pollution control device equipment or element of design of such equipment installed in such vessel;

(C) for any person to fail or refuse to permit access to or copying of records or to fail to make reports or provide information required under this section; and

(D) for a vessel subject to such standards and regulations to operate on the navigable waters of the United States, if such vessel is not equipped with an operable marine sanitation device certified pursuant to this section.

(2) EFFECT OF SUBSECTION.— Nothing in this subsection requires certification of a marine pollution control device for use on any vessel of the Armed Forces.

(i) The district courts of the United States shall have jurisdictions to restrain violations of subsection (g)(1) of this section and subsections (h)(1) through (3) of this section. Actions to restrain such violations shall be brought by, and in, the name of the United States. In case of contumacy or refusal to obey a subpena served upon any person under this subsection, the district court of the United States for any district in which such person is found or resides or transacts business, upon application by the United States and after notice to such person, shall have jurisdiction to issue an order requiring such person to appear and give testimony or to appear and produce documents, and any failure to obey such order of the court may be punished by such court as a contempt thereof.

(j) Any person who violates subsection (g)(1), clause (1) or (2) of subsection (h), or subsection (n)(8) shall be liable to a civil penalty of not more than $5,000 for each violation. Any person who violates clause (4) of subsection (h) of this section or any regulation issued pursuant to this section shall be liable to a civil penalty of not more than $2,000 for each violation. Each violation shall be a separate offense. The Secretary of the department in which the Coast Guard is operating may assess and compromise any such penalty. No penalty shall be assessed until the person charged shall have been given notice and an opportunity for a hearing on such charge. In determining the amount of the penalty, or the amount agreed upon in compromise, the gravity of the violation, and the demonstrated good faith of the person charged in attempting to achieve rapid compliance, after notification of a violation, shall be considered by said Secretary.

(k) ENFORCEMENT AUTHORITY.—

(1) ADMINISTRATOR.— This section shall be enforced by the Administrator, to the extent provided in section 309.

(2) SECRETARY.—

(A) IN GENERAL.— This section shall be enforced by the Secretary of the department in which the Coast Guard is operating, who may use, by agreement, with or without reimbursement, law enforcement officers or other personnel and facilities of the Administrator, other Federal agencies, or the States to carry out the provisions of this section.

(B) INSPECTIONS.— For purposes of ensuring compliance with this section, the Secretary—

(i) may carry out an inspection (including the taking of ballast water samples) of any vessel at any time; and

(ii) shall—

(I) establish procedures for—

(aa) reporting violations of this section; and

(bb) accumulating evidence regarding those violations; and

(II) use appropriate and practicable measures of detection and environmental monitoring of vessels.

(C) DETENTION.— The Secretary may detain a vessel if the Secretary—

(i) has reasonable cause to believe that the vessel—

(I) has failed to comply with an applicable requirement of this section; or

(II) is being operated in violation of such a requirement; and

(ii) the Secretary provides to the owner or operator of the vessel a notice of the intent to detain.

(3) STATES.—

(A) IN GENERAL.— This section may be enforced by a State or political subdivision of a State (including the attorney general of a State), including by filing a civil action in an appropriate Federal district court to enforce any violation of subsection (p).

(B) JURISDICTION.— The appropriate Federal district court shall have jurisdiction with respect to a civil action filed pursuant to subparagraph (A), without regard to the amount in controversy or the citizenship of the parties—

(i) to enforce the requirements of this section; and

(ii) to apply appropriate civil penalties under this section or section 309(d), as appropriate.

(l) Anyone authorized by the Secretary of the department in which the Coast Guard is operating to enforce the provisions of this section may, except as to public vessels, (1) board and inspect any vessel upon the navigable waters of the United States and (2) execute any warrant or other process issued by an officer or court of competent jurisdiction.

(m) In the case of Guam and the Trust Territory of the Pacific Islands, actions arising under this section may be brought in the district court of Guam, and in the case of the Virgin Islands such actions may be brought in the district court of the Virgin Islands. In the case of American Samoa and the Trust Territory of the Pacific Islands, such actions may be brought in the District Court of the United States for the District of Hawaii and such court shall have jurisdiction of such actions. In the case of the Canal Zone, such actions may be brought in the District Court for the District of the Canal Zone.

(n) UNIFORM NATIONAL DISCHARGE STANDARDS FOR VESSELS OF THE ARMED FORCES.—

(1) APPLICABILITY.— This subsection shall apply to vessels of the Armed Forces and discharges, other than sewage, incidental to the normal operation of a vessel of the Armed Forces, unless the Secretary of Defense finds that compliance with this subsection would not be in the national security interests of the United States.

(2) DETERMINATION OF DISCHARGES REQUIRED TO BE CONTROLLED BY MARINE POLLUTION CONTROL DEVICES.—

(A) IN GENERAL.— The Administrator and the Secretary of Defense, after consultation with the Secretary of the department in which the Coast Guard is operating, the Secretary of Commerce, and interested States, shall jointly determine the discharges incidental to the normal operation of a vessel of the Armed Forces for which it is reasonable and practicable to require use of a marine pollution control device to mitigate adverse impacts on the marine environment. Notwithstanding subsection (a)(1) of section 553 of title 5, United States Code, the Administrator and the Secretary of Defense shall promulgate the determinations in accordance with such section. The Secretary of Defense shall require the use of a marine pollution control device on board a vessel of the Armed Forces in any case in which it is determined that the use of such a device is reasonable and practicable.

(B) CONSIDERATIONS.— In making a determination under subparagraph (A), the Administrator and the Secretary of Defense shall take into consideration—

(i) the nature of the discharge;

(ii) the environmental effects of the discharge;

(iii) the practicability of using the marine pollution control device;

(iv) the effect that installation or use of the marine pollution control device would have on the operation or operational capability of the vessel;

(v) applicable United States law;

(vi) applicable international standards; and

(vii) the economic costs of the installation and use of the marine pollution control device.

(3) PERFORMANCE STANDARDS FOR MARINE POLLUTION CONTROL DEVICES.—

(A) IN GENERAL.— For each discharge for which a marine pollution control device is determined to be required under paragraph (2), the Administrator and the Secretary of Defense, in consultation with the Secretary of the department in which the Coast Guard is operating, the Secretary of State, the Secretary of Commerce, other interested Federal agencies, and interested States, shall jointly promulgate Federal standards of performance for each marine pollution control device required with respect to the discharge. Notwithstanding subsection (a)(1) of section 553 of title 5, United States Code, the Administrator and the Secretary of Defense shall promulgate the standards in accordance with such section.

(B) CONSIDERATIONS.— In promulgating standards under this paragraph, the Administrator and the Secretary of Defense shall take into consideration the matters set forth in paragraph (2)(B).

(C) CLASSES, TYPES, AND SIZES OF VESSELS.— The standards promulgated under this paragraph may—

(i) distinguish among classes, types, and sizes of vessels;

(ii) distinguish between new and existing vessels;

and

(iii) provide for a waiver of the applicability of the standards as necessary or appropriate to a particular class, type, age, or size of vessel.

(4) REGULATIONS FOR USE OF MARINE POLLUTION CONTROL DEVICES.— The Secretary of Defense, after consultation with the Administrator and the Secretary of the department in which the Coast Guard is operating, shall promulgate such regulations governing the design, construction, installation, and use of marine pollution control devices on board vessels of the Armed Forces as are necessary to achieve the standards promulgated under paragraph (3).

(5) DEADLINES; EFFECTIVE DATE.—

(A) DETERMINATIONS.— The Administrator and the Secretary of Defense shall—

(i) make the initial determinations under paragraph (2) not later than 2 years after the date of the enactment of this subsection; and

(ii) every 5 years—

(I) review the determinations; and

(II) if necessary, revise the determinations based on significant new information.

(B) STANDARDS.— The Administrator and the Secretary of Defense shall—

(i) promulgate standards of performance for a marine pollution control device under paragraph (3) not later than 2 years after the date of a determination under paragraph (2) that the marine pollution control device is required; and

(ii) every 5 years—

(I) review the standards; and

(II) if necessary, revise the standards, consistent with paragraph (3)(B) and based on significant new information.

(C) REGULATIONS.— The Secretary of Defense shall promulgate regulations with respect to a marine pollution control device under paragraph (4) as soon as practicable after the Administrator and the Secretary of Defense promulgate standards with respect to the device under paragraph (3), but not later than 1 year after the Administrator and the Secretary of Defense promulgate the standards. The regulations promulgated by the Secretary of Defense under paragraph (4) shall become effective upon promulgation unless another effective date is specified in the regulations.

(D) PETITION FOR REVIEW.— The Governor of any State may submit a petition requesting that the Secretary of Defense and the Administrator review a determination under paragraph (2) or a standard under paragraph (3), if there is significant new information, not considered previously, that could reasonably result in a change to the particular determination or standard after consideration of the matters set forth in paragraph (2)(B). The petition shall be accompanied by the scientific and technical information on which the petition is based. The Administrator and the Secretary of Defense shall grant or deny the petition not later than 2 years after the date of receipt of the petition.

(6) EFFECT ON OTHER LAWS.—

(A) PROHIBITION ON REGULATION BY STATES OR POLITICAL SUBDIVISIONS OF STATES.— Beginning on the effective date of—

(i) a determination under paragraph (2) that it is not reasonable and practicable to require use of a marine pollution control device regarding a particular discharge incidental to the normal operation of a vessel of the Armed Forces; or

(ii) regulations promulgated by the Secretary of Defense under paragraph (4);

except as provided in paragraph (7), neither a State nor a political subdivision of a State may adopt or enforce any statute or regulation of the State or political subdivision with respect to the discharge or the design, construction, installation, or use of any marine pollution control device required to control discharges from a vessel of the Armed Forces.

(B) FEDERAL LAWS.— This subsection shall not affect the application of section 311 to discharges incidental to the normal operation of a vessel.

(7) ESTABLISHMENT OF STATE NO-DISCHARGE ZONES.—

(A) STATE PROHIBITION.—

(i) IN GENERAL.— After the effective date of—

(I) a determination under paragraph (2) that it is not reasonable and practicable to require use of a marine pollution control device regarding a particular discharge incidental to the normal operation of a vessel of the Armed Forces; or

(II) regulations promulgated by the Secretary of Defense under paragraph (4);

if a State determines that the protection and enhancement of the quality of some or all of the waters within the State require greater environmental protection, the State may prohibit 1 or more discharges incidental to the normal operation of a vessel, whether treated or not treated, into the waters. No prohibition shall apply until the Administrator makes the determinations described in subclauses (II) and (III) of subparagraph (B)(i).

(ii) DOCUMENTATION.— To the extent that a prohibition under this paragraph would apply to vessels of the Armed Forces and not to other types of vessels, the State shall document the technical or environmental basis for the distinction.

(B) PROHIBITION BY THE ADMINISTRATOR.—

(i) IN GENERAL.— Upon application of a State, the Administrator shall by regulation prohibit the discharge from a vessel of 1 or more discharges incidental to the normal operation of a vessel, whether treated or not treated, into the waters covered by the application if the Administrator determines that—

(I) the protection and enhancement of the quality of the specified waters within the State require a prohibition of the discharge into the waters;

(II) adequate facilities for the safe and sanitary removal of the discharge incidental to the normal operation of a vessel are reasonably available for the waters to which the prohibition would apply; and

(III) the prohibition will not have the effect of discriminating against a vessel of the Armed Forces by reason of the ownership or operation by the Federal Government, or the military function, of the vessel.

(ii) APPROVAL OR DISAPPROVAL.— The Administrator shall approve or disapprove an application submitted under clause (i) not later than 90 days after the date on which the application is submitted to the Administrator. Notwithstanding clause (i)(II), the Administrator shall not disapprove an application for the sole reason that there are not adequate facilities to remove any discharge incidental to the normal operation of a vessel from vessels of the Armed Forces.

(C) APPLICABILITY TO FOREIGN FLAGGED VESSELS.— A prohibition under this paragraph—

(i) shall not impose any design, construction, manning, or equipment standard on a foreign flagged vessel engaged in innocent passage unless the prohibition implements a generally accepted international rule or standard; and

(ii) that relates to the prevention, reduction, and control of pollution shall not apply to a foreign flagged vessel engaged in transit passage unless the prohibition implements an applicable international regulation regarding the discharge of oil, oily waste, or any other noxious substance into the waters.

(8) PROHIBITION RELATING TO VESSELS OF THE ARMED FORCES.— After the effective date of the regulations promulgated by the Secretary of Defense under paragraph (4), it shall be unlawful for any vessel of the Armed Forces subject to the regulations to—

(A) operate in the navigable waters of the United States or the waters of the contiguous zone, if the vessel is not equipped with any required marine pollution control device meeting standards established under this subsection; or

(B) discharge overboard any discharge incidental to the normal operation of a vessel in waters with respect to which a prohibition on the discharge has been established under paragraph (7).

(9) ENFORCEMENT.— This subsection shall be enforceable, as provided in subsections (j) and (k), against any agency of the United States responsible for vessels of the Armed Forces notwithstanding any immunity asserted by the agency.

(o) MANAGEMENT PRACTICES FOR RECREATIONAL VESSELS.—

(1) APPLICABILITY.— This subsection applies to any discharge, other than a discharge of sewage, from a recreational vessel that is—

(A) incidental to the normal operation of the vessel; and

(B) exempt from permitting requirements under section 402(r).

(2) DETERMINATION OF DISCHARGES SUBJECT TO MANAGEMENT PRACTICES.—

(A) DETERMINATION.—

(i) IN GENERAL.— The Administrator, in consultation with the Secretary of the department in which the Coast Guard is operating, the Secretary of Commerce, and interested States, shall determine the discharges incidental to the normal operation of a recreational vessel for which it is reasonable and practicable to develop management practices to mitigate adverse impacts on the waters of the United States.

(ii) PROMULGATION.— The Administrator shall promulgate the determinations under clause (i) in accordance with section 553 of title 5, United States Code.

(iii) MANAGEMENT PRACTICES.— The Administrator shall develop management practices for recreational vessels in any case in which the Administrator determines that the use of those practices is reasonable and practicable.

(B) CONSIDERATIONS.— In making a determination under subparagraph (A), the Administrator shall consider—

(i) the nature of the discharge;

(ii) the environmental effects of the discharge;

(iii) the practicability of using a management practice;

(iv) the effect that the use of a management practice would have on the operation, operational capability, or safety of the vessel;

(v) applicable Federal and State law;

(vi) applicable international standards; and

(vii) the economic costs of the use of the management practice.

(C) TIMING.— The Administrator shall—

(i) make the initial determinations under subparagraph (A) not later than 1 year after the date of enactment of this subsection; and

(ii) every 5 years thereafter—

(I) review the determinations; and

(II) if necessary, revise the determinations based on any new information available to the Administrator.

(3) PERFORMANCE STANDARDS FOR MANAGEMENT PRACTICES.—

(A) IN GENERAL.— For each discharge for which a management practice is developed under paragraph (2), the Administrator, in consultation with the Secretary of the department in which the Coast Guard is operating, the Secretary of Commerce, other interested Federal agencies, and interested States, shall promulgate, in accordance with section 553 of title 5, United States Code, Federal standards of performance for each management practice required with respect to the discharge.

(B) CONSIDERATIONS.— In promulgating standards under this paragraph, the Administrator shall take into account the considerations described in paragraph (2)(B).

(C) CLASSES, TYPES, AND SIZES OF VESSELS.— The standards promulgated under this paragraph may—

(i) distinguish among classes, types, and sizes of vessels;

(ii) distinguish between new and existing vessels; and

(iii) provide for a waiver of the applicability of the standards as necessary or appropriate to a particular class, type, age, or size of vessel.

(D) TIMING.— The Administrator shall—

(i) promulgate standards of performance for a management practice under subparagraph (A) not later than 1 year after the date of a determination under paragraph (2) that the management practice is reasonable and practicable; and

(ii) every 5 years thereafter—

(I) review the standards; and

(II) if necessary, revise the standards, in accordance with subparagraph (B) and based on any new information available to the Administrator.

(4) REGULATIONS FOR THE USE OF MANAGEMENT PRACTICES.—

(A) IN GENERAL.— The Secretary of the department in which the Coast Guard is operating shall promulgate such regulations governing the design, construction, installation, and use of management practices for recreational vessels as are necessary to meet the standards of performance promulgated under paragraph (3).

(B) REGULATIONS.—

(i) IN GENERAL.— The Secretary shall promulgate the regulations under this paragraph as soon as practicable after the Administrator promulgates standards with respect to the practice under paragraph (3), but not later than 1 year after the date on which the Administrator promulgates the standards.

(ii) EFFECTIVE DATE.— The regulations promulgated by the Secretary under this paragraph shall be effective upon promulgation unless another effective date is specified in the regulations.

(iii) CONSIDERATION OF TIME.— In determining the effective date of a regulation promulgated under this paragraph, the Secretary shall consider the period of time necessary to communicate the existence of the regulation to persons affected by the regulation.

(5) EFFECT OF OTHER LAWS.— This subsection shall not affect the application of section 311 to discharges incidental to the normal operation of a recreational vessel.

(6) PROHIBITION RELATING TO RECREATIONAL VESSELS.— After the effective date of the regulations promulgated by the Secretary of the department in which the Coast Guard is operating under paragraph (4), the owner or operator of a recreational vessel shall neither operate in nor discharge any discharge incidental to the normal operation of the vessel into, the waters of the United States or the waters of the contiguous zone, if the owner or operator of the vessel is not using any applicable management practice meeting standards established under this subsection.

(p) UNIFORM NATIONAL STANDARDS FOR DISCHARGES INCIDENTAL TO NORMAL OPERATION OF VESSELS.—

(1) DEFINITIONS.— In this subsection:

(A) AQUATIC NUISANCE SPECIES.— The term "aquatic nuisance species" means a nonindigenous species that threatens—

(i) the diversity or abundance of a native species;

(ii) the ecological stability of—

(I) waters of the United States; or

(II) waters of the contiguous zone; or

(iii) a commercial, agricultural, aquacultural, or recreational activity that is dependent on—

(I) waters of the United States; or

(II) waters of the contiguous zone.

(B) BALLAST WATER.—

(i) IN GENERAL.— The term "ballast water" means any water, suspended matter, and other materials taken onboard a vessel—

(I) to control or maintain trim, draught, stability, or stresses of the vessel, regardless of the means by which any such water or suspended matter is carried; or

(II) during the cleaning, maintenance, or other operation of a ballast tank or ballast water management system of the vessel.

(ii) EXCLUSION.— The term "ballast water" does not include any substance that is added to the water described in clause (i) that is directly related to the operation of a properly functioning ballast water management system.

(C) BALLAST WATER DISCHARGE STANDARD.— The term "ballast water discharge standard" means—

(i) the numerical ballast water discharge standard established by section 151.1511 or 151.2030 of title 33, Code of Federal Regulations (or successor regulations); or

(ii) if a standard referred to in clause (i) is superseded by a numerical standard of performance under this subsection, that superseding standard.

(D) BALLAST WATER EXCHANGE.— The term "ballast water exchange" means the replacement of water in a ballast water tank using 1 of the following methods:

(i) Flow-through exchange, in which ballast water is flushed out by pumping in midocean water at the bottom of the tank if practicable, and continuously overflowing the tank from the top, until 3 full volumes of water have been changed to minimize the number of original organisms remaining in the tank.

(ii) Empty and refill exchange, in which ballast water taken on in ports, estuarine waters, or territorial waters is pumped out until the pump loses suction, after which the ballast tank is refilled with midocean water.

(E) BALLAST WATER MANAGEMENT SYSTEM.— The term

"ballast water management system" means any marine pollution control device (including all ballast water treatment equipment, ballast tanks, pipes, pumps, and all associated control and monitoring equipment) that processes ballast water—

(i) to kill, render nonviable, or remove organisms; or

(ii) to avoid the uptake or discharge of organisms.

(F) BEST AVAILABLE TECHNOLOGY ECONOMICALLY ACHIEVABLE.— The term "best available technology economically achievable" means—

(i) best available technology economically achievable (within the meaning of section 301(b)(2)(A));

(ii) best available technology (within the meaning of section 304(b)(2)(B)); and

(iii) best available technology, as determined in accordance with section 125.3(d)(3) of title 40, Code of Federal Regulations (or successor regulations).

(G) BEST CONVENTIONAL POLLUTANT CONTROL TECHNOLOGY.— The term "best conventional pollutant control technology" means—

(i) best conventional pollutant control technology (within the meaning of section 301(b)(2)(E));

(ii) best conventional pollutant control technology (within the meaning of section 304(b)(4)); and

(iii) best conventional pollutant control technology, as determined in accordance with section 125.3(d)(2) of title 40, Code of Federal Regulations (or successor regulations).

(H) BEST MANAGEMENT PRACTICE.—

(i) IN GENERAL.— The term "best management practice" means a schedule of activities, prohibitions of practices, maintenance procedures, and other management practices to prevent or reduce the pollution of—

(I) the waters of the United States; or

(II) the waters of the contiguous zone.

(ii) INCLUSIONS.— The term "best management practice" includes any treatment requirement, operating procedure, or practice to control—

(I) vessel runoff;

(II) spillage or leaks;

(III) sludge or waste disposal; or

(IV) drainage from raw material storage.

(I) BEST PRACTICABLE CONTROL TECHNOLOGY CURRENTLY AVAILABLE.— The term "best practicable control technology currently available" means—

(i) best practicable control technology currently available (within the meaning of section 301(b)(1)(A));

(ii) best practicable control technology currently available (within the meaning of section 304(b)(1)); and

(iii) best practicable control technology currently available, as determined in accordance with section 125.3(d)(1) of title 40, Code of Federal Regulations (or successor regulations).

(J) CAPTAIN OF THE PORT ZONE.— The term "Captain of the Port Zone" means a Captain of the Port Zone established by the Secretary pursuant to sections 92, 93, and 633 of title 14, United States Code.

(K) EMPTY BALLAST TANK.— The term "empty ballast tank" means a tank that—

(i) has previously held ballast water that has been drained to the limit of the functional or operational capabilities of the tank (such as loss of suction);

(ii) is recorded as empty on a vessel log; and

(iii) contains unpumpable residual ballast water and sediment.

(L) GREAT LAKES COMMISSION.— The term "Great Lakes Commission" means the Great Lakes Commission established by article IV A of the Great Lakes Compact to which Congress granted consent in the Act of July 24, 1968 (Public Law 90–419; 82 Stat. 414).

(M) GREAT LAKES STATE.— The term "Great Lakes State" means any of the States of—

(i) Illinois;

(ii) Indiana;

(iii) Michigan;

(iv) Minnesota;

(v) New York;

(vi) Ohio;

(vii) Pennsylvania; and

(viii) Wisconsin.

(N) GREAT LAKES SYSTEM.— The term "Great Lakes System" has the meaning given the term in section 118(a)(3).

(O) INTERNAL WATERS.— The term "internal waters" has the meaning given the term in section 2.24 of title 33, Code of Federal Regulations (or a successor regulation).

(P) MARINE POLLUTION CONTROL DEVICE.— The term "marine pollution control device" means any equipment or management practice (or combination of equipment and a management practice), for installation or use onboard a vessel, that is—

(i) designed to receive, retain, treat, control, or discharge a discharge incidental to the normal operation of a vessel; and

(ii) determined by the Administrator and the Secretary to be the most effective equipment or management practice (or combination of equipment and a management practice) to reduce the environmental impacts of the discharge, consistent with the factors for consideration described in paragraphs (4) and (5).

(Q) NONINDIGENOUS SPECIES.— The term "nonindigenous species" means an organism of a species that enters an ecosystem beyond the historic range of the species.

(R) ORGANISM.— The term "organism" includes—

(i) an animal, including fish and fish eggs and larvae;

(ii) a plant;

(iii) a pathogen;

(iv) a microbe;

(v) a virus;

(vi) a prokaryote (including any archean or bacterium);

(vii) a fungus; and

(viii) a protist.

(S) PACIFIC REGION.—

(i) IN GENERAL.— The term "Pacific Region" means any Federal or State water—

(I) adjacent to the State of Alaska, California, Hawaii, Oregon, or Washington; and

(II) extending from shore.

(ii) INCLUSION.— The term "Pacific Region" includes the entire exclusive economic zone (as defined in section 1001 of the Oil Pollution Act of 1990 (33 U.S.C. 2701)) adjacent to each State described in clause (i)(I).

(T) PORT OR PLACE OF DESTINATION.— The term "port or place of destination" means a port or place to which a vessel is bound to anchor or moor.

(U) RENDER NONVIABLE.— The term "render nonviable", with respect to an organism in ballast water, means the action of a ballast water management system that renders the organism permanently incapable of reproduction following treatment.

(V) SALTWATER FLUSH.—

(i) IN GENERAL.— The term "saltwater flush" means—

(I) (aa) the addition of as much midocean water into each empty ballast tank of a vessel as is safe for the vessel and crew; and

(bb) the mixing of the flushwater with residual ballast water and sediment through the motion of the vessel; and

(II) the discharge of that mixed water, such that the resultant residual water remaining in the tank—

(aa) has the highest salinity possible; and

(bb) is at least 30 parts per thousand.

(ii) MULTIPLE SEQUENCES.— For purposes of clause (i), a saltwater flush may require more than 1 fill-mix-empty sequence, particularly if only small quantities of water can be safely taken onboard a vessel at 1 time.

(W) SECRETARY.— The term "Secretary" means the Secretary of the department in which the Coast Guard is operating.

(X) SMALL VESSEL GENERAL PERMIT.— The term "Small Vessel General Permit" means the permit that is the subject of the notice of final permit issuance entitled "Final National Pollutant Discharge Elimination System (NPDES) Small Vessel General Permit for Discharges Incidental to the Normal Operation of Vessels Less Than 79 Feet" (79 Fed. Reg. 53702 (September 10, 2014)).

(Y) SMALL VESSEL OR FISHING VESSEL.— The term "small vessel or fishing vessel" means a vessel that is—

(i) less than 79 feet in length; or

(ii) a fishing vessel, fish processing vessel, or fish tender vessel (as those terms are defined in section 2101 of title 46, United States Code), regardless of the length of the vessel.

(Z) VESSEL GENERAL PERMIT.— The term "Vessel General Permit" means the permit that is the subject of the notice of final permit issuance entitled "Final National Pollutant Discharge Elimination System (NPDES) General Permit for Discharges Incidental to the Normal Operation of a Vessel" (78 Fed. Reg. 21938 (April 12, 2013)).

(2) APPLICABILITY.—

(A) IN GENERAL.— Except as provided in subparagraph (B), this subsection applies to—

(i) any discharge incidental to the normal operation of a vessel; and

(ii) any discharge incidental to the normal operation of a vessel (such as most graywater) that is commingled with sewage, subject to the conditions that—

(I) nothing in this subsection prevents a State from regulating sewage discharges; and

(II) any such commingled discharge shall comply with all applicable requirements of—

(aa) this subsection; and

(bb) any law applicable to discharges of sewage.

(B) EXCLUSION.— This subsection does not apply to any discharge incidental to the normal operation of a vessel—

(i) from—

(I) a vessel of the Armed Forces subject to subsection (n);

(II) a recreational vessel subject to subsection (o);

(III) a small vessel or fishing vessel, except that this subsection shall apply to any discharge of ballast water from a small vessel or fishing vessel; or

(IV) a floating craft that is permanently moored to a pier, including a "floating" casino, hotel, restaurant, or bar;

(ii) of ballast water from a vessel

(I) that continuously takes on and discharges ballast water in a flow-through system, if the Administrator determines that system cannot materially contribute to the spread or introduction of an aquatic nuisance species into waters of the United States;

(II) in the National Defense Reserve Fleet that is scheduled for disposal, if the vessel does not have an operable ballast water management system;

(III) that discharges ballast water consisting solely of water taken onboard from a public or commercial source that, at the time the water is

taken onboard, meets the applicable requirements
or permit requirements of the Safe Drinking
Water Act (42 U.S.C. 300f et seq.);

(IV) that carries all permanent ballast water
in sealed tanks that are not subject to discharge;
or

(V) that only discharges ballast water into a
reception facility; or

(iii) that results from, or contains material derived
from, an activity other than the normal operation of
the vessel, such as material resulting from an
industrial or manufacturing process onboard the
vessel.

(3) CONTINUATION IN EFFECT OF EXISTING
REQUIREMENTS.—

(A) VESSEL GENERAL PERMIT.— Notwithstanding the
expiration date of the Vessel General Permit or any other
provision of law, all provisions of the Vessel General Permit
shall remain in force and effect, and shall not be modified,
until the applicable date described in subparagraph (C).

(B) NONINDIGENOUS AQUATIC NUISANCE PREVENTION
AND CONTROL ACT REGULATIONS.— Notwithstanding
section 903(a)(2)(A) of the Vessel Incidental Discharge Act
of 2018, all regulations promulgated by the Secretary
pursuant to section 1101 of the Nonindigenous Aquatic
Nuisance Prevention and Control Act of 1990 (16 U.S.C.
4711) (as in effect on the day before the date of enactment
of this subsection), including the regulations contained in
subparts C and D of part 151 of title 33, Code of Federal
Regulations, and subpart 162.060 of part 162 of title 46,
Code of Federal Regulations (as in effect on the day before
that date of enactment), shall remain in force and effect
until the applicable date described in subparagraph (C).

(C) REPEAL ON EXISTENCE OF FINAL, EFFECTIVE, AND
ENFORCEABLE REQUIREMENTS.— Effective beginning on the
date on which the requirements promulgated by the
Secretary under subparagraphs (A), (B), and (C) of
paragraph (5) with respect to every discharge incidental
to the normal operation of a vessel that is subject to

regulation under this subsection are final, effective, and enforceable, the requirements of the Vessel General Permit and the regulations described in subparagraph (B) shall have no force or effect.

(4) NATIONAL STANDARDS OF PERFORMANCE FOR MARINE POLLUTION CONTROL DEVICES AND WATER QUALITY ORDERS.—

(A) ESTABLISHMENT.—

(i) IN GENERAL.— Not later than 2 years after the date of enactment of this subsection, the Administrator, in concurrence with the Secretary (subject to clause (ii)), and in consultation with interested Governors (subject to clause (iii)), shall promulgate Federal standards of performance for marine pollution control devices for each type of discharge incidental to the normal operation of a vessel that is subject to regulation under this subsection.

(ii) CONCURRENCE WITH SECRETARY.—

(I) REQUEST.— The Administrator shall submit to the Secretary a request for written concurrence with respect to a proposed standard of performance under clause (i).

(II) EFFECT OF FAILURE TO CONCUR.— A failure by the Secretary to concur with the Administrator under clause (i) by the date that is 60 days after the date on which the Administrator submits a request for concurrence under subclause (I) shall not prevent the Administrator from promulgating the relevant standard of performance in accordance with the deadline under clause (i), subject to the condition that the Administrator shall include in the administrative record of the promulgation—

(aa) documentation of the request submitted under subclause (I); and

(bb) the response of the Administrator to any written objections received from the Secretary relating to the proposed standard of performance during the 60-day period beginning on the date of submission of the request.

(iii) CONSULTATION WITH GOVERNORS.—

(I) IN GENERAL.— The Administrator, in promulgating a standard of performance under clause (i), shall develop the standard of performance—

(aa) in consultation with interested Governors; and

(bb) in accordance with the deadlines under that clause.

(II) PROCESS.— The Administrator shall develop a process for soliciting input from interested Governors, including information sharing relevant to such process, to allow interested Governors to inform the development of standards of performance under clause (i).

(III) OBJECTION BY GOVERNORS.—

(aa) SUBMISSION.— An interested Governor that objects to a proposed standard of performance under clause (i) may submit to the Administrator in writing a detailed objection to the proposed standard of performance, describing the scientific, technical, or operational factors that form the basis of the objection.

(bb) RESPONSE.— Before finalizing a standard of performance under clause (i) that is subject to an objection under item (aa) from 1 or more interested Governors, the Administrator shall provide a written response to each interested Governor that submitted an objection under that item that details the scientific, technical, or operational factors that form the basis for that standard of performance.

(cc) JUDICIAL REVIEW.— A response of the Administrator under item (bb) shall not be subject to judicial review.

(iv) PROCEDURE.— The Administrator shall

promulgate the standards of performance under this subparagraph in accordance with—

(I) this paragraph; and

(II) section 553 of title 5, United States Code.

(B) STRINGENCY.—

(i) IN GENERAL.— Subject to clause (iii), the standards of performance promulgated under this paragraph shall require—

(I) with respect to conventional pollutants, toxic pollutants, and nonconventional pollutants (including aquatic nuisance species), the application of the best practicable control technology currently available;

(II) with respect to conventional pollutants, the application of the best conventional pollutant control technology; and

(III) with respect to toxic pollutants and nonconventional pollutants (including aquatic nuisance species), the application of the best available technology economically achievable for categories and classes of vessels, which shall result in reasonable progress toward the national goal of eliminating discharges of all pollutants.

(ii) BEST MANAGEMENT PRACTICES.— The Administrator shall require the use of best management practices to control or abate any discharge incidental to the normal operation of a vessel if—

(I) numeric standards of performance are infeasible under clause (i); or

(II) the best management practices are reasonably necessary—

(aa) to achieve the standards of performance; or

(bb) to carry out the purpose and intent of this subsection.

(iii) MINIMUM REQUIREMENTS.— Subject to subparagraph (D)(ii)(II), the combination of any equipment or best management practice comprising a marine pollution control device shall not be less stringent than the following provisions of the Vessel General Permit:

(I) All requirements contained in parts 2.1 and 2.2 (relating to effluent limits and related requirements), including with respect to waters subject to Federal protection, in whole or in part, for conservation purposes.

(II) All requirements contained in part 5 (relating to vessel class-specific requirements) that concern effluent limits and authorized discharges (within the meaning of that part), including with respect to waters subject to Federal protection, in whole or in part, for conservation purposes.

(C) CLASSES, TYPES, AND SIZES OF VESSELS.— The standards promulgated under this paragraph may distinguish—

(i) among classes, types, and sizes of vessels; and

(ii) between new vessels and existing vessels.

(D) REVIEW AND REVISION.—

(i) IN GENERAL.— Not less frequently than once every 5 years, the Administrator, in consultation with the Secretary, shall—

(I) review the standards of performance in effect under this paragraph; and

(II) if appropriate, revise those standards of performance—

(aa) in accordance with subparagraphs (A) through (C); and

(bb) as necessary to establish requirements for any discharge that is subject to regulation under this subsection.

(ii) MAINTAINING PROTECTIVENESS.—

(I) IN GENERAL.— Except as provided in subclause (II), the Administrator shall not revise a standard of performance under this subsection to be less stringent than an applicable existing requirement.

(II) EXCEPTIONS.— The Administrator may revise a standard of performance to be less stringent than an applicable existing requirement—

(aa) if information becomes available that—

(AA) was not reasonably available when the Administrator promulgated the initial standard of performance or comparable requirement of the Vessel General Permit, as applicable (including the subsequent scarcity or unavailability of materials used to control the relevant discharge); and

(BB) would have justified the application of a less-stringent standard of performance at the time of promulgation; or

(bb) if the Administrator determines that a material technical mistake or misinterpretation of law occurred when promulgating the existing standard of performance or comparable requirement of the Vessel General Permit, as applicable.

(E) BEST MANAGEMENT PRACTICES FOR AQUATIC NUISANCE SPECIES EMERGENCIES AND FURTHER PROTECTION OF WATER QUALITY.—

(i) IN GENERAL.— Notwithstanding any other provision of this subsection, the Administrator, in concurrence with the Secretary (subject to clause (ii)), and in consultation with States, may require, by order, the use of an emergency best management practice for any region or category of vessels in any case in which the Administrator determines that such a best management practice—

(I) is necessary to reduce the reasonably foreseeable risk of introduction or establishment of an aquatic nuisance species; or

(II) will mitigate the adverse effects of a discharge that contributes to a violation of a water quality requirement under section 303, other than a requirement based on the presence of an aquatic nuisance species.

(ii) CONCURRENCE WITH SECRETARY.—

(I) REQUEST.— The Administrator shall submit to the Secretary a request for written concurrence with respect to an order under clause (i).

(II) EFFECT OF FAILURE TO CONCUR.— A failure by the Secretary to concur with the Administrator under clause (i) by the date that is 60 days after the date on which the Administrator submits a request for concurrence under subclause (I) shall not prevent the Administrator from issuing the relevant order, subject to the condition that the Administrator shall include in the administrative record of the issuance—

(aa) documentation of the request submitted under subclause (I); and

(bb) the response of the Administrator to any written objections received from the Secretary relating to the proposed order during the 60-day period beginning on the date of submission of the request.

(iii) DURATION.— An order issued by the Administrator under clause (i) shall expire not later than the date that is 4 years after the date of issuance.

(iv) EXTENSIONS.— The Administrator may reissue an order under clause (i) for such subsequent periods of not longer than 4 years as the Administrator determines to be appropriate.

(5) IMPLEMENTATION, COMPLIANCE, AND ENFORCEMENT REQUIREMENTS.—

(A) ESTABLISHMENT.—

(i) IN GENERAL.— As soon as practicable, but not

later than 2 years, after the date on which the Administrator promulgates any new or revised standard of performance under paragraph (4) with respect to a discharge, the Secretary, in consultation with States, shall promulgate the regulations required under this paragraph with respect to that discharge.

(ii) MINIMUM REQUIREMENTS.— Subject to subparagraph (C)(ii)(II), the regulations promulgated under this paragraph shall not be less stringent with respect to ensuring, monitoring, and enforcing compliance than—

(I) the requirements contained in part 3 of the Vessel General Permit (relating to corrective actions);

(II) the requirements contained in part 4 of the Vessel General Permit (relating to inspections, monitoring, reporting, and recordkeeping), including with respect to waters subject to Federal protection, in whole or in part, for conservation purposes;

(III) the requirements contained in part 5 of the Vessel General Permit (relating to vessel class-specific requirements) regarding monitoring, inspection, and educational and training requirements (within the meaning of that part), including with respect to waters subject to Federal protection, in whole or in part, for conservation purposes; and

(IV) any comparable, existing requirements promulgated under the Nonindigenous Aquatic Nuisance Prevention and Control Act of 1990 (16 U.S.C. 4701 et seq.) (including section 1101 of that Act (16 U.S.C. 4711) (as in effect on the day before the date of enactment of this subsection)) applicable to that discharge.

(iii) COORDINATION WITH STATES.— The Secretary, in coordination with the Governors of the States, shall develop, publish, and periodically update inspection, monitoring, data management, and enforcement procedures for the enforcement by States of Federal standards and requirements under this subsection.

(iv) EFFECTIVE DATE.— In determining the effective date of a regulation promulgated under this paragraph, the Secretary shall take into consideration the period of time necessary—

(I) to communicate to affected persons the applicability of the regulation; and

(II) for affected persons reasonably to comply with the regulation.

(v) PROCEDURE.— The Secretary shall promulgate the regulations under this subparagraph in accordance with—

(I) this paragraph; and

(II) section 553 of title 5, United States Code.

(B) IMPLEMENTATION REGULATIONS FOR MARINE POLLUTION CONTROL DEVICES.— The Secretary shall promulgate such regulations governing the design, construction, testing, approval, installation, and use of marine pollution control devices as are necessary to ensure compliance with the standards of performance promulgated under paragraph (4).

(C) COMPLIANCE ASSURANCE.—

(i) IN GENERAL.— The Secretary shall promulgate requirements (including requirements for vessel owners and operators with respect to inspections, monitoring, reporting, sampling, and recordkeeping) to ensure, monitor, and enforce compliance with—

(I) the standards of performance promulgated by the Administrator under paragraph (4); and

(II) the implementation regulations promulgated by the Secretary under subparagraph (B).

(ii) MAINTAINING PROTECTIVENESS.—

(I) IN GENERAL.— Except as provided in subclause (II), the Secretary shall not revise a requirement under this subparagraph or subparagraph (B) to be less stringent with respect to ensuring, monitoring, or enforcing compliance than an applicable existing requirement.

(II) EXCEPTIONS.— The Secretary may revise a requirement under this subparagraph or subparagraph (B) to be less stringent than an applicable existing requirement—

(aa) in accordance with this subparagraph or subparagraph (B), as applicable;

(bb) if information becomes available that—

(AA) the Administrator determines was not reasonably available when the Administrator promulgated the existing requirement of the Vessel General Permit, or that the Secretary determines was not reasonably available when the Secretary promulgated the existing requirement under the Nonindigenous Aquatic Nuisance Prevention and Control Act of 1990 (16 U.S.C. 4701 et seq.) or the applicable existing requirement under this subparagraph, as applicable (including subsequent scarcity or unavailability of materials used to control the relevant discharge); and

(BB) would have justified the application of a less-stringent requirement at the time of promulgation; or

(cc) if the Administrator determines that a material technical mistake or misinterpretation of law occurred when promulgating an existing requirement of the Vessel General Permit, or if the Secretary determines that a material mistake or misinterpretation of law occurred when promulgating an existing requirement under the Nonindigenous Aquatic Nuisance Prevention and Control Act of 1990 (16 U.S.C. 4701 et seq.) or this subsection.

(D) DATA AVAILABILITY.— Beginning not later than 1 year after the date of enactment of this subsection, the Secretary shall provide to the Governor of a State, on request by the Governor, access to Automated Identification System arrival data for inbound vessels to specific ports or places of destination in the State.

(6) ADDITIONAL PROVISIONS REGARDING BALLAST WATER.—

(A) IN GENERAL.— In addition to the other applicable requirements of this subsection, the requirements of this paragraph shall apply with respect to any discharge incidental to the normal operation of a vessel that is a discharge of ballast water.

(B) EMPTY BALLAST TANKS.—

(i) REQUIREMENTS.— Except as provided in clause (ii), the owner or operator of a vessel with empty ballast tanks bound for a port or place of destination subject to the jurisdiction of the United States shall, prior to arriving at that port or place of destination, conduct a ballast water exchange or saltwater flush—

(I) not less than 200 nautical miles from any shore for a voyage originating outside the United States or Canadian exclusive economic zone; or

(II) not less than 50 nautical miles from any shore for a voyage originating within the United States or Canadian exclusive economic zone.

(ii) EXCEPTIONS.— Clause (i) shall not apply—

(I) if the unpumpable residual waters and sediments of an empty ballast tank were subject to treatment, in compliance with applicable requirements, through a type-approved ballast water management system approved by the Secretary;

(II) except as otherwise required under this subsection, if the unpumpable residual waters and sediments of an empty ballast tank were sourced within—

(aa) the same port or place of destination; or

(bb) contiguous portions of a single Captain of the Port Zone;

(III) if complying with an applicable requirement of clause (i)—

(aa) would compromise the safety of the vessel; or

(bb) is otherwise prohibited by any Federal, Canadian, or international law (including regulations) pertaining to vessel safety;

(IV) if design limitations of the vessel prevent a ballast water exchange or saltwater flush from being conducted in accordance with clause (i); or

(V) if the vessel is operating exclusively within the internal waters of the United States or Canada.

(C) PERIOD OF USE OF INSTALLED BALLAST WATER MANAGEMENT SYSTEMS.—

(i) IN GENERAL.— Except as provided in clause (ii), a vessel shall be deemed to be in compliance with a standard of performance for a marine pollution control device that is a ballast water management system if the ballast water management system—

(I) is maintained in proper working condition, as determined by the Secretary;

(II) is maintained and used in accordance with manufacturer specifications;

(III) continues to meet the ballast water discharge standard applicable to the vessel at the time of installation, as determined by the Secretary; and

(IV) has in effect a valid type-approval certificate issued by the Secretary.

(ii) LIMITATION.— Clause (i) shall cease to apply with respect to any vessel on, as applicable—

(I) the expiration of the service life, as determined by the Secretary, of—

(aa) the ballast water management

system; or

(bb) the vessel;

(II) the completion of a major conversion (as defined in section 2101 of title 46, United States Code) of the vessel; or

(III) a determination by the Secretary that there are other type-approved systems for the vessel or category of vessels, with respect to the use of which the environmental, health, and economic benefits would exceed the costs.

(D) REVIEW OF BALLAST WATER MANAGEMENT SYSTEM TYPE-APPROVAL TESTING METHODS.—

(i) DEFINITION OF LIVE; LIVING.— Notwithstanding any other provision of law (including regulations), for purposes of section 151.1511 of title 33, and part 162 of title 46, Code of Federal Regulations (or successor regulations), the terms "live" and "living" shall not—

(I) include an organism that has been rendered nonviable; or

(II) preclude the consideration of any method of measuring the concentration of organisms in ballast water that are capable of reproduction.

(ii) DRAFT POLICY.— Not later than 180 days after the date of enactment of this subsection, the Secretary, in coordination with the Administrator, shall publish a draft policy letter, based on the best available science, describing type-approval testing methods and protocols for ballast water management systems, if any, that—

(I) render nonviable organisms in ballast water; and

(II) may be used in addition to the methods established under subpart 162.060 of title 46, Code of Federal Regulations (or successor regulations)—

(aa) to measure the concentration of organisms in ballast water that are capable of reproduction;

(bb) to certify the performance of each ballast water management system under this subsection; and

(cc) to certify laboratories to evaluate applicable treatment technologies.

(iii) PUBLIC COMMENT.— The Secretary shall provide a period of not more than 60 days for public comment regarding the draft policy letter published under clause (ii).

(iv) FINAL POLICY.—

(I) IN GENERAL.— Not later than 1 year after the date of enactment of this subsection, the Secretary, in coordination with the Administrator, shall publish a final policy letter describing type-approval testing methods, if any, for ballast water management systems that render nonviable organisms in ballast water.

(II) METHOD OF EVALUATION.— The ballast water management systems under subclause (I) shall be evaluated by measuring the concentration of organisms in ballast water that are capable of reproduction based on the best available science that may be used in addition to the methods established under subpart 162.060 of title 46, Code of Federal Regulations (or successor regulations).

(III) REVISIONS.— The Secretary shall revise the final policy letter under subclause (I) in any case in which the Secretary, in coordination with the Administrator, determines that additional testing methods are capable of measuring the concentration of organisms in ballast water that have not been rendered nonviable.

(v) FACTORS FOR CONSIDERATION.— In developing a policy letter under this subparagraph, the Secretary, in coordination with the Administrator—

(I) shall take into consideration a testing method that uses organism grow-out and most probable number statistical analysis to determine the concentration of organisms in ballast water that are capable of reproduction; and

(II) shall not take into consideration a testing method that relies on a staining method that measures the concentration of—

(aa) organisms greater than or equal to 10 micrometers; and

(bb) organisms less than or equal to 50 micrometers.

(E) INTERGOVERNMENTAL RESPONSE FRAMEWORK.—

(i) IN GENERAL.— The Secretary, in consultation with the Administrator and acting in coordination with, or through, the Aquatic Nuisance Species Task Force established by section 1201(a) of the Nonindigenous Aquatic Nuisance Prevention and Control Act of 1990 (16 U.S.C. 4721(a)), shall establish a framework for Federal and intergovernmental response to aquatic nuisance species risks from discharges from vessels subject to ballast water and incidental discharge compliance requirements under this subsection, including the introduction, spread, and establishment of aquatic nuisance species populations.

(ii) BALLAST DISCHARGE RISK RESPONSE.— The Administrator, in coordination with the Secretary and taking into consideration information from the National Ballast Information Clearinghouse developed under section 1102(f) of the Nonindigenous Aquatic Nuisance Prevention and Control Act of 1990 (16 U.S.C. 4712(f)), shall establish a risk assessment and response framework using ballast water discharge data and aquatic nuisance species monitoring data for the purposes of—

(I) identifying and tracking populations of aquatic invasive species;

(II) evaluating the risk of any aquatic nuisance species population tracked under subclause (I) establishing and spreading in waters of the United States or waters of the contiguous zone; and

(III) establishing emergency best management practices that may be deployed rapidly, in a local or regional manner, to respond to emerging aquatic nuisance species threats.

(7) PETITIONS BY GOVERNORS FOR REVIEW.—

(A) IN GENERAL.— The Governor of a State (or a designee) may submit to the Administrator or the Secretary a petition—

(i) to issue an order under paragraph (4)(E); or

(ii) to review any standard of performance, regulation, or policy promulgated under paragraph (4), (5), or (6), respectively, if there exists new information that could reasonably result in a change to—

(I) the standard of performance, regulation, or policy; or

(II) a determination on which the standard of performance, regulation, or policy was based.

(B) INCLUSION.— A petition under subparagraph (A) shall include a description of any applicable scientific or technical information that forms the basis of the petition.

(C) DETERMINATION.—

(i) TIMING.— The Administrator or the Secretary, as applicable, shall grant or deny—

(I) a petition under subparagraph (A)(i) by not later than the date that is 180 days after the date on which the petition is submitted; and

(II) a petition under subparagraph (A)(ii) by not later than the date that is 1 year after the date on which the petition is submitted.

(ii) EFFECT OF GRANT.— If the Administrator or the Secretary determines under clause (i) to grant a petition—

(I) in the case of a petition under subparagraph (A)(i), the Administrator shall immediately issue the relevant order under paragraph (4)(E); or

(II) in the case of a petition under subparagraph (A)(ii), the Administrator or Secretary shall publish in the Federal Register, by not later than 30 days after the date of that determination, a notice of proposed rulemaking to revise the relevant standard, requirement, regulation, or policy under paragraph (4), (5), or (6), as applicable.

(iii) NOTICE OF DENIAL.— If the Administrator or the Secretary determines under clause (i) to deny a petition, the Administrator or Secretary shall publish in the Federal Register, by not later than 30 days after the date of that determination, a detailed explanation of the scientific, technical, or operational factors that form the basis of the determination.

(iv) REVIEW.— A determination by the Administrator or the Secretary under clause (i) to deny a petition shall be—

(I) considered to be a final agency action; and

(II) subject to judicial review in accordance with section 509, subject to clause (v).

(v) EXCEPTIONS.—

(I) VENUE.— Notwithstanding section 509(b), a petition for review of a determination by the Administrator or the Secretary under clause (i) to deny a petition submitted by the Governor of a State under subparagraph (A) may be filed in any United States district court of competent jurisdiction.

(II) DEADLINE FOR FILING.— Notwithstanding section 509(b), a petition for review of a determination by the Administrator or the Secretary under clause (i) shall be filed by not later than 180 days after the date on which the justification for the determination is published in the Federal Register under clause (iii).

(8) PROHIBITION.—

(A) IN GENERAL.— It shall be unlawful for any person to violate—

(i) a provision of the Vessel General Permit in force and effect under paragraph (3)(A);

(ii) a regulation promulgated pursuant to section 1101 of the Nonindigenous Aquatic Nuisance Prevention and Control Act of 1990 (16 U.S.C. 4711) (as in effect on the day before the date of enactment of this subsection) in force and effect under paragraph (3)(B); or

(iii) an applicable requirement or regulation under this subsection.

(B) COMPLIANCE WITH REGULATIONS.— Effective beginning on the effective date of a regulation promulgated under paragraph (4), (5), (6), or (10), as applicable, it shall be unlawful for the owner or operator of a vessel subject to the regulation—

(i) to discharge any discharge incidental to the normal operation of the vessel into waters of the United States or waters of the contiguous zone, except in compliance with the regulation; or

(ii) to operate in waters of the United States or waters of the contiguous zone, if the vessel is not equipped with a required marine pollution control device that complies with the requirements established under this subsection, unless—

(I) the owner or operator of the vessel denotes in an entry in the official logbook of the vessel that the equipment was not operational; and

(II) either—

(aa) the applicable discharge was avoided; or

(bb) an alternate compliance option approved by the Secretary as meeting the applicable standard was employed.

(C) AFFIRMATIVE DEFENSE.— No person shall be found to be in violation of this paragraph if—

(i) the violation was in the interest of ensuring the safety of life at sea, as determined by the Secretary; and

(ii) the applicable emergency circumstance was not the result of negligence or malfeasance on the part of—

(I) the owner or operator of the vessel;

(II) the master of the vessel; or

(III) the person in charge of the vessel.

(D) TREATMENT.— Each day of continuing violation of an applicable requirement of this subsection shall constitute a separate offense.

(E) IN REM LIABILITY.— A vessel operated in violation of this subsection is liable in rem for any civil penalty assessed for the violation.

(F) REVOCATION OF CLEARANCE.— The Secretary shall withhold or revoke the clearance of a vessel required under section 60105 of title 46, United States Code, if the owner or operator of the vessel is in violation of this subsection.

(9) EFFECT ON OTHER LAWS.—

(A) STATE AUTHORITY.—

(i) IN GENERAL.— Except as provided in clauses (ii) through (v) and paragraph (10), effective beginning on the date on which the requirements promulgated by the Secretary under subparagraphs (A), (B), and (C) of paragraph (5) with respect to every discharge incidental to the normal operation of a vessel that is subject to regulation under this subsection are final, effective, and enforceable, no State, political subdivision of a State, or interstate agency may adopt or enforce any law, regulation, or other requirement of the State, political subdivision, or interstate agency with respect to any such discharge.

(ii) IDENTICAL OR LESSER STATE LAWS.— Clause (i) shall not apply to any law, regulation, or other requirement of a State, political subdivision of a State, or interstate agency in effect on or after the date of enactment of this subsection—

(I) that is identical to a Federal requirement under this subsection applicable to the relevant discharge; or

(II) compliance with which would be achieved concurrently in achieving compliance with a Federal requirement under this subsection applicable to the relevant discharge.

(iii) STATE ENFORCEMENT OF FEDERAL REQUIREMENTS.— A State may enforce any standard of performance or other Federal requirement of this subsection in accordance with subsection (k) or other applicable Federal authority.

(iv) EXCEPTION FOR CERTAIN FEES.—

(I) IN GENERAL.— Subject to subclauses (II) and (III), a State that assesses any fee pursuant to any State or Federal law relating to the regulation of a discharge incidental to the normal operation of a vessel before the date of enactment of this subsection may assess or retain a fee to cover the costs of administration, inspection, monitoring, and enforcement activities by the State to achieve compliance with the applicable requirements of this subsection.

(II) MAXIMUM AMOUNT.—

(aa) IN GENERAL.— Except as provided in item (bb), a State may assess a fee for activities under this clause equal to not more than $1,000 against the owner or operator of a vessel that—

(AA) has operated outside of that State; and

(BB) arrives at a port or place of destination in the State (excluding movement entirely within a single port or place of destination).

(bb) VESSELS ENGAGED IN COASTWISE TRADE.— A State may assess against the owner or operator of a vessel registered in accordance with applicable Federal law and lawfully engaged in the coastwise trade not more than $5,000 in fees under this clause per vessel during a calendar year.

(III) ADJUSTMENT FOR INFLATION.—

(aa) IN GENERAL.— A State may adjust the amount of a fee authorized under this clause not more frequently than once every 5 years to reflect the percentage by which the Consumer Price Index for All Urban Consumers published by the Department of Labor for the month of October immediately preceding the date of adjustment exceeds the Consumer Price Index for All Urban Consumers published by the Department of Labor for the month of October that immediately precedes the date that is 5 years before the date of adjustment.

(bb) EFFECT OF SUBCLAUSE.— Nothing in this subclause prevents a State from adjusting a fee in effect before the date of enactment of this subsection to the applicable maximum amount under subclause (II).

(cc) APPLICABILITY.— This subclause applies only to increases in fees to amounts greater than the applicable maximum amount under subclause (II).

(v) ALASKA GRAYWATER.— Clause (i) shall not apply with respect to any discharge of graywater (as defined in section 1414 of the Consolidated Appropriations Act, 2001 (Public Law 106–554; 114 Stat. 2763A–323)) from a passenger vessel (as defined in section 2101 of title 46, United States Code) in the State of Alaska (including all waters in the Alexander Archipelago) carrying 50 or more passengers.

(vi) PRESERVATION OF AUTHORITY.— Nothing in this subsection preempts any State law, public initiative, referendum, regulation, requirement, or other State action, except as expressly provided in this subsection.

(B) ESTABLISHED REGIMES.— Except as expressly provided in this subsection, nothing in this subsection affects the applicability to a vessel of any other provision of Federal law, including—

(i) this section;

(ii) section 311;

(iii) the Act to Prevent Pollution from Ships (33 U.S.C. 1901 et seq.); and

(iv) title X of the Coast Guard Authorization Act of 2010 (33 U.S.C. 3801 et seq.).

(C) PERMITTING.— Effective beginning on the date of enactment of this subsection—

(i) the Small Vessel General Permit is repealed; and

(ii) the Administrator, or a State in the case of a permit program approved under section 402, shall not require, or in any way modify, a permit under that section for—

(I) any discharge that is subject to regulation under this subsection;

(II) any discharge incidental to the normal operation of a vessel from a small vessel or fishing vessel, regardless of whether that discharge is subject to regulation under this subsection; or

(III) any discharge described in paragraph (2)(B)(ii).

(D) NO EFFECT ON CIVIL OR CRIMINAL ACTIONS.— Nothing in this subsection, or any standard, regulation, or requirement established under this subsection, modifies or otherwise affects, preempts, or displaces—

(i) any cause of action; or

(ii) any provision of Federal or State law establishing a remedy for civil relief or criminal penalty.

(E) NO EFFECT ON CERTAIN SECRETARIAL AUTHORITY.— Nothing in this subsection affects the authority of the Secretary of Commerce or the Secretary of the Interior to administer any land or waters under the administrative control of the Secretary of Commerce or the Secretary of the Interior, respectively.

(F) NO LIMITATION ON STATE INSPECTION AUTHORITY.— Nothing in this subsection limits the authority of a State to inspect a vessel pursuant to paragraph (5)(A)(iii) in order to monitor compliance with an applicable requirement of this section.

(10) ADDITIONAL REGIONAL REQUIREMENTS.—

(A) MINIMUM GREAT LAKES SYSTEM REQUIREMENTS.—

(i) IN GENERAL.— Except as provided in clause (ii), the owner or operator of a vessel entering the St. Lawrence Seaway through the mouth of the St. Lawrence River shall conduct a complete ballast water exchange or saltwater flush—

(I) not less than 200 nautical miles from any shore for a voyage originating outside the United States or Canadian exclusive economic zone; or

(II) not less than 50 nautical miles from any shore for a voyage originating within the United States or Canadian exclusive economic zone.

(ii) EXCEPTIONS.— Clause (i) shall not apply to a vessel if—

(I) complying with an applicable requirement of clause (i)—

(aa) would compromise the safety of the vessel; or

(bb) is otherwise prohibited by any Federal, Canadian, or international law (including regulations) pertaining to vessel safety;

(II) design limitations of the vessel prevent a ballast water exchange from being conducted in accordance with an applicable requirement of clause (i);

(III) the vessel—

(aa) is certified by the Secretary as having no residual ballast water or sediments onboard; or

(bb) retains all ballast water while in waters subject to the requirement; or

(IV) empty ballast tanks on the vessel are sealed and certified by the Secretary in a manner that ensures that—

(aa) no discharge or uptake occurs; and

(bb) any subsequent discharge of ballast water is subject to the requirement.

(B) ENHANCED GREAT LAKES SYSTEM REQUIREMENTS.—

(i) PETITIONS BY GOVERNORS FOR PROPOSED ENHANCED STANDARDS AND REQUIREMENTS.—

(I) IN GENERAL.— The Governor of a Great Lakes State (or a State employee designee) may submit a petition in accordance with subclause (II) to propose that other Governors of Great Lakes States endorse an enhanced standard of performance or other requirement with respect to any discharge that—

(aa) is subject to regulation under this subsection; and

(bb) occurs within the Great Lakes System.

(II) SUBMISSION.— A Governor shall submit a petition under subclause (I), in writing, to—

(aa) the Executive Director of the Great Lakes Commission, in such manner as may be prescribed by the Great Lakes Commission;

(bb) the Governor of each other Great Lakes State; and

(cc) the Director of the Great Lakes National Program Office established by section 118(b).

(III) PRELIMINARY ASSESSMENT BY GREAT LAKES COMMISSION.—

(aa) IN GENERAL.— After the date of receipt of a petition under subclause (II)(aa), the Great Lakes Commission (acting through the Great Lakes Panel on Aquatic Nuisance Species, to the maximum extent practicable) may develop a preliminary assessment regarding each enhanced standard of performance or other requirement described in the petition.

(bb) PROVISIONS.— The preliminary assessment developed by the Great Lakes Commission under item (aa)—

(AA) may be developed in consultation with relevant experts and stakeholders;

(BB) may be narrative in nature;

(CC) may include the preliminary views, if any, of the Great Lakes Commission on the propriety of the proposed enhanced standard of performance or other requirement;

(DD) shall be submitted, in writing, to the Governor of each Great Lakes State and the Director of the Great Lakes National Program Office and published on the internet website of the Great Lakes National Program Office; and

(EE) except as provided in clause (iii), shall not be taken into consideration, or provide a basis for review, by the Administrator or the Secretary for purposes of that clause.

(ii) PROPOSED ENHANCED STANDARDS AND REQUIREMENTS.—

(I) PUBLICATION IN FEDERAL REGISTER.—

(aa) REQUEST BY GOVERNOR.— Not earlier than the date that is 90 days after the date on which the Executive Director of the Great Lakes Commission receives from a Governor of a Great Lakes State a petition under clause (i)(II)(aa), the Governor may request the Director of the Great Lakes National Program Office to publish, for a period requested by the Governor of not less than 30 days, and the Director shall so publish, in the Federal Register for public comment—

(AA) a copy of the petition; and

(BB) if applicable as of the date of publication, any preliminary assessment of the Great Lakes Commission developed under clause (i)(III) relating to the petition.

(bb) REVIEW OF PUBLIC COMMENTS.— On receipt of a written request of a Governor of a Great Lakes State, the Director of the Great Lakes National Program Office shall make available all public comments received in response to the notice under item (aa).

(cc) NO RESPONSE REQUIRED.— Notwithstanding any other provision of law, a Governor of a Great Lakes State or the Director of the Great Lakes National Program Office shall not be required to provide a response to any comment received in response to the publication of a petition or preliminary assessment under item (aa).

(dd) PURPOSE.— Any public comments received in response to the publication of a petition or preliminary assessment under item (aa) shall be used solely for the purpose of providing information and feedback to the Governor of each Great Lakes State regarding the decision to endorse the proposed standard or requirement.

(ee) EFFECT OF PETITION.— A proposed standard or requirement developed under subclause (II) may differ from the proposed standard or requirement described in a petition published under item (aa).

(II) COORDINATION TO DEVELOP PROPOSED STANDARD OR REQUIREMENT.— After the expiration of the public comment period for the petition under subclause (I), any interested Governor of a Great Lakes State may work in coordination with the Great Lakes Commission to develop a proposed standard of performance or other requirement applicable to a discharge referred to in the petition.

(III) REQUIREMENTS.— A proposed standard of performance or other requirement under subclause (II)—

(aa) shall be developed—

(AA) in consultation with representatives from the Federal and provincial governments of Canada;

(BB) after notice and opportunity for public comment on the petition published under subclause (I); and

(CC) taking into consideration the preliminary assessment, if any, of the Great Lakes Commission under clause (i)(III);

(bb) shall be specifically endorsed in writing by—

(AA) the Governor of each Great Lakes State, if the proposed standard or requirement would impose any additional equipment requirement on a vessel; or

(BB) not fewer than 5 Governors of Great Lakes States, if the proposed standard or requirement would not impose any additional equipment requirement on a vessel; and

(cc) in the case of a proposed requirement to prohibit 1 or more types of discharge regulated under this subsection, whether treated or not treated, into waters within the Great Lakes System, shall not apply outside the waters of the Great Lakes States of the Governors endorsing the proposed requirement under item (bb).

(iii) PROMULGATION BY ADMINISTRATOR AND SECRETARY.—

(I) SUBMISSION.—

(aa) IN GENERAL.— The Governors

endorsing a proposed standard or requirement under clause (ii)(III)(bb) may jointly submit to the Administrator and the Secretary for approval each proposed standard of performance or other requirement developed and endorsed pursuant to clause (ii).

(bb) INCLUSION.— Each submission under item (aa) shall include an explanation regarding why the applicable standard of performance or other requirement is—

(AA) at least as stringent as a comparable standard of performance or other requirement under this subsection;

(BB) in accordance with maritime safety; and

(CC) in accordance with applicable maritime and navigation laws and regulations.

(cc) WITHDRAWAL.—

(AA) IN GENERAL.— The Governor of any Great Lakes State that endorses a proposed standard or requirement under clause (ii)(III)(bb) may withdraw the endorsement by not later than the date that is 90 days after the date on which the Administrator and the Secretary receive the proposed standard or requirement.

(BB) EFFECT ON FEDERAL REVIEW.— If, after the withdrawal of an endorsement under subitem (AA), the proposed standard or requirement does not have the applicable number of endorsements under clause (ii)(III)(bb), the Administrator and the Secretary shall terminate the review under this clause.

(dd) DISSENTING OPINIONS.— The Governor of a Great Lakes State that does not endorse a proposed standard or requirement under clause (ii)(III)(bb) may submit to the Administrator and the Secretary any dissenting opinions of the Governor.

(II) JOINT NOTICE.— On receipt of a proposed standard of performance or other requirement under subclause (I), the Administrator and the Secretary shall publish in the Federal Register a joint notice that, at minimum—

(aa) states that the proposed standard or requirement is publicly available; and

(bb) provides an opportunity for public comment regarding the proposed standard or requirement during the 90-day period beginning on the date of receipt by the Administrator and the Secretary of the proposed standard or requirement.

(III) REVIEW.—

(aa) IN GENERAL.— As soon as practicable after the date of publication of a joint notice under subclause (II)—

(AA) the Administrator shall commence a review of each proposed standard of performance or other requirement covered by the notice to determine whether that standard or requirement is at least as stringent as comparable standards and requirements under this subsection; and

(BB) the Secretary shall commence a review of each proposed standard of performance or other requirement covered by the notice to determine whether that standard or requirement is in accordance with maritime safety and applicable maritime and navigation laws and regulations.

(bb) CONSULTATION.— In carrying out item (aa), the Administrator and the Secretary—

(AA) shall consult with the Governor of each Great Lakes State and representatives from the Federal and provincial governments of Canada;

(BB) shall take into consideration any relevant data or public comments received under subclause (II)(bb); and

(CC) shall not take into consideration any preliminary assessment by the Great Lakes Commission under clause (i)(III), or any dissenting opinion under subclause (I)(dd), except to the extent that such an assessment or opinion is relevant to the criteria for the applicable determination under item (aa).

(IV) APPROVAL OR DISAPPROVAL.— Not later than 180 days after the date of receipt of each proposed standard of performance or other requirement under subclause (I), the Administrator and the Secretary shall—

(aa) determine, as applicable, whether each proposed standard or other requirement satisfies the criteria under subclause (III)(aa);

(bb) approve each proposed standard or other requirement, unless the Administrator or the Secretary, as applicable, determines under item (aa) that the proposed standard or other requirement does not satisfy the criteria under subclause (III)(aa); and

(cc) submit to the Governor of each Great Lakes State, and publish in the Federal Register, a notice of the determination under item (aa).

(V) ACTION ON DISAPPROVAL.—

(aa) RATIONALE AND RECOMMENDATIONS.— If the Administrator and the Secretary disapprove a proposed standard of performance or other requirement under subclause (IV)(bb), the notices under subclause (IV)(cc) shall include—

(AA) a description of the reasons why the standard or requirement is, as applicable, less stringent than a comparable standard or requirement under this subsection, inconsistent with maritime safety, or inconsistent with applicable maritime and navigation laws and regulations; and

(BB) any recommendations regarding changes the Governors of the Great Lakes States could make to conform the disapproved portion of the standard or requirement to the requirements of this subparagraph.

(bb) REVIEW.— Disapproval of a proposed standard or requirement by the Administrator and the Secretary under this subparagraph shall be considered to be a final agency action subject to judicial review under section 509.

(VI) ACTION ON APPROVAL.— On approval by the Administrator and the Secretary of a proposed standard of performance or other requirement under subclause (IV)(bb)—

(aa) the Administrator shall establish, by regulation, the proposed standard or requirement within the Great Lakes System in lieu of any comparable standard or other requirement promulgated under paragraph (4); and

(bb) the Secretary shall establish, by regulation, any requirements necessary to implement, ensure compliance with, and enforce the standard or requirement under item (aa), or to apply the proposed requirement, within the Great Lakes System in lieu of any comparable requirement promulgated under paragraph (5).

(VII) NO JUDICIAL REVIEW FOR CERTAIN

ACTIONS.— An action or inaction of a Governor of a Great Lakes State or the Great Lakes Commission under this subparagraph shall not be subject to judicial review.

(VIII) GREAT LAKES COMPACT.— Nothing in this subsection limits, alters, or amends the Great Lakes Compact to which Congress granted consent in the Act of July 24, 1968 (Public Law 90–419; 82 Stat. 414).

(IX) AUTHORIZATION OF APPROPRIATIONS.— There is authorized to be appropriated to the Great Lakes Commission $5,000,000, to be available until expended.

(C) MINIMUM PACIFIC REGION REQUIREMENTS.—

(i) DEFINITION OF COMMERCIAL VESSEL.— In this subparagraph, the term "commercial vessel" means a vessel operating between—

(I) 2 ports or places of destination within the Pacific Region; or

(II) a port or place of destination within the Pacific Region and a port or place of destination on the Pacific Coast of Canada or Mexico north of parallel 20 degrees north latitude, inclusive of the Gulf of California.

(ii) BALLAST WATER EXCHANGE.—

(I) IN GENERAL.— Except as provided in subclause (II) and clause (iv), the owner or operator of a commercial vessel shall conduct a complete ballast water exchange in waters more than 50 nautical miles from shore.

(II) EXEMPTIONS.— Subclause (I) shall not apply to a commercial vessel—

(aa) using, in compliance with applicable requirements, a type-approved ballast water management system approved by the Secretary; or

(bb) voyaging—

(AA) between or to a port or place of

destination in the State of Washington, if the ballast water to be discharged from the commercial vessel originated solely from waters located between the parallel 46 degrees north latitude, including the internal waters of the Columbia River, and the internal waters of Canada south of parallel 50 degrees north latitude, including the waters of the Strait of Georgia and the Strait of Juan de Fuca;

(BB) between ports or places of destination in the State of Oregon, if the ballast water to be discharged from the commercial vessel originated solely from waters located between the parallel 40 degrees north latitude and the parallel 50 degrees north latitude;

(CC) between ports or places of destination in the State of California within the San Francisco Bay area east of the Golden Gate Bridge, including the Port of Stockton and the Port of Sacramento, if the ballast water to be discharged from the commercial vessel originated solely from ports or places within that area;

(DD) between the Port of Los Angeles, the Port of Long Beach, and the El Segundo offshore marine oil terminal, if the ballast water to be discharged from the commercial vessel originated solely from the Port of Los Angeles, the Port of Long Beach, or the El Segundo offshore marine oil terminal;

(EE) between a port or place of destination in the State of Alaska within a single Captain of the Port Zone;

(FF) between ports or places of destination in different counties of the State of Hawaii, if the vessel may conduct a complete ballast water exchange in waters that are more than 10 nautical miles from shore and at least 200 meters deep; or

(GG) between ports or places of destination within the same county of the State of Hawaii, if the vessel does not transit outside State marine waters during the voyage.

(iii) LOW-SALINITY BALLAST WATER.—

(I) IN GENERAL.— Except as provided in subclause (II) and clause (iv), the owner or operator of a commercial vessel that transports ballast water sourced from waters with a measured salinity of less than 18 parts per thousand and voyages to a Pacific Region port or place of destination with a measured salinity of less than 18 parts per thousand shall conduct a complete ballast water exchange—

(aa) not less than 50 nautical miles from shore, if the ballast water was sourced from a Pacific Region port or place of destination; or

(bb) more than 200 nautical miles from shore, if the ballast water was not sourced from a Pacific Region port or place of destination.

(II) EXCEPTION.— Subclause (I) shall not apply to a commercial vessel voyaging to a port or place of destination in the Pacific Region that is using, in compliance with applicable requirements, a type-approved ballast water management system approved by the Secretary to achieve standards of performance of—

(aa) less than 1 organism per 10 cubic meters, if that organism—

(AA) is living, or has not been rendered nonviable; and

(BB) is 50 or more micrometers in minimum dimension;

(bb) less than 1 organism per 10 milliliters, if that organism—

(AA) is living, or has not been rendered nonviable; and

(BB) is more than 10, but less than 50, micrometers in minimum dimension;

(cc) concentrations of indicator microbes that are less than—

(AA) 1 colony-forming unit of toxicogenic Vibrio cholera (serotypes O1 and O139) per 100 milliliters or less than 1 colony-forming unit of that microbe per gram of wet weight of zoological samples;

(BB) 126 colony-forming units of escherichia coli per 100 milliliters; and

(CC) 33 colony-forming units of intestinal enterococci per 100 milliliters; and

(dd) concentrations of such additional indicator microbes and viruses as may be specified in the standards of performance established by the Administrator under paragraph (4).

(iv) GENERAL EXCEPTIONS.— The requirements of clauses (ii) and (iii) shall not apply to a commercial vessel if—

(I) complying with the requirement would compromise the safety of the commercial vessel;

(II) design limitations of the commercial vessel prevent a ballast water exchange from being conducted in accordance with clause (ii) or (iii), as applicable;

(III) the commercial vessel—

(aa) is certified by the Secretary as having no residual ballast water or sediments onboard; or

(bb) retains all ballast water while in waters subject to those requirements; or

(IV) empty ballast tanks on the commercial vessel are sealed and certified by the Secretary in a manner that ensures that—

(aa) no discharge or uptake occurs; and

(bb) any subsequent discharge of ballast water is subject to those requirements.

(D) ESTABLISHMENT OF STATE NO-DISCHARGE ZONES.—

(i) STATE PROHIBITION.— Subject to clause (ii), after the effective date of regulations promulgated by the Secretary under paragraph (5), if any State determines that the protection and enhancement of the quality of some or all of the waters within the State require greater environmental protection, the State may prohibit 1 or more types of discharge regulated under this subsection, whether treated or not treated, into such waters.

(ii) APPLICABILITY.— A prohibition by a State under clause (i) shall not apply until the date on which the Administrator makes the applicable determinations described in clause (iii).

(iii) PROHIBITION BY ADMINISTRATOR.—

(I) DETERMINATION.— On application of a State, the Administrator, in concurrence with the Secretary (subject to subclause (II)), shall, by regulation, prohibit the discharge from a vessel of 1 or more discharges subject to regulation under this subsection, whether treated or not treated, into the waters covered by the application if the Administrator determines that—

(aa) prohibition of the discharge would protect and enhance the quality of the specified waters within the State;

(bb) adequate facilities for the safe and sanitary removal and treatment of the discharge are reasonably available for the water and all vessels to which the prohibition would apply;

(cc) the discharge can be safely collected and stored until a vessel reaches a discharge facility or other location; and

(dd) in the case of an application for the prohibition of discharges of ballast water in a port (or in any other location where cargo, passengers, or fuel are loaded and unloaded)—

(AA) the adequate facilities described in item (bb) are reasonably available for commercial vessels, after considering, at a minimum, water depth, dock size, pumpout facility capacity and flow rate, availability of year-round operations, proximity to navigation routes, and the ratio of pumpout facilities to the population and discharge capacity of commercial vessels operating in those waters; and

(BB) the prohibition will not unreasonably interfere with the safe loading and unloading of cargo, passengers, or fuel.

(II) CONCURRENCE WITH SECRETARY.—

(aa) REQUEST.— The Administrator shall submit to the Secretary a request for written concurrence with respect to a prohibition under subclause (I).

(bb) EFFECT OF FAILURE TO CONCUR.— A failure by the Secretary to concur with the Administrator under subclause (I) by the date that is 60 days after the date on which the Administrator submits a request for concurrence under item (aa) shall not prevent the Administrator from prohibiting the relevant discharge in accordance with subclause (III), subject to the condition that the Administrator shall include in the administrative record of the promulgation—

(AA) documentation of the request submitted under item (aa); and

(BB) the response of the Administrator to any written objections received from the Secretary relating to the proposed standard of performance during the 60-day period beginning on the date of submission of the request.

(III) TIMING.— The Administrator shall approve or disapprove an application submitted under subclause (I) by not later than 90 days after the date on which the application is submitted to the Administrator.

(E) MAINTENANCE IN EFFECT OF MORE-STRINGENT STANDARDS.— In any case in which a requirement established under this paragraph is more stringent or environmentally protective than a comparable requirement established under paragraph (4), (5), or (6), the more-stringent or more-protective requirement shall control.

[33 U.S.C. 1322]

* * * * * * *

DEEPWATER PORT ACT OF 1974

PUBLIC LAW 93-627
AS AMENDED THROUGH P.L. 118-159

DEEPWATER PORT ACT OF 1974

[Public Law 93-627]

[As Amended Through P.L. 118–159, Enacted December 23, 2024]

AN ACT To regulate commerce, promote efficiency in transportation, and protect the environment, by establishing procedures for the location, construction, and operation of deepwater ports off the coasts of the United States, and for other purposes.

Be it enacted by the Senate and House of Representatives of the United States of America in Congress assembled,

That this Act may be cited as the "Deepwater Port Act of 1974".
[33 U.S.C. 1501 nt]

SEC. 2.

(a) PURPOSES.—The purposes of this Act are—

(1) to authorize and regulate the location, ownership, construction, and operation of deepwater ports in waters beyond the territorial limits of the United States;

(2) to provide for the protection of the marine and coastal environment to prevent or minimize any adverse impact which might occur as a consequence of the development of deepwater ports;

(3) to protect the interests of the United States and those of adjacent coastal States in the location, construction, and operation of deepwater ports;

(4) to protect the rights and responsibilities of States and communities to regulate growth, determine land use, and otherwise protect the environment in accordance with law;

(5) to promote the construction and operation of deepwater ports as a safe and effective means of importing oil or natural gas into the United States and transporting oil or natural gas from the outer Continental Shelf while minimizing tanker traffic and the risks associated with that traffic; and

(6) to promote oil or natural gas production on the outer Continental Shelf by affording an economic and safe means of transportation of outer Continental Shelf oil or natural gas to the United States mainland.

(b) EFFECT OF ACT.—Nothing in this Act affects the legal status of the high seas, the superjacent airspace, or the seabed and subsoil, including the Continental Shelf.

[33 U.S.C. 1501]

SEC. 3. DEFINITIONS.

In this Act:

(1) ADJACENT COASTAL STATE.—The term"adjacent coastal State" means any coastal State which (A) would be directly connected by pipeline to a deepwater port, as proposed in an application; (B) would be located within 15 miles of any such proposed deepwater port; or (C) is designated by the Secretary in accordance with section 9(a)(2) of this Act.

(2) AFFILIATE.—The term"affiliate" means any entity owned or controlled by, any person who owns or controls, or any entity which is under common ownership or control with an applicant, licensee, or any person required to be disclosed pursuant to subparagraph (A) or (B) of section 5(c)(2).

(3) APPLICATION.—The term "application" means an application submitted under this Act for a license for the ownership, construction, and operation of a deepwater port.

(4) CITIZEN OF THE UNITED STATES.—The term "citizen of the United States" means any person who is a United States citizen by law, birth, or naturalization, any State, any agency of a State or a group of States, or any corporation, partnership, or association organized under the laws of any State which has as its president or other executive officer and as its chairman of the board of directors, or holder of a similar office, a person who is a United States citizen by law, birth or naturalization and which has no more of its directors who are not United States citizens by law, birth or naturalization than constitute

a minority of the number required for a quorum necessary to conduct the business of the board.

(5) COASTAL ENVIRONMENT.—The term "coastal environment" means the navigable waters (including the lands therein and thereunder) and the adjacent shorelines including[1] waters therein and thereunder). The term includes transitional and intertidal areas, bays, lagoons, salt marshes, estuaries, and beaches; the fish, wildlife and other living resources thereof; and the recreational and scenic values of such lands, waters and resources.

---

[1] So in original. Probably should be preceded by an opening parenthesis.

(6) COASTAL STATE.—The term "coastal State" means any State of the United States in or bordering on the Atlantic, Pacific, or Arctic Oceans, or the Gulf of Mexico.

(7) CONSTRUCTION.—The term "construction" means the supervising, inspection, actual building, and all other activities incidental to the building, repairing, or expanding of a deepwater port or any of its components, including, but not limited to, pile driving and bulkheading, and alterations, modifications, or additions to the deepwater port.

(8) CONTROL.—The term"control" means the power, directly or indirectly, to determine the policy, business practices, or decisionmaking process of another person, whether by stock or other ownership interest, by representation on a board of directors or similar body, by contract or other agreement with stockholders or others, or otherwise.

(9) DEEPWATER PORT.—The term"deepwater port"—

(A) means any fixed or floating manmade structure other than a vessel, or any group of such structures, that are located beyond State seaward boundaries and that are used or intended for use as a port or terminal for the transportation, storage, or further handling of oil or natural gas for transportation to or from any State, except as otherwise provided in section 23, and for other uses not inconsistent with the purposes of this Act, including transportation of oil or natural gas from the United States outer continental shelf;

(B) includes all components and equipment, including

pipelines, pumping stations, service platforms, buoys, mooring lines, and similar facilities to the extent they are located seaward of the high water mark;

(C) in the case of a structure used or intended for such use with respect to natural gas, includes all components and equipment, including pipelines, pumping or compressor stations, service platforms, buoys, mooring lines, and similar facilities that are proposed or approved for construction and operation as part of a deepwater port, to the extent that they are located seaward of the high water mark and do not include interconnecting facilities; and

(D) shall be considered a "new source" for purposes of the Clean Air Act (42 U.S.C. 7401 et seq.), and the Federal Water Pollution Control Act (33 U.S.C. 1251 et seq.).

(10) GOVERNOR.—The term "Governor" means the Governor of a State or the person designated by State law to exercise the powers granted to the Governor pursuant to this Act.

(11) LICENSEE.—The term "licensee" means a citizen of the United States holding a valid license for the ownership, construction, and operation of a deepwater port that was issued, transferred, or renewed pursuant to this Act.

(12) MARINE ENVIRONMENT.—The term"marine environment" includes the coastal environment, waters of the contiguous zone, and waters of the high seas; the fish, wildlife, and other living resources of such waters; and the recreational and scenic values of such waters and resources.

(13) NATURAL GAS.—The term "natural gas" means either natural gas unmixed, or any mixture of natural or artificial gas, including compressed or liquefied natural gas, natural gas liquids, liquefied petroleum gas, and condensate recovered from natural gas, natural gas liquids, liquefied petroleum gas, and condensate recovered from natural gas.

(14) OIL.—The term "oil" means petroleum, crude oil, and any substance refined from petroleum or crude oil.

(15) PERSON.—The term "person" includes an individual, a public or private corporation, a partnership or other association, or a government entity.

(16) SAFETY ZONE.—The term "safety zone" means the safety zone established around a deepwater port as determined by the Secretary in accordance with section 10(d) of this Act.

(17) SECRETARY.—The term"Secretary" means the Secretary of Transportation.

(18) STATE.—The term"State" includes each of the States of the United States, the District of Columbia, the Commonwealth of Puerto Rico, and the territories and possessions of the United States.

(19) VESSEL.—The term"vessel" means every description of watercraft or other artificial contrivance used as a means of transportation on or through the water.

[33 U.S.C. 1502]

LICENSE FOR THE OWNERSHIP, CONSTRUCTION, AND OPERATION
OF A DEEPWATER PORT

SEC. 4. (a) No person may engage in the ownership, construction, or operation of a deepwater port except in accordance with a license issued pursuant to this Act. No person may transport or otherwise transfer any oil or natural gas between a deepwater port and the United States unless such port has been so licensed and the license is in force.

(b) The Secretary may—

(1) on application, issue a license for the ownership, construction, and operation of a deepwater port; and

(2) on petition of the licensee, amend, transfer, or reinstate a license issued under this Act.

(c) The Secretary may issue a license in accordance with the provisions of this Act if—

(1) the Secretary determines that the applicant is financially responsible and will meet the requirements of section 1016 of the Oil Pollution Act of 1990;

(2) the Secretary determines that the applicant can and will comply with applicable laws, regulations, and license conditions;

(3) the Secretary determines that the construction and operation of the deepwater port will be in the national interest and consistent with national security and other national policy

goals and objectives, including energy sufficiency and environmental quality;

(4) the Secretary determines that the deepwater port will not unreasonably interfere with international navigation or other reasonable uses of the high seas, as defined by treaty, convention, or customary international law;

(5) the Secretary determines, in accordance with the environmental review criteria established pursuant to section 6 of this Act, that the applicant has demonstrated that the deepwater port will be constructed and operated using best available technology, so as to prevent or minimize adverse impact on the marine environment;

(6) the Secretary has not been informed, within 45 days of the last public hearing on a proposed license for a designated application area, by the Administrator of the Environmental Protection Agency that the deepwater port will not conform with all applicable provisions of the Clean Air Act, as amended, the Federal Water Pollution Control Act, as amended, or the Marine Protection, Research and Sanctuaries Act, as amended;

(7) the Secretary has consulted with the Secretary of the Army, the Secretary of State, and the Secretary of Defense, to determine their views on the adequacy of the application, and its effect on programs within their respective jurisdictions;

(8) the Governor of each adjacent coastal State or States, pursuant to section 9 of this Act,[2] approves, or is presumed to approve, the issuance of the license pursuant to section 9(b)(1), if applicable; and

---

[2] Section 3514(k)(3)(A)(iii)(II) of division C of Public Law 118–31 attempts to amend paragraph (8) by striking "of States, pursuant to section 9 of this Act,". Such amendment should have been to strike "or States, pursuant to section 9 of this Act,".

---

(9) the adjacent coastal State to which the deepwater port is to be directly connected by pipeline has developed, or is making, at the time the application is submitted, reasonable progress, as determined in accordance with section 9(c) of this Act, toward developing, an approved coastal zone management program pursuant to the Coastal Zone Management Act of 1972.

(d) If an application is made under this Act for a license to

construct a deepwater port facility off the coast of a State, and a port of the State which will be directly connected by pipeline with such deepwater port, on the date of such application—

(1) has existing plans for construction of a deep draft channel and harbor; and

(2) has either (A) an active study by the Secretary of the Army relating to the construction of a deep draft channel and harbor, or (B) a pending application for a permit under section 10 of the Act of March 3, 1899 (30 Stat. 1121), for such construction; and

(3) applies to the Secretary for a determination under this section within 30 days of the date of the license application;

the Secretary shall not issue a license under this Act until he has examined and compared the economic, social, and environmental effects of the construction and operation of the deepwater port with the economic, social and environmental effects of the construction, expansion, deepening, and operation of such State port, and has determined which project best serves the national interest or that both developments are warranted. The Secretary's determination shall be discretionary and nonreviewable.

(e)(1) In issuing a license for the ownership, construction, and operation of a deepwater port, the Secretary shall prescribe those conditions which the Secretary deems necessary to carry out the provisions and requirements of this title or which are otherwise required by any Federal department or agency pursuant to the terms of this title. To the extent practicable, conditions required to carry out the provisions and requirements of this Act shall be addressed in license conditions rather than by regulation and, to the extent practicable, the license shall allow a deepwater port's operating procedures to be stated in an operations manual, approved by the Coast Guard, in accordance with section 10(a), rather than in detailed and specific license conditions or regulations, except that basic standards and conditions shall be addressed in regulations. On petition of a licensee, the Secretary shall review any condition of license issued under this Act to determine if that condition is uniform, insofar as practicable, with the conditions of other licenses issued under this Act, reasonable, and necessary to meet the objectives of this Act. The Secretary shall amend or rescind any condition that is no longer necessary or otherwise required by any Federal department or agency under this

Act.

(2) No license shall be issued, transferred, or renewed under this Act unless the licensee or transferee first agrees in writing that (A) there will be no substantial change from the plans, operational systems, and methods, procedures, and safeguards set forth in his license, as approved, without prior approval in writing from the Secretary; and (B) the licensee or transferee will comply with any condition the Secretary may prescribe in accordance with the provisions of this Act.

(3) The Secretary shall establish such bonding requirements or other assurances as the Secretary determines to be necessary to ensure that, upon the revocation or termination of a license, the licensee will remove all components of the deepwater port. In the case of components lying in the subsoil below the seabed, the Secretary is authorized to waive the removal requirements if the Secretary finds that such removal is not otherwise necessary and that the remaining components do not constitute any threat to navigation or to the environment. At the request of the licensee, the Secretary, after consultation with the Secretary of the Interior, is authorized to waive the removal requirement as to any components which the Secretary determines may be utilized in connection with the transportation of oil, natural gas, or other minerals, pursuant to a lease granted under the provisions of the Outer Continental Shelf Lands Act (43 U.S.C. 1331 et seq.), after which waiver the utilization of such components shall be governed by the terms of that Act.

(f) AMENDMENTS, TRANSFERS, AND REINSTATEMENTS.—The Secretary may amend, transfer, or reinstate a license issued under this Act if the Secretary finds that the amendment, transfer, or reinstatement is consistent with the requirements of this Act.

(g) Any citizen of the United States who otherwise qualifies under the terms of this Act shall be eligible to be issued a license for the ownership, construction, and operation of a deepwater port.

(h) A license issued under this Act remains in effect unless suspended or revoked by the Secretary or until surrendered by the licensee.

(i) To promote the security of the United States, the Secretary shall give top priority to the processing of a license under this Act for liquefied natural gas facilities that will be supplied with or that

will supply liquefied natural gas by United States flag vessels.
[33 U.S.C. 1503]

PROCEDURE

SEC. 5. (a) The Secretary shall, as soon as practicable after the date of enactment of this Act, and after consultation with other Federal agencies, issue regulations to carry out the purposes and provisions of this Act, in accordance with the provisions of section 553 of title 5, United States Code, without regard to subsection (a) thereof. Such regulations shall pertain to, but need not be limited to, application, issuance, transfer, renewal, suspension, and termination of licenses. Such regulations shall provide for full consultation and cooperation with all other interested Federal agencies and departments and with any potentially affected coastal State, and for consideration of the views of any interested members of the general public. The Secretary is further authorized, consistent with the purposes and provisions of this Act, to amend or rescind any such regulation.

(b) The Secretary, in consultation with the Secretary of the Interior and the Administrator of the National Oceanic and Atmospheric Administration, shall, as soon as practicable after the date of enactment of this Act, prescribe regulations relating to those activities involved in site evaluation and preconstruction testing at potential deepwater port locations that may (1) adversely affect the environment; (2) interfere with authorized uses of the Outer Continental Shelf; or (3) pose a threat to human health and welfare. Such activity may thenceforth not be undertaken except in accordance with regulations prescribed pursuant to this subsection. Such regulations shall be consistent with the purposes of this Act.

(c) APPLICATIONS.—

(1) REQUIREMENTS.—

(A) IN GENERAL.—Each person that submits to the Secretary an application shall include in the application a detailed plan that contains all information required under paragraph (2).

(B) ACTION BY SECRETARY.—Not later than 21 days after the date of receipt of an application, the Secretary shall—

(i) determine whether the application contains all information required under paragraph (2); and (ii)(I) if the Secretary determines that such information is contained in the application, not later than 5 days after making the determination, publish in the Federal Register—

(aa) a notice of the application; and

(bb) a summary of the plans; or

(II) if the Secretary determines that all required information is not contained in the application—

(aa) notify the applicant of the applicable deficiencies; and

(bb) take no further action with respect to the application until those deficiencies have been remedied.

(C) APPLICABILITY.—On publication of a notice relating to an application under subparagraph (B)(ii)(I), the Secretary shall be subject to subsection (f).

(2) INCLUSIONS.—Each application shall include such financial, technical, and other information as the Secretary determines to be necessary or appropriate, including—

(A) the name, address, citizenship, telephone number, and the ownership interest in the applicant, of each person having any ownership interest in the applicant of greater than 3 per centum;

(B) to the extent feasible, the name, address, citizenship, and telephone number of any person with whom the applicant has made, or proposes to make, a significant contract for the construction or operation of the deepwater port, and a copy of any such contract;

(C) the name, address, citizenship, and telephone number of each affiliate of the applicant and of any person required to be disclosed pursuant to subparagraphs (A) or (B), together with a description of the manner in which such affiliate is associated with the applicant or any person required to be disclosed under subparagraph (A) or (B);

(D) the proposed location and capacity of the deepwater port, including all components thereof;

(E) the type and design of all components of the

deepwater port and any storage facilities associated with the deepwater port;

(F) with respect to construction in phases, a detailed description of each phase, including anticipated dates of completion for each of the specific components thereof;

(G) the location and capacity of existing and proposed storage facilities and pipelines which will store or transport oil transported through the deepwater port, to the extent known by the applicant or any person required to be disclosed pursuant to subparagraphs (A), (B), or (C);

(H) with respect to any existing and proposed refineries which will receive oil transported through the deepwater port, the location and capacity of each such refinery and the anticipated volume of such oil to be refined by each such refinery, to the extent known by the applicant or any person required to be disclosed pursuant to subparagraphs (A), (B), or (C);

(I) the financial and technical capabilities of the applicant to construct or operate the deepwater port;

(J) other qualifications of the applicant to hold a license under this Act;

(K) the nation of registry for, and the nationality or citizenship of officers and crew serving on board, vessels transporting natural gas that are reasonably anticipated to be servicing the deepwater port;

(L) a description of procedures to be used in constructing, operating, and maintaining the deepwater port, including systems of oil spill prevention, containment, and cleanup; and

(M) such other information as may be required by the Secretary to determine the environmental impact of the proposed deepwater port.

(3) Upon written request of any person subject to this subsection, the Secretary may make a determination in writing to exempt such person from any of the informational filing provisions enumerated in this subsection or the regulations implementing this section if the Secretary determines that such information is not necessary to facilitate the Secretary's determinations under section 4 of this Act and that such

exemption will not limit public review and evaluation of the deepwater port project.

(d)(1) At the time notice of an application is published pursuant to subsection (c) of this section, the Secretary shall publish a description in the Federal Register of an application area encompassing the deepwater port site proposed by such application and within which construction of the proposed deepwater port would eliminate, at the time such application was submitted, the need for any other deepwater port within that application area.

(2) As used in this section, "application area" means any reasonable geographical area within which a deepwater port may be constructed and operated. Such application area shall not exceed a circular zone, the center of which is the principal point of loading and unloading at the port, and the radius of which is the distance from such point to the high water mark of the nearest adjacent coastal State.

(3) the Secretary shall accompany such publication with a call for submission of any other applications for licenses for the ownership, construction, and operation of a deepwater port within the designated application area. Persons intending to file applications for such license shall submit a notice of intent to file an application with the Secretary not later than 60 days after the publication of notice pursuant to subsection (c) of this section and shall submit the completed application no later than 90 days after publication of such notice. The Secretary shall publish notice of any such application received in accordance with subsection (c) of this section. No application for a license for the ownership, construction, and operation of a deepwater port within the designated application area for which a notice of intent to file was received after such 60-day period, or which is received after such 90-day period has elapsed, shall be considered until the application pending with respect to such application area have been denied pursuant to this Act.

(4) This subsection shall not apply to deepwater ports for natural gas.

(e)(1) Not later than 30 days after the date of enactment of this Act, the Secretary of the Interior, the Administrator of the Environmental Protection Agency, the Chief of Engineers of the United States Army Corps of Engineers, the Administrator of the

National Oceanic and Atmospheric Administration, and the heads of any other Federal departments or agencies having expertise concerning, or jurisdiction over, any aspect of the construction or operation of deepwater ports shall transmit to the Secretary written comments as to their expertise or statutory responsibilities pursuant to this Act or any other Federal law.

(2) An application filed with the Secretary shall constitute an application for all Federal authorizations required for ownership, construction, and operation of a deepwater port. At the time notice of any application is published pursuant to subsection (c) of this section, the Secretary shall forward a copy of such application to those Federal agencies and departments with jurisdiction over any aspect of such ownership, construction, or operation for comment, review, or recommendation as to conditions and for such other action as may be required by law. Each agency or department involved shall review the application and, based upon legal considerations within its area of responsibility, recommend to the Secretary the approval or disapproval of the application not later than 45 days after the last public hearing on a proposed license for a designated application area. In any case in which the agency or department recommends disapproval, it shall set forth in detail the manner in which the application does not comply with any law or regulation within its area of responsibility and shall notify the Secretary how the application may be amended so as to bring it into compliance with the law or regulation involved.

(f) NEPA COMPLIANCE.—For all applications, the Secretary, in cooperation with other involved Federal agencies and departments, shall comply with the National Environmental Policy Act of 1969 (42 U.S.C. 4332). Such compliance shall fulfill the requirement of all Federal agencies in carrying out their responsibilities under the National Environmental Policy Act of 1969 pursuant to this Act.

(g) A license may be issued only after public notice and public hearings in accordance with this subsection. At least one such public hearing shall be held in each adjacent coastal State. Any interested person may present relevant material at any hearing. After hearings in each adjacent coastal State are concluded, if the Secretary determines that there exists one or more specific and material factual issues which may be resolved by a formal evidentiary hearing, at least one adjudicatory hearing shall be held in accordance with the provisions of section 554 of title 5, United States Code, in the District of Columbia. The record developed in any such adjudicatory hearing shall be basis for the Secretary's decision to approve or deny a license. Hearings held pursuant to this subsection shall be consolidated insofar as practicable with hearings held by other agencies. All public hearings on all applications for any designated application area shall be consolidated and shall be concluded not later than 240 days after notice of the initial application has been published pursuant to subsection (c).

(h) FEES.—

(1) REQUIREMENT.—

(A) IN GENERAL.—Each person applying for a license pursuant to this Act shall remit to the Secretary at the time the application is filed a nonrefundable application fee established by regulation by the Secretary.

(B) REIMBURSEMENT.—In addition to a fee under subparagraph (A), an applicant shall also reimburse the United States and the appropriate adjacent coastal State for any additional costs incurred in processing an application.

(2) USAGE FEES.—

(A) DEFINITION OF DIRECTLY RELATED LAND-BASED FACILITY.—In this paragraph, the term "directly related land-based facility", with respect to a deepwater port facility, means an onshore tank farm and any pipelines connecting the tank farm to the deepwater port facility.

(B) AUTHORIZATION.—Notwithstanding any other provision of this Act, and unless prohibited by law, an adjacent coastal State may fix reasonable fees for the use of a deepwater port facility, and such State and any other State in which land-based facilities directly related to a deepwater port facility are located may set reasonable fees for the use of such land-based facilities.

(C) TREATMENT.—A fee may be established pursuant to this paragraph as compensation for any economic cost attributable to the construction and operation of the applicable deepwater port and the applicable land-based facilities, which cannot be recovered under other authority of the applicable State or political subdivision thereof, including, but not limited to, ad valorem taxes, and for environmental and administrative costs attributable to the construction and operation of the applicable deepwater port and the applicable land-based facilities.

(D) AMOUNT.—The amount of a fee established under this paragraph shall not exceed the applicable economic, environmental, and administrative costs of the applicable State.

(E) APPROVAL.—A fee established under this paragraph shall be subject to the approval of the Secretary.

(3) RENTAL PAYMENT.—A licensee shall pay annually in advance the fair market rental value (as determined by the Secretary of the Interior) of the subsoil and seabed of the outer Continental Shelf of the United States to be utilized by the deepwater port, including the fair market rental value of the right-of-way necessary for the pipeline segment of the port located on such subsoil and seabed.

(i)(1) The Secretary shall approve or deny any application for a designated application area submitted pursuant to this Act not later than 90 days after the last public hearing on a proposed license for that area.

(2) In the event more than one application is submitted for an application area, the Secretary, unless one of the proposed deepwater ports clearly best serves the national interest, shall issue a license according to the following order of priorities:

(A) First, to an adjacent coastal State (or combination of States), any political subdivision thereof, or agency or instrumentality, including a wholly owned corporation of any such government.

(B) Second, to a person who is neither (i) engaged in producing, refining, or marketing oil, nor (ii) an affiliate of any person who is engaged in producing, refining, or marketing oil or an affiliate of any such affiliate.

(C) Third, to any other person.

(3) In determining whether any one proposed deepwater port clearly best serves the national interest, the Secretary shall consider the following factors:

(A) The degree to which the proposed deepwater ports

affect the environment, as determined under criteria established pursuant to section 6.

(B) National security, including an assessment of the implications for the national security of the United States or an allied country (as that term is defined in section 2350f(d)(1) of title 10, United States Code) of the United States.

(C) Any significant differences between anticipated completion dates for the proposed deepwater ports.

(D) Any differences in costs of construction and operation of the proposed deepwater ports, to the extent that such differential may significantly affect the ultimate cost of oil to the consumer.

(4) APPLICATIONS FOR DEEPWATER PORTS FOR NATURAL GAS.—

(A) DEADLINE FOR DETERMINATION.—The Secretary shall approve or deny any application for a deepwater port for natural gas submitted pursuant to this Act not later than 90 days after the last public hearing on a proposed license.

(B) EFFECT OF FAILURE TO DETERMINE.—If the Secretary fails to approve or deny an application for a deepwater port for natural gas by the applicable deadline under subparagraph (A), the reporting requirements under paragraphs (1), (2), and (3) shall not apply to the application.

(5) DECISION ON AMENDED LICENSE APPLICATIONS.—

(A) DEFINITION OF AMENDED LICENSE APPLICATION.—In this paragraph, the term "amended license application" means a license application for a deepwater port for natural gas—

(i) that was originally submitted to the Secretary prior to the issuance of the proclamation issued by the President on March 13, 2020, with respect to the Coronavirus Disease 2019 (COVID–19) pandemic; and

(ii) with respect to which the applicant, based on guidance offered by the Secretary, has made subsequent revisions since the submission of the initial license application and submitted such revised application.

(B) EXPEDITED REVIEW AND APPROVAL.—The Secretary shall expedite the review and subsequent approval or denial of amended license applications submitted pursuant to this section that meet the eligibility criteria described in subparagraph (C).

(C) ELIGIBILITY CRITERIA.—To be eligible for review under this paragraph, an amended license application shall meet the following criteria:

(i) The amended license application is for a natural gas deepwater port facility.

(ii) The Secretary had determined that the project as specified in the initial license application was not likely to have any significant adverse environmental impact on species and habitat, consistent with law including National Environmental Policy Act of 1969 (42 U.S.C. 4321 et seq.).

(iii) The Secretary has determined that the results of the environmental review conducted for the initial license application is still applicable to the amended license application and an additional environmental review is not required.

(iv) The Secretary had published an affirmative Record of Decision for the initial license application.

(D) DEADLINE FOR DECISION.—The Secretary shall approve or deny an amended license application submitted pursuant to this paragraph by no later than 270 consecutive days after the date on which the Secretary determines that the amended license application is complete and meets the requirements under this section.

(j) LNG TANKERS.—

(1) PROGRAM.—The Secretary shall develop and implement a program to promote the transportation of liquefied natural gas to and from the United States on United States flag vessels.

(2) INFORMATION TO BE PROVIDED.—When the Coast Guard is operating as a contributing agency in the Federal Energy Regulatory Commission's shoreside licensing process for a liquefied natural gas or liquefied petroleum gas terminal located on shore or within State seaward boundaries, the Coast

Guard shall provide to the Commission the information described in section 5(c)(2)(K) of the Deepwater Port Act of 1974 (33 U.S.C. 1504(c)(2)(K)) with respect to vessels reasonably anticipated to be servicing that port.

(k) TRANSPARENCY IN ISSUANCE OF LICENSES AND PERMITS.—

(1) DEFINITION OF APPLICABLE DEADLINE.—In this subsection, the term "applicable deadline", with respect to an applicant, means the deadline or date applicable to the applicant under any of the following:

(A) Section 4(c)(6).

(B) Section 4(d)(3).

(C) Subsection (c)(1)(B) (including clause (ii)(I) of that subsection).

(D) Subsection (d)(3).

(E) Paragraph (1) or (2) of subsection (e).

(F) Subsection (g).

(G) Paragraph (1) or (4)(A) of subsection (i).

(2) SUSPENSIONS AND DELAYS.—If the Secretary suspends or delays an applicable deadline, the Secretary shall submit to the applicant, and publish in the Federal Register, a written statement—

(A) describing the reasons for the suspension or delay;

(B) describing and requesting any information necessary to issue the applicable license or permit and the status of applicable license or permit application at the lead agency and any cooperating agencies; and

(C) identifying the applicable deadline with respect to the statement.

(3) APPLICANT RIGHTS TO TECHNICAL ASSISTANCE.—

(A) IN GENERAL.—An applicant that receives a statement under paragraph (2) may submit to the Secretary a request for a meeting with appropriate personnel of the Department of Transportation and representatives of each cooperating Federal agency, as appropriate, determined by the Secretary to be relevant with respect to the application, including such officials as are appropriate, who shall provide technical assistance, status, process, and timeline updates and additional information as necessary.

(B) TIMING.—A meeting requested under clause (i) shall be held not later than 30 days after the date on which the Secretary receives the request under that clause.

(4) REQUIREMENTS.—On receipt of a request under paragraph (3)(A), and not less frequently than once every 30 days thereafter until the date on which the application process is no longer suspended or delayed, the Secretary shall submit a notice of the delay, including a description of the time elapsed since the applicable deadline and the nature and circumstances of the applicable suspension or delay, to—

(A) the Committee on Commerce, Science, and Transportation of the Senate; and

(B) the Committee on Transportation and Infrastructure of the House of Representatives.

(5) BRIEFING.—If the Secretary suspends or delays an applicable deadline, not later than 120 days after that applicable deadline, and not less frequently than once every 120 days thereafter until the date on which the application process is no longer suspended or delayed, the Secretary (or a designee of the Secretary) shall provide a briefing regarding the time elapsed since the applicable deadline and the nature and circumstances of the applicable suspension or delay to—

(A) the Committee on Commerce, Science, and Transportation of the Senate; and

(B) the Committee on Transportation and Infrastructure of the House of Representatives.

[33 U.S.C. 1504]

ENVIRONMENTAL REVIEW CRITERIA

SEC. 6. (a) ESTABLISHMENT.—The Secretary, in accordance with the recommendations of the Administrator of the Environmental Protection Agency and the Administrator of the National Oceanic and Atmospheric Administration and after consultation with any other Federal departments and agencies having jurisdiction over any aspect of the construction or operation of a deepwater port, shall establish, as soon as practicable after the date of enactment of this Act, environmental review criteria consistent with the National

Environmental Policy Act. Such criteria shall be used to evaluate a deepwater port as proposed in an application, including—

(1) the effect on the marine environment;

(2) the effect on oceanographic currents and wave patterns;

(3) the effect on alternate uses of the oceans and navigable water, such as scientific study, fishing, and exploitation of other living and nonliving resources;

(4) the potential dangers to a deepwater port from waves, winds, weather, and geological conditions, and the steps which can be taken to protect against or minimize such dangers;

(5) effects of land-based developments related to deepwater port development;

(6) the effect on human health and welfare; and

(7) such other considerations as the Secretary deems necessary or appropriate.

(b) REVIEW AND REVISION.—The Secretary shall periodically review and, whenever necessary, revise in the same manner as originally developed, criteria established pursuant to subsection (a)

(c) REQUIREMENT.—The criteria established pursuant to this section shall be developed concurrently with the regulations promulgated pursuant to section 5(a) and in accordance with that section.

[33 U.S.C. 1505]

[Section 7 repealed by section 506 of Public Law 104–324 (110 Stat. 3927).]

SEC. 8.[3] (a) A deepwater port and a storage facility serviced directly by that deepwater port shall operate as a common carrier under applicable provisions of part I of the Interstate Commerce Act and subtitle IV of title 49, United States Code, and shall accept, transport, or convey without discrimination all oil delivered to the deepwater port with respect to which its license is issued, except as provided by subsection (b) of this section.

---

[3]   So in original. Section 3(a) of P.L. 98–419, 98 Stat. 1608 struck section 8 and inserted a new section 8 shown above. Probably should have a section heading.

(b) A licensee is not discriminating under this section and is not subject to common carrier regulations under subsection (a) of this section when that licensee—

(1) is subject to effective competition for the transportation of oil from alternative transportation systems; and

(2) sets its rates, fees, charges, and conditions of service on the basis of competition, giving consideration to other relevant business factors such as the market value of services provided, licensee's cost of operation, and the licensee's investment in the deepwater port and a storage facility, and components thereof, serviced directly by that deepwater port.

(c) When the Secretary has reason to believe that a licensee is not in compliance with this section, the Secretary shall commence an appropriate proceeding before the Federal Energy Regulatory Commission or request the Attorney General to take appropriate steps to enforce compliance with this section and, when appropriate, to secure the imposition of appropriate sanctions. In addition, the Secretary may suspend or revoke the license of a licensee not complying with its obligations under this section.

(d) MANAGED ACCESS.—Subsections (a) and (b) shall not apply to deepwater ports for natural gas. A licensee of a deepwater port for natural gas, or an affiliate thereof, may exclusively utilize the entire capacity of the deepwater port and storage facilities for the acceptance, transport, storage, regasification, or conveyance of natural gas produced, processed, marketed, or otherwise obtained by agreement by such licensee or its affiliates. The licensee may make unused capacity of the deepwater port and storage facilities available to other persons, pursuant to reasonable terms and conditions imposed by the licensee, if such use does not otherwise interfere in any way with the acceptance, transport, storage, regasification, or conveyance of natural gas produced, processed, marketed, or otherwise obtained by agreement by such licensee or its affiliates.

(e) JURISDICTION.—Notwithstanding any provision of the Natural Gas Act (15 U.S.C. 717 et seq.), any regulation or rule issued thereunder, or section 19 as it pertains to such Act, this Act shall apply with respect to the licensing, siting, construction, or operation of a deepwater natural gas port or the acceptance, transport, storage, regasification, or conveyance of natural gas at or through a deepwater port, to the exclusion of the Natural Gas Act or any regulation or rule issued thereunder.

[33 U.S.C. 1507]

ADJACENT COASTAL STATES

SEC. 9.

(a) DESIGNATION.—In issuing a notice relating to an application for a deepwater port under section 5(c)(1)(B)(ii)(I), the Secretary shall designate as an adjacent coastal State, with respect to the deepwater port, any coastal State that would be—

(1) directly connected by pipeline to that deepwater port; or

(2) located within 15 miles of that deepwater port.

(b) INPUT FROM ADJACENT COASTAL STATES AND OTHER INTERESTED STATES.—

(1) SUBMISSION OF APPLICATIONS TO GOVERNORS FOR APPROVAL.—

(A) IN GENERAL.—Not later than 10 days after the date on which the Secretary designates adjacent coastal States under subsection (a) with respect to a deepwater port proposed in an application, the Secretary shall transmit a complete copy of the application to the Governor of each adjacent coastal State.

(B) PROHIBITION.—The Secretary shall not issue a license without the approval of the Governor of each adjacent coastal State.

(C) PRESUMED APPROVAL.—If the Governor of an adjacent coastal State fails to transmit a required approval or disapproval to the Secretary not later than 45 days after the last public hearing on applications for a particular application area, such approval shall be conclusively presumed.

(D) INCONSISTENCY WITH CERTAIN STATE PROGRAMS.—If the Governor of an adjacent coastal State notifies the Secretary that an application, which would otherwise be approved pursuant to this paragraph, is inconsistent with State programs relating to environmental protection, land and water use, and coastal zone management, the Secretary shall condition the license granted so as to make it consistent with such State programs.

(2) OTHER INTERESTED STATES.—Any other State with an interest relating to the deepwater port proposed in an application shall have the opportunity to make its views known to, and shall be given full consideration by, the Secretary regarding the location, construction, and operation of the deepwater port.

(c) The Secretary shall not issue a license unless the adjacent coastal State to which the deepwater port is to be directly connected by pipeline has developed, or is making, at the time the application is submitted, reasonable progress toward developing an approved coastal zone management program pursuant to the Coastal Zone Management Act of 1972 in the area to be directly and primarily impacted by land and water development in the coastal zone resulting from such deepwater port. For the purposes of this Act, a State shall be considered to be making reasonable progress if it is receiving a planning grant pursuant to section 305 of the Coastal Zone Management Act.

(d) The consent of Congress is given to two or more coastal States to negotiate and enter into agreements or compacts, not in conflict with any law or treaty of the United States, (1) to apply for a license for the ownership, construction, and operation of a deepwater port or for the transfer of such license, and (2) to establish such agencies, joint or otherwise, as are deemed necessary or appropriate for implementing and carrying out the provisions of any such agreement or compact. Such agreement or compact shall be binding and obligatory upon any State or party thereto without further approval by Congress.

[33 U.S.C. 1508]

MARINE ENVIRONMENTAL PROTECTION AND NAVIGATIONAL
SAFETY

SEC. 10. (a) Subject to recognized principles of international law and the provision of adequate opportunities for public involvement, the Secretary shall prescribe and enforce procedures, either by regulation (for basic standards and conditions) or by the licensee's operations manual, with respect to rules governing vessel movement, loading and unloading procedures, designation and marking of anchorage areas, maintenance, law enforcement, and the equipment, training, and maintenance required (A) to prevent pollution of the marine environment, (B) to clean up any pollutants which may be discharged, and (C) to otherwise prevent or minimize any adverse impact from the construction and operation of such deepwater port.

(b) The Secretary shall issue and enforce regulation with respect to lights and other warning devices, safety equipment, and other matters relating to the promotion of safety of life and property in any deepwater port and the waters adjacent thereto.

(c) The Secretary shall mark, for the protection of navigation, any component of a deepwater port whenever the licensee fails to mark such component in accordance with applicable regulations. The licensee shall pay the cost of such marking.

(d)(1) Subject to recognized principles of international law and after consultation with the Secretary of the Interior, the Secretary of Commerce, the Secretary of State, and the Secretary of Defense, the Secretary shall designate a zone of appropriate size around and including any deepwater port for the purpose of navigational safety. In such zone, no installations, structures, or uses will be permitted that are incompatible with the operation of the deepwater port. The Secretary shall by regulation define permitted activities within such zone. The Secretary shall, not later than 30 days after publication of notice pursuant to section 5(c) of this Act, designate such safety zone with respect to any proposed deepwater port.

(2) In addition to any other regulations, the Secretary is authorized, in accordance with this subsection, to establish a safety zone to be effective during the period of construction of a deepwater port and to issue rules and regulations relating thereto.

[33 U.S.C. 1509]

INTERNATIONAL AGREEMENTS

SEC. 11. The Secretary of State, in consultation with the Secretary, shall seek effective international action and cooperation in support of the policy and purposes of this Act and may formulate, present, or support specific proposals in the United Nations and other competent international organizations for the development of appropriate international rules and regulations relative to the construction, ownership, and operation of deepwater ports, with particular regard for measures that assure protection of such facilities as well as the promotion of navigational safety in the vicinity thereof.

[33 U.S.C. 1510]

SUSPENSION OR TERMINATION OF LICENSES

SEC. 12. (a) Whenever a licensee fails to comply with any applicable provision of this title or any applicable rule, regulation, restriction, or condition issued or imposed by the Secretary under the authority of this title, the Attorney General, at the request of the Secretary, may file an appropriate action in the United States district court nearest to the location of the proposed or actual deepwater port, as the case may be, or in the district in which the licensee resides or may be found, to—

(1) suspend the license; or

(2) if such failure is knowing and continues for a period of thirty days after the Secretary mails notification of such failure by registered letter to the licensee at his record post office address, revoke such license.

No proceeding under this subsection is necessary if the license, by its terms, provides for automatic suspension or termination upon the occurrence of a fixed or agreed upon condition, event, or time.

(b) If the Secretary determines that immediate suspension of the construction or operation of a deepwater port or any component thereof is necessary to protect public health or safety or to eliminate imminent and substantial danger to the environment, he shall order the licensee to cease or alter such construction or operation pending the completion of a judicial proceeding pursuant to subsection (a) of this section.

[33 U.S.C. 1511]

RECORDKEEPING AND INSPECTION

SEC. 13. (a) Each licensee shall establish and maintain such records, make such reports, and provide such information as the Secretary, after consultation with other interested Federal departments and agencies, shall by regulation prescribe to carry out the provision of this Act. Such regulations shall not amend, contradict or duplicate regulations established pursuant to part I of the Interstate Commerce Act or any other law. Each licensee shall submit such reports and shall make such records and information available as the Secretary may request.

(b) All United States officials, including those officials

responsible for the implementation and enforcement of United States laws applicable to a deepwater port, shall at all times be afforded reasonable access to a deepwater port licensed under this Act for the purpose of enforcing laws under their jurisdiction or otherwise carrying out their responsibilities. Each such official may inspect, at reasonable times, records, files, papers, processes, controls, and facilities and may test any feature of a deepwater port. Each inspection shall be conducted with reasonable promptness, and such licensee shall be notified of the results of such inspection.

[33 U.S.C. 1512]

PUBLIC ACCESS TO INFORMATION

SEC. 14. (a) Copies of any communication, document, report, or information transmitted between any official of the Federal Government and any person concerning a deepwater port (other than contracts referred to in section 5(c)(2)(B) of this Act) shall be made available to the public for inspection, and shall be available for the purpose of reproduction at a reasonable cost, to the public upon identifiable request, unless such information may not be publicly released under the terms of subsection (b) of this section. Except as provided in subsection (b) of this section, nothing contained in this section shall be construed to require the release of any information of the kind described in subsection (b) of section 552 of title 5, United States Code, or which is otherwise protected by law from disclosure to the public.

(b) The Secretary shall not disclose information obtained by him under this Act that concerns or relates to a trade secret, referred to in section 1905 of title 18, United States Code, or to a contract referred to in section 5(c)(2)(B) of this Act, except that such information may be disclosed, in a manner which is designed to maintain confidentiality—

(1) to other Federal and adjacent coastal State government departments and agencies for official use, upon request;

(2) to any committee of Congress having jurisdiction over the subject matter to which the information relates, upon request;

(3) to any person in any judicial proceeding, under a court order formulated to preserve such confidentiality without impairing the proceedings; and

(4) to public in order to protect health and safety, after notice and opportunity for comment in writing or for discussion in closed session within fifteen days by the party to which the information pertains (if the delay resulting from such notice and opportunity for comment would not be detrimental to the public health and safety).

[33 U.S.C. 1513]

REMEDIES

SEC. 15. (a) Any person who willfully violates any provision of this Act or any rule, order, or regulation issued pursuant thereto commits a class A misdemeanor for each day of violation.

(b)(1) Whenever on the basis of any information available to him the Secretary finds that any person is in violation of any provision of this Act or any rule, regulation, order, license, or condition thereof, or other requirements under this Act, he shall issue an order requiring such person to comply with such provision or requirement, or he shall bring a civil action in accordance with paragraph (3) of this subsection.

(2) Any order issued under this subsection shall state with reasonable specificity the nature of the violation and a time for compliance, not to exceed thirty days, which the Secretary determines is reasonable, taking into account the seriousness of the violation and any good faith efforts to comply with applicable requirements.

(3) Upon a request by the Secretary, the Attorney General shall commence a civil action for appropriate relief, including a permanent or temporary injunction or a civil penalty not to exceed $25,000 per day of such violation, for any violation for which the Secretary is authorized to issue a compliance order under paragraph (1) of this subsection. Any action under this subsection may be brought in the district court of the United States for the district in which the defendant is located or resides or is doing business, and such court shall have jurisdiction to restrain such violation, require compliance, or impose such penalty.

(c) Upon a request by the Secretary, the Attorney General shall bring an action in an appropriate district court of the United States for equitable relief to redress a violation by any person of any provision of this Act, any regulation under this Act, or any license condition. The district courts of the United States shall have jurisdiction to grant such relief as is necessary or appropriate, including mandatory or prohibitive injunctive relief, interim equitable relief, compensatory damages, and punitive damages.

(d) Any vessel, except a public vessel engaged in noncommercial activities, used in a violation of this Act or of any rule or regulation issued pursuant to this Act, shall be liable in rem for any civil penalty assessed or criminal fine imposed and may be proceeded against in any district court of the United States having jurisdiction thereof; but no vessel shall be liable unless it shall appear that one or more of the owners, or bareboat charterers, was at the time of the violation, a consenting party or privy to such violation.

[33 U.S.C. 1514]

CITIZEN CIVIL ACTION

SEC. 16. (a) Except as provided in subsection (b) of this section, any person may commence a civil action for equitable relief on his own behalf, whenever such action constitutes a case or controversy—

(1) against any person (including (A) the United States, and (B) any other governmental instrumentality or agency to the extent permitted by the eleventh amendment to the Constitution) who is alleged to be in violation of any provision of this Act or any condition of a license issued pursuant to this Act; or

(2) against the Secretary where there is alleged a failure of the Secretary to perform any act or duty under this Act which is not discretionary with the Secretary. Any action brought against the Secretary under this paragraph shall be brought in the district court for the District of Columbia or the district of the appropriate adjacent coastal State.

In suits brought under this Act, the district court shall have jurisdiction, without regard to the amount in controversy or the citizenship of the parties, to enforce any provision of this Act or any condition of a license issued pursuant to this Act, or to order the Secretary to perform such act or duty, as the case may be.

(b) No civil action may be commenced—

(1) under subsection (a)(1) of this section—

(A) prior to 60 days after the plaintiff has given notice of the violation (i) to the Secretary and (ii) to any alleged violator; or

(B) if the Secretary or the Attorney General has commenced and is diligently prosecuting a civil or criminal action with respect to such matters in a court of the United States, but in any such action any person may intervene as a matter of right; or

(2) under subsection (a)(2) of this section prior to 60 days after the plaintiff has given notice of such action to the Secretary.

Notice under this subsection shall be given in such a manner as the Secretary shall prescribe by regulation.

(c) In any action under this section, the Secretary or the Attorney General, if not a party, may intervene as a matter of right.

(d) The Court, in issuing any final order in any action brought pursuant to subsection (a) of this section, may award costs of litigation (including reasonable attorney and expert witness fees) to any party whenever the court determines that such an award is appropriate.

(e) Nothing in this section shall restrict any right which any person (or class of persons) may have under any statute or common law to seek enforcement or to seek any other relief.

[33 U.S.C. 1515]

JUDICIAL REVIEW

SEC. 17. Any person suffering legal wrong, or who is adversely affected or aggrieved by the Secretary's decision to issue, transfer, modify, renew, suspend, or revoke a license may, not later than 60 days after any such decision is made, seek judicial review of such decision in the United States Court of Appeals for the circuit within which the nearest adjacent coastal State is located. A person shall be deemed to be aggrieved by the Secretary's decision within the meaning of this Act if he—

(A) has participated in the administrative proceedings before the Secretary (or if he did not so participate, he can show that his failure to do so was caused by the Secretary's failure to provide the required notice); and

(B) is adversely affected by the Secretary's action.

[33 U.S.C. 1516]

[Section 18 repealed by section 2003(a)(2) of P.L. 101–380, 104 Stat. 507]

RELATIONSHIP TO OTHER LAWS

SEC. 19. (a)(1) The Constitution, laws, and treaties of the United States shall apply to a deepwater port licensed under this Act and to activities connected, associated, or potentially interfering with the use or operation of any such port, in the same manner as if such port were an area of exclusive Federal jurisdiction located within a State. Nothing in this Act shall be construed to relieve, exempt, or immunize any person from any other requirement imposed by Federal law, regulation, or treaty. Deepwater ports licensed under this Act do not possess the status of islands and have no territorial seas of their own.

(2) Except as otherwise provided by this Act, nothing in this Act shall in any way alter the responsibilities and authorities of a State or the United States within the territorial seas of the United States.

(3) The Secretary of State shall notify the government of each foreign state having vessels registered under its authority or flying its flag which may call at or otherwise utilize a deepwater port but which do not currently have an agreement in effect as provided in subsection (c)(2)(A)(i) of this section that the United States intends to exercise jurisdiction over vessels calling at or otherwise utilizing a deepwater port and the persons on board such vessels. The Secretary of State shall notify the government of each such state that, absent its objection, its vessels will be subject to the jurisdiction of the United States whenever they—

(A) are calling at or otherwise utilizing a deepwater port; and

(B) are within the safety zone of such a deepwater port and are engaged in activities connected, associated, or potentially interfering with the use and operation of the deepwater port.

The Secretary of State shall promptly inform licensees of deepwater ports of all objections received from governments of foreign states in response to notifications made under this paragraph.

(b) The law of the nearest adjacent coastal State, not in effect or hereafter adopted, amended, or repealed, is declared to be the law of the United States, and shall apply to any deepwater port licensed pursuant to this Act, to the extent applicable and not inconsistent with any provision or regulation under this Act or other Federal laws and regulations now in effect or hereafter adopted, amended, or repealed. All such applicable laws shall be administered and enforced by the appropriate officers and courts of the United States. For purposes of this subsection, the nearest adjacent coastal State shall be that State whose seaward boundaries, if extended beyond 3 miles, would encompass the site of the deepwater port.

(c)(1) The jurisdiction of the United States shall apply to vessels of the United States and persons on board such vessels. The jurisdiction of the United States shall also apply to vessels, and persons on board such vessels, registered in or flying the flags of foreign states, whenever such vessels are—

(A) calling at or otherwise utilizing a deepwater port; and

(B) are within the safety zone of such a deepwater port, and are engaged in activities connected, associated, or potentially interfering with the use and operation of the deepwater port.

The jurisdiction of the United States under this paragraph shall not, however, apply to vessels registered in or flying the flag of any foreign state that has objected to the application of such jurisdiction.

(2) Except in a situation involving force majeure, a licensee shall not permit a vessel registered in or flying the flag of a foreign state to call at or otherwise utilize a deepwater port licensed under this Act unless—

(A)(i) the foreign state involved, by specific agreement with the United States, has agreed to recognize the jurisdiction of the United States over the vessels registered in or flying the flag of that state and persons on board such vessels in accordance with the provisions of paragraph (1) of this subsection, while the vessel is located within the safety zone, or

(ii) the foreign state has not objected to the application of the jurisdiction of the United States to any vessel, or persons on board such vessel, while the vessel is located within the safety zone; and

(B) the vessel owner or operator has designated an agent in the United States for receipt of service of process in the event of any claim or legal proceeding resulting from activities of the vessel or its personnel while located within such a safety zone.

(3) For purposes of paragraph (2)(A)(ii) of this subsection, a licensee shall not be obliged to prohibit a call at or use of a deepwater port by a vessel registered in or flying the flag of an objecting state unless the licensee has been informed by the Secretary of State as required by subsection (a)(3) of this section.

(d) The customs laws administered by the Secretary of the Treasury shall not apply to any deepwater port licensed under this Act, but all foreign articles to be used in the construction of any such deepwater port, including any component thereof, shall first be made subject to all applicable duties and taxes which would be imposed upon or by reason of their importation if they were imported for consumption in the United States. Duties and taxes shall be paid thereon in accordance with laws applicable to merchandise imported into the customs territory of the United States.

(e) The United States district courts shall have original jurisdiction of cases and controversies arising out of or in connection with the construction and operation of deepwater ports, and proceedings with respect to any such case or controversy may be instituted in the judicial district in which any defendant resides or may be found, or in the judicial district of the adjacent coastal State nearest the place where the cause of action arose.

[33 U.S.C. 1518]

(f) Section 4(a)(2) of the Act of August 7, 1953 (67 Stat. 462) is amended by deleting the words "as of the effective date of this Act" in the first sentence thereof and inserting in lieu thereof the words ", now in effect or hereafter adopted, amended, or repealed".

[Section 20 repealed by section 1121(a) of Public Law 104–66 (109 Stat. 724).]

PIPELINE SAFETY AND OPERATION

SEC. 21. (a) The Secretary, in cooperation with the Secretary of the Interior, shall establish and enforce such standards and regulations as may be necessary to assure the safe construction and operation of oil or natural gas pipelines on the Outer Continental Shelf.

(b) The Secretary, in cooperation with the Secretary of the Interior, is authorized and directed to report to the Congress within 60 days after the date of enactment of this Act on appropriations and staffing needed to monitor pipelines on Federal lands and the Outer Continental Shelf so as to assure that they meet all applicable standards for construction, operation, and maintenance.

(c) The Secretary, in cooperation with the Secretary of the Interior, is authorized and directed to review all laws and regulations relating to the construction, operation, and maintenance of pipelines on Federal lands and the Outer Continental Shelf and to report to Congress thereon within 6 months after the date of enactment of this Act on administrative changes needed and recommendations for new legislation.

[33 U.S.C. 1520]

NEGOTIATIONS WITH CANADA AND MEXICO

SEC. 22. The President of the United States is authorized and requested to enter into negotiations with the Governments of Canada and Mexico to determine:

(1) the need for intergovernmental understandings, agreements, or treaties to protect the interests of the people of Canada, Mexico, and the United States and of any party or parties involved with the construction or operation of deepwater ports; and

(2) the desirability of undertaking joint studies and investigations designed to insure protection of the environment and to eliminate any legal and regulatory uncertainty, to assure that the interests of the people of Canada, Mexico, and the United States are adequately met.

The President shall report to the Congress the actions taken, the progress achieved, the areas of disagreement, and the matters about which more information is needed, together with his recommendations for further action.

[33 U.S.C. 1521]

PUBLIC LAW 93–153

SEC. 23. Nothing in this Act shall be construed to amend, restrict,

or otherwise limit the application of section 28(u) of the Mineral
Leasing Act of 1920, as amended by Public Law 93–153.
[33 U.S.C. 1522]

GENERAL PROCEDURES

SEC. 24. The Secretary or his delegate shall have the authority
to issue and enforce orders during proceedings brought under this
Act. Such authority shall include the authority to issue subpenas,
administer oaths, compel the attendance and testimony of witnesses
and the production of books, papers, documents, and other evidence,
to take depositions before any designated individual competent to
administer oaths, and to examine witnesses.
[33 U.S.C. 1523]

ACT TO PREVENT POLLUTION FROM SHIPS

PUBLIC LAW 96-478
AS AMENDED THROUGH P.L. 116-283

ACT TO PREVENT POLLUTION FROM SHIPS

[Public Law 96-478]

[As Amended Through P.L. 116–283, Enacted January 1, 2021]

AN ACT To implement the Protocol of 1978 Relating to the International Convention for the Prevention of Pollution from Ships, 1973, and for other purposes.

Be it enacted by the Senate and House of Representatives of the United States of America in Congress assembled,

That this Act may be cited as the "Act to Prevent Pollution from Ships".

SEC. 2. (a) Unless the context indicates otherwise, as used in this Act—

(1) "Administrator" means the Administrator of the Environmental Protection Agency;

(2) "Antarctica" means the area south of 60 degrees south latitude;

(3) "Antarctic Protocol" means the Protocol on Environmental Protection to the Antarctic Treaty, signed October 4, 1991, in Madrid, and all annexes thereto, and includes any future amendments thereto which have entered into force;

(4) "MARPOL Protocol" means the Protocol of 1978 relating to the International Convention for the Prevention of Pollution from Ships, 1973, and includes the Convention;

(5) "Convention" means the International Convention for the Prevention of Pollution from Ships, 1973, including Protocols I and II and Annexes I, II, V, and VI thereto, including any modification or amendments to the Convention,

Protocols or Annexes which have entered into force for the United States;

(6) "discharge", "emission", "garbage", "harmful substance", and "incident" shall have the meanings provided in the Convention;

(7) "navigable waters" includes the territorial sea of the United States (as defined in Presidential Proclamation 5928 of December 27, 1988) and the internal waters of the United States;

(8) "owner" means any person holding title to, or in the absence of title, any other indicia of ownership of, a ship or terminal, but does not include a person who, without participating in the management or operation of a ship or terminal, holds indicia of ownership primarily to protect a security interest in the ship or terminal;

(9) "operator" means—

(a) in the case of a ship, a charterer by demise or any other person, except the owner, who is responsible for the operation, manning, victualing, and supplying of the vessel, or

(b) in the case of a terminal, any person, except the owner, responsible for the operation of the terminal by agreement with the owner;

(10) "person" means an individual, firm, public or private corporation, partnership, association, State, municipality, commission, political subdivision of a State, or any interstate body;

(11) "Secretary" means the Secretary of the department in which the Coast Guard is operating;

(12) "ship" means a vessel of any type whatsoever, including hydrofoils, air-cushion vehicles, submersibles, floating craft whether self-propelled or not, and fixed or floating platforms;

(13) "submersible" means a submarine, or any other vessel designed to operate under water; and

(14) "terminal" means an onshore facility or an offshore structure located in the navigable waters of the United States or subject to the jurisdiction of the United States and used, or intended to be used, as a port or facility for the transfer or other

handling of a harmful substance.

(b) For purposes of this Act, the requirements of Annex V shall apply to the navigable waters of the United States, as well as to all other waters and vessels over which the United States has jurisdiction.

(c) For the purposes of this Act, the requirements of Annex IV to the Antarctic Protocol shall apply in Antarctica to all vessels over which the United States has jurisdiction.

[33 U.S.C. 1901]

SEC. 3. (a) This Act shall apply—

(1) to a ship of United States registry or nationality, or one operated under the authority of the United States, wherever located;

(2) with respect to Annexes I and II to the Convention, to a ship, other than a ship referred to in paragraph (1), while in the navigable waters of the United States;

(3) with respect to the requirements of Annex V to the Convention, to a ship, other than a ship referred to in paragraph (1), while in the navigable waters or the exclusive economic zone of the United States;

(4) with respect to regulations prescribed under section 6 of this Act, any port or terminal in the United States; and

(5) with respect to Annex VI to the Convention, and other than with respect to a ship referred to in paragraph (1)—

(A) to a ship that is in a port, shipyard, offshore terminal, or the internal waters of the United States;

(B) to a ship that is bound for, or departing from, a port, shipyard, offshore terminal, or the internal waters of the United States, and is in—

(i) the navigable waters or the exclusive economic zone of the United States;

(ii) an emission control area designated pursuant to section 4; or

(iii) any other area that the Administrator, in consultation with the Secretary and each State in which any part of the area is located, has designated by order as being an area from which emissions from ships are of concern with respect to protection of public health, welfare, or the environment;

(C) to a ship that is entitled to fly the flag of, or operating under the authority of, a party to Annex VI, and is in—

(i) the navigable waters or the exclusive economic zone of the United States;

(ii) an emission control area designated under section 4; or

(iii) any other area that the Administrator, in consultation with the Secretary and each State in which any part of the area is located, has designated by order as being an area from which emissions from ships are of concern with respect to protection of public health, welfare, or the environment; and

(D) to any other ship, to the extent that, and in the same manner as, such ship may be boarded by the Secretary to implement or enforce any other law of the United States or Annex I, II, or V of the Convention, and is in—

(i) the exclusive economic zone of the United States;

(ii) the navigable waters of the United States;

(iii) an emission control area designated under section 4; or

(iv) any other area that the Administrator, in consultation with the Secretary and each State in which any part of the area is located, has designated by order as being an area from which emissions from ships are of concern with respect to protection of public health, welfare, or the environment.

(b)(1) Except as provided in paragraph (3), this Act shall not apply to—

(A) a ship of the Armed Forces described in paragraph (2); or

(B) any other ship specifically excluded by the MARPOL Protocol or the Antarctic Protocol.

(2) A ship described in this paragraph is a ship that is

owned or operated by the Secretary, with respect to the Coast Guard, or by the Secretary of a military department, and that, as determined by the Secretary concerned—

(A) has unique military design, construction, manning, or operating requirements; and

(B) cannot fully comply with the discharge requirements of Annex V to the Convention because compliance is not technologically feasible or would impair the operations or operational capability of the ship.

(3)(A) Notwithstanding any provision of the MARPOL Protocol, the requirements of Annex V to the Convention shall apply to all ships referred to in subsection (a) other than those described in paragraph (2).

(B) A ship that is described in paragraph (2) shall limit the discharge into the sea of garbage as follows:

(i) The discharge into the sea of plastics, including synthetic ropes, synthetic fishing nets, plastic garbage bags, and incinerator ashes from plastic products that may contain toxic chemicals or heavy metals, or the residues thereof, is prohibited.

(ii) Garbage consisting of the following material may be discharged into the sea, subject to subparagraph (C):

(I) A non-floating slurry of seawater, paper, cardboard, or food waste that is capable of passing through a screen with openings no larger than 12 millimeters in diameter.

(II) Metal and glass that have been shredded and bagged (in compliance with clause (i)) so as to ensure negative buoyancy.

(III) With regard to a submersible, nonplastic garbage that has been compacted and weighted to ensure negative buoyancy.

(IV) Ash from incinerators or other thermal destruction systems not containing toxic chemicals, heavy metals, or incompletely burned plastics.

(C)(i) Garbage described in subparagraph (B)(ii)(I) may

not be discharged within 3 nautical miles of land.

(ii) Garbage described in subclauses (II), (III), and (IV) of subparagraph (B)(ii) may not be discharged within 12 nautical miles of land.

(D) Notwithstanding subparagraph (C), a ship described in paragraph (2) that is not equipped with garbage-processing equipment sufficient to meet the requirements of subparagraph (B)(ii) may discharge garbage that has not been processed in accordance with subparagraph (B)(ii) if such discharge occurs as far as practicable from the nearest land, but in any case not less than—

(i) 12 nautical miles from the nearest land, in the case of food wastes and non-floating garbage, including paper products, cloth, glass, metal, bottles, crockery, and similar refuse; and

(ii) 25 nautical miles from the nearest land, in the case of all other garbage.

(E) This paragraph shall not apply when discharge of any garbage is necessary for the purpose of securing the safety of the ship, the health of the ship's personnel, or saving life at sea. In the event that there is such a discharge, the discharge shall be reported to the Secretary, with respect to the Coast Guard, or the Secretary concerned.

(F) This paragraph shall not apply during time of war or a national emergency declared by the President or Congress.

(c) APPLICATION TO OTHER PERSONS.—This Act shall apply to all persons to the extent necessary to ensure compliance with Annex VI to the Convention.

(d) DISCHARGES IN SPECIAL AREAS.—(1) Except as provided in paragraphs (2) and (3), not later than December 31, 2000, all surface ships owned or operated by the Department of the Navy, and not later than December 31, 2008, all submersibles owned or operated by the Department of the Navy, shall comply with the special area requirements of Regulation 5 of Annex V to the Convention.

(2)(A) Subject to subparagraph (B), any ship described in

subparagraph (C) may discharge, without regard to the special area requirements of Regulation 5 of Annex V to the Convention, the following non-plastic, non-floating garbage:

(i) A slurry of seawater, paper, cardboard, or food waste that is capable of passing through a screen with openings no larger than 12 millimeters in diameter.

(ii) Metal and glass that have been shredded and bagged so as to ensure negative buoyancy.

(iii) With regard to a submersible, nonplastic garbage that has been compacted and weighted to ensure negative buoyancy.

(B)(i) Garbage described in subparagraph (A)(i) may not be discharged within 3 nautical miles of land.

(ii) Garbage described in clauses (ii) and (iii) of subparagraph (A) may not be discharged within 12 nautical miles of land.

(C) This paragraph applies to any ship that is owned or operated by the Department of the Navy that, as determined by the Secretary of the Navy—

(i) has unique military design, construction, manning, or operating requirements; and

(ii) cannot fully comply with the special area requirements of Regulation 5 of Annex V to the Convention because compliance is not technologically feasible or would impair the operations or operational capability of the ship.

(3)(A) Not later than December 31, 2000, the Secretary of the Navy shall prescribe and publish in the Federal Register standards to ensure that each ship described in subparagraph (B) is, to the maximum extent practicable without impairing the operations or operational capabilities of the ship, operated in a manner that is consistent with the special area requirements of Regulation 5 of Annex V to the Convention.

(B) Subparagraph (A) applies to surface ships that are owned or operated by the Department of the Navy that the Secretary plans to decommission during the period beginning on January 1, 2001, and ending on December 31, 2005.

(C) At the same time that the Secretary publishes standards under subparagraph (A), the Secretary shall publish in the Federal Register a list of the ships covered by subparagraph (B).

(e) DISCHARGE OF AGRICULTURAL CARGO RESIDUE.—Notwithstanding any other provision of law, the discharge from a vessel of any agricultural cargo residue material in the form of hold washings shall be governed exclusively by the provisions of this Act that implement Annex V to the International Convention for the Prevention of Pollution from Ships.

(f) The Secretary or the Administrator, consistent with section 4 of this Act, shall prescribe regulations applicable to the ships of a country not a party to the MARPOL Protocol (or the applicable Annex), including regulations conforming to and giving effect to the requirements of Annex V and Annex VI as they apply under subsection (a) of this section,[1] to ensure that their treatment is not more favorable than that accorded ships to parties to the MARPOL Protocol.

---

[1] Section 4(4)(B) of Public Law 110–280 provides for an amendment to subsection (e) (as redesignated by such Public Law) by striking "of section (3)," and inserting "of this section,". The amendment probably should have been made to strike "of section 3,". Such amendment was executed to reflect the probable intent of Congress.

(g) COMPLIANCE BY EXCLUDED VESSELS.—(1) The Secretary of the Navy shall develop and, as appropriate, support the development of technologies and practices for solid waste management aboard ships owned or operated by the Department of the Navy, including technologies and practices for the reduction of the waste stream generated aboard such ships, that are necessary to ensure the compliance of such ships with subsection (b) of this section.

(2) Notwithstanding any effective date of the application of this section to a ship, the provisions of Annex V to the Convention and subsection (b)(3)(B)(i) of this section with respect to the disposal of plastic shall apply to ships equipped with plastic processors required for the long-term collection and storage of plastic aboard ships of the Navy upon the installation of such processors in such ships.

(3) Except when necessary for the purpose of securing the

safety of the ship, the health of the ship's personnel, or saving life at sea, it shall be a violation of this Act for a ship referred to in subsection (b)(1)(A) of this section that is owned or operated by the Department of the Navy:

(A) With regard to a submersible, to discharge buoyant garbage or plastic.

(B) With regard to a surface ship, to discharge plastic contaminated by food during the last 3 days before the ship enters port.

(C) With regard to a surface ship, to discharge plastic, except plastic that is contaminated by food, during the last 20 days before the ship enters port.

(4) The Secretary of Defense shall publish in the Federal Register:

(A) Beginning on October 1, 1994, and each year thereafter until October 1, 2000, the amount and nature of the discharges in special areas, not otherwise authorized under Annex V to the Convention, during the preceding year from ships referred to in subsection (b)(1)(A) of this section owned or operated by the Department of the Navy.

(B) Beginning on October 1, 1996, and each year thereafter until October 1, 1998, a list of the names of such ships equipped with plastic processors pursuant to section 1003(e) of the National Defense Authorization Act for Fiscal Year 1994.

(h) WAIVER AUTHORITY.—The President may waive the effective dates of the requirements set forth in subsection (c) of this section and in subsection 1003(e) of the National Defense Authorization Act for Fiscal Year 1994 if the President determines it to be in the paramount interest of the United States to do so. Any such waiver shall be for a period not in excess of one year. The President shall submit to the Congress each January a report on all waivers from the requirements of this section granted during the preceding calendar year, together with the reasons for granting such waivers.

(i) The heads of Federal departments and agencies shall prescribe standards applicable to ships excluded from this Act by subsection (b)(1) of this section and for which they are responsible. Standards prescribed under this subsection shall ensure, so far as is reasonable and practicable without impairing the operations or operational capabilities of such ships, that such ships act in a manner consistent with the MARPOL Protocol.

(j) SAVINGS CLAUSE.—Nothing in this section shall be construed to restrict in a manner inconsistent with international law navigational rights and freedoms as defined by United States law, treaty, convention, or customary international law.

[33 U.S.C. 1902]

SEC. 4. (a) Unless otherwise specified herein, the Secretary shall administer and enforce the MARPOL Protocol and this Act. In the administration and enforcement of the MARPOL Protocol and this Act, Annexes I and II of the MARPOL Protocol, Annex IV to the Antarctic Protocol, shall be applicable only to seagoing ships.

(b) DUTY OF THE ADMINISTRATOR.—In addition to other duties specified in this Act, the Administrator and the Secretary, respectively, shall have the following duties and authorities:

(1) The Administrator shall, and no other person may, issue Engine International Air Pollution Prevention certificates in accordance with Annex VI and the International Maritime Organization's Technical Code on Control of Emissions of Nitrogen Oxides from Marine Diesel Engines, on behalf of the United States for a vessel of the United States as that term is defined in section 116 of title 46, United States Code. The issuance of Engine International Air Pollution Prevention certificates shall be consistent with any applicable requirements of the Clean Air Act or regulations prescribed under that Act.

(2) The Administrator shall have authority to administer regulations 12, 13, 14, 15, 16, 17, 18, and 19 of Annex VI to the Convention.

(3) The Administrator shall, only as specified in section 8(f), have authority to enforce Annex VI of the Convention.

(c)(1) The Secretary shall prescribe any necessary or desired regulations to carry out the provisions of the MARPOL Protocol, Annex IV to the Antarctic Protocol, or this Act.

(2) In addition to the authority the Secretary has to prescribe regulations under this Act, the Administrator shall also prescribe any necessary or desired regulations to carry out

the provisions of regulations 12, 13, 14, 15, 16, 17, 18, and 19 of Annex VI to the Convention.

(3) In prescribing any regulations under this section, the Secretary and the Administrator shall consult with each other, and with respect to regulation 19, with the Secretary of the Interior.

(4) The Secretary of the department in which the Coast Guard is operating shall—

(A) prescribe regulations which—

(i) require certain ships described in section 3(a)(1) to maintain refuse record books and shipboard management plans, and to display placards which notify the crew and passengers of the requirements of Annex V to the Convention and of Annex IV to the Antarctic Protocol" after ``the Convention; and

(ii) specify the ships described in section 3(a)(1) to which the regulations apply;

(B) seek an international agreement or international agreements which apply requirements equivalent to those described in subparagraph (A)(i) to all vessels subject to Annex V to the Convention; and

(C) within 2 years after the effective date of this paragraph, report to the Congress—

(i) regarding activities of the Secretary under subparagraph (B); and

(ii) if the Secretary has not obtained agreements pursuant to subparagraph (B) regarding the desirability of applying the requirements described in subparagraph (A)(i) to all vessels described in section 3(a) which call at United States ports.

(5) No standard issued by any person or Federal authority, with respect to emissions from tank vessels subject to regulation 15 of Annex VI to the Convention, shall be effective until 6 months after the required notification to the International Maritime Organization by the Secretary.

(d) The Secretary may utilize by agreement, with or without reimbursement, personnel, facilities, or equipment of other Federal departments and agencies in administering the MARPOL Protocol, this Act, or the regulations thereunder.

[33 U.S.C. 1903]

SEC. 5. (a) Except as provided in section 4(b)(1), the Secretary shall designate those persons authorized to issue on behalf of the United States the certificates required by the MARPOL Protocol. A certificate required by the MARPOL Protocol shall not be issued to a ship which is registered in or of the nationality of a country which is not a party to the MARPOL Protocol.

(b) A certificate issued by a country which is a party to the MARPOL Protocol has the same validity as a certificate issued by the Secretary or the Administrator under the authority of this Act.[2]

---

[2] The amendment made by section 6(2) of Public Law 110–280 to strike "Secretary under the authority of the MARPOL protocol." and insert "Secretary or the Administrator under the authority of this Act." was carried out to reflect the probable intent of Congress. The issue relates to the capitalization of the word "protocol" in the stricken matter which appears in uppercase (i.e. "Protocol") in the original law.

(c) A ship required by the MARPOL Protocol to have a certificate—

(1) shall carry a valid certificate onboard in the manner prescribed by the authority issuing the certificate; and

(2) is subject to inspection while in a port or terminal under the jurisdiction of the United States.

(d) An inspection conducted under subsection (c)(2) of this section is limited to verifying whether or not a valid certificate is onboard, unless clear grounds exist which reasonably indicate that the condition of the ship or its equipment does not substantially agree with the particulars of its certificate. This section shall not limit the authority of any official or employee of the United States under any other treaty, law, or regulation to board and inspect a ship or its equipment.

(e) In addition to the penalties prescribed in section 9 of the Act, a ship required by the MARPOL Protocol to have a certificate—

(1) which does not have a valid certificate onboard; or

(2) whose condition or whose equipment's condition does not substantially agree with the particulars of the certificate onboard;

shall be detained by order of the Secretary at the port or terminal where the violation is discovered until, in the opinion of the Secretary, the ship can proceed to sea without presenting an unreasonable threat of harm to the marine environment or the public health and welfare. The detention order may authorize the ship to proceed to the nearest appropriate available shipyard rather than remaining at the place where the violation was discovered.

(f) SHIP CLEARANCE; REFUSAL OR REVOCATION.—If a ship is under a detention order under this section, the Secretary may refuse or revoke the clearance required by section 60105 of title 46, United States Code.

(g) A person whose ship is subject to a detention order under this section may petition the Secretary, in the manner prescribed by regulation, to review the detention order. Upon receipt of a petition under this subsection, the Secretary shall affirm, modify, or withdraw the detention order within the time prescribed by regulation.

(h) A ship unreasonably detained or delayed by the Secretary acting under the authority of this Act is entitled to compensation for any loss or damage suffered thereby.

[33 U.S.C. 1904]

SEC. 6. (a)(1) The Secretary, after consultation with the Administrator of the Environmental Protection Agency, shall establish regulations setting criteria for determining the adequacy of a port's or terminal's reception facilities for mixtures containing oil or noxious liquid substances and shall establish procedures whereby a person in charge of a port or terminal may request the Seretary to certify that the port's or terminal's facilities for receiving the residues and mixtures containing oil or noxious liquid substance from seagoing ships are adequate.

(2) The Secretary, after consulting with appropriate Federal agencies, shall establish regulations setting criteria for determining the adequacy of reception facilities for garbage at a port or terminal, and stating such additional measures and requirements as are appropriate to ensure such adequacy. Persons in charge of ports and terminals shall provide reception facilities, or ensure that such facilities are available, for receiving garbage in accordance with those regulations.

(3) The Secretary and the Administrator, after consulting with appropriate Federal agencies, shall jointly prescribe

regulations setting criteria for determining the adequacy of reception facilities for receiving ozone depleting substances, equipment containing such substances, and exhaust gas cleaning residues at a port or terminal, and stating any additional measures and requirements as are appropriate to ensure such adequacy. Persons in charge of ports and terminals shall provide reception facilities, or ensure that reception facilities are available, in accordance with those regulations. The Secretary and the Administrator may jointly prescribe regulations to certify, and may issue certificates to the effect, that a port's or terminal's facilities for receiving ozone depleting substances, equipment containing such substances, and exhaust gas cleaning residues from ships are adequate.

(b) In determining the adequacy of reception facilities required by the MARPOL Protocol or the Antarctic Protocol at a port or terminal, and in establishing regulations under subsection (a) of this section, the Secretary or the Administrator may consider, among other things, the number and types of ships or seagoing ships using the port or terminal, including their principal trades.

(c)(1) If reception facilities of a port or terminal meet the requirements of Annex I and Annex II to the Convention and the regulations prescribed under subsection (a)(1), the Secretary shall, after consultation with the Administrator of the Environmental Protection Agency, issue a certificate to that effect to the applicant.

(2)(A) Subject to subparagraph (B), if reception facilities of a port or terminal meet the requirements of Annex V to the Convention and the regulations prescribed under subsection (a)(2), the Secretary may, after consultation with appropriate Federal agencies, issue a certificate to that effect to the person in charge of the port or terminal.

(B) The Secretary may not issue a certificate attesting to the adequacy of reception facilities under this paragraph unless, prior to the issuance of the certificate, the Secretary conducts an inspection of the reception facilities of the port or terminal that is the subject of the certificate.

(C) The Secretary may, with respect to certificates issued under this paragraph prior to the date of enactment of the Coast Guard Authorization Act of 1996, prescribe by regulation differing periods of validity for such certificates.

(3) A certificate issued under this subsection—

(A) is valid for the 5-year period beginning on the date of issuance of the certificate, except that if—

(i) the charge for operation of the port or terminal is transferred to a person or entity other than the person or entity that is the operator on the date of issuance of the certificate—

(I) the certificate shall expire on the date that is 30 days after the date of the transfer; and

(II) the new operator shall be required to submit an application for a certificate before a certificate may be issued for the port or terminal; or

(ii) the certificate is suspended or revoked by the Secretary, the certificate shall cease to be valid; and

(B) shall be available for inspection upon the request of the master, other person in charge, or agent of a ship using or intending to use the port or terminal.

(4) The suspension or revocation of a certificate issued under this subsection may be appealed to the Secretary and acted on by the Secretary in the manner prescribed by regulation.

(d)(1) The Secretary shall maintain a list of ports or terminals with respect to which a certificate issued under this section—

(A) is in effect; or

(B) has been revoked or suspended.

(2) The Secretary shall make the list referred to in paragraph (1) available to the general public.

(e)(1) Except in the case of force majeure, the Secretary shall deny entry to a seagoing ship required by the Convention or the Antarctic Protocol to retain onboard while at sea, residues and mixtures containing oil or noxious liquid substances, if—

(A) the port or terminal is one required by the Annexes I and II of the Convention or Article 9 of Annex IV to the Antarctic Protocol or regulations hereunder to have adequate reception facilities; and

(B) the port or terminal does not hold a valid certificate issued by the Secretary under this section.

(2) The Secretary may deny the entry of a ship to a port

or terminal required by the MARPOL Protocol, this Act, or regulations prescribed under this section relating to the provision of adequate reception facilities for garbage, ozone depleting substances, equipment containing those substances, or exhaust gas cleaning residues, if the port or terminal is not in compliance with the MARPOL Protocol, this Act, or those regulations.

(f)(1) The Secretary and the Administrator are authorized to conduct surveys of existing reception facilities in the United States to determine measures needed to comply with the MARPOL Protocol or the Antarctic Protocol.

(2) Not later than 18 months after the date of enactment of the Coast Guard Authorization Act of 1996, the Secretary shall promulgate regulations that require the operator of each port or terminal that is subject to any requirement of the MARPOL Protocol relating to reception facilities to post a placard in a location that can easily be seen by port and terminal users. The placard shall state, at a minimum, that a user of a reception facility of the port or terminal should report to the Secretary any inadequacy of the reception facility.

[33 U.S.C. 1905]

SEC. 7. (a) The master, person in charge, owner, charterer, manager, or operator of a ship involved in an incident shall report the incident in the manner prescribed by Article 8 of the Convention in accordance with regulations promulgated by the Secretary for that purpose.

(b) The master or person in charge of—

(1) a ship of United States registry or nationality, or operated under the authority of the United States, wherever located;

(2) another ship while in the navigable waters of the United States; or

(3) a sea port or oil handling facility subject to the jurisdiction of the United States,

shall report a discharge, probable discharge, or presence of oil in the manner prescribed by Article 4 of the International Convention on Oil Pollution Preparedness, Response and Cooperation, 1990 (adopted at London, November 30, 1990), in accordance with

regulations promulgated by the Secretary for that purpose.
[33 U.S.C. 1906]

SEC. 8. (a) It is unlawful to act in violation of the MARPOL Protocol, Annex IV to the Antarctic Protocol, this Act, or the regulations issued thereunder. The Secretary shall cooperate with other parties to the MARPOL Protocol or to the Antarctic Protocol in the detection of violations and in enforcement of the MARPOL Protocol and Annex IV to the Antarctic Protocol. The Secretary shall use all appropriate and practical measures of detection and environmental monitoring, and shall establish adequate procedures for reporting violations and accumulating evidence.

(b) Upon receipt of evidence that a violation has occurred, the Secretary shall cause the matter to be investigated. In any investigation under this section the Secretary may issue subpenas to require the attendance of any witness and the production of documents and other evidence. In case of refusal to obey a subpena issued to any person, the Secretary may request the Attorney General to invoke the aid of the appropriate district court of the United States to compel compliance. Upon completion of the investigation, the Secretary shall take the action required by the MARPOL Protocol or the Antarctic Protocol and whatever further action he considers appropriate under the circumstances. If the initial evidence was provided by a party to the MARPOL Protocol or the Antarctic Protocol, the Secretary, acting through the Secretary of State, shall inform that party of the action taken or proposed.

(c)(1) This subsection applies to inspections relating to possible violations of Annex I or Annex II to the Convention, of Article 3 or Article 4 of Annex IV to the Antarctic Protocol, or of this Act by any seagoing ship referred to in section 3(a)(2) of this Act.

(2) While at a port or terminal subject to the jurisdiction of the United States, a ship to which the MARPOL Protocol or the Antarctic Protocol applies may be inspected by the Secretary—

(A) to verify whether or not the ship has discharged a harmful substance in violation of the MARPOL Protocol, Annex IV to the Antarctic Protocol, or this Act; or

(B) to comply with a request from a party to the MARPOL Protocol or the Antarctic Protocol for an investigation as to whether the ship may have discharged a harmful substance anywhere in violation of the MARPOL

Protocol or Annex IV to the Antarctic Protocol. An investigation may be undertaken under this clause only when the requesting party has furnished sufficient evidence to allow the Secretary reasonably to believe that a discharge has occurred.

If an inspection under this subsection indicates that a violation has occurred, the investigating officer shall forward a report to the Secretary for appropriate action. The Secretary shall undertake to notify the master of the ship concerned and, acting in coordination with the Secretary of State, shall take any additional action required by Article 6 of the Convention.

(d)(1) The Secretary may inspect a ship referred to in section 3(a)(3) of this Act to verify whether the ship has disposed of garbage in violation of Annex V to the Convention, Article 5 of Annex IV to the Antarctic Protocol, or this Act.

(2) If an inspection under this subsection indicates that a violation has occurred, the Secretary may undertake enforcement action under section 9 of this Act.

(e)(1) The Secretary may inspect at any time a ship of United States registry or nationality or operating under the authority of the United States to which the MARPOL Protocol or the Antarctic Protocol applies to verify whether the ship has discharged a harmful substance or disposed of garbage in violation of those Protocols or this Act.

(2) If an inspection under this subsection indicates that a violation of the MARPOL Protocol, of Annex IV to the Antarctic Protocol, or of this Act has occurred the Secretary may undertake enforcement action under section 9 of this Act.

(f)(1) The Secretary may inspect a ship to which this Act applies as provided under section 3(a)(5), to verify whether the ship is in compliance with Annex VI to the Convention and this Act.

(2) If an inspection under this subsection or any other information indicates that a violation has occurred, the Secretary, or the Administrator in a matter referred by the Secretary, may undertake enforcement action under this section.

(3) Notwithstanding subsection (b) and paragraph (2) of this subsection, the Administrator shall have all of the authorities of the Secretary, as specified in subsection (b) of

this section, for the purposes of enforcing regulations 17 and 18 of Annex VI to the Convention to the extent that shoreside violations are the subject of the action and in any other matter referred to the Administrator by the Secretary.

[33 U.S.C. 1907]

SEC. 9. (a) A person who knowingly violates the MARPOL Protocol, Annex IV to the Antarctic Protocol, This Act, or the regulations issued thereunder commits a class D felony. In the discretion of the Court, an amount equal to not more than ½ of such fine may be paid to the person giving information leading to conviction.

(b) A person who is found by the Secretary, or the Administrator as provided for in this Act, after notice and an opportunity for a hearing, to have—

(1) violated the MARPOL Protocol, Annex IV to the Antarctic Protocol, this Act, or the regulations issued thereunder shall be liable to the United States for a civil penalty, not to exceed $25,000 for each violation; or

(2) made a false, fictitious, or fraudulent statement or representation in any matter in which a statement or representation is required to be made to the Secretary, or the Administrator as provided for in this Act, under the MARPOL Protocol, Annex IV to the Antarctic Protocol, this Act, or the regulations thereunder, shall be liable to the United States for a civil penalty, not to exceed $5,000 for each statement or representation.

Each day of a continuing violation shall constitute a separate violation. The amount of the civil penalty shall be assessed by the Secretary, or the Administrator as provided for in this Act or his designee, by written notice. In determining the amount of the penalty, the Secretary, or the Administrator as provided for in this Act, shall take into account the nature, circumstances, extent, and gravity of the prohibited acts committed and, with respect to the violator, the degree of culpability, any history of prior offenses, ability to pay, and other matters as justice may require. An amount equal to not more than ½ of such penalties may be paid by the Secretary, or the Administrator as provided for in this Act, to the person giving information leading to the assessment of such penalties.

(c) The Secretary, or the Administrator as provided for in this Act, may compromise, modify, or remit, with or without conditions, any civil penalty which is subject to assessment or which has been assessed under this section. If any person fails to pay an assessment of a civil penalty after it has become final, the Secretary, or the Administrator as provided for in this Act, may refer the matter to the Attorney General of the United States for collection in any appropriate district court of the United States.

(d) A ship operated in violation of the MARPOL Protocol, Annex IV to the Antarctic Protocol, this Act, or the regulations thereunder is liable in rem for any fine imposed under subsection (a) or civil penalty assessed pursuant to subsection (b), and may be proceeded against in the United States district court of any district in which the ship may be found.

(e) If any ship subject to the MARPOL Protocol, Annex IV to the Antarctic Protocol, or this Act, its owner, operator, or person in charge is liable for a fine or civil penalty under this section, or if reasonable cause exists to believe that the ship, its owner, operator, or person in charge may be subject to a fine or civil penalty under this section, the Secretary of the Treasury, upon the request of the Secretary, shall refuse or revoke the clearance required by section 4197 of the Revised Statutes of the United States (46 U.S.C. App. 91). Clearance may be granted upon the filing of a bond or other surety satisfactory to the Secretary.

(f) Notwithstanding subsection (a), (b), or (d) of this section, if the violation is by a ship registered in or of the nationality of a country party to the MARPOL Protocol or the Antarctic Protocol, or one operated under the authority of a country party to the MARPOL Protocol or the Antarctic Protocol, the Secretary, or the Administrator as provided for in this Act acting in coordination with the Secretary of State, may refer the matter to the government of the country of the ship's registry or nationality, or under whose authority the ship is operating for appropriate action, rather than taking the actions required or authorized by this section.

(g) Any penalty collected under subsection (a) or (b) that is not paid under that subsection to the person giving information leading to the conviction or assessment of such penalties shall be deposited in the Abandoned Seafarers Fund established under section 11113 of title 46, United States Code.

[33 U.S.C. 1908]

SEC. 10. (a) A proposed amendment to the MARPOL Protocol received by the United States from the Secretary-General of the International Maritime Organization pursuant to Article VI of the MARPOL Protocol, may be accepted on behalf of the United States by the President following the advice and consent of the Senate, except as provided for in subsection (b) of this section.

(b) A proposed amendment to Annex I, II, V, or VI to the Convention, appendices to those Annexes, or Protocol I of the Convention received by the United States from the Secretary-General of the International Maritime Organization pursuant to Article VI of the MARPOL Protocol, may be the subject of appropriate action on behalf of the United States by the Secretary of State following consultation with the Secretary, or the Administrator as provided for in this Act, who shall inform the Secretary of State as to what action he considers appropriate at least 30 days prior to the expiration of the period specified in Article VI of the MARPOL Protocol during which objection may be made to any amendment received.

(c) Following consultation with the Secretary, the Secretary of State may make a declaration that the United States does not accept an amendment proposed pursuant to Article VI of the MARPOL Protocol.

[33 U.S.C. 1909]

SEC. 11. (a) Except as provided in subsection (b) of this section, any person having an interest which is, or can be, adversely affected, may bring an action on his own behalf—

(1) against any person alleged to be in violation of the provisions of this Act, or regulations issued hereunder;

(2) against the Secretary where there is alleged a failure of the Secretary to perform any act or duty under this Act which is not discretionary with the Secretary;

(3) against the Administrator where there is alleged a failure of the Administrator to perform any act or duty under this Act which is not discretionary; or

(4) against the Secretary of the Treasury where there is alleged a failure of the Secretary of the Treasury to take action under section 9(e) of this Act.

(b) No action may be commenced under subsection (a) of this

section—

(1) prior to 60 days after the plaintiff has given notice, in writing and under oath, to the alleged violator, the Secretary concerned or the Administrator, and the Attorney General; or

(2) if the Secretary or the Administrator has commenced enforcement or penalty action with respect to the alleged violation and is conducting such procedures diligently.

(c) Any suit brought under this section shall be brought—

(1) in a case concerning an onshore facility or port, in the United States district court for the judicial district where the onshore facility or port is located;

(2) in a case concerning an offshore facility or offshore structure under the jurisdiction of the United States, in the United States district court for the judicial district nearest the offshore facility or offshore structure;

(3) in a case concerning a ship, in the United States district court for any judicial district wherein the ship or its owner or operator may be found; or

(4) in any case, in the District Court for the District of Columbia.

(d) The court, in issuing any final order in any action brought pursuant to this section, may award costs of litigation (including reasonable attorney and expert witness fees) to any party including the Federal Government.

(e) In any action brought under this section, if the Secretary or Attorney General are not parties of record, the United States, though the Attorney General, shall have the right to intervene.

[33 U.S.C. 1910]

SEC. 12. On the effective date of this Act—

(a) the Oil Pollution Act, 1961, as amended (75 Stat. 402; 33 U.S.C. 1001 et seq.) is repealed. Any criminal or civil penalty proceeding under that Act for a violation which occurred prior to the effective date of this Act may be initiated or continued to conclusion as though that Act had not been repealed; and

(b) the Oil Pollution Act Amendments of 1973 (87 Stat. 428, Public Law 93–119) are repealed.

SEC. 13. (a) Section 4417a of the Revised Statutes of the United

States (46 U.S.C. 391a) is amended as follows—

(1) by amending subparagraph (C) of paragraph (2) by deleting the word "or" in clause (ii); by deleting the period at the end of clause (iii) and inserting "; or"; and by adding a new clause (iv) as follows:

"(iv) designated as a noxious liquid substance under Annex II of the Protocol of 1978 Relating to the International Convention for the Prevention of Pollution from Ships, 1973."

(2) by amending subparagraph (E) of paragraph (3) to read as follows:

"(E) which is constructed or adapted to carry, or which carries, oil or any hazardous materials in bulk as cargo or in residue."

(b) The Federal Water Pollution Control Act, as amended, is further amended in the first sentence of section 311(b)(3), after the words "except (A) in the case of such discharges", by striking the words "of oil"; and by striking the phrase "the International Convention for the Prevention of Pollution of the Sea by Oil, 1954, as amended" and inserting in lieu thereof the phrase "the Protocol of 1978 Relating to the International Convention for the Prevention of Pollution from Ships, 1973".

SEC. 14. (a) Except as provided in subsection (b) of this section, this Act is effective upon the date of enactment, or on the date the MARPOL Protocol becomes effective as to the United States, whichever is later.

(b) The Secretary and the heads of Federal departments shall have the authority to issue regulations, standards, and certifications under sections 3(c), 3(d), 4(b), 5(a), 6(a), 6(c), and 6(f) effective on the date of enactment of this Act. Section 13(a)(2) is effective upon the date of enactment of this Act.

(c) Any rights or liabilities existing on the effective date of this Act shall not be affected by this enactment. Any regulations or procedures promulgated or effected pursuant to the Oil Pollution Act, 1961, as amended, remain in effect until modified or superseded by regulations promulgated under the authority of the MARPOL Protocol or this act.

SEC. 15. EFFECT ON OTHER LAWS.

Authorities, requirements, and remedies of this Act supplement and neither amend nor repeal any other authorities, requirements, or remedies conferred by any other provision of law. Nothing in this Act shall limit, deny, amend, modify, or repeal any other authority, requirement, or remedy available to the United States or any other person, except as expressly provided in this Act.
[33 U.S.C. 1911]

SEC. 16. (a) Subsection (c) of section 4 of the Act of 1956 (16 U.S.C. 742c(c)) is amended—

(1) by striking out "September 30, 1980," each place it appears therein and inserting in lieu thereof "September 30, 1982,"; and

(2) by striking out the third, fourth, and fifth sentences thereof.

(b) The amendments made by subsection (a) shall take effect on September 1, 1980.

SEC. 17. Any action taken under this Act shall be taken in accordance with international law.
[33 U.S.C. 1912]

MARINE DEBRIS ACT

PUBLIC LAW 109-449
AS AMENDED THROUGH P.L. 116-224

Marine Debris Act

[(Public Law 109–449)]

[As Amended Through P.L. 116–224, Enacted December 18, 2020]

AN ACT To establish a program within the National Oceanic and Atmospheric Administration and the United States Coast Guard to help identify, determine sources of, assess, reduce, and prevent marine debris and its adverse impacts on the marine environment and navigation safety, in coordination with non-Federal entities, and for other purposes.

Be it enacted by the Senate and House of Representatives of the United States of America in Congress assembled,

SECTION 1. [33 U.S.C. 1951 note] SHORT TITLE.

This Act may be cited as the "Marine Debris Act".

SEC. 2. [33 U.S.C. 1951] PURPOSE.

The purpose of this Act is to address the adverse impacts of marine debris on the United States economy, the marine environment (including waters in the jurisdiction of the United States, the high seas, and waters in the jurisdiction of other countries), and navigation safety through the identification, determination of sources, assessment, prevention, reduction, and removal of marine debris.

SEC. 3. [33 U.S.C. 1952] NOAA MARINE DEBRIS PROGRAM.

(a) ESTABLISHMENT OF PROGRAM.—There is established, within the National Oceanic and Atmospheric Administration, a Marine Debris Program to identify, determine sources of, assess, prevent, reduce, and remove marine debris and address the adverse impacts of marine debris on the economy of the United States, the marine environment, and navigation safety.

(b) PROGRAM COMPONENTS.—The Administrator, acting through the Program and subject to the availability of appropriations, shall—

(1) identify, determine sources of, assess, prevent, reduce, and remove marine debris, with a focus on marine debris posing a threat to living marine resources and navigation safety;

(2) provide national and regional coordination to assist States, Indian tribes, and regional organizations in the identification, determination of sources, assessment, prevention, reduction, and removal of marine debris;

(3) undertake efforts to reduce the adverse impacts of lost and discarded fishing gear on living marine resources and navigation safety, including—

(A) research and development of alternatives to gear posing threats to the marine environment and methods for marking gear used in certain fisheries to enhance the tracking, recovery, and identification of lost and discarded gear; and

(B) the development of effective nonregulatory measures and incentives to cooperatively reduce the volume of lost and discarded fishing gear and to aid in gear recovery;

(4) undertake outreach and education activities for the public and other stakeholders on sources of marine debris, threats associated with marine debris, and approaches to identifying, determining sources of, assessing, preventing, reducing, and removing marine debris and its adverse impacts on the United States economy, the marine environment, and navigation safety, including outreach and education activities through public-private initiatives;

(5) develop, in consultation with the Interagency Committee, interagency plans for the timely response to events determined by the Administrator to be severe marine debris events, including plans to—

(A) coordinate across agencies and with relevant State, tribal, and local governments to ensure adequate, timely, and efficient response;

(B) assess the composition, volume, and trajectory of marine debris associated with a severe marine debris event; and

(C) estimate the potential impacts of a severe marine debris event, including economic impacts on human health, navigation safety, natural resources, tourism, and livestock, including aquaculture;

(6) work to develop outreach and education strategies with other Federal agencies to address sources of marine debris;

(7) except for discharges of marine debris from vessels, in consultation with the Department of State and other Federal agencies, promote international action, as appropriate, to reduce the incidence of marine debris, including providing technical assistance to expand waste management systems internationally; and

(8) in the case of an event determined to be a severe marine debris event under subsection (c)—

(A) assist in the cleanup and response required by the severe marine debris event; or

(B) conduct such other activity as the Administrator determines is appropriate in response to the severe marine debris event.

(c) SEVERE MARINE DEBRIS EVENTS.—At the discretion of the Administrator or at the request of the Governor of an affected State, the Administrator shall determine whether there is a severe marine debris event.

(d) GRANTS, COOPERATIVE AGREEMENTS, AND CONTRACTS.—

(1) IN GENERAL.—The Administrator, acting through the Program, shall enter into cooperative agreements and contracts and provide financial assistance in the form of grants for projects to accomplish the purpose set forth in section 2.

(2) GRANT COST SHARING REQUIREMENT.—

(A) IN GENERAL.—Except as provided in subparagraphs (B) and (C), Federal funds for any grant under this section may not exceed 50 percent of the total cost of such project. For purposes of this subparagraph, the non-Federal share of project costs may be provided by in-kind contributions and other noncash support.

(B) WAIVER.—The Administrator may waive all or part of the matching requirement under subparagraph (A) if the

Administrator determines that no reasonable means are available through which applicants can meet the matching requirement and the probable benefit of such project outweighs the public interest in such matching requirement.

(C) SEVERE MARINE DEBRIS EVENTS.—Notwithstanding subparagraph (A), the Federal share of the cost of an activity carried out under a determination made under subsection (c) shall be—

(i) 100 percent of the cost of the activity, for an activity funded wholly by funds made available by a person, including the government of a foreign country, to the Federal Government for the purpose of responding to a severe marine debris event; or

(ii) 75 percent of the cost of the activity, for any activity other than an activity funded as described in clause (i).

(3) AMOUNTS PAID AND SERVICES RENDERED UNDER CONSENT.—

(A) CONSENT DECREES AND ORDERS.—If authorized by the Administrator or the Attorney General, as appropriate, the non-Federal share of the cost of a project carried out under this Act may include money paid pursuant to, or the value of any in-kind service performed under, an administrative order on consent or judicial consent decree that will remove or prevent marine debris.

(B) OTHER DECREES AND ORDERS.—The non-Federal share of the cost of a project carried out under this Act may not include any money paid pursuant to, or the value of any in-kind service performed under, any other administrative order or court order.

(4) ELIGIBILITY.—Any State, local, or tribal government whose activities affect research or regulation of marine debris, and any institution of higher education, nonprofit organization, or commercial organization with expertise in a field related to marine debris, is eligible to submit to the Administrator a marine debris proposal under the grant program.

(5) PROJECT REVIEW AND APPROVAL.—The Administrator shall—

(A) review each marine debris project proposal to determine if it meets the grant criteria and supports the goals of this Act;

(B) after considering any written comments and recommendations based on the review, approve or disapprove the proposal; and

(C) provide notification of that approval or disapproval to the person who submitted the proposal.

(6) PROJECT REPORTING.—Each grantee under this section shall provide periodic reports as required by the Administrator. Each report shall include all information required by the Administrator for evaluating the progress and success in meeting its stated goals, and impact of the grant activities on the marine debris problem.

SEC. 4. [33 U.S.C. 1953] COAST GUARD PROGRAM.

The Commandant of the Coast Guard, in consultation with the Interagency Committee, shall—

(1) take actions to reduce violations of and improve implementation of MARPOL Annex V and the Act to Prevent Pollution from Ships (33 U.S.C. 1901 et seq.) with respect to the discard of plastics and other garbage from vessels;

(2) take actions to cost-effectively monitor and enforce compliance with MARPOL Annex V and the Act to Prevent Pollution from Ships (33 U.S.C. 1901 et seq.), including through cooperation and coordination with other Federal and State enforcement programs;

(3) take actions to improve compliance with requirements under MARPOL Annex V and section 6 of the Act to Prevent Pollution from Ships (33 U.S.C. 1905) that all United States ports and terminals maintain and monitor the adequacy of receptacles for the disposal of plastics and other garbage, including through promoting voluntary government-industry partnerships;

(4) develop and implement a plan, in coordination with industry and recreational boaters, to improve ship-board waste management, including recordkeeping, and access to waste reception facilities for ship-board waste;

(5) take actions to improve international cooperation to

reduce marine debris; and

(6) establish a voluntary reporting program for commercial vessel operators and recreational boaters to report incidents of damage to vessels and disruption of navigation caused by marine debris, and observed violations of laws and regulations relating to the disposal of plastics and other marine debris.

SEC. 5. [33 U.S.C. 1954] COORDINATION.

(a) ESTABLISHMENT OF INTERAGENCY MARINE DEBRIS COORDINATING COMMITTEE.—There is established an Interagency Marine Debris Coordinating Committee to coordinate a comprehensive program of marine debris research and activities among Federal agencies, in cooperation and coordination with non-governmental organizations, industry, universities, and research institutions, States, Indian tribes, and other nations, as appropriate.

(b) MEMBERSHIP.—The Committee shall include a senior official from—

(1) the National Oceanic and Atmospheric Administration,who shall serve as the Chairperson of the Committee;

(2) the Environmental Protection Agency;

(3) the United States Coast Guard;

(4) the United States Navy;

(5) the Department of State;

(6) the Department of the Interior; and

(7) such other Federal agencies that have an interest in ocean issues or water pollution prevention and control as the Secretary of Commerce determines appropriate.

(c) MEETINGS.—Committee shall meet at least twice a year to provide a public, interagency forum to ensure the coordination of national and international research, monitoring, education, and regulatory actions addressing the persistent marine debris problem.

(d) MONITORING.—Secretary of Commerce, acting through the Administrator of the National Oceanic and Atmospheric Administration, in cooperation with the Administrator of the Environmental Protection Agency, shall utilize the marine debris data derived under title V of the Marine Protection, Research, and

Sanctuaries Act of 1972 (33 U.S.C. 2801 et seq.) to assist—

(1) the Committee in ensuring coordination of research,monitoring, education and reguiatory actions; and

(2) the United States Coast Guard in assessing the effectiveness of the Marine Plastic Pollution Research and Control Act of 1987 and the Act to Prevent Pollution from Ships in ensuring compliance under section 2201 of the Marine Plastic Pollution Research and Control Act of 1987.

(e) BIENNIAL PROGRESS REPORTS.—Biennially, the Committee, through the Chairperson, shall submit to the Committee on Commerce, Science, and Transportation of the Senate and the Committee on Transportation and Infrastructure and the Committee on Natural Resources of the House of Representatives a report that evaluates United States and international progress in meeting the purpose of this Act. The report shall include—

(1) the status of implementation of any recommendations and strategies of the Committee and analysis of their effectiveness;

(2) a summary of the marine debris inventory to be maintained by the National Oceanic and Atmospheric Administration;

(3) a review of the National Oceanic and Atmospheric Administration program authorized by section 3, including projects funded and accomplishments relating to reduction and prevention of marine debris;

(4) a review of Coast Guard programs and accomplishments relating to marine debris removal, including enforcement and compliance with MARPOL requirements; and

(5) estimated Federal and non-Federal funding provided for marine debris and recommendations for priority funding needs.

SEC. 6. [33 U.S.C. 1955] FEDERAL INFORMATION CLEARINGHOUSE.

The Administrator, in coordination with the Interagency Committee, shall—

(1) maintain a Federal information clearinghouse on marine debris that will be available to researchers and other interested persons to improve marine debris source identification, data sharing, and monitoring efforts through

collaborative research and open sharing of data; and

(2) take the necessary steps to ensure the confidentiality of such information (especially proprietary information), for any information required by the Administrator to be submitted under this section.

SEC. 7. [33 U.S.C. 1956] DEFINITIONS.

In this Act:

(1) ADMINISTRATOR.—The term "Administrator" means the Administrator of the National Oceanic and Atmospheric Administration.

(2) INTERAGENCY COMMITTEE.—The term "Interagency Committee" means the Interagency Marine Debris Coordinating Committee established under section 5 of this Act.

(3) MARINE DEBRIS.—The term "marine debris" means any persistent solid material that is manufactured or processed and directly or indirectly, intentionally or unintentionally, disposed of or abandoned into the marine environment or the Great Lakes.

(4) MARPOL; ANNEX V; CONVENTION.—The terms "MARPOL", "Annex V", and "Convention" have the meaning given those terms under section 2(a) of the Act to Prevent Pollution from Ships (33 U.S.C. 1901(a)).

(6) SEVERE MARINE DEBRIS EVENT.—The term "severe marine debris event" means atypically large amounts of marine debris caused by a natural disaster, including a tsunami, flood, landslide, or hurricane, or other source.

(5) PROGRAM.—The term "Program" means the Marine Debris Program established under section 3.[1]

---

[1] The placement of paragraph (5), as redesignated by section 608(4) of Public Law 112–213, is so in law. Such amendment probably should have included an instruction to transfer paragraph (5) (as redesignated) to appear after paragraph (4).

---

(7) STATE.—The term "State" means—

(A) any State of the United States that is impacted by marine debris within its seaward or Great Lakes boundaries;

(B) the District of Columbia;

(C) American Samoa, Guam, the Northern Mariana Islands, Puerto Rico, and the Virgin Islands; and

(D) any other territory or possession of the United States, or separate sovereign in free association with the United States, that is impacted by marine debris within its seaward boundaries.

SEC. 8. [33 U.S.C. 1957] RELATIONSHIP TO OUTER CONTINENTAL SHELF LANDS ACT.

Nothing in this Act supersedes, or limits the authority of the Secretary of the Interior under, the Outer Continental Shelf Lands Act (43 U.S.C. 1331 et seq.).

SEC. 9.[2] [33 U.S.C. 1958] AUTHORIZATION OF APPROPRIATIONS.

(a) IN GENERAL.—There is authorized to be appropriated to the Administrator $15,000,000 for each of fiscal years 2018 through 2022 for carrying out sections 3, 5, and 6, of which not more than 7 percent is authorized for each fiscal year for administrative costs.

(b) AMOUNTS AUTHORIZED FOR COAST GUARD.—Of the amounts authorized for each fiscal year under section 2702(1) of title 14, United States Code, up to $2,000,000 is authorized for the Secretary of the department in which the Coast Guard is operating for use by the Commandant of the Coast Guard to carry out section 4 of this Act, of which not more than 5 percent is authorized for each fiscal year for administrative costs.

---

[2] Section 11328(b) of Public Law 117–263 attempts to amend section 9, however, the reference to the amended law states "Maritime Debris Act" and should have been made to the "Marine Debris Act". As a result, these amendments are not reflected here.

SEC. 10. [33 U.S.C. 1959] PRIORITIZATION OF MARINE DEBRIS IN EXISTING INNOVATION AND ENTREPRENEURSHIP PROGRAMS.

In carrying out any relevant innovation and entrepreneurship programs that improve the innovation, effectiveness, and efficiency of the Marine Debris Program established under section 3 without undermining the purpose for which such program was established, the Secretary of Commerce, the Secretary of Energy, the Administrator of the Environmental Protection Agency, and the heads of other relevant Federal agencies, shall prioritize efforts to combat marine debris, including by—

(1) increasing innovation in methods and the effectiveness of efforts to identify, determine sources of, assess, prevent, reduce, and remove marine debris; and

(2) addressing the impacts of marine debris on—

(A) the economy of the United States;

(B) the marine environment; and

(C) navigation safety.

OIL POLLUTION ACT OF 1990

PUBLIC LAW 101-380
AS AMENDED THROUGH P.L. 117-286

OIL POLLUTION ACT OF 1990

[Public Law 101-380]

[As Amended Through P.L. 117–286, Enacted December 27, 2022]

AN ACT To establish limitations on liability for damages resulting from oil pollution, to establish a fund for the payment of compensation for such damages, and for other purposes.

Be it enacted by the Senate and House of Representatives of the United States of America in Congress assembled,

SECTION 1. SHORT TITLE.

This Act may be cited as the "Oil Pollution Act of 1990".

[33 U.S.C. 2701 note]

SEC. 2. TABLE OF CONTENTS.

The contents of this Act are as follows:

TITLE I—OIL POLLUTION LIABILITY AND COMPENSATION

TITLE I—OIL POLLUTION LIABILITY AND COMPENSATION

SEC. 1001. DEFINITIONS.

For the purposes of this Act, the term—

(1) "act of God" means an unanticipated grave natural disaster or other natural phenomenon of an exceptional, inevitable, and irresistible character the effects of which could not have been prevented or avoided by the exercise of due care or foresight;

(2) "barrel" means 42 United States gallons at 60 degrees fahrenheit;

(3) "claim" means a request, made in writing for a sum certain, for compensation for damages or removal costs resulting from an incident;

(4) "claimant" means any person or government who presents a claim for compensation under this title;

(5) "damages" means damages specified in section 1002(b) of this Act, and includes the cost of assessing these damages;

(6) "deepwater port" is a facility licensed under the Deepwater Port Act of 1974 (33 U.S.C. 1501–1524);

(7) "discharge" means any emission (other than natural seepage), intentional or unintentional, and includes, but is not limited to, spilling, leaking, pumping, pouring, emitting, emptying, or dumping;

(8) "exclusive economic zone" means the zone established by Presidential Proclamation Numbered 5030, dated March 10, 1983, including the ocean waters of the areas referred to as "eastern special areas" in Article 3(1) of the Agreement between the United States of America and the Union of Soviet Socialist Republics on the Maritime Boundary, signed June 1, 1990;

(9) "facility" means any structure, group of structures, equipment, or device (other than a vessel) which is used for one or more of the following purposes: exploring for, drilling for, producing, storing, handling, transferring, processing, or transporting oil. This term includes any motor vehicle, rolling stock, or pipeline used for one or more of these purposes;

(10) "foreign offshore unit" means a facility which is

located, in whole or in part, in the territorial sea or on the continental shelf of a foreign country and which is or was used for one or more of the following purposes: exploring for, drilling for, producing, storing, handling, transferring, processing, or transporting oil produced from the seabed beneath the foreign country's territorial sea or from the foreign country's continental shelf;

(11) "Fund" means the Oil Spill Liability Trust Fund, established by section 9509 of the Internal Revenue Code of 1986 (26 U.S.C. 9509);

(12) "gross ton" has the meaning given that term by the Secretary under part J of title 46, United States Code;

(13) "guarantor" means any person, other than the responsible party, who provides evidence of financial responsibility for a responsible party under this Act;

(14) "incident" means any occurrence or series of occurrences having the same origin, involving one or more vessels, facilities, or any combination thereof, resulting in the discharge or substantial threat of discharge of oil;

(15) "Indian tribe" means any Indian tribe, band, nation, or other organized group or community, but not including any Alaska Native regional or village corporation, which is recognized as eligible for the special programs and services provided by the United States to Indians because of their status as Indians and has governmental authority over lands belonging to or controlled by the tribe;

(16) "lessee" means a person holding a leasehold interest in an oil or gas lease on lands beneath navigable waters (as that term is defined in section 2(a) of the Submerged Lands Act (43 U.S.C. 1301(a))) or on submerged lands of the Outer Continental Shelf, granted or maintained under applicable State law or the Outer Continental Shelf Lands Act (43 U.S.C. 1331 et seq.);

(17) "liable" or "liability" shall be construed to be the standard of liability which obtains under section 311 of the Federal Water Pollution Control Act (33 U.S.C. 1321);

(18) "mobile offshore drilling unit" means a vessel (other than a self-elevating lift vessel) capable of use as an offshore facility;

(19) "National Contingency Plan" means the National Contingency Plan prepared and published under section 311(d) of the Federal Water Pollution Control Act, as amended by this Act, or revised under section 105 of the Comprehensive Environmental Response, Compensation, and Liability Act (42 U.S.C. 9605);

(20) "natural resources" includes land, fish, wildlife, biota, air, water, ground water, drinking water supplies, and other such resources belonging to, managed by, held in trust by, appertaining to, or otherwise controlled by the United States (including the resources of the exclusive economic zone), any State or local government or Indian tribe, or any foreign government;

(21) "navigable waters" means the waters of the United States, including the territorial sea;

(22) "offshore facility" means any facility of any kind located in, on, or under any of the navigable waters of the United States, and any facility of any kind which is subject to the jurisdiction of the United States and is located in, on, or under any other waters, other than a vessel or a public vessel;

(23) "oil" means oil of any kind or in any form, including petroleum, fuel oil, sludge, oil refuse, and oil mixed with wastes other than dredged spoil, but does not include any substance which is specifically listed or designated as a hazardous substance under subparagraphs (A) through (F) of section 101(14) of the Comprehensive Environmental Response, Compensation, and Liability Act (42 U.S.C. 9601) and which is subject to the provisions of that Act;

(24) "onshore facility" means any facility (including, but not limited to, motor vehicles and rolling stock) of any kind located in, on, or under, any land within the United States other than submerged land;

(25) the term "Outer Continental Shelf facility" means an offshore facility which is located, in whole or in part, on the Outer Continental Shelf and is or was used for one or more of the following purposes: exploring for, drilling for, producing, storing, handling, transferring, processing, or transporting oil produced from the Outer Continental Shelf;

(26) "owner or operator"—

(A) means—

(i) in the case of a vessel, any person owning, operating, or chartering by demise, the vessel;

(ii) in the case of an onshore facility, offshore facility, or foreign offshore unit or other facility located seaward of the exclusive economic zone, any person or entity owning or operating such facility;

(iii) in the case of any abandoned offshore facility or foreign offshore unit or other facility located seaward of the exclusive economic zone, the person or entity that owned or operated such facility immediately prior to such abandonment;

(iv) in the case of any facility, title or control of which was conveyed due to bankruptcy, foreclosure, tax delinquency, abandonment, or similar means to a unit of State or local government, any person who owned, operated, or otherwise controlled activities at such facility immediately beforehand;

(v) notwithstanding subparagraph (B)(i), and in the same manner and to the same extent, both procedurally and substantively, as any nongovernmental entity, including for purposes of liability under section 1002, any State or local government that has caused or contributed to a discharge or substantial threat of a discharge of oil from a vessel or facility ownership or control of which was acquired involuntarily through—

(I) seizure or otherwise in connection with law enforcement activity;

(II) bankruptcy;

(III) tax delinquency;

(IV) abandonment; or

(V) other circumstances in which the government involuntarily acquires title by virtue of its function as sovereign;

(vi) notwithstanding subparagraph (B)(ii), a person that is a lender and that holds indicia of ownership primarily to protect a security interest in a vessel or facility if, while the borrower is still in possession of the vessel or facility encumbered by the security interest, the person—

(I) exercises decision making control over the environmental compliance related to the vessel or facility, such that the person has undertaken responsibility for oil handling or disposal practices related to the vessel or facility; or

(II) exercises control at a level comparable to that of a manager of the vessel or facility, such that the person has assumed or manifested responsibility—

(aa) for the overall management of the vessel or facility encompassing day-to-day decision making with respect to environmental compliance; or

(bb) over all or substantially all of the operational functions (as distinguished from financial or administrative functions) of the vessel or facility other than the function of environmental compliance; and

(B) does not include—

(i) A unit of state or local government that acquired ownership or control of a vessel or facility involuntarily through—

(I) seizure or otherwise in connection with law enforcement activity;

(II) bankruptcy;

(III) tax delinquency;

(IV) abandonment; or

(V) other circumstances in which the government involuntarily acquires title by virtue of its function as sovereign;

(ii) a person that is a lender that does not participate in management of a vessel or facility, but holds indicia of ownership primarily to protect the security interest of the person in the vessel or facility; or

(iii) a person that is a lender that did not participate in management of a vessel or facility prior to foreclosure, notwithstanding that the person—

(I) forecloses on the vessel or facility; and

(II) after foreclosure, sells, re-leases (in the case of a lease finance transaction), or liquidates the vessel or facility, maintains business activities, winds up operations, undertakes a removal action under section 311(c) of the Federal Water Pollution Control Act (33 U.S.C. 1321(c)) or under the direction of an on-scene coordinator appointed under the National Contingency Plan, with respect to the vessel or facility, or takes any other measure to preserve, protect, or prepare the vessel or facility prior to sale or disposition,

if the person seeks to sell, re-lease (in the case of a lease finance transaction), or otherwise divest the person of the vessel or facility at the earliest practicable, commercially reasonable time, on commercially reasonable terms, taking into account market conditions and legal and regulatory requirements;

(27) "person" means an individual, corporation, partnership, association, State, municipality, commission, or political subdivision of a State, or any interstate body;

(28) "permittee" means a person holding an authorization, license, or permit for geological exploration issued under section 11 of the Outer Continental Shelf Lands Act (43 U.S.C. 1340) or applicable State law;

(29) "public vessel" means a vessel owned or bareboat chartered and operated by the United States, or by a State or political subdivision thereof, or by a foreign nation, except when the vessel is engaged in commerce;

(30) "remove" or "removal" means containment and removal of oil or a hazardous substance from water and shorelines or the taking of other actions as may be necessary to minimize or mitigate damage to the public health or welfare, including, but not limited to, fish, shellfish, wildlife, and public and private property, shorelines, and beaches;

(31) "removal costs" means the costs of removal that are incurred after a discharge of oil has occurred or, in any case in which there is a substantial threat of a discharge of oil, the costs to prevent, minimize, or mitigate oil pollution from such an incident;

(32) "responsible party" means the following:

(A) VESSELS.—In the case of a vessel, any person owning, operating, or demise chartering the vessel. In the case of a vessel, the term "responsible party" also includes the owner of oil being transported in a tank vessel with a single hull after December 31, 2010.

(B) ONSHORE FACILITIES.—In the case of an onshore facility (other than a pipeline), any person owning or operating the facility, except a Federal agency, State, municipality, commission, or political subdivision of a State, or any interstate body, that as the owner transfers possession and right to use the property to another person by lease, assignment, or permit.

(C) OFFSHORE FACILITIES.—In the case of an offshore facility (other than a pipeline or a deepwater port licensed under the Deepwater Port Act of 1974 (33 U.S.C. 1501 et seq.)), the lessee or permittee of the area in which the facility is located or the holder of a right of use and easement granted under applicable State law or the Outer Continental Shelf Lands Act (43 U.S.C. 1301–1356) for the area in which the facility is located (if the holder is a different person than the lessee or permittee), except a Federal agency, State, municipality, commission, or political subdivision of a State, or any interstate body, that as owner transfers possession and right to use the property to another person by lease, assignment, or permit.

(D) FOREIGN FACILITIES.—In the case of a foreign offshore unit or other facility located seaward of the exclusive economic zone, any person or other entity owning or operating the facility, and any leaseholder, permit holder, assignee, or holder of a right of use and easement granted under applicable foreign law for the area in which the facility is located.

(E) DEEPWATER PORTS.—In the case of a deepwater port licensed under the Deepwater Port Act of 1974 (33

U.S.C. 1501–1524), the licensee.

(F) PIPELINES.—In the case of a pipeline, any person owning or operating the pipeline.

(G) ABANDONMENT.—In the case of an abandoned vessel, onshore facility, deepwater port, pipeline, ,[1] offshore facility, or foreign offshore unit or other facility located seaward of the exclusive economic zone, the persons or entities that would have been responsible parties immediately prior to the abandonment of the vessel or facility.

---

[1]   Two commas are so in law. See amendment made by section 3508(b)(1)(A)(ii)(III) of division C of Public Law 115–91.

---

(33) "Secretary" means the Secretary of the department in which the Coast Guard is operating;

(34) "tank vessel" means a vessel that is constructed or adapted to carry, or that carries, oil or hazardous material in bulk as cargo or cargo residue, and that—

(A) is a vessel of the United States;

(B) operates on the navigable waters; or

(C) transfers oil or hazardous material in a place subject to the jurisdiction of the United States;

(35) "territorial seas" means the belt of the seas measured from the line of ordinary low water along that portion of the coast which is in direct contact with the open sea and the line marking the seaward limit of inland waters, and extending seaward a distance of 3 miles;

(36) "United States" and "State" mean the several States of the United States, the District of Columbia, the Commonwealth of Puerto Rico, Guam, American Samoa, the United States Virgin Islands, the Commonwealth of the Northern Marianas, and any other territory or possession of the United States;

(37) "vessel" means every description of watercraft or other artificial contrivance used, or capable of being used, as a means of transportation on water, other than a public vessel;

(38) "participate in management"—

(A)(i) means actually participating in the management or operational affairs of a vessel or facility; and

(ii) does not include merely having the capacity to influence, or the unexercised right to control, vessel or facility operations; and

(B) does not include—

(i) performing an act or failing to act prior to the time at which a security interest is created in a vessel or facility;

(ii) holding a security interest or abandoning or releasing a security interest;

(iii) including in the terms of an extension of credit, or in a contract or security agreement relating to the extension, a covenant, warranty, or other term or condition that relates to environmental compliance;

(iv) monitoring or enforcing the terms and conditions of the extension of credit or security interest;

(v) monitoring or undertaking one or more inspections of the vessel or facility;

(vi) requiring a removal action or other lawful means of addressing a discharge or substantial threat of a discharge of oil in connection with the vessel or facility prior to, during, or on the expiration of the term of the extension of credit;

(vii) providing financial or other advice or counseling in an effort to mitigate, prevent, or cure default or diminution in the value of the vessel or facility;

(viii) restructuring, renegotiating, or otherwise agreeing to alter the terms and conditions of the extension of credit or security interest, exercising forbearance;

(ix) exercising other remedies that may be available under applicable law for the breach of a term or condition of the extension of credit or security agreement; or

(x) conducting a removal action under 311(c) of the Federal Water Pollution Control Act (33 U.S.C. 1321(c)) or under the direction of an on-scene coordinator appointed under the National Contingency Plan,

if such actions do not rise to the level of participating in management under subparagraph (A) of this paragraph and paragraph (26)(A)(vi);

(39) "extension of credit" has the meaning provided in section 101(20)(G)(i) of the Comprehensive Environmental Response, Compensation and Liability Act of 1980 (42 U.S.C. 9601(20)(G)(i));

(40) "financial or administrative function" has the meaning provided in section 101(20)(G)(ii) of the Comprehensive Environmental Response, Compensation and Liability Act of 1980 (42 U.S.C. 9601(20)(G)(ii));

(41) "foreclosure" and "foreclose" each has the meaning provided in section 101(20)(G)(iii) of the Comprehensive Environmental Response, Compensation and Liability Act of 1980 (42 U.S.C. 9601(20)(G)(iii));

(42) "lender" has the meaning provided in section 101(20)(G)(iv) of the Comprehensive Environmental Response, Compensation and Liability Act of 1980 (42 U.S.C. 9601(20)(G)(iv));

(43) "operational function" has the meaning provided in section 101(20)(G)(v) of the Comprehensive Environmental Response, Compensation and Liability Act of 1980 (42 U.S.C. 9601(20)(G)(v)); and

(44) "security interest" has the meaning provided in section 101(20)(G)(vi) of the Comprehensive Environmental Response, Compensation and Liability Act of 1980 (42 U.S.C. 9601(20)(G)(vi)).

[33 U.S.C. 2701]

SEC. 1002. ELEMENTS OF LIABILITY.

(a) IN GENERAL.—Notwithstanding any other provision or rule of law, and subject to the provisions of this Act, each responsible party for a vessel or a facility from which oil is discharged, or which poses the substantial threat of a discharge of oil, into or upon the navigable waters or adjoining shorelines or the exclusive economic zone is liable for the removal costs and damages specified in subsection (b) that result from such incident.

(b) COVERED REMOVAL COSTS AND DAMAGES.—

(1) REMOVAL COSTS.—The removal costs referred to in subsection (a) are—

(A) all removal costs incurred by the United States, a State, or an Indian tribe under subsection (c), (d), (e), or (l) of section 311 of the Federal Water Pollution Control Act (33 U.S.C. 1321), as amended by this Act, under the Intervention on the High Seas Act (33 U.S.C. 1471 et seq.), or under State law; and

(B) any removal costs incurred by any person for acts taken by the person which are consistent with the National Contingency Plan.

(2) DAMAGES.—The damages referred to in subsection (a) are the following:

(A) NATURAL RESOURCES.—Damages for injury to, destruction of, loss of, or loss of use of, natural resources, including the reasonable costs of assessing the damage, which shall be recoverable by a United States trustee, a State trustee, an Indian tribe trustee, or a foreign trustee.

(B) REAL OR PERSONAL PROPERTY.—Damages for injury to, or economic losses resulting from destruction of, real or personal property, which shall be recoverable by a claimant who owns or leases that property.

(C) SUBSISTENCE USE.—Damages for loss of subsistence use of natural resources, which shall be recoverable by any claimant who so uses natural resources which have been injured, destroyed, or lost, without regard to the ownership or management of the resources.

(D) REVENUES.—Damages equal to the net loss of taxes, royalties, rents, fees, or net profit shares due to the injury, destruction, or loss of real property, personal property, or natural resources, which shall be recoverable by the Government of the United States, a State, or a political subdivision thereof.

(E) PROFITS AND EARNING CAPACITY.—Damages equal to the loss of profits or impairment of earning capacity due to the injury, destruction, or loss of real property, personal property, or natural resources, which shall be recoverable by any claimant.

(F) PUBLIC SERVICES.—Damages for net costs of providing increased or additional public services during or after removal activities, including protection from fire, safety, or health hazards, caused by a discharge of oil, which shall be recoverable by a State, or a political subdivision of a State.

(c) EXCLUDED DISCHARGES.—This title does not apply to any discharge—

(1) permitted by a permit issued under Federal, State, or local law;

(2) from a public vessel; or

(3) from an onshore facility which is subject to the Trans-Alaska Pipeline Authorization Act (43 U.S.C. 1651 et seq.).

(d) LIABILITY OF THIRD PARTIES.—

(1) IN GENERAL.—

(A) THIRD PARTY TREATED AS RESPONSIBLE PARTY.—Except as provided in subparagraph (B), in any case in which a responsible party establishes that a discharge or threat of a discharge and the resulting removal costs and damages were caused solely by an act or omission of one or more third parties described in section 1003(a)(3) (or solely by such an act or omission in combination with an act of God or an act of war), the third party or parties shall be treated as the responsible party or parties for purposes of determining liability under this title.

(B) SUBROGATION OF RESPONSIBLE PARTY.—If the responsible party alleges that the discharge or threat of a discharge was caused solely by an act or omission of a third party, the responsible party—

(i) in accordance with section 1013, shall pay removal costs and damages to any claimant; and

(ii) shall be entitled by subrogation to all rights of the United States Government and the claimant to recover removal costs or damages from the third party or the Fund paid under this subsection.

(2) LIMITATION APPLIED.—

(A) OWNER OR OPERATOR OF VESSEL OR FACILITY.—If

the act or omission of a third party that causes an incident occurs in connection with a vessel or facility owned or operated by the third party, the liability of the third party shall be subject to the limits provided in section 1004 as applied with respect to the vessel or facility.

(B) OTHER CASES.—In any other case, the liability of a third party or parties shall not exceed the limitation which would have been applicable to the responsible party of the vessel or facility from which the discharge actually occurred if the responsible party were liable.

[33 U.S.C. 2702]

SEC. 1003. DEFENSES TO LIABILITY.

(a) COMPLETE DEFENSES.—A responsible party is not liable for removal costs or damages under section 1002 if the responsible party establishes, by a preponderance of the evidence, that the discharge or substantial threat of a discharge of oil and the resulting damages or removal costs were caused solely by—

(1) an act of God;

(2) an act of war;

(3) an act or omission of a third party, other than an employee or agent of the responsible party or a third party whose act or omission occurs in connection with any contractual relationship with the responsible party (except where the sole contractual arrangement arises in connection with carriage by a common carrier by rail), if the responsible party establishes, by a preponderance of the evidence, that the responsible party—

(A) exercised due care with respect to the oil concerned, taking into consideration the characteristics of the oil and in light of all relevant facts and circumstances; and

(B) took precautions against foreseeable acts or omissions of any such third party and the foreseeable consequences of those acts or omissions; or

(4) any combination of paragraphs (1), (2), and (3).

(b) DEFENSES AS TO PARTICULAR CLAIMANTS.—A responsible party is not liable under section 1002 to a claimant, to the extent that the incident is caused by the gross negligence or willful misconduct of the claimant.

(c) LIMITATION ON COMPLETE DEFENSE.—Subsection (a) does not apply with respect to a responsible party who fails or refuses—

(1) to report the incident as required by law if the responsible party knows or has reason to know of the incident;

(2) to provide all reasonable cooperation and assistance requested by a responsible official in connection with removal activities; or

(3) without sufficient cause, to comply with an order issued under subsection (c) or (e) of section 311 of the Federal Water Pollution Control Act (33 U.S.C. 1321), as amended by this Act, or the Intervention on the High Seas Act (33 U.S.C. 1471 et seq.).

(d) DEFINITION OF CONTRACTUAL RELATIONSHIP.—

(1) IN GENERAL.—For purposes of subsection (a)(3) the term "contractual relationship" includes, but is not limited to, land contracts, deeds, easements, leases, or other instruments transferring title or possession, unless—

(A) the real property on which the facility concerned is located was acquired by the responsible party after the placement of the oil on, in, or at the real property on which the facility concerned is located;

(B) one or more of the circumstances described in subparagraph (A), (B), or (C) of paragraph (2) is established by the responsible party by a preponderance of the evidence; and

(C) the responsible party complies with paragraph (3).

(2) REQUIRED CIRCUMSTANCE.—The circumstances referred to in paragraph (1)(B) are the following:

(A) At the time the responsible party acquired the real property on which the facility is located the responsible party did not know and had no reason to know that oil that is the subject of the discharge or substantial threat of discharge was located on, in, or at the facility.

(B) The responsible party is a government entity that acquired the facility—

(i) by escheat;

(ii) through any other involuntary transfer or acquisition; or

(iii) through the exercise of eminent domain authority by purchase or condemnation.

(C) The responsible party acquired the facility by inheritance or bequest.

(3) ADDITIONAL REQUIREMENTS.—For purposes of paragraph (1)(C), the responsible party must establish by a preponderance of the evidence that the responsible party—

(A) has satisfied the requirements of section 1003(a)(3)(A) and (B);

(B) has provided full cooperation, assistance, and facility access to the persons that are authorized to conduct removal actions, including the cooperation and access necessary for the installation, integrity, operation, and maintenance of any complete or partial removal action;

(C) is in compliance with any land use restrictions established or relied on in connection with the removal action; and

(D) has not impeded the effectiveness or integrity of any institutional control employed in connection with the removal action.

(4) REASON TO KNOW.—

(A) APPROPRIATE INQUIRIES.—To establish that the responsible party had no reason to know of the matter described in paragraph (2)(A), the responsible party must demonstrate to a court that—

(i) on or before the date on which the responsible party acquired the real property on which the facility is located, the responsible party carried out all appropriate inquiries, as provided in subparagraphs (B) and (D), into the previous ownership and uses of the real property on which the facility is located in accordance with generally accepted good commercial and customary standards and practices; and

(ii) the responsible party took reasonable steps to—

(I) stop any continuing discharge;

(II) prevent any substantial threat of discharge; and

(III) prevent or limit any human, environmental, or natural resource exposure to any previously discharged oil.

(B) REGULATIONS ESTABLISHING STANDARDS AND PRACTICES.—Not later than 2 years after the date of the enactment of this paragraph, the Secretary, in consultation with the Administrator of the Environmental Protection Agency, shall by regulation establish standards and practices for the purpose of satisfying the requirement to carry out all appropriate inquiries under subparagraph (A).

(C) CRITERIA.—In promulgating regulations that establish the standards and practices referred to in subparagraph (B), the Secretary shall include in such standards and practices provisions regarding each of the following:

(i) The results of an inquiry by an environmental professional.

(ii) Interviews with past and present owners, operators, and occupants of the facility and the real property on which the facility is located for the purpose of gathering information regarding the potential for oil at the facility and on the real property on which the facility is located.

(iii) Reviews of historical sources, such as chain of title documents, aerial photographs, building department records, and land use records, to determine previous uses and occupancies of the real property on which the facility is located since the property was first developed.

(iv) Searches for recorded environmental cleanup liens against the facility and the real property on which the facility is located that are filed under Federal, State, or local law.

(v) Reviews of Federal, State, and local government records, waste disposal records, underground storage tank records, and waste handling, generation, treatment, disposal, and spill records, concerning oil at or near the facility and on the real property on which the facility is located.

(vi) Visual inspections of the facility, the real property on which the facility is located, and adjoining properties.

(vii) Specialized knowledge or experience on the part of the responsible party.

(viii) The relationship of the purchase price to the value of the facility and the real property on which the facility is located, if oil was not at the facility or on the real property.

(ix) Commonly known or reasonably ascertainable information about the facility and the real property on which the facility is located.

(x) The degree of obviousness of the presence or likely presence of oil at the facility and on the real property on which the facility is located, and the ability to detect the oil by appropriate investigation.

(D) INTERIM STANDARDS AND PRACTICES.—

(i) REAL PROPERTY PURCHASED BEFORE MAY 31, 1997.—With respect to real property purchased before May 31, 1997, in making a determination with respect to a responsible party described in subparagraph (A), a court shall take into account—

(I) any specialized knowledge or experience on the part of the responsible party;

(II) the relationship of the purchase price to the value of the facility and the real property on which the facility is located, if the oil was not at the facility or on the real property;

(III) commonly known or reasonably ascertainable information about the facility and the real property on which the facility is located;

(IV) the obviousness of the presence or likely presence of oil at the facility and on the real property on which the facility is located; and

(V) the ability of the responsible party to detect oil by appropriate inspection.

(ii) REAL PROPERTY PURCHASED ON OR AFTER MAY 31, 1997.—With respect to real property purchased on or after May 31, 1997, until the Secretary promulgates the regulations described in clause (ii), the procedures of the American Society for Testing and Materials, including the document known as "Standard E1527–97", entitled "Standard Practice for Environmental Site Assessment: Phase I Environmental Site Assessment Process", shall satisfy the requirements in subparagraph (A).

(E) SITE INSPECTION AND TITLE SEARCH.—In the case of real property for residential use or other similar use purchased by a nongovernmental or noncommercial entity, inspection and title search of the facility and the real property on which the facility is located that reveal no basis for further investigation shall be considered to satisfy the requirements of this paragraph.

(5) PREVIOUS OWNER OR OPERATOR.—Nothing in this paragraph or in section 1003(a)(3) shall diminish the liability of any previous owner or operator of such facility who would otherwise be liable under this Act. Notwithstanding this paragraph, if a responsible party obtained actual knowledge of the discharge or substantial threat of discharge of oil at such facility when the responsible party owned the facility and then subsequently transferred ownership of the facility or the real property on which the facility is located to another person without disclosing such knowledge, the responsible party shall be treated as liable under section 1002(a) and no defense under section 1003(a) shall be available to such responsible party.

(6) LIMITATION ON DEFENSE.—Nothing in this paragraph shall affect the liability under this Act of a responsible party who, by any act or omission, caused or contributed to the discharge or substantial threat of discharge of oil which is the subject of the action relating to the facility.

[33 U.S.C. 2703]

SEC. 1004. LIMITS ON LIABILITY.

(a) GENERAL RULE.—Except as otherwise provided in this section, the total of the liability of a responsible party under section 1002 and any removal costs incurred by, or on behalf of, the responsible party, with respect to each incident shall not exceed—

(1) for a tank vessel, the greater of—

(A) with respect to a single-hull vessel, including a single-hull vessel fitted with double sides only or a double bottom only, $3,000 per gross ton;

(B) with respect to a vessel other than a vessel referred to in subparagraph (A), $1,900 per gross ton; or

(C)(i) with respect to a vessel greater than 3,000 gross tons that is—

(I) a vessel described in subparagraph (A), $22,000,000; or

(II) a vessel described in subparagraph (B), $16,000,000; or

(ii) with respect to a vessel of 3,000 gross tons or less that is—

(I) a vessel described in subparagraph (A), $6,000,000; or

(II) a vessel described in subparagraph (B), $4,000,000;

(2) for any other vessel, $950 per gross ton or $800,000, whichever is greater;

(3) for an offshore facility except a deepwater port, the total of all removal costs plus $75,000,000; and

(4) for any onshore facility and a deepwater port, $350,000,000.

(b) DIVISION OF LIABILITY FOR MOBILE OFFSHORE DRILLING UNITS.—

(1) TREATED FIRST AS TANK VESSEL.—For purposes of determining the responsible party and applying this Act and except as provided in paragraph (2), a mobile offshore drilling unit which is being used as an offshore facility is deemed to be a tank vessel with respect to the discharge, or the substantial threat of a discharge, of oil on or above the surface of the water.

(2) TREATED AS FACILITY FOR EXCESS LIABILITY.—To the extent that removal costs and damages from any incident described in paragraph (1) exceed the amount for which a responsible party is liable (as that amount may be limited under subsection (a)(1)), the mobile offshore drilling unit is deemed to be an offshore facility. For purposes of applying subsection (a)(3), the amount specified in that subsection shall

be reduced by the amount for which the responsible party is liable under paragraph (1).

(c) EXCEPTIONS.—

(1) ACTS OF RESPONSIBLE PARTY.—Subsection (a) does not apply if the incident was proximately caused by—

(A) gross negligence or willful misconduct of, or

(B) the violation of an applicable Federal safety, construction, or operating regulation by,

the responsible party, an agent or employee of the responsible party, or a person acting pursuant to a contractual relationship with the responsible party (except where the sole contractual arrangement arises in connection with carriage by a common carrier by rail).

(2) FAILURE OR REFUSAL OF RESPONSIBLE PARTY.—Subsection (a) does not apply if the responsible party fails or refuses—

(A) to report the incident as required by law and the responsible party knows or has reason to know of the incident;

(B) to provide all reasonable cooperation and assistance requested by a responsible official in connection with removal activities; or

(C) without sufficient cause, to comply with an order issued under subsection (c) or (e) of section 311 of the Federal Water Pollution Control Act (33 U.S.C. 1321), as amended by this Act, or the Intervention on the High Seas Act (33 U.S.C. 1471 et seq.).

(3) OCS FACILITY OR VESSEL.—Notwithstanding the limitations established under subsection (a) and the defenses of section 1003, all removal costs incurred by the United States Government or any State or local official or agency in connection with a discharge or substantial threat of a discharge of oil from any Outer Continental Shelf facility or a vessel carrying oil as cargo from such a facility shall be borne by the owner or operator of such facility or vessel.

(4) CERTAIN TANK VESSELS.—Subsection (a)(1) shall not apply to—

(A) a tank vessel on which the only oil carried as cargo

is an animal fat or vegetable oil, as those terms are used in section 2 of the Edible Oil Regulatory Reform Act; and

(B) a tank vessel that is designated in its certificate of inspection as an oil spill response vessel (as that term is defined in section 2101 of title 46, United States Code) and that is used solely for removal.

(d) ADJUSTING LIMITS OF LIABILITY.—

(1) ONSHORE FACILITIES.—Subject to paragraph (2), the President may establish by regulation, with respect to any class or category of onshore facility, a limit of liability under this section of less than $350,000,000, but not less than $8,000,000, taking into account size, storage capacity, oil throughput, proximity to sensitive areas, type of oil handled, history of discharges, and other factors relevant to risks posed by the class or category of facility.

(2) DEEPWATER PORTS AND ASSOCIATED VESSELS.—

(A) STUDY.—The Secretary shall conduct a study of the relative operational and environmental risks posed by the transportation of oil by vessel to deepwater ports (as defined in section 3 of the Deepwater Port Act of 1974 (33 U.S.C. 1502)) versus the transportation of oil by vessel to other ports. The study shall include a review and analysis of offshore lightering practices used in connection with that transportation, an analysis of the volume of oil transported by vessel using those practices, and an analysis of the frequency and volume of oil discharges which occur in connection with the use of those practices.

(B) REPORT.—Not later than 1 year after the date of the enactment of this Act, the Secretary shall submit to the Congress a report on the results of the study conducted under subparagraph (A).

(C) RULEMAKING PROCEEDING.—If the Secretary determines, based on the results of the study conducted under subparagraph (A), that the use of deepwater ports in connection with the transportation of oil by vessel results in a lower operational or environmental risk than the use of other ports, the Secretary shall initiate, not later than the 180th day following the date of submission of the report to the Congress under subparagraph (B), a rulemaking proceeding to lower the limits of liability under this section for deepwater ports as the Secretary determines appropriate. The Secretary may establish a limit of liability of less than $350,000,000, but not less than $50,000,000, in accordance with paragraph (1).

(3) PERIODIC REPORTS.—The President shall, within 6 months after the date of the enactment of this Act, and from time to time thereafter, report to the Congress on the desirability of adjusting the limits of liability specified in subsection (a).

(4) ADJUSTMENT TO REFLECT CONSUMER PRICE INDEX.—The President, by regulations issued not later than 3 years after the date of enactment of the Delaware River Protection Act of 2006 and not less than every 3 years thereafter, shall adjust the limits on liability specified in subsection (a) to reflect significant increases in the Consumer Price Index.

[33 U.S.C. 2704]

SEC. 1005. INTEREST; PARTIAL PAYMENT OF CLAIMS.

(a) GENERAL RULE.—The responsible party or the responsible party's guarantor is liable to a claimant for interest on the amount paid in satisfaction of a claim under this Act for the period described in subsection (b). The responsible party shall establish a procedure for the payment or settlement of claims for interim, short-term damages. Payment or settlement of a claim for interim, short-term damages representing less than the full amount of damages to which the claimant ultimately may be entitled shall not preclude recovery by the claimant for damages not reflected in the paid or settled partial claim.

(b) PERIOD.—

(1) IN GENERAL.—Except as provided in paragraph (2), the period for which interest shall be paid is the period beginning on the 30th day following the date on which the claim is presented to the responsible party or guarantor and ending on the date on which the claim is paid.

(2) EXCLUSION OF PERIOD DUE TO OFFER BY GUARANTOR.—If the guarantor offers to the claimant an amount equal to or greater than that finally paid in satisfaction of the claim, the period described in paragraph (1) does not include the period beginning on the date the offer is made and ending on the

date the offer is accepted. If the offer is made within 60 days after the date on which the claim is presented under section 1013(a), the period described in paragraph (1) does not include any period before the offer is accepted.

(3) EXCLUSION OF PERIODS IN INTERESTS OF JUSTICE.—If in any period a claimant is not paid due to reasons beyond the control of the responsible party or because it would not serve the interests of justice, no interest shall accrue under this section during that period.

(4) CALCULATION OF INTEREST.—

(A) IN GENERAL.—The interest paid for claims, other than Federal Government cost recovery claims, under this section shall be calculated at the average of the highest rate for commercial and finance company paper of maturities of 180 days or less obtaining on each of the days included within the period for which interest must be paid to the claimant, as published in the Federal Reserve Bulletin.

(B) FEDERAL COST RECOVERY CLAIMS.—The interest paid for Federal Government cost recovery claims under this section shall be calculated in accordance with section 3717 of title 31, United States Code.

(5) INTEREST NOT SUBJECT TO LIABILITY LIMITS.—

(A) IN GENERAL.—Interest (including prejudgment interest) under this paragraph is in addition to damages and removal costs for which claims may be asserted under section 1002 and shall be paid without regard to any limitation of liability under section 1004.

(B) PAYMENT BY GUARANTOR.—The payment of interest under this subsection by a guarantor is subject to section 1016(g).

[33 U.S.C. 2705]

SEC. 1006. NATURAL RESOURCES.

(a) LIABILITY.—In the case of natural resource damages under section 1002(b)(2)(A), liability shall be—

(1) to the United States Government for natural resources belonging to, managed by, controlled by, or appertaining to the United States;

(2) to any State for natural resources belonging to, managed by, controlled by, or appertaining to such State or political subdivision thereof;

(3) to any Indian tribe for natural resources belonging to, managed by, controlled by, or appertaining to such Indian tribe; and

(4) in any case in which section 1007 applies, to the government of a foreign country for natural resources belonging to, managed by, controlled by, or appertaining to such country.

(b) DESIGNATION OF TRUSTEES.—

(1) IN GENERAL.—The President, or the authorized representative of any State, Indian tribe, or foreign government, shall act on behalf of the public, Indian tribe, or foreign country as trustee of natural resources to present a claim for and to recover damages to the natural resources.

(2) FEDERAL TRUSTEES.—The President shall designate the Federal officials who shall act on behalf of the public as trustees for natural resources under this Act.

(3) STATE TRUSTEES.—The Governor of each State shall designate State and local officials who may act on behalf of the public as trustee for natural resources under this Act and shall notify the President of the designation.

(4) INDIAN TRIBE TRUSTEES.—The governing body of any Indian tribe shall designate tribal officials who may act on behalf of the tribe or its members as trustee for natural resources under this Act and shall notify the President of the designation.

(5) FOREIGN TRUSTEES.—The head of any foreign government may designate the trustee who shall act on behalf of that government as trustee for natural resources under this Act.

(c) FUNCTIONS OF TRUSTEES.—

(1) FEDERAL TRUSTEES.—The Federal officials designated under subsection (b)(2)—

(A) shall assess natural resource damages under section 1002(b)(2)(A) for the natural resources under their trusteeship;

(B) may, upon request of and reimbursement from a

State or Indian tribe and at the Federal officials' discretion, assess damages for the natural resources under the State's or tribe's trusteeship; and

(C) shall develop and implement a plan for the restoration, rehabilitation, replacement, or acquisition of the equivalent, of the natural resources under their trusteeship.

(2) STATE TRUSTEES.—The State and local officials designated under subsection (b)(3)—

(A) shall assess natural resource damages under section 1002(b)(2)(A) for the purposes of this Act for the natural resources under their trusteeship; and

(B) shall develop and implement a plan for the restoration, rehabilitation, replacement, or acquisition of the equivalent, of the natural resources under their trusteeship.

(3) INDIAN TRIBE TRUSTEES.—The tribal officials designated under subsection (b)(4)—

(A) shall assess natural resource damages under section 1002(b)(2)(A) for the purposes of this Act for the natural resources under their trusteeship; and

(B) shall develop and implement a plan for the restoration, rehabilitation, replacement, or acquisition of the equivalent, of the natural resources under their trusteeship.

(4) FOREIGN TRUSTEES.—The trustees designated under subsection (b)(5)—

(A) shall assess natural resource damages under section 1002(b)(2)(A) for the purposes of this Act for the natural resources under their trusteeship; and

(B) shall develop and implement a plan for the restoration, rehabilitation, replacement, or acquisition of the equivalent, of the natural resources under their trusteeship.

(5) NOTICE AND OPPORTUNITY TO BE HEARD.—Plans shall be developed and implemented under this section only after adequate public notice, opportunity for a hearing, and consideration of all public comment.

(d) MEASURE OF DAMAGES.—

(1) IN GENERAL.—The measure of natural resource damages under section 1002(b)(2)(A) is—

(A) the cost of restoring, rehabilitating, replacing, or acquiring the equivalent of, the damaged natural resources;

(B) the diminution in value of those natural resources pending restoration; plus

(C) the reasonable cost of assessing those damages.

(2) DETERMINE COSTS WITH RESPECT TO PLANS.—Costs shall be determined under paragraph (1) with respect to plans adopted under subsection (c).

(3) NO DOUBLE RECOVERY.—There shall be no double recovery under this Act for natural resource damages, including with respect to the costs of damage assessment or restoration, rehabilitation, replacement, or acquisition for the same incident and natural resource.

(e) DAMAGE ASSESSMENT REGULATIONS.—

(1) REGULATIONS.—The President, acting through the Under Secretary of Commerce for Oceans and Atmosphere and in consultation with the Administrator of the Environmental Protection Agency, the Director of the United States Fish and Wildlife Service, and the heads of other affected agencies, not later than 2 years after the date of the enactment of this Act, shall promulgate regulations for the assessment of natural resource damages under section 1002(b)(2)(A) resulting from a discharge of oil for the purpose of this Act.

(2) REBUTTABLE PRESUMPTION.—Any determination or assessment of damages to natural resources for the purposes of this Act made under subsection (d) by a Federal, State, or Indian trustee in accordance with the regulations promulgated under paragraph (1) shall have the force and effect of a rebuttable presumption on behalf of the trustee in any administrative or judicial proceeding under this Act.

(f) USE OF RECOVERED SUMS.—Sums recovered under this Act by a Federal, State, Indian, or foreign trustee for natural resource damages under section 1002(b)(2)(A) shall be retained by the trustee in a revolving trust account, without further appropriation, for use only to reimburse or pay costs incurred by the trustee under subsection (c) with respect to the damaged natural resources. Any amounts in excess of those required for these reimbursements and costs shall be deposited in the Fund.

(g) COMPLIANCE.—Review of actions by any Federal official where there is alleged to be a failure of that official to perform a duty under this section that is not discretionary with that official may be had by any person in the district court in which the person resides or in which the alleged damage to natural resources occurred. The court may award costs of litigation (including reasonable attorney and expert witness fees) to any prevailing or substantially prevailing party. Nothing in this subsection shall restrict any right which any person may have to seek relief under any other provision of law.

[33 U.S.C. 2706]

SEC. 1007. RECOVERY BY FOREIGN CLAIMANTS.

(a) REQUIRED SHOWING BY FOREIGN CLAIMANTS.—

(1) IN GENERAL.—In addition to satisfying the other requirements of this Act, to recover removal costs or damages resulting from an incident a foreign claimant shall demonstrate that—

(A) the claimant has not been otherwise compensated for the removal costs or damages; and

(B) recovery is authorized by a treaty or executive agreement between the United States and the claimant's country, or the Secretary of State, in consultation with the Attorney General and other appropriate officials, has certified that the claimant's country provides a comparable remedy for United States claimants.

(2) EXCEPTIONS.—Paragraph (1)(B) shall not apply with respect to recovery by a resident of Canada in the case of an incident described in subsection (b)(4).

(b) DISCHARGES IN FOREIGN COUNTRIES.—A foreign claimant may make a claim for removal costs and damages resulting from a discharge, or substantial threat of a discharge, of oil in or on the territorial sea, internal waters, or adjacent shoreline of a foreign country, only if the discharge is from—

(1) an Outer Continental Shelf facility or a deepwater port;

(2) a vessel in the navigable waters;

(3) a vessel carrying oil as cargo between 2 places in the United States; or

(4) a tanker that received the oil at the terminal of the pipeline constructed under the Trans-Alaska Pipeline Authorization Act (43 U.S.C. 1651 et seq.), for transportation to a place in the United States, and the discharge or threat occurs prior to delivery of the oil to that place.

(c) FOREIGN CLAIMANT DEFINED.—In this section, the term "foreign claimant" means—

(1) a person residing in a foreign country;

(2) the government of a foreign country; and

(3) an agency or political subdivision of a foreign country.

[33 U.S.C. 2707]

SEC. 1008. RECOVERY BY RESPONSIBLE PARTY.

(a) IN GENERAL.—The responsible party for a vessel or facility from which oil is discharged, or which poses the substantial threat of a discharge of oil, may assert a claim for removal costs and damages under section 1013 only if the responsible party demonstrates that—

(1) the responsible party is entitled to a defense to liability under section 1003; or

(2) the responsible party is entitled to a limitation of liability under section 1004.

(b) EXTENT OF RECOVERY.—A responsible party who is entitled to a limitation of liability may assert a claim under section 1013 only to the extent that the sum of the removal costs and damages incurred by the responsible party plus the amounts paid by the responsible party, or by the guarantor on behalf of the responsible party, for claims asserted under section 1013 exceeds the amount to which the total of the liability under section 1002 and removal costs and damages incurred by, or on behalf of, the responsible party is limited under section 1004.

[33 U.S.C. 2708]

SEC. 1009. CONTRIBUTION.

A person may bring a civil action for contribution against any other person who is liable or potentially liable under this Act or another law. The action shall be brought in accordance with section

1017.

[33 U.S.C. 2709]

SEC. 1010. INDEMNIFICATION AGREEMENTS.

(a) AGREEMENTS NOT PROHIBITED.—Nothing in this Act prohibits any agreement to insure, hold harmless, or indemnify a party to such agreement for any liability under this Act.

(b) LIABILITY NOT TRANSFERRED.—No indemnification, hold harmless, or similar agreement or conveyance shall be effective to transfer liability imposed under this Act from a responsible party or from any person who may be liable for an incident under this Act to any other person.

(c) RELATIONSHIP TO OTHER CAUSES OF ACTION.—Nothing in this Act, including the provisions of subsection (b), bars a cause of action that a responsible party subject to liability under this Act, or a guarantor, has or would have, by reason of subrogation or otherwise, against any person.

[33 U.S.C. 2710]

SEC. 1011. CONSULTATION ON REMOVAL ACTIONS.

The President shall consult with the affected trustees designated under section 1006 on the appropriate removal action to be taken in connection with any discharge of oil. For the purposes of the National Contingency Plan, removal with respect to any discharge shall be considered completed when so determined by the President in consultation with the Governor or Governors of the affected States. However, this determination shall not preclude additional removal actions under applicable State law.

[33 U.S.C. 2711]

SEC. 1012. USES OF THE FUND.

(a) USES GENERALLY.—The Fund shall be available to the President for—

(1) the payment of removal costs, including the costs of monitoring removal actions, determined by the President to be consistent with the National Contingency Plan—

(A) by Federal authorities; or

(B) by a State, a political subdivision of a State, or an Indian tribe, pursuant to a cost-reimbursable agreement under subsection (d);

(2) the payment of costs incurred by Federal, State, or Indian tribe trustees in carrying out their functions under section 1006 for assessing natural resource damages and for developing and implementing plans for the restoration, rehabilitation, replacement, or acquisition of the equivalent of damaged resources determined by the President to be consistent with the National Contingency Plan;

(3) the payment of removal costs determined by the President to be consistent with the National Contingency Plan as a result of, and damages resulting from, a discharge, or a substantial threat of a discharge, of oil from a foreign offshore unit;

(4) the payment of claims in accordance with section 1013 for uncompensated removal costs determined by the President to be consistent with the National Contingency Plan or uncompensated damages, including, in the case of a spill of national significance that results in extraordinary Coast Guard claims processing activities, the administrative and personnel costs of the Coast Guard to process such claims (including the costs of commercial claims processing, expert services, training, and technical services), subject to the condition that the Coast Guard shall submit to Congress a report describing each spill of national significance not later than 30 days after the date on which the Coast Guard determines it necessary to process such claims; and

(5) the payment of Federal administrative, operational, and personnel costs and expenses reasonably necessary for and incidental to the implementation, administration, and enforcement of this Act (including, but not limited to, sections 1004(d)(2), 1006(e), 4107, 4110, 4111, 4112, 4117, 5006, 8103, and title VII) and subsections (b), (c), (d), (j), and (l) of section 311 of the Federal Water Pollution Control Act (33 U.S.C. 1321), as amended by this Act, with respect to prevention, removal, and enforcement related to oil discharges, provided that—

(A) not more than $25,000,000 in each fiscal year shall be available to the Secretary for operations and support incurred by the Coast Guard;

(B) not more than $15,000,000 in each fiscal year shall be available to the Under Secretary of Commerce for

Oceans and Atmosphere for expenses incurred by, and activities related to, response and damage assessment capabilities of the National Oceanic and Atmospheric Administration;

(C) not more than $30,000,000 each year through the end of fiscal year 1992 shall be available to establish the National Response System under section 311(j) of the Federal Water Pollution Control Act, as amended by this Act, including the purchase and prepositioning of oil spill removal equipment; and

(D) not more than $27,250,000 in each fiscal year shall be available to carry out title VII of this Act.

(b) DEFENSE TO LIABILITY FOR FUND.—

(1) IN GENERAL.—The Fund shall not be available to pay any claim for removal costs or damages to a particular claimant, to the extent that the incident, removal costs, or damages are caused by the gross negligence or willful misconduct of that claimant.

(2) SUBROGATED RIGHTS.—Except for a guarantor claim pursuant to a defense under section 1016(f)(1), Fund compensation of any claim by an insurer or other indemnifier of a responsible party or injured third party is subject to the subrogated rights of that responsible party or injured third party to such compensation.

(c) OBLIGATION OF FUND BY FEDERAL OFFICIALS.—The President may promulgate regulations designating one or more Federal officials who may obligate money in accordance with subsection (a).

(d) COST-REIMBURSABLE AGREEMENT.—

(1) IN GENERAL.—In carrying out section 311(c) of the Federal Water Pollution Control Act (33 U.S.C. 1321(c)), the President may enter into cost-reimbursable agreements with a State, a political subdivision of a State, or an Indian tribe to obligate the Fund for the payment of removal costs consistent with the National Contingency Plan.

(2) INAPPLICABILITY.—Chapter 63 and section 1535 of title 31, United States Code shall not apply to a cost-reimbursable agreement entered into under this subsection.

(e) RIGHTS OF SUBROGATION.—Payment of any claim or

obligation by the Fund under this Act shall be subject to the United States Government acquiring by subrogation all rights of the claimant or State to recover from the responsible party.

(f) PERIOD OF LIMITATIONS FOR CLAIMS.—

(1) REMOVAL COSTS.—No claim may be presented under this title for recovery of removal costs for an incident unless the claim is presented within 6 years after the date of completion of all removal actions for that incident.

(2) DAMAGES.—No claim may be presented under this section for recovery of damages unless the claim is presented within 3 years after the date on which the injury and its connection with the discharge in question were reasonably discoverable with the exercise of due care, or in the case of natural resource damages under section 1002(b)(2)(A), if later, the date of completion of the natural resources damage assessment under section 1006(e).

(3) MINORS AND INCOMPETENTS.—The time limitations contained in this subsection shall not begin to run—

(A) against a minor until the earlier of the date when such minor reaches 18 years of age or the date on which a legal representative is duly appointed for the minor, or

(B) against an incompetent person until the earlier of the date on which such incompetent's incompetency ends or the date on which a legal representative is duly appointed for the incompetent.

(g) LIMITATION ON PAYMENT FOR SAME COSTS.—In any case in which the President has paid an amount from the Fund for any removal costs or damages specified under subsection (a), no other claim may be paid from the Fund for the same removal costs or damages.

(h) OBLIGATION IN ACCORDANCE WITH PLAN.—

(1) IN GENERAL.—Except as provided in paragraph (2), amounts may be obligated from the Fund for the restoration, rehabilitation, replacement, or acquisition of natural resources only in accordance with a plan adopted under section 1006(c).

(2) EXCEPTION.—Paragraph (1) shall not apply in a situation requiring action to avoid irreversible loss of natural resources or to prevent or reduce any continuing danger to natural resources or similar need for emergency action.

(i) PREFERENCE FOR PRIVATE PERSONS IN AREA AFFECTED BY DISCHARGE.—

(1) IN GENERAL.—In the expenditure of Federal funds for removal of oil, including for distribution of supplies, construction, and other reasonable and appropriate activities, under a contract or agreement with a private person, preference shall be given, to the extent feasible and practicable, to private persons residing or doing business primarily in the area affected by the discharge of oil.

(2) LIMITATION.—This subsection shall not be considered to restrict the use of Department of Defense resources.

(j) REPORTS.—

(1) IN GENERAL.—Each year, on the date on which the President submits to Congress a budget under section 1105 of title 31, United States Code, the President, through the Secretary of the Department in which the Coast Guard is operating, shall—

(A) provide a report on disbursements for the preceding fiscal year from the Fund, regardless of whether those disbursements were subject to annual appropriations, to—

(i) the Senate Committee on Commerce, Science, and Transportation; and

(ii) the House of Representatives Committee on Transportation and Infrastructure; and

(B) make the report available to the public on the National Pollution Funds Center Internet website.

(2) CONTENTS.—The report shall include—

(A) a list of each incident that—

(i) occurred in the preceding fiscal year; and

(ii) resulted in disbursements from the Fund, for removal costs and damages, totaling $500,000 or more;

(B) a list of each incident that—

(i) occurred in the fiscal year preceding the preceding fiscal year; and

(ii) resulted in disbursements from the Fund, for removal costs and damages, totaling $500,000 or more;

and

(C) an accounting of any amounts reimbursed to the Fund in the preceding fiscal year that were recovered from a responsible party for an incident that resulted in disbursements from the Fund, for removal costs and damages, totaling $500,000 or more.

(3) AGENCY RECORDKEEPING.—Each Federal agency that receives amounts from the Fund shall maintain records describing the purposes for which such funds were obligated or expended in such detail as the Secretary may require for purposes of the report required under paragraph (1).

[33 U.S.C. 2712]

SEC. 1013. CLAIMS PROCEDURE.

(a) PRESENTATION.—Except as provided in subsection (b), all claims for removal costs or damages shall be presented first to the responsible party or guarantor of the source designated under section 1014(a).

(b) PRESENTATION TO FUND.—

(1) IN GENERAL.—Claims for removal costs or damages may be presented first to the Fund—

(A) if the President has advertised or otherwise notified claimants in accordance with section 1014(c);

(B) by a responsible party who may assert a claim under section 1008;

(C) by the Governor of a State for removal costs incurred by that State; or

(D) by a United States claimant in a case where a foreign offshore unit has discharged oil causing damage for which the Fund is liable under section 1012(a).

(2) LIMITATION ON PRESENTING CLAIM.—No claim of a person against the Fund may be approved or certified during the pendency of an action by the person in court to recover costs which are the subject of the claim.

(c) ELECTION.—If a claim is presented in accordance with subsection (a) and—

(1) each person to whom the claim is presented denies all liability for the claim, or

(2) the claim is not settled by any person by payment within 90 days after the date upon which (A) the claim was presented, or (B) advertising was begun pursuant to section 1014(b), whichever is later,

the claimant may elect to commence an action in court against the responsible party or guarantor or to present the claim to the Fund.

(d) UNCOMPENSATED DAMAGES.—If a claim is presented in accordance with this section, including a claim for interim, short-term damages representing less than the full amount of damages to which the claimant ultimately may be entitled, and full and adequate compensation is unavailable, a claim for the uncompensated damages and removal costs may be presented to the Fund.

(e) PROCEDURE FOR CLAIMS AGAINST FUND.—The President shall promulgate, and may from time to time amend, regulations for the presentation, filing, processing, settlement, and adjudication of claims under this Act against the Fund.

[33 U.S.C. 2713]

SEC. 1014. DESIGNATION OF SOURCE AND ADVERTISEMENT.

(a) DESIGNATION OF SOURCE AND NOTIFICATION.—When the President receives information of an incident, the President shall, where possible and appropriate, designate the source or sources of the discharge or threat. If a designated source is a vessel or a facility, the President shall immediately notify the responsible party and the guarantor, if known, of that designation.

(b) ADVERTISEMENT BY RESPONSIBLE PARTY OR GUARANTOR.—(1) If a responsible party or guarantor fails to inform the President, within 5 days after receiving notification of a designation under subsection (a), of the party's or the guarantor's denial of the designation, such party or guarantor shall advertise the designation and the procedures by which claims may be presented, in accordance with regulations promulgated by the President. Advertisement under the preceding sentence shall begin no later than 15 days after the date of the designation made under subsection (a). If advertisement is not otherwise made in accordance with this subsection, the President shall promptly and at the expense of the responsible party or the guarantor involved, advertise the designation and the procedures by which claims may be presented to the responsible party or guarantor. Advertisement under this subsection shall continue for a period of no less than 30 days.

(2) An advertisement under paragraph (1) shall state that a claimant may present a claim for interim, short-term damages representing less than the full amount of damages to which the claimant ultimately may be entitled and that payment of such a claim shall not preclude recovery for damages not reflected in the paid or settled partial claim.

(c) ADVERTISEMENT BY PRESIDENT.—If—

(1) the responsible party and the guarantor both deny a designation within 5 days after receiving notification of a designation under subsection (a),

(2) the source of the discharge or threat was a public vessel, or

(3) the President is unable to designate the source or sources of the discharge or threat under subsection (a),

the President shall advertise or otherwise notify potential claimants of the procedures by which claims may be presented to the Fund.

[33 U.S.C. 2714]

SEC. 1015. SUBROGATION.[2]

(a) IN GENERAL.—Any person, including the Fund, who pays compensation pursuant to this Act to any claimant for removal costs or damages shall be subrogated to all rights, claims, and causes of action that the claimant has under any other law.

---

[2]   Section 1142(d) of Public Law 104–324 (110 Stat. 3991) stated that "[s]ection 1015(a) of the Oil Pollution Act of 1990 (33 U.S.C. 2715(a)) is amended" by redesignating subsection (b) as subsection (c) and by inserting after subsection (a) a new subsection (b). The amendments were executed as amendments to section 1015.

(b) INTERIM DAMAGES.—

(1) IN GENERAL.—If a responsible party, a guarantor, or the Fund has made payment to a claimant for interim, short-term damages representing less than the full amount of damages to which the claimant ultimately may be entitled, subrogation under subsection (a) shall apply only with respect to the portion of the claim reflected in the paid interim claim.

(2) FINAL DAMAGES.—Payment of such a claim shall not

foreclose a claimant's right to recovery of all damages to which the claimant otherwise is entitled under this Act or under any other law.

(c) ACTIONS ON BEHALF OF FUND.—At the request of the Secretary, the Attorney General shall commence an action on behalf of the Fund to recover any compensation paid by the Fund to any claimant pursuant to this Act, and all costs incurred by the Fund by reason of the claim, including interest (including prejudgment interest), administrative and adjudicative costs, and attorney's fees. Such an action may be commenced against any responsible party or (subject to section 1016) guarantor, or against any other person who is liable, pursuant to any law, to the compensated claimant or to the Fund, for the cost or damages for which the compensation was paid. Such an action shall be commenced against the responsible foreign government or other responsible party to recover any removal costs or damages paid from the Fund as the result of the discharge, or substantial threat of discharge, of oil from a foreign offshore unit or other facility located seaward of the exclusive economic zone.

(d) AUTHORITY TO SETTLE.—The head of any department or agency responsible for recovering amounts for which a person is liable under this title may consider, compromise, and settle a claim for such amounts, including such costs paid from the Fund, if the claim has not been referred to the Attorney General. In any case in which the total amount to be recovered may exceed $500,000 (excluding interest), a claim may be compromised and settled under the preceding sentence only with the prior written approval of the Attorney General.

[33 U.S.C. 2715]

SEC. 1016. FINANCIAL RESPONSIBILITY.

(a) REQUIREMENT.—The responsible party for—

(1) any vessel over 300 gross tons (except a non-self-propelled vessel that does not carry oil as cargo or fuel) using any place subject to the jurisdiction of the United States;

(2) any vessel using the waters of the exclusive economic zone to transship or lighter oil destined for a place subject to the jurisdiction of the United States; or

(3) any tank vessel over 100 gross tons using any place subject to the jurisdiction of the United States;

shall establish and maintain, in accordance with regulations promulgated by the Secretary, evidence of financial responsibility sufficient to meet the maximum amount of liability to which the responsible party could be subjected under section 1004(a) or (d) of this Act, in a case where the responsible party would be entitled to limit liability under that section. If the responsible party owns or operates more than one vessel, evidence of financial responsibility need be established only to meet the amount of the maximum liability applicable to the vessel having the greatest maximum liability.

(b) SANCTIONS.—

(1) WITHHOLDING CLEARANCE.—The Secretary of the Treasury shall withhold or revoke the clearance required by section 4197 of the Revised Statutes of the United States of any vessel subject to this section that does not have the evidence of financial responsibility required for the vessel under this section.

(2) DENYING ENTRY TO OR DETAINING VESSELS.—The Secretary may—

(A) deny entry to any vessel to any place in the United States, or to the navigable waters, or

(B) detain at the place,

any vessel that, upon request, does not produce the evidence of financial responsibility required for the vessel under this section.

(3) SEIZURE OF VESSEL.—Any vessel subject to the requirements of this section which is found in the navigable waters without the necessary evidence of financial responsibility for the vessel shall be subject to seizure by and forfeiture to the United States.

(c) OFFSHORE FACILITIES.—

(1) IN GENERAL.—

(A) EVIDENCE OF FINANCIAL RESPONSIBILITY REQUIRED.—Except as provided in paragraph (2), a responsible party with respect to an offshore facility that—

(i)(I) is located seaward of the line of ordinary low water along that portion of the coast that is in direct contact with the open sea and the line marking the seaward limit of inland waters; or

>> (II) is located in coastal inland waters, such as bays or estuaries, seaward of the line of ordinary low water along that portion of the coast that is not in direct contact with the open sea;

> (ii) is used for exploring for, drilling for, producing, or transporting oil from facilities engaged in oil exploration, drilling, or production; and

> (iii) has a worst-case oil spill discharge potential of more than 1,000 barrels of oil (or a lesser amount if the President determines that the risks posed by such facility justify it),

shall establish and maintain evidence of financial responsibility in the amount required under subparagraph (B) or (C), as applicable.

(B) AMOUNT REQUIRED GENERALLY.—Except as provided in subparagraph (C), the amount of financial responsibility for offshore facilities that meet the criteria of subparagraph (A) is—

> (i) $35,000,000 for an offshore facility located seaward of the seaward boundary of a State; or

> (ii) $10,000,000 for an offshore facility located landward of the seaward boundary of a State.

(C) GREATER AMOUNT.—If the President determines that an amount of financial responsibility for a responsible party greater than the amount required by subparagraph (B) is justified based on the relative operational, environmental, human health, and other risks posed by the quantity or quality of oil that is explored for, drilled for, produced, or transported by the responsible party, the evidence of financial responsibility required shall be for an amount determined by the President not exceeding $150,000,000.

(D) MULTIPLE FACILITIES.—In a case in which a person is a responsible party for more than one facility subject to this subsection, evidence of financial responsibility need be established only to meet the amount applicable to the facility having the greatest financial responsibility requirement under this subsection.

(E) DEFINITION.—For the purpose of this paragraph, the seaward boundary of a State shall be determined in accordance with section 2(b) of the Submerged Lands Act (43 U.S.C. 1301(b)).

(2) DEEPWATER PORTS.—Each responsible party with respect to a deepwater port shall establish and maintain evidence of financial responsibility sufficient to meet the maximum amount of liability to which the responsible party could be subjected under section 1004(a) of this Act in a case where the responsible party would be entitled to limit liability under that section. If the Secretary exercises the authority under section 1004(d)(2) to lower the limit of liability for deepwater ports, the responsible party shall establish and maintain evidence of financial responsibility sufficient to meet the maximum amount of liability so established. In a case in which a person is the responsible party for more than one deepwater port, evidence of financial responsibility need be established only to meet the maximum liability applicable to the deepwater port having the greatest maximum liability.

(e) METHODS OF FINANCIAL RESPONSIBILITY.—Financial responsibility under this section may be established by any one, or by any combination, of the following methods which the Secretary (in the case of a vessel) or the President (in the case of a facility) determines to be acceptable: evidence of insurance, surety bond, guarantee, letter of credit, qualification as a self-insurer, or other evidence of financial responsibility. Any bond filed shall be issued by a bonding company authorized to do business in the United States. In promulgating requirements under this section, the Secretary or the President, as appropriate, may specify policy or other contractual terms, conditions, or defenses which are necessary, or which are unacceptable, in establishing evidence of financial responsibility to effectuate the purposes of this Act.

(f) CLAIMS AGAINST GUARANTOR.—

(1) IN GENERAL.—Subject to paragraph (2), a claim for which liability may be established under section 1002 may be asserted directly against any guarantor providing evidence of financial responsibility for a responsible party liable under that section for removal costs and damages to which the claim pertains. In defending against such a claim, the guarantor may invoke—

(A) all rights and defenses which would be available to the responsible party under this Act;

(B) any defense authorized under subsection (e); and

(C) the defense that the incident was caused by the willful misconduct of the responsible party.

The guarantor may not invoke any other defense that might be available in proceedings brought by the responsible party against the guarantor.

(2) FURTHER REQUIREMENT.—A claim may be asserted pursuant to paragraph (1) directly against a guarantor providing evidence of financial responsibility under subsection (c)(1) with respect to an offshore facility only if—

(A) the responsible party for whom evidence of financial responsibility has been provided has denied or failed to pay a claim under this Act on the basis of being insolvent, as defined under section 101(32) of title 11, United States Code, and applying generally accepted accounting principles;

(B) the responsible party for whom evidence of financial responsibility has been provided has filed a petition for bankruptcy under title 11, United States Code; or

(C) the claim is asserted by the United States for removal costs and damages or for compensation paid by the Fund under this Act, including costs incurred by the Fund for processing compensation claims.

(3) RULEMAKING AUTHORITY.—Not later than 1 year after the date of enactment of this paragraph, the President shall promulgate regulations to establish a process for implementing paragraph (2) in a manner that will allow for the orderly and expeditious presentation and resolution of claims and effectuate the purposes of this Act.

(g) LIMITATION ON GUARANTOR'S LIABILITY.—Nothing in this Act shall impose liability with respect to an incident on any guarantor for damages or removal costs which exceed, in the aggregate, the amount of financial responsibility which that guarantor has provided for a responsible party pursuant to this section. The total liability of the guarantor on direct action for claims brought under this Act with respect to an incident shall be limited to that amount.

(h) CONTINUATION OF REGULATIONS.—Any regulation relating to financial responsibility, which has been issued pursuant to any provision of law repealed or superseded by this Act, and which is in effect on the date immediately preceding the effective date of this Act, is deemed and shall be construed to be a regulation issued pursuant to this section. Such a regulation shall remain in full force and effect unless and until superseded by a new regulation issued under this section.

(i) UNIFIED CERTIFICATE.—The Secretary may issue a single unified certificate of financial responsibility for purposes of this Act and any other law.

[33 U.S.C. 2716]

SEC. 1017. LITIGATION, JURISDICTION, AND VENUE.

(a) REVIEW OF REGULATIONS.—Review of any regulation promulgated under this Act may be had upon application by any interested person only in the Circuit Court of Appeals of the United States for the District of Columbia. Any such application shall be made within 90 days from the date of promulgation of such regulations. Any matter with respect to which review could have been obtained under this subsection shall not be subject to judicial review in any civil or criminal proceeding for enforcement or to obtain damages or recovery of response costs.

(b) JURISDICTION.—Except as provided in subsections (a) and (c), the United States district courts shall have exclusive original jurisdiction over all controversies arising under this Act, without regard to the citizenship of the parties or the amount in controversy. Venue shall lie in any district in which the discharge or injury or damages occurred, or in which the defendant resides, may be found, has its principal office, or has appointed an agent for service of process. For the purposes of this section, the Fund shall reside in the District of Columbia.

(c) STATE COURT JURISDICTION.—A State trial court of competent jurisdiction over claims for removal costs or damages, as defined under this Act, may consider claims under this Act or State law and any final judgment of such court (when no longer subject to ordinary forms of review) shall be recognized, valid, and enforceable for all purposes of this Act.

(d) ASSESSMENT AND COLLECTION OF TAX.—The provisions of

subsections (a), (b), and (c) shall not apply to any controversy or other matter resulting from the assessment or collection of any tax, or to the review of any regulation promulgated under the Internal Revenue Code of 1986.

(e) SAVINGS PROVISION.—Nothing in this title shall apply to any cause of action or right of recovery arising from any incident which occurred prior to the date of enactment of this title. Such claims shall be adjudicated pursuant to the law applicable on the date of the incident.

(f) PERIOD OF LIMITATIONS.—

(1) DAMAGES.—Except as provided in paragraphs (3) and (4), an action for damages under this Act shall be barred unless the action is brought within 3 years after—

(A) the date on which the loss and the connection of the loss with the discharge in question are reasonably discoverable with the exercise of due care, or

(B) in the case of natural resource damages under section 1002(b)(2)(A), the date of completion of the natural resources damage assessment under section 1006(c).

(2) REMOVAL COSTS.—An action for recovery of removal costs referred to in section 1002(b)(1) must be commenced within 3 years after completion of the removal action. In any such action described in this subsection, the court shall enter a declaratory judgment on liability for removal costs or damages that will be binding on any subsequent action or actions to recover further removal costs or damages. Except as otherwise provided in this paragraph, an action may be commenced under this title for recovery of removal costs at any time after such costs have been incurred.

(3) CONTRIBUTION.—No action for contribution for any removal costs or damages may be commenced more than 3 years after—

(A) the date of judgment in any action under this Act for recovery of such costs or damages, or

(B) the date of entry of a judicially approved settlement with respect to such costs or damages.

(4) SUBROGATION.—No action based on rights subrogated pursuant to this Act by reason of payment of a claim may be commenced under this Act more than 3 years after the date of

payment of such claim.

(5) COMMENCEMENT.—The time limitations contained herein shall not begin to run—

(A) against a minor until the earlier of the date when such minor reaches 18 years of age or the date on which a legal representative is duly appointed for such minor, or

(B) against an incompetent person until the earlier of the date on which such incompetent's incompetency ends or the date on which a legal representative is duly appointed for such incompetent.

[33 U.S.C. 2717]

SEC. 1018. RELATIONSHIP TO OTHER LAW.

(a) PRESERVATION OF STATE AUTHORITIES; SOLID WASTE DISPOSAL ACT.—Nothing in this Act or the Act of March 3, 1851 shall—

(1) affect, or be construed or interpreted as preempting, the authority of any State or political subdivision thereof from imposing any additional liability or requirements with respect to—

(A) the discharge of oil or other pollution by oil within such State; or

(B) any removal activities in connection with such a discharge; or

(2) affect, or be construed or interpreted to affect or modify in any way the obligations or liabilities of any person under the Solid Waste Disposal Act (42 U.S.C. 6901 et seq.) or State law, including common law.

(b) PRESERVATION OF STATE FUNDS.—Nothing in this Act or in section 9509 of the Internal Revenue Code of 1986 (26 U.S.C. 9509) shall in any way affect, or be construed to affect, the authority of any State—

(1) to establish, or to continue in effect, a fund any purpose of which is to pay for costs or damages arising out of, or directly resulting from, oil pollution or the substantial threat of oil pollution; or

(2) to require any person to contribute to such a fund.

(c) ADDITIONAL REQUIREMENTS AND LIABILITIES;

PENALTIES.—Nothing in this Act, the Act of March 3, 1851 (46 U.S.C. 183 et seq.), or section 9509 of the Internal Revenue Code of 1986 (26 U.S.C. 9509), shall in any way affect, or be construed to affect, the authority of the United States or any State or political subdivision thereof—

(1) to impose additional liability or additional requirements; or

(2) to impose, or to determine the amount of, any fine or penalty (whether criminal or civil in nature) for any violation of law;

relating to the discharge, or substantial threat of a discharge, of oil.

(d) FEDERAL EMPLOYEE LIABILITY.—For purposes of section 2679(b)(2)(B) of title 28, United States Code, nothing in this Act shall be construed to authorize or create a cause of action against a Federal officer or employee in the officer's or employee's personal or individual capacity for any act or omission while acting within the scope of the officer's or employee's office or employment.

[33 U.S.C. 2718]

SEC. 1019. STATE FINANCIAL RESPONSIBILITY.

A State may enforce, on the navigable waters of the State, the requirements for evidence of financial responsibility under section 1016.

[33 U.S.C. 2719]

SEC. 1020. APPLICATION.

This Act shall apply to an incident occurring after the date of the enactment of this Act.

[33 U.S.C. 2701 note]

TITLE II—CONFORMING AMENDMENTS

* * * * * * *

SEC. 2002. FEDERAL WATER POLLUTION CONTROL ACT.

(a) APPLICATION.—Subsections (f), (g), (h), and (i) of section 311 of the Federal Water Pollution Control Act (33 U.S.C. 1321) shall not apply with respect to any incident for which liability is established under section 1002 of this Act.

(b)

* * *

[33 U.S.C. 1321 note]

SEC. 2003. DEEPWATER PORT ACT.

(a)

* * *

(b) AMOUNTS REMAINING IN DEEPWATER PORT FUND.—Any amounts remaining in the Deepwater Port Liability Fund established under section 18(f) of the Deepwater Port Act of 1974 (33 U.S.C. 1517(f)) shall be deposited in the Oil Spill Liability Trust Fund established under section 9509 of the Internal Revenue Code of 1986 (26 U.S.C. 9509). The Oil Spill Liability Trust Fund shall assume all liability incurred by the Deepwater Port Liability Fund.

[26 U.S.C. 9509 note]

SEC. 2004. OUTER CONTINENTAL SHELF LANDS ACT AMENDMENTS OF 1978.

Title III of the Outer Continental Shelf Lands Act Amendments of 1978 (43 U.S.C. 1811–1824) is repealed. Any amounts remaining in the Offshore Oil Pollution Compensation Fund established under section 302 of that title (43 U.S.C. 1812) shall be deposited in the Oil Spill Liability Trust Fund established under section 9509 of the Internal Revenue Code of 1986 (26 U.S.C. 9509). The Oil Spill Liability Trust Fund shall assume all liability incurred by the Offshore Oil Pollution Compensation Fund.

[26 U.S.C. 9509 note]

TITLE III—INTERNATIONAL OIL POLLUTION PREVENTION AND REMOVAL

SEC. 3001. SENSE OF CONGRESS REGARDING PARTICIPATION IN INTERNATIONAL REGIME.

It is the sense of the Congress that it is in the best interests of the United States to participate in an international oil pollution liability and compensation regime that is at least as effective as Federal and State laws in preventing incidents and in guaranteeing full and prompt compensation for damages resulting from incidents.

SEC. 3002. UNITED STATES-CANADA GREAT LAKES OIL SPILL COOPERATION.

(a) REVIEW.—The Secretary of State shall review relevant international agreements and treaties with the Government of Canada, including the Great Lakes Water Quality Agreement, to determine whether amendments or additional international agreements are necessary to—

(1) prevent discharges of oil on the Great Lakes;

(2) ensure an immediate and effective removal of oil on the Great Lakes; and

(3) fully compensate those who are injured by a discharge of oil on the Great Lakes.

(b) CONSULTATION.—In carrying out this section, the Secretary of State shall consult with the Department of Transportation, the Environmental Protection Agency, the National Oceanic and Atmospheric Administration, the Great Lakes States, the International Joint Commission, and other appropriate agencies.

(c) REPORT.—The Secretary of State shall submit a report to the Congress on the results of the review under this section within 6 months after the date of the enactment of this Act.

SEC. 3003. UNITED STATES-CANADA LAKE CHAMPLAIN OIL SPILL COOPERATION.

(a) REVIEW.—The Secretary of State shall review relevant international agreements and treaties with the Government of Canada, to determine whether amendments or additional international agreements are necessary to—

(1) prevent discharges of oil on Lake Champlain;

(2) ensure an immediate and effective removal of oil on Lake Champlain; and

(3) fully compensate those who are injured by a discharge of oil on Lake Champlain.

(b) CONSULTATION.—In carrying out this section, the Secretary of State shall consult with the Department of Transportation, the Environmental Protection Agency, the National Oceanic and Atmospheric Administration, the States of Vermont and New York, the International Joint Commission, and other appropriate agencies.

(c) REPORT.—The Secretary of State shall submit a report to the Congress on the results of the review under this section within 6 months after the date of the enactment of this Act.

SEC. 3004. INTERNATIONAL INVENTORY OF REMOVAL EQUIPMENT AND PERSONNEL.

The President shall encourage appropriate international organizations to establish an international inventory of spill removal equipment and personnel.

SEC. 3005. NEGOTIATIONS WITH CANADA CONCERNING TUG ESCORTS IN PUGET SOUND.

Congress urges the Secretary of State to enter into negotiations with the Government of Canada to ensure that tugboat escorts are required for all tank vessels with a capacity over 40,000 deadweight tons in the Strait of Juan de Fuca and in Haro Strait.

TITLE IV—PREVENTION AND REMOVAL

Subtitle A—Prevention

* * * * * * *

SEC. 4102. TERM OF LICENSES, CERTIFICATES OF REGISTRY, AND MERCHANT MARINERS' DOCUMENTS; CRIMINAL RECORD REVIEWS IN RENEWALS.

(a)

* * *

* * * * * * *

(d) TERMINATION OF EXISTING LICENSES, CERTIFICATES, AND DOCUMENTS.—A license, certificate of registry, or merchant mariner's document issued before the date of the enactment of this section terminates on the day it would have expired if—

(1) subsections (a), (b), and (c) were in effect on the date it was issued; and

(2) it was renewed at the end of each 5-year period under section 7106, 7107, or 7302 of title 46, United States Code.

[46 U.S.C. 7106 note]

* * * * * * *

SEC. 4107. VESSEL TRAFFIC SERVICE SYSTEMS.

(a)

* * *

(b) DIRECTION OF VESSEL MOVEMENT.—

(1) STUDY.—The Secretary shall conduct a study—

(A) of whether the Secretary should be given additional authority to direct the movement of vessels on navigable waters and should exercise such authority; and

(B) to determine and prioritize the United States ports and channels that are in need of new, expanded, or improved vessel traffic service systems, by evaluating—

(i) the nature, volume, and frequency of vessel traffic;

(ii) the risks of collisions, spills, and damages associated with that traffic;

(iii) the impact of installation, expansion, or improvement of a vessel traffic service system; and

(iv) all other relevant costs and data.

(2) REPORT.—Not later than 1 year after the date of the enactment of this Act, the Secretary shall submit to the Congress a report on the results of the study conducted under paragraph (1) and recommendations for implementing the results of that study.

* * * * * * *

SEC. 4109. PERIODIC GAUGING OF PLATING THICKNESS OF COMMERCIAL VESSELS.

Not later than 1 year after the date of the enactment of this Act, the Secretary shall issue regulations for vessels constructed or adapted to carry, or that carry, oil in bulk as cargo or cargo residue—

(1) establishing minimum standards for plating thickness; and

(2) requiring, consistent with generally recognized

principles of international law, periodic gauging of the plating thickness of all such vessels over 30 years old operating on the navigable waters or the waters of the exclusive economic zone.

[46 U.S.C. 3703 note]

SEC. 4110. OVERFILL AND TANK LEVEL OR PRESSURE MONITORING DEVICES.

(a) STANDARDS.—The Secretary may establish, by regulation, minimum standards for devices for warning persons of overfills and tank levels of oil in cargo tanks and devices for monitoring the pressure of oil cargo tanks.

(b) USE.—No sooner than 1 year after the Secretary prescribes regulations under subsection (a), the Secretary may issue regulations establishing, consistent with generally recognized principles of international law, requirements concerning the use of—

(1) overfill devices, and

(2) tank level or pressure monitoring devices,

which are referred to in subsection (a) and which meet any standards established by the Secretary under subsection (a), on vessels constructed or adapted to carry, or that carry, oil in bulk as cargo or cargo residue on the navigable waters and the waters of the exclusive economic zone.

[46 U.S.C. 3703 note]

SEC. 4111. STUDY ON TANKER NAVIGATION SAFETY STANDARDS.

(a) IN GENERAL.— Not later than 1 year after the date of enactment of this Act, the Secretary shall initiate a study to determine whether existing laws and regulations are adequate to ensure the safe navigation of vessels transporting oil or hazardous substances in bulk on the navigable waters and the waters of the exclusive economic zone.

(b) CONTENT.—In conducting the study required under subsection (a), the Secretary shall—

(1) determine appropriate crew sizes on tankers;

(2) evaluate the adequacy of qualifications and training of crewmembers on tankers;

(3) evaluate the ability of crewmembers on tankers to take emergency actions to prevent or remove a discharge of oil or a

hazardous substance from their tankers;

(4) evaluate the adequacy of navigation equipment and systems on tankers (including sonar, electronic chart display, and satellite technology);

(5) evaluate and test electronic means of position-reporting and identification on tankers, consider the minimum standards suitable for equipment for that purpose, and determine whether to require that equipment on tankers;

(6) evaluate the adequacy of navigation procedures under different operating conditions, including such variables as speed, daylight, ice, tides, weather, and other conditions;

(7) evaluate whether areas of navigable waters and the exclusive economic zone should be designated as zones where the movement of tankers should be limited or prohibited;

(8) evaluate whether inspection standards are adequate;

(9) review and incorporate the results of past studies, including studies conducted by the Coast Guard and the Office of Technology Assessment;

(10) evaluate the use of computer simulator courses for training bridge officers and pilots of vessels transporting oil or hazardous substances on the navigable waters and waters of the exclusive economic zone, and determine the feasibility and practicality of mandating such training;

(11) evaluate the size, cargo capacity, and flag nation of tankers transporting oil or hazardous substances on the navigable waters and the waters of the exclusive economic zone—

(A) identifying changes occurring over the past 20 years in such size and cargo capacity and in vessel navigation and technology; and

(B) evaluating the extent to which the risks or difficulties associated with tanker navigation, vessel traffic control, accidents, oil spills, and the containment and cleanup of such spills are influenced by or related to an increase in tanker size and cargo capacity; and

(12) evaluate and test a program of remote alcohol testing for masters and pilots aboard tankers carrying significant quantities of oil.

(c) REPORT.—Not later than 2 years after the date of enactment of this Act, the Secretary shall transmit to the Congress a report on the results of the study conducted under subsection (a), including recommendations for implementing the results of that study.

[46 U.S.C. 3703 note]

SEC. 4112. DREDGE MODIFICATION STUDY.

(a) STUDY.—The Secretary of the Army shall conduct a study and demonstration to determine the feasibility of modifying dredges to make them usable in removing discharges of oil and hazardous substances.

(b) REPORT.—Not later than 1 year after the date of enactment of this Act, the Secretary of the Army shall submit to the Congress a report on the results of the study conducted under subsection (a) and recommendations for implementing the results of that study.

SEC. 4113. USE OF LINERS.

(a) STUDY.—The President shall conduct a study to determine whether liners or other secondary means of containment should be used to prevent leaking or to aid in leak detection at onshore facilities used for the bulk storage of oil and located near navigable waters.

(b) REPORT.—Not later than 1 year after the date of enactment of this Act, the President shall submit to the Congress a report on the results of the study conducted under subsection (a) and recommendations to implement the results of the study.

(c) IMPLEMENTATION.—Not later than 6 months after the date the report required under subsection (b) is submitted to the Congress, the President shall implement the recommendations contained in the report.

SEC. 4114. TANK VESSEL MANNING.

(a) RULEMAKING.—In order to protect life, property, and the environment, the Secretary shall initiate a rulemaking proceeding within 180 days after the date of the enactment of this Act to define the conditions under, and designate the waters upon, which tank vessels subject to section 3703 of title 46, United States Code, may operate in the navigable waters with the auto-pilot engaged or with an unattended engine room.

(b)

* * *

* * * * * * *

[46 U.S.C. 3703 note]

SEC. 4115. ESTABLISHMENT OF DOUBLE HULL REQUIREMENT FOR TANK VESSELS.

(a)

* * *

(b) RULEMAKING.—The Secretary shall, within 12 months after the date of the enactment of this Act, complete a rulemaking proceeding and issue a final rule to require that tank vessels over 5,000 gross tons affected by section 3703a of title 46, United States Code, as added by this section, comply until January 1, 2015, with structural and operational requirements that the Secretary determines will provide as substantial protection to the environment as is economically and technologically feasible.

[46 U.S.C. 3703a note]

* * * * * * *

(e) SECRETARIAL STUDIES.—

(1) OTHER REQUIREMENTS.—Not later than 6 months after the date of enactment of this Act, the Secretary shall determine, based on recommendations from the National Academy of Sciences or other qualified organizations, whether other structural and operational tank vessel requirements will provide protection to the marine environment equal to or greater than that provided by double hulls, and shall report to the Congress that determination and recommendations for legislative action.

(2) REVIEW AND ASSESSMENT.—The Secretary shall—

(A) periodically review recommendations from the National Academy of Sciences and other qualified organizations on methods for further increasing the environmental and operational safety of tank vessels;

(B) not later than 5 years after the date of enactment of this Act, assess the impact of this section on the safety of the marine environment and the economic viability and operational makeup of the maritime oil transportation industry; and

(C) report the results of the review and assessment to the Congress with recommendations for legislative or other action.

(3) No later than one year after the date of enactment of the Coast Guard and Maritime Transportation Act of 2004, the Secretary shall, taking into account the recommendations contained in the report by the Marine Board of the National Research Council entitled "Environmental Performance of Tanker Design in Collision and Grounding" and dated 2001, establish and publish an environmental equivalency evaluation index (including the methodology to develop that index) to assess overall outflow performance due to collisions and groundings for double hull tank vessels and alternative designs.

* * * * * * *

SEC. 4116. PILOTAGE.

(a)

* * *

* * * * * * *

(c) ESCORTS FOR CERTAIN TANKERS.—(1)[3] IN GENERAL.—The Secretary shall initiate issuance of regulations under section 3703(a)(3) of title 46, United States Code, to define those areas, including Prince William Sound, Alaska, and Rosario Strait and Puget Sound, Washington (including those portions of the Strait of Juan de Fuca east of Port Angeles, Haro Strait, and the Strait of Georgia subject to United States jurisdiction), on which single hulled tankers over 5,000 gross tons transporting oil in bulk shall be escorted by at least two towing vessels (as defined under section 2101 of title 46, United States Code) or other vessels considered appropriate by the Secretary.

---

[3] Margin of paragraph (1) so in law. The amendment made by section 711(b)(1)(A) of Public Law 111–281 amends subsection (c) which is reflected above. The amendment results in designation of text in subsection (c) as paragraph (1); however, the margin for paragraph (1) probably should appear on its own margin rather than run-in to the heading for subsection (c).

(2) PRINCE WILLIAM SOUND, ALASKA.—

(A) IN GENERAL.—The requirement in paragraph (1) relating to single hulled tankers in Prince William Sound, Alaska, described in that paragraph being escorted by at least 2 towing vessels or other vessels considered to be appropriate by the Secretary (including regulations promulgated in accordance with section 3703(a)(3) of title 46, United States Code, as set forth in part 168 of title 33, Code of Federal Regulations (as in effect on March 1, 2009) implementing this subsection with respect to those tankers) shall apply to double hulled tankers over 5,000 gross tons transporting oil in bulk in Prince William Sound, Alaska.

(B) IMPLEMENTATION OF REQUIREMENTS.—The Secretary of the department in which the Coast Guard is operating shall prescribe interim final regulations to carry out subparagraph (A) as soon as practicable without notice and hearing pursuant to section 553 of title 5 of the United States Code.

(d) TANKER DEFINED.—In this section the term "tanker" has the same meaning the term has in section 2101 of title 46, United States Code.

[46 U.S.C. 3703 note]

SEC. 4117. MARITIME POLLUTION PREVENTION TRAINING PROGRAM STUDY.

The Secretary shall conduct a study to determine the feasibility of a Maritime Oil Pollution Prevention Training program to be carried out in cooperation with approved maritime training institutions. The study shall assess the costs and benefits of transferring suitable vessels to selected maritime training institutions, equipping the vessels for oil spill response, and training students in oil pollution response skills. The study shall be completed and transmitted to the Congress no later than one year after the date of the enactment of this Act.

[46 U.S.C. app. 1295 note]

SEC. 4118. VESSEL COMMUNICATION EQUIPMENT REGULATIONS.

The Secretary shall, not later than one year after the date of the enactment of this Act, issue regulations necessary to ensure that vessels subject to the Vessel Bridge-to-Bridge Radiotelephone Act of

1971 (33 U.S.C. 1203) are also equipped as necessary to—

(1) receive radio marine navigation safety warnings; and

(2) engage in radio communications on designated frequencies with the Coast Guard, and such other vessels and stations as may be specified by the Secretary.

[33 U.S.C. 1203 note]

Subtitle B—Removal

SEC. 4201. FEDERAL REMOVAL AUTHORITY.

(a)

* * *

* * * * * * *

(c)[4] REVISION OF NATIONAL CONTINGENCY PLAN.—Not later than one year after the date of the enactment of this Act, the President shall revise and republish the National Contingency Plan prepared under section 311(c)(2) of the Federal Water Pollution Control Act (as in effect immediately before the date of the enactment of this Act) to implement the amendments made by this section and section 4202.

---

[4]   So in law. Probably should be redesignated as subsection (d).

[33 U.S.C. 1321 note]

SEC. 4202. NATIONAL PLANNING AND RESPONSE SYSTEM.

(a)

* * *

(b) IMPLEMENTATION.—

(1) AREA COMMITTEES AND CONTINGENCY PLANS.—(A) Not later than 6 months after the date of the enactment of this Act, the President shall designate the areas for which Area Committees are established under section 311(j)(4) of the Federal Water Pollution Control Act, as amended by this Act. In designating such areas, the President shall ensure that all navigable waters, adjoining shorelines, and waters of the exclusive economic zone are subject to an Area Contingency

Plan under that section.

(B) Not later than 18 months after the date of the enactment of this Act, each Area Committee established under that section shall submit to the President the Area Contingency Plan required under that section.

(C) Not later than 24 months after the date of the enactment of this Act, the President shall—

(i) promptly review each plan;

(ii) require amendments to any plan that does not meet the requirements of section 311(j)(4) of the Federal Water Pollution Control Act; and

(iii) approve each plan that meets the requirements of that section.

(2) NATIONAL RESPONSE UNIT.—Not later than one year after the date of the enactment of this Act, the Secretary of the department in which the Coast Guard is operating shall establish a National Response Unit in accordance with section 311(j)(2) of the Federal Water Pollution Control Act, as amended by this Act.

(3) COAST GUARD DISTRICT RESPONSE GROUPS.—Not later than 1 year after the date of the enactment of this Act, the Secretary of the department in which the Coast Guard is operating shall establish Coast Guard District Response Groups in accordance with section 311(j)(3) of the Federal Water Pollution Control Act, as amended by this Act.

(4) TANK VESSEL AND FACILITY RESPONSE PLANS; TRANSITION PROVISION; EFFECTIVE DATE OF PROHIBITION.—(A) Not later than 24 months after the date of the enactment of this Act, the President shall issue regulations for tank vessel and facility response plans under section 311(j)(5) of the Federal Water Pollution Control Act, as amended by this Act.

(B) During the period beginning 30 months after the date of the enactment of this paragraph and ending 36 months after that date of enactment, a tank vessel or facility for which a response plan is required to be prepared under section 311(j)(5) of the Federal Water Pollution Control Act, as amended by this Act, may not handle, store, or transport oil unless the owner or operator thereof has submitted such a plan to the President.

(C) Subparagraph (E) of section 311(j)(5) of the Federal Water Pollution Control Act, as amended by this Act, shall take effect 36 months after the date of the enactment of this Act.

[33 U.S.C. 1321 note]

* * * * * * *

SEC. 4203. COAST GUARD VESSEL DESIGN.

The Secretary shall ensure that vessels designed and constructed to replace Coast Guard buoy tenders are equipped with oil skimming systems that are readily available and operable, and that complement the primary mission of servicing aids to navigation.

* * * * * * *

Subtitle C—Penalties and Miscellaneous

* * * * * * *

SEC. 4303. FINANCIAL RESPONSIBILITY CIVIL PENALTIES.

(a) ADMINISTRATIVE.—Any person who, after notice and an opportunity for a hearing, is found to have failed to comply with the requirements of section 1016 or the regulations issued under that section, or with a denial or detention order issued under subsection (b)(2) of that section, shall be liable to the United States for a civil penalty, not to exceed $25,000 per day of violation. The amount of the civil penalty shall be assessed by the President by written notice. In determining the amount of the penalty, the President shall take into account the nature, circumstances, extent, and gravity of the violation, the degree of culpability, any history of prior violation, ability to pay, and such other matters as justice may require. The President may compromise, modify, or remit, with or without conditions, any civil penalty which is subject to imposition or which has been imposed under this paragraph. If any person fails to pay an assessed civil penalty after it has become final, the President may refer the matter to the Attorney General for collection.

(b) JUDICIAL.—In addition to, or in lieu of, assessing a penalty under subsection (a), the President may request the Attorney General to secure such relief as necessary to compel compliance with section 1016, including a judicial order terminating operations. The district courts of the United States shall have jurisdiction to grant any relief as the public interest and the equities of the case may require.

[33 U.S.C. 2716a]

SEC. 4304. DEPOSIT OF CERTAIN PENALTIES INTO OIL SPILL LIABILITY TRUST FUND.

Penalties paid pursuant to section 311 of the Federal Water Pollution Control Act, section 309(c) of that Act, as a result of violations of section 311 of that Act, and the Deepwater Port Act of 1974, shall be deposited in the Oil Spill Liability Trust Fund created under section 9509 of the Internal Revenue Code of 1986 (26 U.S.C. 9509).

[26 U.S.C. 9509 note]

* * * * * * *

TITLE V—PRINCE WILLIAM SOUND PROVISIONS

SEC. 5001. OIL SPILL RECOVERY INSTITUTE.

(a) ESTABLISHMENT OF INSTITUTE.—The Secretary of Commerce shall provide for the establishment of a Prince William Sound Oil Spill Recovery Institute (hereinafter in this section referred to as the "Institute") through the Prince William Sound Science and Technology Institute located in Cordova, Alaska.

(b) FUNCTIONS.—The Institute shall conduct research and carry out educational and demonstration projects designed to—

(1) identify and develop the best available techniques, equipment, and materials for dealing with oil spills in the arctic and subarctic marine environment; and

(2) complement Federal and State damage assessment efforts and determine, document, assess, and understand the long-range effects of Arctic or Subarctic oil spills on the natural resources of Prince William Sound and its adjacent waters (as generally depicted on the map entitled "EXXON VALDEZ oil

spill dated March 1990"), and the environment, the economy, and the lifestyle and well-being of the people who are dependent on them, except that the Institute shall not conduct studies or make recommendations on any matter which is not directly related to Arctic or Subarctic oil spills or the effects thereof.

(c) ADVISORY BOARD.—

(1) IN GENERAL.—The policies of the Institute shall be determined by an advisory board, composed of 16 members appointed as follows:

(A) One representative appointed by each of the Commissioners of Fish and Game, Environmental Conservation, and Natural Resources of the State of Alaska, all of whom shall be State employees.

(B) One representative appointed by each of the Secretaries of Commerce and the Interior and the Commandant of the Coast Guard, who shall be Federal employees.

(C) Two representatives from the fishing industry appointed by the Governor of the State of Alaska from among residents of communities in Alaska that were affected by the EXXON VALDEZ oil spill, who shall serve terms of 2 years each. Interested organizations from within the fishing industry may submit the names of qualified individuals for consideration by the Governor.

(D) Two Alaska Natives who represent Native entities affected by the EXXON VALDEZ oil spill, at least one of whom represents an entity located in Prince William Sound, appointed by the Governor of Alaska from a list of 4 qualified individuals submitted by the Alaska Federation of Natives, who shall serve terms of 2 years each.

(E) Two representatives from the oil and gas industry to be appointed by the Governor of the State of Alaska who shall serve terms of 2 years each. Interested organizations from within the oil and gas industry may submit the names of qualified individuals for consideration by the Governor.

(F) Two at-large representatives from among residents of communities in Alaska that were affected by the EXXON VALDEZ oil spill who are knowledgeable about the marine environment and wildlife within Prince William Sound, and who shall serve terms of 2 years each, appointed by the remaining members of the Advisory Board. Interested parties may submit the names of qualified individuals for consideration by the Advisory Board.

(G) One nonvoting representative of the Institute of Marine Science.

(H) One nonvoting representative appointed by the Prince William Sound Science and Technology Institute.

(2) CHAIRMAN.—The representative of the Secretary of Commerce shall serve as Chairman of the Advisory Board.

(3) POLICIES.—Policies determined by the Advisory Board under this subsection shall include policies for the conduct and support, through contracts and grants awarded on a nationally competitive basis, of research, projects, and studies to be supported by the Institute in accordance with the purposes of this section.

(4) SCIENTIFIC REVIEW.—The Advisory Board may request a scientific review of the research program every five years by the National Academy of Sciences which shall perform the review, if requested, as part of its responsibilities under section 7001(b)(2).

(d) SCIENTIFIC AND TECHNICAL COMMITTEE.—

(1) IN GENERAL.—The Advisory Board shall establish a scientific and technical committee, composed of specialists in matters relating to oil spill containment and cleanup technology, arctic and subarctic marine ecology, and the living resources and socioeconomics of Prince William Sound and its adjacent waters, from the University of Alaska, the Institute of Marine Science, the Prince William Sound Science and Technology Institute, and elsewhere in the academic community.

(2) FUNCTIONS.—The Scientific and Technical Committee shall provide such advice to the Advisory Board as the Advisory Board shall request, including recommendations regarding the conduct and support of research, projects, and studies in accordance with the purposes of this section. The Advisory Board shall not request, and the Committee shall not provide, any advice which is not directly related to Arctic or Subarctic

oil spills or the effects thereof.

(e) DIRECTOR.—The Institute shall be administered by a Director appointed by the Advisory Board. The Prince William Sound Science and Technology Institute and the Scientific and Technical Committee may each submit independent recommendations for the Advisory Board's consideration for appointment as Director. The Director may hire such staff and incur such expenses on behalf of the Institute as are authorized by the Advisory Board.

(f) EVALUATION.—The Secretary of Commerce may conduct an ongoing evaluation of the activities of the Institute to ensure that funds received by the Institute are used in a manner consistent with this section.

(g) AUDIT.—The Comptroller General of the United States, and any of his or her duly authorized representatives, shall have access, for purposes of audit and examination, to any books, documents, papers, and records of the Institute and its administering agency that are pertinent to the funds received and expended by the Institute and its administering agency.

(h) STATUS OF EMPLOYEES.—Employees of the Institute shall not, by reason of such employment, be considered to be employees of the Federal Government for any purpose.

(i) TERMINATION.—The authorization in section 5006(b) providing funding for the Institute shall terminate 1 year after the date on which the Secretary, in consultation with the Secretary of the Interior, determines that oil and gas exploration, development, and production in the State of Alaska have ceased.

(j) USE OF FUNDS.—No funds made available to carry out this section may be used to initiate litigation. No funds made available to carry out this section may be used for the acquisition of real property (including buildings) or construction of any building. No more than 20 percent of funds made available to carry out this section may be used to lease necessary facilities and to administer the Institute. The Advisory Board may compensate its Federal representatives for their reasonable travel costs. None of the funds authorized by this section shall be used for any purpose other than the functions specified in subsection (b).

(k) RESEARCH.—The Institute shall publish and make available to any person upon request the results of all research, educational, and demonstration projects conducted by the Institute. The Administrator shall provide a copy of all research, educational, and demonstration projects conducted by the Institute to the National Oceanic and Atmospheric Administration.

(l) DEFINITIONS.—In this section, the term "Prince William Sound and its adjacent waters" means such sound and waters as generally depicted on the map entitled "EXXON VALDEZ oil spill dated March 1990".

[33 U.S.C. 2731]

SEC. 5002. TERMINAL AND TANKER OVERSIGHT AND MONITORING.

(a) SHORT TITLE AND FINDINGS.—

(1) SHORT TITLE.—This section may be cited as the "Oil Terminal and Oil Tanker Environmental Oversight and Monitoring Act of 1990".

(2) FINDINGS.—The Congress finds that—

(A) the March 24, 1989, grounding and rupture of the fully loaded oil tanker, the EXXON VALDEZ, spilled 11 million gallons of crude oil in Prince William Sound, an environmentally sensitive area;

(B) many people believe that complacency on the part of the industry and government personnel responsible for monitoring the operation of the Valdez terminal and vessel traffic in Prince William Sound was one of the contributing factors to the EXXON VALDEZ oil spill;

(C) one way to combat this complacency is to involve local citizens in the process of preparing, adopting, and revising oil spill contingency plans;

(D) a mechanism should be established which fosters the long-term partnership of industry, government, and local communities in overseeing compliance with environmental concerns in the operation of crude oil terminals;

(E) such a mechanism presently exists at the Sullom Voe terminal in the Shetland Islands and this terminal should serve as a model for others;

(F) because of the effective partnership that has developed at Sullom Voe, Sullom Voe is considered the safest terminal in Europe;

(G) the present system of regulation and oversight of crude oil terminals in the United States has degenerated into a process of continual mistrust and confrontation;

(H) only when local citizens are involved in the process will the trust develop that is necessary to change the present system from confrontation to consensus;

(I) a pilot program patterned after Sullom Voe should be established in Alaska to further refine the concepts and relationships involved; and

(J) similar programs should eventually be established in other major crude oil terminals in the United States because the recent oil spills in Texas, Delaware, and Rhode Island indicate that the safe transportation of crude oil is a national problem.

(b) DEMONSTRATION PROGRAMS.—

(1) ESTABLISHMENT.—There are established 2 Oil Terminal and Oil Tanker Environmental Oversight and Monitoring Demonstration Programs (hereinafter referred to as "Programs") to be carried out in the State of Alaska.

(2) ADVISORY FUNCTION.—The function of these Programs shall be advisory only.

(3) PURPOSE.—The Prince William Sound Program shall be responsible for environmental monitoring of the terminal facilities in Prince William Sound and the crude oil tankers operating in Prince William Sound. The Cook Inlet Program shall be responsible for environmental monitoring of the terminal facilities and crude oil tankers operating in Cook Inlet located South of the latitude at Point Possession and North of the latitude at Amatuli Island, including offshore facilities in Cook Inlet.

(4) SUITS BARRED.—No program, association, council, committee or other organization created by this section may sue any person or entity, public or private, concerning any matter arising under this section except for the performance of contracts.

(c) OIL TERMINAL FACILITIES AND OIL TANKER OPERATIONS ASSOCIATION.—

(1) ESTABLISHMENT.—There is established an Oil Terminal Facilities and Oil Tanker Operations Association (hereinafter in this section referred to as the "Association") for each of the Programs established under subsection (b).

(2) MEMBERSHIP.—Each Association shall be comprised of 4 individuals as follows:

(A) One individual shall be designated by the owners and operators of the terminal facilities and shall represent those owners and operators.

(B) One individual shall be designated by the owners and operators of the crude oil tankers calling at the terminal facilities and shall represent those owners and operators.

(C) One individual shall be an employee of the State of Alaska, shall be designated by the Governor of the State of Alaska, and shall represent the State government.

(D) One individual shall be an employee of the Federal Government, shall be designated by the President, and shall represent the Federal Government.

(3) RESPONSIBILITIES.—Each Association shall be responsible for reviewing policies relating to the operation and maintenance of the oil terminal facilities and crude oil tankers which affect or may affect the environment in the vicinity of their respective terminals. Each Association shall provide a forum among the owners and operators of the terminal facilities, the owners and operators of crude oil tankers calling at those facilities, the United States, and the State of Alaska to discuss and to make recommendations concerning all permits, plans, and site-specific regulations governing the activities and actions of the terminal facilities which affect or may affect the environment in the vicinity of the terminal facilities and of crude oil tankers calling at those facilities.

(4) DESIGNATION OF EXISTING ORGANIZATION.—The Secretary may designate an existing nonprofit organization as an Association under this subsection if the organization is organized to meet the purposes of this section and consists of at least the individuals listed in paragraph (2).

(d) REGIONAL CITIZENS' ADVISORY COUNCILS.—

(1) MEMBERSHIP.—There is established a Regional

Citizens' Advisory Council (hereinafter in this section referred to as the "Council") for each of the programs established by subsection (b).

(2) MEMBERSHIP.—Each Council shall be composed of voting members and nonvoting members, as follows:

(A) VOTING MEMBERS.—Voting members shall be Alaska residents and, except as provided in clause (vii) of this paragraph, shall be appointed by the Governor of the State of Alaska from a list of nominees provided by each of the following interests, with one representative appointed to represent each of the following interests, taking into consideration the need for regional balance on the Council:

(i) Local commercial fishing industry organizations, the members of which depend on the fisheries resources of the waters in the vicinity of the terminal facilities.

(ii) Aquaculture associations in the vicinity of the terminal facilities.

(iii) Alaska Native Corporations and other Alaska Native organizations the members of which reside in the vicinity of the terminal facilities.

(iv) Environmental organizations the members of which reside in the vicinity of the terminal facilities.

(v) Recreational organizations the members of which reside in or use the vicinity of the terminal facilities.

(vi) The Alaska State Chamber of Commerce, to represent the locally based tourist industry.

(vii)(I) For the Prince William Sound Terminal Facilities Council, one representative selected by each of the following municipalities: Cordova, Whittier, Seward, Valdez, Kodiak, the Kodiak Island Borough, and the Kenai Peninsula Borough.

(II) For the Cook Inlet Terminal Facilities Council, one representative selected by each of the following municipalities: Homer, Seldovia, Anchorage, Kenai, Kodiak, the Kodiak Island Borough, and the Kenai Peninsula Borough.

(B) NONVOTING MEMBERS.—One ex-officio, nonvoting representative shall be designated by, and represent, each of the following:

(i) The Environmental Protection Agency.

(ii) The Coast Guard.

(iii) The National Oceanic and Atmospheric Administration.

(iv) The United States Forest Service.

(v) The Bureau of Land Management.

(vi) The Alaska Department of Environmental Conservation.

(vii) The Alaska Department of Fish and Game.

(viii) The Alaska Department of Natural Resources.

(ix) The Division of Emergency Services, Alaska Department of Military and Veterans Affairs.

(3) TERMS.—

(A) DURATION OF COUNCILS.—The term of the Councils shall continue throughout the life of the operation of the Trans-Alaska Pipeline System and so long as oil is transported to or from Cook Inlet.

(B) THREE YEARS.—The voting members of each Council shall be appointed for a term of 3 years except as provided for in subparagraph (C).

(C) INITIAL APPOINTMENTS.—The terms of the first appointments shall be as follows:

(i) For the appointments by the Governor of the State of Alaska, one-third shall serve for 3 years, one-third shall serve for 2 years, and one-third shall serve for one year.

(ii) For the representatives of municipalities required by subsection (d)(2)(A)(vii), a drawing of lots among the appointees shall determine that one-third of that group serves for 3 years, one-third serves for 2 years, and the remainder serves for 1 year.

(4) SELF-GOVERNING.—Each Council shall elect its own chairperson, select its own staff, and make policies with regard

to its internal operating procedures. After the initial organizational meeting called by the Secretary under subsection (i), each Council shall be self-governing.

(5) DUAL MEMBERSHIP AND CONFLICTS OF INTEREST PROHIBITED.—(A) No individual selected as a member of the Council shall serve on the Association.

(B) No individual selected as a voting member of the Council shall be engaged in any activity which might conflict with such individual carrying out his functions as a member thereof.

(6) DUTIES.—Each Council shall—

(A) provide advice and recommendations to the Association on policies, permits, and site-specific regulations relating to the operation and maintenance of terminal facilities and crude oil tankers which affect or may affect the environment in the vicinity of the terminal facilities;

(B) monitor through the committee established under subsection (e), the environmental impacts of the operation of the terminal facilities and crude oil tankers;

(C) monitor those aspects of terminal facilities' and crude oil tankers' operations and maintenance which affect or may affect the environment in the vicinity of the terminal facilities;

(D) review through the committee established under subsection (f), the adequacy of oil spill prevention and contingency plans for the terminal facilities and the adequacy of oil spill prevention and contingency plans for crude oil tankers, operating in Prince William Sound or in Cook Inlet;

(E) provide advice and recommendations to the Association on port operations, policies and practices;

(F) recommend to the Association—

(i) standards and stipulations for permits and site-specific regulations intended to minimize the impact of the terminal facilities' and crude oil tankers' operations in the vicinity of the terminal facilities;

(ii) modifications of terminal facility operations

and maintenance intended to minimize the risk and mitigate the impact of terminal facilities, operations in the vicinity of the terminal facilities and to minimize the risk of oil spills;

(iii) modifications of crude oil tanker operations and maintenance in Prince William Sound and Cook Inlet intended to minimize the risk and mitigate the impact of oil spills; and

(iv) modifications to the oil spill prevention and contingency plans for terminal facilities and for crude oil tankers in Prince William Sound and Cook Inlet intended to enhance the ability to prevent and respond to an oil spill; and

(G) create additional committees of the Council as necessary to carry out the above functions, including a scientific and technical advisory committee to the Prince William Sound Council.

(7) NO ESTOPPEL.—No Council shall be held liable under State or Federal law for costs or damages as a result of rendering advice under this section. Nor shall any advice given by a voting member of a Council, or program representative or agent, be grounds for estopping the interests represented by the voting Council members from seeking damages or other appropriate relief.

(8) SCIENTIFIC WORK.—In carrying out its research, development and monitoring functions, each Council is authorized to conduct its own scientific research and shall review the scientific work undertaken by or on behalf of the terminal operators or crude oil tanker operators as a result of a legal requirement to undertake that work. Each Council shall also review the relevant scientific work undertaken by or on behalf of any government entity relating to the terminal facilities or crude oil tankers. To the extent possible, to avoid unnecessary duplication, each Council shall coordinate its independent scientific work with the scientific work performed by or on behalf of the terminal operators and with the scientific work performed by or on behalf of the operators of the crude oil tankers.

(e) COMMITTEE FOR TERMINAL AND OIL TANKER OPERATIONS AND ENVIRONMENTAL MONITORING.—

(1) MONITORING COMMITTEE.—Each Council shall establish a standing Terminal and Oil Tanker Operations and Environmental Monitoring Committee (hereinafter in this section referred to as the "Monitoring Committee") to devise and manage a comprehensive program of monitoring the environmental impacts of the operations of terminal facilities and of crude oil tankers while operating in Prince William Sound and Cook Inlet. The membership of the Monitoring Committee shall be made up of members of the Council, citizens, and recognized scientific experts selected by the Council.

(2) DUTIES.—In fulfilling its responsibilities, the Monitoring Committee shall—

(A) advise the Council on a monitoring strategy that will permit early detection of environmental impacts of terminal facility operations and crude oil tanker operations while in Prince William Sound and Cook Inlet;

(B) develop monitoring programs and make recommendations to the Council on the implementation of those programs;

(C) at its discretion, select and contract with universities and other scientific institutions to carry out specific monitoring projects authorized by the Council pursuant to an approved monitoring strategy;

(D) complete any other tasks assigned by the Council; and

(E) provide written reports to the Council which interpret and assess the results of all monitoring programs.

(f) COMMITTEE FOR OIL SPILL PREVENTION, SAFETY, AND EMERGENCY RESPONSE.—

(1) TECHNICAL OIL SPILL COMMITTEE.—Each Council shall establish a standing technical committee (hereinafter referred to as "Oil Spill Committee") to review and assess measures designed to prevent oil spills and the planning and preparedness for responding to, containing, cleaning up, and mitigating impacts of oil spills. The membership of the Oil Spill Committee shall be made up of members of the Council, citizens, and recognized technical experts selected by the Council.

(2) DUTIES.—In fulfilling its responsibilities, the Oil Spill Committee shall—

(A) periodically review the respective oil spill prevention and contingency plans for the terminal facilities and for the crude oil tankers while in Prince William Sound or Cook Inlet, in light of new technological developments and changed circumstances;

(B) monitor periodic drills and testing of the oil spill contingency plans for the terminal facilities and for crude oil tankers while in Prince William Sound and Cook Inlet;

(C) study wind and water currents and other environmental factors in the vicinity of the terminal facilities which may affect the ability to prevent, respond to, contain, and clean up an oil spill;

(D) identify highly sensitive areas which may require specific protective measures in the event of a spill in Prince William Sound or Cook Inlet;

(E) monitor developments in oil spill prevention, containment, response, and cleanup technology;

(F) periodically review port organization, operations, incidents, and the adequacy and maintenance of vessel traffic service systems designed to assure safe transit of crude oil tankers pertinent to terminal operations;

(G) periodically review the standards for tankers bound for, loading at, exiting from, or otherwise using the terminal facilities;

(H) complete any other tasks assigned by the Council; and

(I) provide written reports to the Council outlining its findings and recommendations.

(g) AGENCY COOPERATION.—On and after the expiration of the 180-day period following the date of the enactment of this section, each Federal department, agency, or other instrumentality shall, with respect to all permits, site-specific regulations, and other matters governing the activities and actions of the terminal facilities which affect or may affect the vicinity of the terminal facilities, consult with the appropriate Council prior to taking substantive action with respect to the permit, site-specific regulation, or other matter. This consultation shall be carried out with a view to enabling the appropriate Association and Council to review the permit, site-specific regulation, or other matters and make appropriate recommendations regarding operations, policy or agency actions. Prior consultation shall not be required if an authorized Federal agency representative reasonably believes that an emergency exists requiring action without delay.

(h) RECOMMENDATIONS OF THE COUNCIL.—In the event that the Association does not adopt, or significantly modifies before adoption, any recommendation of the Council made pursuant to the authority granted to the Council in subsection (d), the Association shall provide to the Council, in writing, within 5 days of its decision, notice of its decision and a written statement of reasons for its rejection or significant modification of the recommendation.

(i) ADMINISTRATIVE ACTIONS.—Appointments, designations, and selections of individuals to serve as members of the Associations and Councils under this section shall be submitted to the Secretary prior to the expiration of the 120-day period following the date of the enactment of this section. On or before the expiration of the 180-day period following that date of enactment of this section, the Secretary shall call an initial meeting of each Association and Council for organizational purposes.

(j) LOCATION AND COMPENSATION.—

(1) LOCATION.—Each Association and Council established by this section shall be located in the State of Alaska.

(2) COMPENSATION.—No member of an Association or Council shall be compensated for the member's services as a member of the Association or Council, but shall be allowed travel expenses, including per diem in lieu of subsistence, at a rate established by the Association or Council not to exceed the rates authorized for employees of agencies under sections 5702 and 5703 of title 5, United States Code. However, each Council may enter into contracts to provide compensation and expenses to members of the committees created under subsections (d), (e), and (f).

(k) FUNDING.—

(1) REQUIREMENT.—Approval of the contingency plans required of owners and operators of the Cook Inlet and Prince William Sound terminal facilities and crude oil tankers while operating in Alaskan waters in commerce with those terminal

facilities shall be effective only so long as the respective Association and Council for a facility are funded pursuant to paragraph (2).

(2) PRINCE WILLIAM SOUND PROGRAM.—The owners or operators of terminal facilities or crude oil tankers operating in Prince William Sound shall provide, on an annual basis, an aggregate amount of not more than $2,000,000, as determined by the Secretary. Such amount—

(A) shall provide for the establishment and operation on the environmental oversight and monitoring program in Prince William Sound;

(B) shall be adjusted annually by the Anchorage Consumer Price Index; and

(C) may be adjusted periodically upon the mutual consent of the owners or operators of terminal facilities or crude oil tankers operating in Prince William Sound and the Prince William Sound terminal facilities Council.

(3) COOK INLET PROGRAM.—The owners or operators of terminal facilities, offshore facilities, or crude oil tankers operating in Cook Inlet shall provide, on an annual basis, an aggregate amount of not less than $1,400,000, as determined by the Secretary. Such amount—

(A) shall provide for the establishment and operation of the environmental oversight and monitoring program in Cook Inlet;

(B) shall be adjusted annually by the Anchorage Consumer Price Index; and

(C) may be adjusted periodically upon the mutual consent of the owners or operators of terminal facilities, offshore facilities, or crude oil tankers operating in Cook Inlet and the Cook Inlet Council.

(l) REPORTS.—

(1) ASSOCIATIONS AND COUNCILS.—Prior to the expiration of the 36-month period following the date of the enactment of this section, each Association and Council established by this section shall report to the President and the Congress concerning its activities under this section, together with its recommendations.

(2) GAO.—Prior to the expiration of the 36-month period following the date of the enactment of this section, the Government Accountability Office shall report to the President and the Congress as to the handling of funds, including donated funds, by the entities carrying out the programs under this section, and the effectiveness of the demonstration programs carried out under this section, together with its recommendations.

(m) DEFINITIONS.—As used in this section, the term—

(1) "terminal facilities" means—

(A) in the case of the Prince William Sound Program, the entire oil terminal complex located in Valdez, Alaska, consisting of approximately 1,000 acres including all buildings, docks (except docks owned by the City of Valdez if those docks are not used for loading of crude oil), pipes, piping, roads, ponds, tanks, crude oil tankers only while at the terminal dock, tanker escorts owned or operated by the operator of the terminal, vehicles, and other facilities associated with, and necessary for, assisting tanker movement of crude oil into and out of the oil terminal complex; and

(B) in the case of the Cook Inlet Program, the entire oil terminal complex including all buildings, docks, pipes, piping, roads, ponds, tanks, vessels, vehicles, crude oil tankers only while at the terminal dock, tanker escorts owned or operated by the operator of the terminal, emergency spill response vessels owned or operated by the operator of the terminal, and other facilities associated with, and necessary for, assisting tanker movement of crude oil into and out of the oil terminal complex;

(2) "crude oil tanker" means a tanker (as that term is defined under section 2101 of title 46, United States Code)—

(A) in the case of the Prince William Sound Program, calling at the terminal facilities for the purpose of receiving and transporting oil to refineries, operating north of Middleston Island and bound for or exiting from Prince William Sound; and

(B) in the case of the Cook Inlet Program, calling at the terminal facilities for the purpose of receiving and transporting oil to refineries and operating in Cook Inlet and the Gulf of Alaska north of Amatuli Island, including tankers transiting to Cook Inlet from Prince William Sound;

(3) "vicinity of the terminal facilities" means that geographical area surrounding the environment of terminal facilities which is directly affected or may be directly affected by the operation of the terminal facilities; and

(4) "Secretary" means the Secretary of the department in which the Coast Guard is operating.

(n) SAVINGS CLAUSE.—

(1) REGULATORY AUTHORITY.—Nothing in this section shall be construed as modifying, repealing, superseding, or preempting any municipal, State or Federal law or regulation, or in any way affecting litigation arising from oil spills or the rights and responsibilities of the United States or the State of Alaska, or municipalities thereof, to preserve and protect the environment through regulation of land, air, and water uses, of safety, and of related development. The monitoring provided for by this section shall be designed to help assure compliance with applicable laws and regulations and shall only extend to activities—

(A) that would affect or have the potential to affect the vicinity of the terminal facilities and the area of crude oil tanker operations included in the Programs; and

(B) are subject to the United States or State of Alaska, or municipality thereof, law, regulation, or other legal requirement.

(2) RECOMMENDATIONS.—This subsection is not intended to prevent the Association or Council from recommending to appropriate authorities that existing legal requirements should be modified or that new legal requirements should be adopted.

(o) ALTERNATIVE VOLUNTARY ADVISORY GROUP IN LIEU OF COUNCIL.—The requirements of subsections (c) through (l), as such subsections apply respectively to the Prince William Sound Program and the Cook Inlet Program, are deemed to have been satisfied so long as the following conditions are met:

(1) PRINCE WILLIAM SOUND.—With respect to the Prince William Sound Program, the Alyeska Pipeline Service

Company or any of its owner companies enters into a contract for the duration of the operation of the Trans-Alaska Pipeline System with the Alyeska Citizens Advisory Committee in existence on the date of enactment of this section, or a successor organization, to fund that Committee or organization on an annual basis in the amount provided for by subsection (k)(2)(A) and the President annually certifies that the Committee or organization fosters the general goals and purposes of this section and is broadly representative of the communities and interests in the vicinity of the terminal facilities and Prince William Sound.

(2) COOK INLET.—With respect to the Cook Inlet Program, the terminal facilities, offshore facilities, or crude oil tanker owners and operators enter into a contract with a voluntary advisory organization to fund that organization on an annual basis and the President annually certifies that the organization fosters the general goals and purposes of this section and is broadly representative of the communities and interests in the vicinity of the terminal facilities and Cook Inlet.

[33 U.S.C. 2732]

SEC. 5003. BLIGH REEF LIGHT.

The Secretary of Transportation shall within one year after the date of the enactment of this title install and ensure operation of an automated navigation light on or adjacent to Bligh Reef in Prince William Sound, Alaska, of sufficient power and height to provide long-range warning of the location of Bligh Reef.

[33 U.S.C. 2733]

SEC. 5004. VESSEL TRAFFIC SERVICE SYSTEM.

The Secretary of Transportation shall within one year after the date of the enactment of this title—

(1) acquire, install, and operate such additional equipment (which may consist of radar, closed circuit television, satellite tracking systems, or other shipboard dependent surveillance), train and locate such personnel, and issue such final regulations as are necessary to increase the range of the existing VTS system in the Port of Valdez, Alaska, sufficiently to track the locations and movements of tank vessels carrying oil from the Trans-Alaska Pipeline when such vessels are transiting Prince William Sound, Alaska, and to sound an

audible alarm when such tankers depart from designated navigation routes; and

(2) submit to the Committee on Commerce, Science, and Transportation of the Senate and the Committee on Transportation and Infrastructure of the House of Representatives a report on the feasibility and desirability of instituting positive control of tank vessel movements in Prince William Sound by Coast Guard personnel using the Port of Valdez, Alaska, VTS system, as modified pursuant to paragraph (1).

[33 U.S.C. 2734]

SEC. 5005. EQUIPMENT AND PERSONNEL REQUIREMENTS UNDER TANK VESSEL AND FACILITY RESPONSE PLANS.

(a) IN GENERAL.—In addition to the requirements for response plans for vessels established by section 311(j) of the Federal Water Pollution Control Act, as amended by this Act, a response plan for a tanker loading cargo at a facility permitted under the Trans-Alaska Pipeline Authorization Act (43 U.S.C. 1651 et seq.),[5] shall provide for—

---

[5]   Section 354(2) of P.L. 102–388 attempted to amend section 5005(a) by inserting "and a response plan for such a facility," after "(43 U.S.C. 1651 et seq.).". The amendment probably should have made the insertion after "(43 U.S.C. 1651 et seq.),".

---

(1) prepositioned oil spill containment and removal equipment in communities and other strategic locations within the geographic boundaries of Prince William Sound, including escort vessels with skimming capability; barges to receive recovered oil; heavy duty sea boom, pumping, transferring, and lightering equipment; and other appropriate removal equipment for the protection of the environment, including fish hatcheries;

(2) the establishment of an oil spill removal organization at appropriate locations in Prince William Sound, consisting of trained personnel in sufficient numbers to immediately remove, to the maximum extent practicable, a worst case discharge or a discharge of 200,000 barrels of oil, whichever is greater;

(3) training in oil removal techniques for local residents and individuals engaged in the cultivation or production of fish

or fish products in Prince William Sound;

(4) practice exercises not less than 2 times per year which test the capacity of the equipment and personnel required under this paragraph; and

(5) periodic testing and certification of equipment required under this paragraph, as required by the Secretary.

(b) DEFINITIONS.—In this section—

(1) the term "Prince William Sound" means all State and Federal waters within Prince William Sound, Alaska, including the approach to Hinchenbrook Entrance out to and encompassing Seal Rocks; and

(2) the term "worst case discharge" means—

(A) in the case of a vessel, a discharge in adverse weather conditions of its entire cargo; and

(B) in the case of a facility, the largest foreseeable discharge in adverse weather conditions.

[33 U.S.C. 2735]

SEC. 5006. FUNDING.

(a) SECTIONS 5001, 5003 AND 5004.—Amounts in the Fund shall be available, without further appropriations and without fiscal year limitation, to carry out section 5001 in the amount as determined in section 5006(b), and to carry out sections 5003 and 5004, in an amount not to exceed $5,000,000.

(b) USE OF INTEREST ONLY.—The amount of funding to be made available annually to carry out section 5001 shall be the interest produced by the Fund's investment of the $22,500,000 remaining funding authorized for the Prince William Sound Oil Spill Recovery Institute and currently deposited in the Fund and invested by the Secretary of the Treasury in income producing securities along with other funds comprising the Fund. The National Pollution Funds Center shall transfer all such accrued interest, including the interest earned from the date funds in the Trans-Alaska Liability Pipeline Fund were transferred into the Oil Spill Liability Trust Fund pursuant to section 8102(a)(2)(B)(ii), to the Prince William Sound Oil Spill Recovery Institute annually, beginning 60 days after the date of enactment of the Coast Guard Authorization Act of 1996.

(c) USE FOR SECTION 1012.—Beginning 1 year after the date

on which the Secretary, in consultation with the Secretary of the Interior, determines that oil and gas exploration, development, and production in the State of Alaska have ceased, the funding authorized for the Prince William Sound Oil Spill Recovery Institute and deposited in the Fund shall thereafter be made available for purposes of section 1012 in Alaska.

(d) SECTION 5008.—Amounts in the Fund shall be available, without further appropriation and without fiscal year limitation, to carry out section 5008(b), in an annual[6] amount not to exceed $5,000,000 of which up to $3,000,000 may be used for the lease payment to the Alaska SeaLife Center under section 5008(b)(2): *Provided*, That the entire amount is designated by the Congress as an emergency requirement pursuant to section 251(b)(2)(A) of the Balanced Budget and Emergency Deficit Control Act of 1985, as amended: *Provided further*, That the entire amount shall be available only to the extent an official budget request that includes designation of the entire amount of the request as an emergency requirement as defined in the Balanced Budget and Emergency Deficit Control Act of 1985, as amended, is transmitted by the President to the Congress.

---

[6] Section 4413 of Public Law 109–59 (119 Stat. 1779) amended this subsection by inserting "annual" before "amount". The amendment has been carried out by inserting "annual" before "amount" the first place it appears to reflect the probable intent of Congress.

[33 U.S.C. 2736]

SEC. 5007. LIMITATION.

Notwithstanding any other law, tank vessels that have spilled more than 1,000,000 gallons of oil into the marine environment after March 22, 1989, are prohibited from operating on the navigable waters of Prince William Sound, Alaska.

[33 U.S.C. 2737]

SEC. 5008. NORTH PACIFIC MARINE RESEARCH INSTITUTE.

(a) INSTITUTE ESTABLISHED.—The Secretary of Commerce shall establish a North Pacific Marine Research Institute (hereafter in this section referred to as the "Institute") to be administered at the Alaska SeaLife Center by the North Pacific Research Board.

(b) FUNCTIONS.—The Institute shall—

(1) conduct research and carry out education and

demonstration projects on or relating to the North Pacific marine ecosystem with particular emphasis on marine mammal, sea bird, fish, and shellfish populations in the Bering Sea and Gulf of Alaska including populations located in or near Kenai Fjords National Park and the Alaska Maritime National Wildlife Refuge; and

(2) lease, maintain, operate, and upgrade the necessary research equipment and related facilities necessary to conduct such research at the Alaska SeaLife Center.

(c) EVALUATION AND AUDIT.—The Secretary of Commerce may periodically evaluate the activities of the Institute to ensure that funds received by the Institute are used in a manner consistent with this section. Chapter 10 of title 5, United States Code, shall not apply to the Institute.

(d) STATUS OF EMPLOYEES.—Employees of the Institute shall not, by reason of such employment, be considered to be employees of the Federal Government for any purpose.

(e) USE OF FUNDS.—No funds made available to carry out this section may be used to initiate litigation, or for the acquisition of real property (other than facilities leased at the Alaska SeaLife Center). No more than 10 percent of the funds made available to carry out subsection (b)(1) may be used to administer the Institute. The administrative funds of the Institute and the administrative funds of the North Pacific Research Board created under Public Law 105–83 may be used to jointly administer such programs at the discretion of the North Pacific Research Board.

(f) AVAILABILITY OF RESEARCH.—The Institute shall publish and make available to any person on request the results of all research, educational, and demonstration projects conducted by the Institute. The Institute shall provide a copy of all research, educational, and demonstration projects conducted by the Institute to the National Park Service, the United States Fish and Wildlife Service, and the National Oceanic and Atmospheric Administration.

[33 U.S.C. 2738]

TITLE VI—MISCELLANEOUS

SEC. 6001. SAVINGS PROVISIONS.

(a) CROSS-REFERENCES.—A reference to a law replaced by this

Act, including a reference in a regulation, order, or other law, is deemed to refer to the corresponding provision of this Act.

(b) CONTINUATION OF REGULATIONS.—An order, rule, or regulation in effect under a law replaced by this Act continues in effect under the corresponding provision of this Act until repealed, amended, or superseded.

(c) RULE OF CONSTRUCTION.—An inference of legislative construction shall not be drawn by reason of the caption or catch line of a provision enacted by this Act.

(d) ACTIONS AND RIGHTS.—Nothing in this Act shall apply to any rights and duties that matured, penalties that were incurred, and proceedings that were begun before the date of enactment of this Act, except as provided by this section, and shall be adjudicated pursuant to the law applicable on the date prior to the date of the enactment of this Act.

(e) ADMIRALTY AND MARITIME LAW.—Except as otherwise provided in this Act, this Act does not affect—

(1) admiralty and maritime law; or

(2) the jurisdiction of the district courts of the United States with respect to civil actions under admiralty and maritime jurisdiction, saving to suitors in all cases all other remedies to which they are otherwise entitled.

[33 U.S.C. 2751]

SEC. 6002. ANNUAL APPROPRIATIONS.

(a) REQUIRED.—Except as provided in subsection (b), amounts in the Fund shall be available only as provided in annual appropriation Acts.

(b) EXCEPTIONS.—

(1) IN GENERAL.—Subsection (a) shall not apply to—

(A) section 1006(f), 1012(a)(4), or 5006; or

(B) an amount, which may not exceed $50,000,000 in any fiscal year, made available by the President from the Fund—

(i) to carry out section 311(c) of the Federal Water Pollution Control Act (33 U.S.C. 1321(c)); and

(ii) to initiate the assessment of natural resources damages required under section 1006.

(2) FUND ADVANCES.—

(A) IN GENERAL.—To the extent that the amount described in subparagraph (B) of paragraph (1) is not adequate to carry out the activities described in such subparagraph, the Coast Guard may obtain 1 or more advances from the Fund as may be necessary, up to a maximum of $100,000,000 for each advance, with the total amount of advances not to exceed the amounts available under section 9509(c)(2) of the Internal Revenue Code of 1986.

(B) NOTIFICATION TO CONGRESS.—Not later than 30 days after the date on which the Coast Guard obtains an advance under subparagraph (A), the Coast Guard shall notify Congress of—

(i) the amount advanced; and

(ii) the facts and circumstances that necessitated the advance.

(C) REPAYMENT.—Amounts advanced under this paragraph shall be repaid to the Fund when, and to the extent that, removal costs are recovered by the Coast Guard from responsible parties for the discharge or substantial threat of discharge.

(3) AVAILABILITY.—Amounts to which this subsection applies shall remain available until expended.

[33 U.S.C. 2752]

[Section 6003—Repealed by section 109 of P.L. 104–134]

SEC. 6004. COOPERATIVE DEVELOPMENT OF COMMON HYDROCARBON-BEARING AREAS.

(a)

* * *

(b) EXCEPTION FOR WEST DELTA FIELD.—Section 5(j) of the Outer Continental Shelf Lands Act, as added by this section, shall not be applicable with respect to Blocks 17 and 18 of the West Delta Field offshore Louisiana.

(c) AUTHORIZATION OF APPROPRIATIONS.—There are hereby authorized to be appropriated such sums as may be necessary to provide compensation, including interest, to the State of Louisiana and its lessees, for net drainage of oil and gas resources as determined in the Third Party Factfinder Louisiana Boundary Study dated March 21, 1989. For purposes of this section, such lessees shall include those persons with an ownership interest in State of Louisiana leases SL10087, SL10088 or SL10187, or ownership interests in the production or proceeds therefrom, as established by assignment, contract or otherwise. Interest shall be computed for the period March 21, 1989 until the date of payment.

TITLE VII—OIL POLLUTION RESEARCH AND DEVELOPMENT PROGRAM

SEC. 7001. OIL POLLUTION RESEARCH AND DEVELOPMENT PROGRAM.

(a) DEFINITIONS.—In this section—

(1) the term "Chair" means the Chairperson of the Interagency Committee designated under subsection (c)(2);

(2) the term "Commandant" means the Commandant of the Coast Guard;

(3) the term "institution of higher education" means an institution of higher education, as defined in section 101(a) of the Higher Education Act of 1965 (20 U.S.C. 1001(a));

(4) the term "Interagency Committee" means the Interagency Coordinating Committee on Oil Pollution Research established under subsection (b);

(5) the term "Under Secretary" means the Under Secretary of Commerce for Oceans and Atmosphere; and

(6) the term "Vice Chair" means the Vice Chairperson of the Interagency Committee designated under subsection (c)(3).

(b) ESTABLISHMENT OF INTERAGENCY COORDINATING COMMITTEE ON OIL POLLUTION RESEARCH.—

(1) ESTABLISHMENT.—There is established an Interagency Coordinating Committee on Oil Pollution Research.

(2) PURPOSE.—The Interagency Committee shall coordinate a comprehensive program of oil pollution research, technology development, and demonstration among the Federal agencies, in cooperation and coordination with industry, 4-year institutions of higher education and research institutions, State

governments, and other nations, as appropriate, and shall foster cost-effective research mechanisms, including the joint funding of research.

(c) MEMBERSHIP.—

(1) COMPOSITION.—The Interagency Committee shall be composed of—

(A) at least 1 representative of the Coast Guard;

(B) at least 1 representative of the National Oceanic and Atmospheric Administration;

(C) at least 1 representative of the Environmental Protection Agency;

(D) at least 1 representative of the Department of the Interior;

(E) at least 1 representative of the Bureau of Safety and Environmental Enforcement;

(F) at least 1 representative of the Bureau of Ocean Energy Management;

(G) at least 1 representative of the United States Fish and Wildlife Service;

(H) at least 1 representative of the Department of Energy;

(I) at least 1 representative of the Pipeline and Hazardous Materials Safety Administration;

(J) at least 1 representative of the Federal Emergency Management Agency;

(K) at least 1 representative of the Navy;

(L) at least 1 representative of the Corps of Engineers;

(M) at least 1 representative of the United States Arctic Research Commission; and

(N) at least 1 representative of each of such other Federal agencies as the President considers to be appropriate.

(2) CHAIRPERSON.—The Commandant shall designate a Chairperson from among the members of the Interagency Committee selected under paragraph (1)(A).

(3) VICE CHAIRPERSON.—The Under Secretary shall designate a Vice Chairperson from among the members of the

Interagency Committee selected under paragraph (1)(B).

(4) MEETINGS.—

(A) QUARTERLY MEETINGS.—At a minimum, the members of the Interagency Committee shall meet once each quarter.

(B) PUBLIC SUMMARIES.—After each meeting, a summary shall be made available by the Chair or Vice Chair, as appropriate.

(d) DUTIES OF THE INTERAGENCY COMMITTEE.—

(1) RESEARCH.—The Interagency Committee shall—

(A) coordinate a comprehensive program of oil pollution research, technology development, and demonstration among the Federal agencies, in cooperation and coordination with industry, 4-year institutions of higher education and research institutions, States, Indian tribes, and other countries, as appropriate; and

(B) foster cost-effective research mechanisms, including the joint funding of research and the development of public-private partnerships for the purpose of expanding research.

(2) OIL POLLUTION RESEARCH AND TECHNOLOGY PLAN.—

(A) IMPLEMENTATION PLAN.—Not later than 180 days after the date of enactment of the Elijah E. Cummings Coast Guard Authorization Act of 2020, the Interagency Committee shall submit to Congress a research plan to report on the state of oil discharge prevention and response capabilities that—

(i) identifies current research programs conducted by Federal agencies, States, Indian tribes, 4-year institutions of higher education, and corporate entities;

(ii) assesses the current status of knowledge on oil pollution prevention, response, and mitigation technologies and effects of oil pollution on the environment;

(iii) identifies significant oil pollution research gaps, including an assessment of major technological deficiencies in responses to past oil discharges;

(iv) establishes national research priorities and goals for oil pollution technology development related to prevention, response, mitigation, and environmental effects;

(v) assesses the research on the applicability and effectiveness of the prevention, response, and mitigation technologies to each class of oil;

(vi) estimates the resources needed to conduct the oil pollution research and development program established pursuant to subsection (e), and timetables for completing research tasks;

(vii) summarizes research on response equipment in varying environmental conditions, such as in currents, ice cover, and ice floes; and

(viii) includes such other information or recommendations as the Interagency Committee determines to be appropriate.

(B) ADVICE AND GUIDANCE.—

(i) NATIONAL ACADEMY OF SCIENCES CONTRACT.—The Chair, through the department in which the Coast Guard is operating, shall contract with the National Academy of Sciences to—

(I) provide advice and guidance in the preparation and development of the research plan;

(II) assess the adequacy of the plan as submitted, and submit a report to Congress on the conclusions of such assessment; and

(III) provide organization guidance regarding the implementation of the research plan, including delegation of topics and research among Federal agencies represented on the Interagency Committee.

(ii) NIST ADVICE AND GUIDANCE.—The National Institute of Standards and Technology shall provide the Interagency Committee with advice and guidance on issues relating to quality assurance and standards measurements relating to its activities under this section.

(C) 10-YEAR UPDATES.—Not later than 10 years after the date of enactment of the Elijah E. Cummings Coast Guard Authorization Act of 2020, and every 10 years thereafter, the Interagency Committee shall submit to Congress a research plan that updates the information contained in the previous research plan submitted under this subsection.

(e) OIL POLLUTION RESEARCH AND DEVELOPMENT PROGRAM.—

(1) ESTABLISHMENT.—The Interagency Committee shall coordinate the establishment, by the agencies represented on the Interagency Committee, of a program for conducting oil pollution research, technology, and development, as provided in this subsection.

(2) INNOVATIVE OIL POLLUTION TECHNOLOGY.—The program established under paragraph (1) shall provide for research, development, and demonstration of new or improved technologies and methods that are effective in preventing, mitigating, or restoring damage from oil discharges and that protect the environment, including—

(A) development of improved designs for vessels and facilities, and improved operational practices;

(B) research, development, and demonstration of improved technologies to measure the ullage of a vessel tank, prevent discharges from tank vents, prevent discharges during lightering and bunkering operations, contain discharges on the deck of a vessel, prevent discharges through the use of vacuums in tanks, and otherwise contain discharges of oil from vessels and facilities;

(C) research, development, and demonstration of new or improved systems of mechanical, chemical, biological, and other methods (including the use of dispersants, solvents, and bioremediation) for the recovery, removal, and disposal of oil, including evaluation of the environmental effects of the use of such systems;

(D) research and training, in consultation with the National Response Team, to improve industry's and Government's ability to quickly and effectively remove an oil discharge, including the long-term use, as appropriate, of the National Spill Control School in Corpus Christi, Texas, and the Center for Marine Training and Safety in Galveston, Texas;

(E) research to improve information systems for decisionmaking, including the use of data from coastal mapping, baseline data, and other data related to the environmental effects of oil discharges, and cleanup technologies;

(F) development of technologies and methods to protect public health and safety from oil discharges, including the population directly exposed to an oil discharge;

(G) development of technologies, methods, and standards for protecting removal personnel, including training, adequate supervision, protective equipment, maximum exposure limits, and decontamination procedures;

(H) research and development of methods to restore and rehabilitate natural resources damaged by oil discharges;

(I) research to evaluate the relative effectiveness and environmental impacts of bioremediation technologies; and

(J) the demonstration of a satellite-based, dependent surveillance vessel traffic system in Narragansett Bay to evaluate the utility of such system in reducing the risk of oil discharges from vessel collisions and groundings in confined waters.

(3) OIL POLLUTION TECHNOLOGY EVALUATION.—The program established under paragraph (1) shall provide for oil pollution prevention and mitigation technology evaluation including—

(A) the evaluation and testing of technologies developed independently of the research and development program established under paragraph (1);

(B) the establishment, where appropriate, of standards and testing protocols traceable to national standards to measure the performance of oil pollution prevention or mitigation technologies; and

(C) the use, where appropriate, of controlled field testing to evaluate real-world application of oil discharge prevention or mitigation technologies.

(4) OIL POLLUTION EFFECTS RESEARCH.—(A) The Committee shall establish a research program to monitor and evaluate the environmental effects of acute and chronic oil discharges on coastal and marine resources (including impacts on protected areas such as sanctuaries) and protected species, and such program shall include the following elements:

(i) The development of improved models and capabilities for predicting the environmental fate, transport, and effects of oil discharges.

(ii) The development of methods, including economic methods, to assess damages to natural resources resulting from oil discharges.

(iii) Research to understand and quantify the effects of sublethal impacts of oil discharge on living natural marine resources, including impacts on pelagic fish species, marine mammals, and commercially and recreationally targeted fish and shellfish species.

(iv) The identification of types of ecologically sensitive areas at particular risk to oil discharges and the preparation of scientific monitoring and evaluation plans, one for each of several types of ecological conditions, to be implemented in the event of major oil discharges in such areas.

(v) The collection of environmental baseline data in ecologically sensitive areas at particular risk to oil discharges where such data are insufficient.

(vi) Research to understand the long-term effects of major oil discharges and the long-term effects of smaller endemic oil discharges.

(vii) The identification of potential impacts on ecosystems, habitat, and wildlife from the additional toxicity, heavy metal concentrations, and increased corrosiveness of mixed crude, such as diluted bitumen crude.

(viii) The development of methods to restore and rehabilitate natural resources and ecosystem functions damaged by oil discharges.

(B) The Department of Commerce in consultation with

the Environmental Protection Agency shall monitor and scientifically evaluate the long-term environmental effects of oil discharges if—

(i) the amount of oil discharged exceeds 250,000 gallons;

(ii) the oil discharge has occurred on or after January 1, 1989; and

(iii) the Interagency Committee determines that a study of the long-term environmental effects of the discharge would be of significant scientific value, especially for preventing or responding to future oil discharges.

Areas for study may include the following sites where oil discharges have occurred: the New York/New Jersey Harbor area, where oil was discharged by an Exxon underwater pipeline, the T/B CIBRO SAVANNAH, and the M/V BT NAUTILUS; Narragansett Bay where oil was discharged by the WORLD PRODIGY; the Houston Ship Channel where oil was discharged by the RACHEL B; the Delaware River, where oil was discharged by the PRESIDENTE RIVERA and the T/V ATHOS I, and Huntington Beach, California, where oil was discharged by the AMERICAN TRADER.

(C) Research conducted under this paragraph by, or through, the United States Fish and Wildlife Service shall be directed and coordinated by the National Wetland Research Center.

(5) MARINE SIMULATION RESEARCH.—The program established under paragraph (1) shall include research on the greater use and application of geographic and vessel response simulation models, including the development of additional data bases and updating of existing data bases using, among others, the resources of the National Maritime Research Center. It shall include research and vessel simulations for—

(A) contingency plan evaluation and amendment;

(B) removal and strike team training;

(C) tank vessel personnel training; and

(D) those geographic areas where there is a significant likelihood of a major oil discharge.

(6) DEMONSTRATION PROJECTS.—The United States Coast Guard, in conjunction with such agencies as the President may designate, shall conduct 4[7] port oil pollution minimization demonstration projects, one each with (A) the Port Authority of New York and New Jersey, (B) the Ports of Los Angeles and Long Beach, California,[7] (C) the Port of New Orleans, Louisiana, and (D) a port on the Great Lakes[7] for the purpose of developing and demonstrating integrated port oil pollution prevention and cleanup systems which utilize the information and implement the improved practices and technologies developed from the research, development, and demonstration program established in this section. Such systems shall utilize improved technologies and management practices for reducing the risk of oil discharges, including, as appropriate, improved data access, computerized tracking of oil shipments, improved vessel tracking and navigation systems, advanced technology to monitor pipeline and tank conditions, improved oil spill response capability, improved capability to predict the flow and effects of oil discharges in both the inner and outer harbor areas for the purposes of making infrastructure decisions, and such other activities necessary to achieve the purposes of this section.

---

[7] Section 2002(1) of P.L. 101–537 and section 4002(1) of P.L. 101–646 made almost identical amendments to section 7001(c)(6). The amendments made by P.L. 101–537 have been executed.

---

(7) SIMULATED ENVIRONMENTAL TESTING.—

(A) IN GENERAL.—Agencies represented on the Interagency Committee shall ensure the long-term use and operation of the Oil and Hazardous Materials Simulated Environmental Test Tank (OHMSETT) Research Center in New Jersey for oil pollution technology testing and evaluations.

(B) OTHER TESTING FACILITIES.—Nothing in subparagraph (A) shall be construed as limiting the ability of the Interagency Committee to contract or partner with a facility or facilities other than the Center described in subparagraph (A) for the purpose of oil pollution technology testing and evaluations, provided such a facility or facilities have testing and evaluation capabilities equal to or greater than those of such Center.

(C) IN-KIND CONTRIBUTIONS.—

(i) IN GENERAL.—The Secretary of the department in which the Coast Guard is operating and the Administrator of the Environmental Protection Agency may accept donations of crude oil and crude oil product samples in the form of in-kind contributions for use by the Federal Government for product testing, research and development, and for other purposes as the Secretary and the Administrator determine appropriate.

(ii) USE OF DONATED OIL.—Oil accepted under clause (i) may be used directly by the Secretary and shall be provided to other Federal agencies or departments through interagency agreements to carry out the purposes of this Act.

(8) REGIONAL RESEARCH PROGRAM.—(A) Consistent with the research plan in subsection (d), the Interagency Committee shall coordinate a program of competitive grants to universities or other research institutions, or groups of universities or research institutions, for the purposes of conducting a coordinated research program related to the regional aspects of oil pollution, such as prevention, removal, mitigation, and the effects of discharged oil on regional environments. For the purposes of this paragraph, a region means a Coast Guard district as set out in part 3 of title 33, Code of Federal Regulations (2010).

(B) The Interagency Committee shall coordinate the publication by the agencies represented on the Interagency Committee of a solicitation for grants under this subsection. The application shall be in such form and contain such information as may be required in the published solicitation. The applications shall be reviewed by the Interagency Committee, which shall make recommendations to the appropriate granting agency represented on the Interagency Committee for awarding the grant. The granting agency shall award the grants recommended by the Interagency Committee unless the agency decides not to award the grant due to budgetary or other compelling considerations and publishes its reasons for such a determination in the Federal Register. No grants may be made by any agency from any funds authorized for this paragraph unless such grant award has first been recommended by the Interagency Committee.

(C) Any university or other research institution, or group of universities or research institutions, may apply for a grant for the regional research program established by this paragraph. The applicant must be located in the region, or in a State a part of which is in the region, for which the project is proposed as part of the regional research program. With respect to a group application, the entity or entities which will carry out the substantial portion of the proposed research must be located in the region, or in a State a part of which is in the region, for which the project is proposed as part of the regional research program.

(D) The Interagency Committee shall make recommendations on grants in such a manner as to ensure an appropriate balance within a region among the various aspects of oil pollution research, including prevention, removal, mitigation, and the effects of discharged oil on regional environments. In addition, the Interagency Committee shall make recommendations for grants based on the following criteria:

(i) There is available to the applicant for carrying out this paragraph demonstrated research resources.

(ii) The applicant demonstrates the capability of making a significant contribution to regional research needs.

(iii) The projects which the applicant proposes to carry out under the grant are consistent with the research plan under subsection (d) and would further the objectives of the research and development program established in this section.

(E) Grants provided under this paragraph shall be for a period up to 3 years, subject to annual review by the granting agency, and provide not more than 80 percent of the costs of the research activities carried out in connection with the grant.

(F) No funds made available to carry out this subsection may be used for the acquisition of real property (including buildings) or construction of any building.

(G) Nothing in this paragraph is intended to alter or abridge the authority under existing law of any Federal agency to make grants, or enter into contracts or cooperative agreements, using funds other than those authorized in this Act for the purposes of carrying out this paragraph.

(9) FUNDING.—For each of the fiscal years 1991, 1992, 1993, 1994, and 1995, $6,000,000 of amounts in the Fund shall be available to carry out the regional research program in paragraph (8), such amounts to be available in equal amounts for the regional research program in each region; except that if the agencies represented on the Interagency Committee determine that regional research needs exist which cannot be addressed within such funding limits, such agencies may use their authority under paragraph (10) to make additional grants to meet such needs. For the purposes of this paragraph, the research program carried out by the Prince William Sound Oil Spill Recovery Institute established under section 5001, shall not be eligible to receive grants under this paragraph until the authorization for funding under section 5006(b) expires.

(10) GRANTS.—In carrying out the research and development program established under paragraph (1), the Under Secretary may enter into contracts and cooperative agreements and make grants to universities, research institutions, and other persons, and States and Indian tribes. Such contracts, cooperative agreements, and grants shall address research and technology priorities set forth in the oil pollution research plan under subsection (d).

(11) In carrying out research under this section, the Department of Transportation shall continue to utilize the resources of the Pipeline and Hazardous Materials Safety Administration of the Department of Transportation, to the maximum extent practicable.

(f) INTERNATIONAL COOPERATION.—In accordance with the research plan submitted under subsection (d), the Interagency Committee shall coordinate and cooperate with other nations and foreign research entities in conducting oil pollution research, development, and demonstration activities, including controlled field tests of oil discharges.

(g) BIENNIAL REPORTS.—The Chair shall submit to Congress every 2 years on October 30 a report on the activities carried out under this section in the preceding 2 fiscal years, and on activities proposed to be carried out under this section in the current 2 fiscal year period.

(h) FUNDING.—Not to exceed $22,000,000[8] of amounts in the Fund shall be available annually to carry out this section except for subsection (e)(8). Of such sums—

---

[8]   Section 2002(2) of P.L. 101–537 and section 4002(2) of P.L. 101–646 made almost identical amendments to section 7001(f). The amendments made by P.L. 101–537 have been executed.

---

(1) funds authorized to be appropriated to carry out the activities under subsection (c)(4) shall not exceed $5,000,000 for fiscal year 1991 or $3,500,000 for any subsequent fiscal year; and

(2) not less than $3,000,000[8] shall be available for carrying out the activities in subsection (c)(6) for fiscal years 1992, 1993, 1994, and 1995.

All activities authorized in this section, including subsection (e)(8), are subject to appropriations.

[33 U.S.C. 2761]

SEC. 7002. SUBMERGED OIL PROGRAM.

(a) PROGRAM.—

(1) ESTABLISHMENT.—The Under Secretary of Commerce for Oceans and Atmosphere, in conjunction with the Commandant of the Coast Guard, shall establish a program to detect, monitor, and evaluate the environmental effects of submerged oil in the Delaware River and Bay region. The program shall include the following elements:

(A) The development of methods to remove, disperse, or otherwise diminish the persistence of submerged oil.

(B) The development of improved models and capacities for predicting the environmental fate, transport, and effects of submerged oil.

(C) The development of techniques to detect and

monitor submerged oil.

(2) REPORT.—Not later than 3 years after the date of enactment of the Delaware River Protection Act of 2006, the Secretary of Commerce shall submit to the Committee on Commerce, Science, and Transportation of the Senate and the Committee on Transportation and Infrastructure of the House of Representatives a report on the activities carried out under this subsection and activities proposed to be carried out under this subsection.

(b) DEMONSTRATION PROJECT.—

(1) REMOVAL OF SUBMERGED OIL.—The Commandant of the Coast Guard, in conjunction with the Under Secretary of Commerce for Oceans and Atmosphere, shall conduct a demonstration project for the purpose of developing and demonstrating technologies and management practices to remove submerged oil from the Delaware River and other navigable waters.

(2) FUNDING.—There is authorized to be appropriated to the Commandant of the Coast Guard $2,000,000 for each of fiscal years 2006 through 2010 to carry out this subsection.

[33 U.S.C. 2762]

TITLE VIII—TRANS-ALASKA PIPELINE SYSTEM

SEC. 8001. SHORT TITLE.

This title may be cited as the "Trans-Alaska Pipeline System Reform Act of 1990".

Subtitle A—Improvements to Trans-Alaska Pipeline System

* * * * * * *

SEC. 8102. TRANS-ALASKA PIPELINE LIABILITY FUND.

(a) TERMINATION OF CERTAIN PROVISIONS.—

(1)

* * *

(2) DISPOSITION OF FUND BALANCE.—

(A) RESERVATION OF AMOUNTS.—The trustees of the Trans-Alaska Pipeline Liability Fund (hereafter in this subsection referred to as the "TAPS Fund") shall reserve the following amounts in the TAPS Fund—

(i) necessary to pay claims arising under section 204(c) of the Trans-Alaska Pipeline Authorization Act (43 U.S.C. 1653(c)); and

(ii) administrative expenses reasonably necessary for and incidental to the implementation of section 204(c) of that Act.

(B) DISPOSITION OF THE BALANCE.—After the Comptroller General of the United States certifies that the requirements of subparagraph (A) have been met, the trustees of the TAPS Fund shall dispose of the balance in the TAPS Fund after the reservation of amounts are made under subparagraph (A) by—

(i) rebating the pro rata share of the balance to the State of Alaska for its contributions as an owner of oil, which, except as otherwise provided under article IX, section 15, of the Alaska Constitution, shall be used for the remediation of above-ground storage tanks; and then

(ii) transferring and depositing the remainder of the balance into the Oil Spill Liability Trust Fund established under section 9509 of the Internal Revenue Code of 1986 (26 U.S.C. 9509).

(C) DISPOSITION OF THE RESERVED AMOUNTS.—After payment of all claims arising from an incident for which funds are reserved under subparagraph (A) and certification by the Comptroller General of the United States that the claims arising from that incident have been paid, the excess amounts, if any, for that incident shall be disposed of as set forth under subparagraphs (A) and (B).

(D) AUTHORIZATION.—The amounts transferred and deposited in the Fund shall be available for the purposes of section 1012 of the Oil Pollution Act of 1990 after funding sections 5001 and 8103 to the extent that funds have not otherwise been provided for the purposes of such sections.

(3) SAVINGS CLAUSE.—The repeal made by paragraph (1) shall have no effect on any right to recover or responsibility that arises from incidents subject to section 204(c) of the Trans-Alaska Pipeline Authorization Act (43 U.S.C. 1653(c)) occurring prior to the date of enactment of this Act.

(4)

* * *

(5) EFFECTIVE DATE.—(A) The repeal by paragraph (1) shall be effective 60 days after the date on which the Comptroller General of the United States certifies to the Congress that—

(i) all claims arising under section 204(c) of the Trans-Alaska Pipeline Authorization Act (43 U.S.C. 1653(c)) have been resolved,

(ii) all actions for the recovery of amounts subject to section 204(c) of the Trans-Alaska Pipeline Authorization Act have been resolved, and

(iii) all administrative expenses reasonably necessary for and incidental to the implementation of section 204(c) of the Trans-Alaska Pipeline Authorization Act have been paid.

(B) Upon the effective date of the repeal pursuant to subparagraph (A), the trustees of the TAPS Fund shall be relieved of all responsibilities under section 204(c) of the Trans-Alaska Pipeline Authorization Act, but not any existing legal liability.

(6) TUCKER ACT.—This subsection is intended expressly to preserve any and all rights and remedies of contributors to the TAPS Fund under section 1491 of title 28, United States Code (commonly referred to as the "Tucker Act").

* * * * * * *

SEC. 8103. PRESIDENTIAL TASK FORCE.

(a) ESTABLISHMENT OF TASK FORCE.—

(1) ESTABLISHMENT AND MEMBERS.—(A) There is hereby established a Presidential Task Force on the Trans-Alaska Pipeline System (hereinafter referred to as the "Task Force")

composed of the following members appointed by the President:

(i) Three members, one of whom shall be nominated by the Secretary of the Interior, one by the Administrator of the Environmental Protection Agency, and one by the Secretary of Transportation.

(ii) Three members nominated by the Governor of the State of Alaska, one of whom shall be an employee of the Alaska Department of Natural Resources and one of whom shall be an employee of the Alaska Department of Environmental Conservation.

(iii) One member nominated by the Office of Technology Assessment.

(B) Any member appointed to fill a vacancy occurring before the expiration of the term for which his or her predecessor was appointed shall be appointed only for the remainder of such term. A member may serve after the expiration of his or her term until a successor, if applicable, has taken office.

(2) COCHAIRMEN.—The President shall appoint a Federal cochairman from among the Federal members of the Task Force appointed pursuant to paragraph (1)(A) and the Governor shall designate a State cochairman from among the State members of the Task Force appointed pursuant to paragraph (1)(B).

(3) COMPENSATION.—Members shall, to the extent approved in appropriations Acts, receive the daily equivalent of the minimum annual rate of basic pay in effect for grade GS–15 of the General Schedule for each day (including travel time) during which they are engaged in the actual performance of duties vested in the Task Force, except that members who are State, Federal, or other governmental employees shall receive no compensation under this paragraph in addition to the salaries they receive as such employees.

(4) STAFF.—The cochairman of the Task Force shall appoint a Director to carry out administrative duties. The Director may hire such staff and incur such expenses on behalf of the Task Force for which funds are available.

(5) RULE.—Employees of the Task Force shall not, by reason of such employment, be considered to be employees of the Federal Government for any purpose.

(b) DUTIES OF THE TASK FORCE.—

(1) AUDIT.—The Task Force shall conduct an audit of the Trans-Alaska Pipeline System (hereinafter referred to as "TAPS") including the terminal at Valdez, Alaska, and other related onshore facilities, make recommendations to the President, the Congress, and the Governor of Alaska.

(2) COMPREHENSIVE REVIEW.—As part of such audit, the Task Force shall conduct a comprehensive review of the TAPS in order to specifically advise the President, the Congress, and the Governor of Alaska concerning whether—

(A) the holder of the Federal and State right-of-way is, and has been, in full compliance with applicable laws, regulations, and agreements;

(B) the laws, regulations, and agreements are sufficient to prevent the release of oil from TAPS and prevent other damage or degradation to the environment and public health;

(C) improvements are necessary to TAPS to prevent release of oil from TAPS and to prevent other damage or degradation to the environment and public health;

(D) improvements are necessary in the onshore oil spill response capabilities for the TAPS; and

(E) improvements are necessary in security for TAPS.

(3) CONSULTANTS.—(A) The Task Force shall retain at least one independent consulting firm with technical expertise in engineering, transportation, safety, the environment, and other applicable areas to assist the Task Force in carrying out this subsection.

(B) Contracts with any such firm shall be entered into on a nationally competitive basis, and the Task Force shall not select any firm with respect to which there may be a conflict of interest in assisting the Task Force in carrying out the audit and review. All work performed by such firm shall be under the direct and immediate supervision of a registered engineer.

(4) PUBLIC COMMENT.—The Task Force shall provide an opportunity for public comment on its activities including at a minimum the following:

(A) Before it begins its audit and review, the Task Force shall review reports prepared by other Government entities conducting reviews of TAPS and shall consult with those Government entities that are conducting ongoing investigations including the General Accounting Office. It shall also hold at least 2 public hearings, at least 1 of which shall be held in a community affected by the Exxon Valdez oil spill. Members of the public shall be given an opportunity to present both oral and written testimony.

(B) The Task Force shall provide a mechanism for the confidential receipt of information concerning TAPS, which may include a designated telephone hotline.

(5) TASK FORCE REPORT.—The Task Force shall publish a draft report which it shall make available to the public. The public will have at least 30 days to provide comments on the draft report. Based on its draft report and the public comments thereon, the Task Force shall prepare a final report which shall include its findings, conclusions, and recommendations made as a result of carrying out such audit. The Task Force shall transmit (and make available to the public), no later than 2 years after the date on which funding is made available under paragraph (7), its final report to the President, the Congress, and the Governor of Alaska.

(6) PRESIDENTIAL REPORT.—The President shall, within 90 days after receiving the Task Force's report, transmit a report to the Congress and the Governor of Alaska outlining what measures have been taken or will be taken to implement the Task Force's recommendations. The President's report shall include recommended changes, if any, in Federal and State law to enhance the safety and operation of TAPS.

(7) EARMARK.—Of amounts in the Fund, $5,000,000 shall be available, subject to appropriations, annually without fiscal year limitation to carry out the requirements of this section.

(c) GENERAL ADMINISTRATION AND POWERS OF THE TASK FORCE.—

(1) AUDIT ACCESS.—The Comptroller General of the United States, and any of his or her duly appointed representatives, shall have access, for purposes of audit and examination, to any books, documents, papers, and records of the Task Force that are pertinent to the funds received and expended by the Task

Force.

(2) TERMINATION.—The Task Force shall cease to exist on the date on which the final report is provided pursuant to subsection (b)(5).

(3) FUNCTIONS LIMITATION.—With respect to safety, operations, and other matters related to the pipeline facilities (as such term is defined in section 202(4) of the Hazardous Liquid Pipeline Safety Act of 1979) of the TAPS, the Task Force shall not perform any functions which are the responsibility of the Secretary of Transportation under the Hazardous Liquid Pipeline Safety Act of 1979, as amended. The Secretary may use the information gathered by and reports issued by the Task Force in carrying out the Secretary's responsibilities under that Act.

(4) POWERS.—The Task Force may, to the extent necessary to carry out its responsibilities, conduct investigations, make reports, issue subpoenas, require the production of relevant documents and records, take depositions, and conduct directly or, by contract, or otherwise, research, testing, and demonstration activities.

(5) EXAMINATION OF RECORDS AND PROPERTIES.—The Task Force, and the employees and agents it so designates, are authorized, upon presenting appropriate credentials to the person in charge, to enter upon, inspect, and examine, at reasonable times and in a reasonable manner, the records and properties of persons to the extent such records and properties are relevant to determining whether such persons have acted or are acting in compliance with applicable laws and agreements.

(6) FOIA.—The information gathered by the Task Force pursuant to subsection (b) shall not be subject to section 552 of title 5, United States Code (commonly referred to as the "Freedom of Information Act"), until its final report is issued pursuant to subsection (b)(6).

[43 U.S.C. 1651 note]

* * * * * * *

AMERICAN FISHERIES ACT TITLE II OF DIVISION C OF THE OMNIBUS CONSOLIDATED AND EMERGENCY SUPPLEMENTAL APPROPRIATIONS ACT, 1999

PUBLIC LAW 105-277
AS AMENDED THROUGH P.L. 117-328

[Copy of our comp to add title V of Div. A]

[(Public Law 105–277; 112 Stat. 2681–856; approved Oct. 21,
1998)]

[As Amended Through P.L. 117–328, Enacted December 29, 2022]

* * * * * * *

DIVISION C—OTHER MATTERS

* * * * * * *

TITLE II—FISHERIES[4]

---

[4] This title was enacted as part of division C of Public Law 105–277 (112 Stat.
2681–616).

---

subtitle I—Fishery Endorsements

SEC. 201. [46 U.S.C. 2101 note] SHORT TITLE.
This title may be cited as the "American Fisheries Act".

SEC. 202. STANDARD FOR FISHERY ENDORSEMENTS.
[(a) STANDARD.—Made amendments to section 12102(c) of title
46, United States Code.]

[(b) PREFERRED MORTGAGE.—Made amendments to section
31322(a) of title 46, United States Code.]

SEC. 203. ENFORCEMENT OF STANDARD.

(a) [46 U.S.C. 12102 note] EFFECTIVE DATE.—The amendments made by section 202 shall take effect on October 1, 2001.

(b) [46 U.S.C. 12102 note] REGULATIONS.—Final regulations to implement this subtitle shall be published in the Federal Register by April 1, 2000. Letter rulings and other interim interpretations about the effect of this subtitle and amendments made by this subtitle on specific vessels may not be issued prior to the publication of such final regulations. The regulations to implement this subtitle shall prohibit impermissible transfers of ownership or control, specify any transactions which require prior approval of an implementing agency, identify transactions which do not require prior agency approval, and to the extent practicable, minimize disruptions to the commercial fishing industry, to the traditional financing arrangements of such industry, and to the opportunity to form fishery cooperatives.

(c) [46 U.S.C. 12102 note] VESSELS MEASURING 100 FEET AND GREATER.—(1) The Administrator of the Maritime Administration shall administer section 12102(c) of title 46, United States Code, as amended by this subtitle, with respect to vessels 100 feet or greater in registered length. The owner of each such vessel shall file a statement of citizenship setting forth all relevant facts regarding vessel ownership and control with the Administrator of the Maritime Administration on an annual basis to demonstrate compliance with such section. Regulations to implement this subsection shall conform to the extent practicable with the regulations establishing the form of citizenship affidavit set forth in part 355 of title 46, Code of Federal Regulations, as in effect on September 25, 1997, except that the form of the statement under this paragraph shall be written in a manner to allow the owner of each such vessel to satisfy any annual renewal requirements for a certificate of documentation for such vessel and to comply with this subsection and section 12102(c) of title 46, United States Code, as amended by this Act, and shall not be required to be notarized.

(2) After October 1, 2001, transfers of ownership and control of vessels subject to section 12102(c) of title 46, United States Code, as amended by this Act, which are 100 feet or greater in registered length, shall be rigorously scrutinized for violations of such section, with particular attention given to leases, charters, mortgages, financing, and similar arrangements, to the control of persons not eligible to own a

vessel with a fishery endorsement under section 12102(c) of title 46, United States Code, as amended by this Act, over the management, sales, financing, or other operations of an entity, and to contracts involving the purchase over extended periods of time of all, or substantially all, of the living marine resources harvested by a fishing vessel.

(d) [46 U.S.C. 12102 note] VESSELS MEASURING LESS THAN 100 FEET.—The Secretary of Transportation shall establish such requirements as are reasonable and necessary to demonstrate compliance with section 12102(c) of title 46, United States Code, as amended by this Act, with respect to vessels measuring less than 100 feet in registered length, and shall seek to minimize the administrative burden on individuals who own and operate such vessels.

(e) [46 U.S.C. 12102 note] ENDORSEMENTS REVOKED.—The Secretary of Transportation shall revoke the fishery endorsement of any vessel subject to section 12102(c) of title 46, United States Code, as amended by this Act, whose owner does not comply with such section.

[(f) PENALTY.—Made an amendment to section 12122 of title 46, United States Code.]

SEC. 204. REPEAL OF OWNERSHIP SAVINGS CLAUSE.

(a) REPEAL.—Section 7(b) of the Commercial Fishing Industry Vessel Anti-Reflagging Act of 1987 (Public Law 100–239; 46 U.S.C. 12102 note) is hereby repealed.

(b) [46 U.S.C. 12102 note] EFFECTIVE DATE.—Subsection (a) shall take effect on October 1, 2001.

subtitle II—Bering Sea Pollock Fishery

SEC. 205. [16 U.S.C. 1851 note] DEFINITIONS.

As used in this subtitle—

(1) the term "Bering Sea and Aleutian Islands Management Area" has the same meaning as the meaning given for such term in part 679.2 of title 50, Code of Federal Regulations, as in effect on October 1, 1998;

(2) the term "catcher/processor" means a vessel that is used for harvesting fish and processing that fish;

(3) the term "catcher vessel" means a vessel that is used for harvesting fish and that does not process pollock onboard;

(4) the term "directed pollock fishery" means the fishery for the directed fishing allowances allocated under paragraphs (1), (2), and (3) of section 206(b);

(5) the term "harvest" means to commercially engage in the catching, taking, or harvesting of fish or any activity that can reasonably be expected to result in the catching, taking, or harvesting of fish;

(6) the term "inshore component" means the following categories that process groundfish harvested in the Bering Sea and Aleutian Islands Management Area:

(A) shoreside processors, including those eligible under section 208(f); and

(B) vessels less than 125 feet in length overall that process less than 126 metric tons per week in round-weight equivalents of an aggregate amount of pollock and Pacific cod;

(7) the term "Magnuson-Stevens Act" means the Magnuson-Stevens Fishery Conservation and Management Act (16 U.S.C. 1801 et seq.);

(8) the term "mothership" means a vessel that receives and processes fish from other vessels in the exclusive economic zone of the United States and is not used for, or equipped to be used for, harvesting fish;

(9) the term "North Pacific Council" means the North Pacific Fishery Management Council established under section 302(a)(1)(G) of the Magnuson-Stevens Act (16 U.S.C. 1852(a)(1)(G));

(10) the term "offshore component" means all vessels not included in the definition of "inshore component" that process groundfish harvested in the Bering Sea and Aleutian Islands Management Area;

(11) the term "Secretary" means the Secretary of Commerce; and

(12) the term "shoreside processor" means any person or vessel that receives unprocessed fish, except catcher/processors, motherships, buying stations, restaurants, or persons receiving

fish for personal consumption or bait.

SEC. 206. [16 U.S.C. 1851 note] ALLOCATIONS.

(a) POLLOCK COMMUNITY DEVELOPMENT QUOTA.—Effective January 1, 1999, 10 percent of the total allowable catch of pollock in the Bering Sea and Aleutian Islands Management Area shall be allocated as a directed fishing allowance to the western Alaska community development quota program established under section 305(i) of the Magnuson-Stevens Act (16 U.S.C. 1855(i)).

(b) INSHORE/OFFSHORE.—Effective January 1, 1999, the remainder of the pollock total allowable catch in the Bering Sea and Aleutian Islands Management Area, after the subtraction of the allocation under subsection (a) and the subtraction of allowances for the incidental catch of pollock by vessels harvesting other groundfish species (including under the western Alaska community development quota program) shall be allocated as directed fishing allowances as follows—

(1) 50 percent to catcher vessels harvesting pollock for processing by the inshore component;

(2) 40 percent to catcher/processors and catcher vessels harvesting pollock for processing by catcher/processors in the offshore component; and

(3) 10 percent to catcher vessels harvesting pollock for processing by motherships in the offshore component.

SEC. 207. [16 U.S.C. 1851 note] BUYOUT.

(a) FEDERAL LOAN.—Under the authority of sections 1111 and 1112 of title XI of the Merchant Marine Act, 1936 (46 U.S.C. App. 1279f and 1279g) and notwithstanding the requirements of section 312 of the Magnuson-Stevens Act (16 U.S.C. 1861a), the Secretary shall, subject to the availability of appropriations for the cost of the direct loan, provide up to $75,000,000 through a direct loan obligation for the payments required under subsection (d).

(b) INSHORE FEE SYSTEM.—Notwithstanding the requirements of section 304(d) or 312 of the Magnuson-Stevens Act (16 U.S.C. 1854(d) and 1861a), the Secretary shall establish a fee for the repayment of such loan obligation which—

(1) shall be six-tenths (0.6) of one cent for each pound round-weight of all pollock harvested from the directed fishing

allowance under section 206(b)(1); and

(2) shall begin with such pollock harvested on or after January 1, 2000, and continue without interruption until such loan obligation is fully repaid; and

(3) shall be collected in accordance with section 312(d)(2)(C) of the Magnuson-Stevens Act (16 U.S.C. 1861a(d)(2)(C)) and in accordance with such other conditions as the Secretary establishes.

(c) FEDERAL APPROPRIATION.—Under the authority of section 312(c)(1)(B) of the Magnuson-Stevens Act (16 U.S.C. 1861a(c)(1)(B)), there are authorized to be appropriated $20,000,000 for the payments required under subsection (d).

(d) PAYMENTS.—Subject to the availability of appropriations for the cost of the direct loan under subsection (a) and funds under subsection (c), the Secretary shall pay by not later than December 31, 1998—

(1) up to $90,000,000 to the owner or owners of the catcher/processors listed in paragraphs (1) through (9) of section 209, in such manner as the owner or owners, with the concurrence of the Secretary, agree, except that—

(A) the portion of such payment with respect to the catcher/processor listed in paragraph (1) of section 209 shall be made only after the owner submits a written certification acceptable to the Secretary that neither the owner nor a purchaser from the owner intends to use such catcher/processor outside of the exclusive economic zone of the United States to harvest any stock of fish (as such term is defined in section 3 of the Magnuson-Stevens Act (16 U.S.C. 1802)) that occurs within the exclusive economic zone of the United States; and

(B) the portion of such payment with respect to the catcher/processors listed in paragraphs (2) through (9) of section 209 shall be made only after the owner or owners of such catcher/processors submit a written certification acceptable to the Secretary that such catcher/processors will be scrapped by December 31, 2000 and will not, before that date, be used to harvest or process any fish; and

(2)(A) if a contract has been filed under section 210(a) by the catcher/processors listed in section 208(e), $5,000,000 to the owner or owners of the catcher/processors listed in paragraphs (10) through (14) of such section in such manner as the owner or owners, with the concurrence of the Secretary, agree; or

(B) if such a contract has not been filed by such date, $5,000,000 to the owners of the catcher vessels eligible under section 208(b) and the catcher/processors eligible under paragraphs (1) through (20) of section 208(e), divided based on the amount of the harvest of pollock in the directed pollock fishery by each such vessel in 1997 in such manner as the Secretary deems appropriate,

except that any such payments shall be reduced by any obligation to the federal government that has not been satisfied by such owner or owners of any such vessels.

(e) PENALTY.—If the catcher/processor under paragraph (1) of section 209 is used outside of the exclusive economic zone of the United States to harvest any stock of fish that occurs within the exclusive economic zone of the United States while the owner who received the payment under subsection (d)(1)(A) has an ownership interest in such vessel, or if the catcher/processors listed in paragraphs (2) through (9) of section 209 are determined by the Secretary not to have been scrapped by December 31, 2000 or to have been used in a manner inconsistent with subsection (d)(1)(B), the Secretary may suspend any or all of the federal permits which allow any vessels owned in whole or in part by the owner or owners who received payments under subsection (d)(1) to harvest or process fish within the exclusive economic zone of the United States until such time as the obligations of such owner or owners under subsection (d)(1) have been fulfilled to the satisfaction of the Secretary.

(f) PROGRAM DEFINED; MATURITY.—For the purposes of section 1111 of the Merchant Marine Act, 1936 (46 U.S.C. App. 1279f), the fishing capacity reduction program in this subtitle shall be within the meaning of the term "program" as defined and used in such section. Notwithstanding section 1111(b)(4) of such Act (46 U.S.C. App. 1279f(b)(4)), the debt obligation under subsection (a) of this section may have a maturity not to exceed 30 years.

(g) FISHERY CAPACITY REDUCTION REGULATIONS.—The Secretary of Commerce shall by not later than October 15, 1998 publish proposed regulations to implement subsections (b), (c), (d), and (e) of section 312 of the Magnuson-Stevens Act (16 U.S.C.

1861a) and sections 1111 and 1112 of title XI of the Merchant Marine Act, 1936 (46 U.S.C. App. 1279f and 1279g).

SEC. 208. [16 U.S.C. 1851 note] ELIGIBLE VESSELS AND PROCESSORS.

(a) CATCHER VESSELS ONSHORE.—Effective January 1, 2000, only catcher vessels which are—

(1) determined by the Secretary—

(A) to have delivered at least 250 metric tons of pollock; or

(B) to be less than 60 feet in length overall and to have delivered at least 40 metric tons of pollock,

for processing by the inshore component in the directed pollock fishery in any one of the years 1996 or 1997, or between January 1, 1998 and September 1, 1998;

(2) eligible to harvest pollock in the directed pollock fishery under the license limitation program recommended by the North Pacific Council and approved by the Secretary; and

(3) not listed in subsection (b),

shall be eligible to harvest the directed fishing allowance under section 206(b)(1) pursuant to a federal fishing permit.

(b) CATCHER VESSELS TO CATCHER/PROCESSORS.—Effective January 1, 1999, only the following catcher vessels shall be eligible to harvest the directed fishing allowance under section 206(b)(2) pursuant to a federal fishing permit:

(1) AMERICAN CHALLENGER (United States official number 633219);

(2) FORUM STAR (United States official number 925863);

(3) MUIR MILACH (United States official number 611524);

(4) NEAHKAHNIE (United States official number 599534);

(5) OCEAN HARVESTER (United States official number 549892);

(6) SEA STORM (United States official number 628959);

(7) TRACY ANNE (United States official number 904859); and

(8) any catcher vessel—

(A) determined by the Secretary to have delivered at

least 250 metric tons and at least 75 percent of the pollock it harvested in the directed pollock fishery in 1997 to catcher/processors for processing by the offshore component; and

(B) eligible to harvest pollock in the directed pollock fishery under the license limitation program recommended by the North Pacific Council and approved by the Secretary.

(c) CATCHER VESSELS TO MOTHERSHIPS.—Effective January 1, 2000, only the following catcher vessels shall be eligible to harvest the directed fishing allowance under section 206(b)(3) pursuant to a federal fishing permit:

(1) ALEUTIAN CHALLENGER (United States official number 603820);

(2) ALYESKA (United States official number 560237);

(3) AMBER DAWN (United States official number 529425);

(4) AMERICAN BEAUTY (United States official number 613847);

(5) CALIFORNIA HORIZON (United States official number 590758);

(6) MAR-GUN (United States official number 525608);

(7) MARGARET LYN (United States official number 615563);

(8) MARK I (United States official number 509552);

(9) MISTY DAWN (United States official number 926647);

(10) NORDIC FURY (United States official number 542651);

(11) OCEAN LEADER (United States official number 561518);

(12) OCEANIC (United States official number 602279);

(13) PACIFIC ALLIANCE (United States official number 612084);

(14) PACIFIC CHALLENGER (United States official number 518937);

(15) PACIFIC FURY (United States official number 561934);

(16) PAPADO II (United States official number 536161);

(17) TRAVELER (United States official number 929356);

(18) VESTERAALEN (United States official number 611642);

(19) WESTERN DAWN (United States official number 524423); and

(20) any vessel—

(A) determined by the Secretary to have delivered at least 250 metric tons of pollock for processing by motherships in the offshore component of the directed pollock fishery in any one of the years 1996 or 1997, or between January 1, 1998 and September 1, 1998;

(B) eligible to harvest pollock in the directed pollock fishery under the license limitation program recommended by the North Pacific Council and approved by the Secretary; and

(C) not listed in subsection (b).

(d) MOTHERSHIPS.—Effective January 1, 2000, only the following motherships shall be eligible to process the directed fishing allowance under section 206(b)(3) pursuant to a federal fishing permit:

(1) EXCELLENCE (United States official number 967502);

(2) GOLDEN ALASKA (United States official number 651041); and

(3) OCEAN PHOENIX (United States official number 296779).

(e) CATCHER/PROCESSORS.—Effective January 1, 1999, only the following catcher/processors shall be eligible to harvest the directed fishing allowance under section 206(b)(2) pursuant to a federal fishing permit:

(1) AMERICAN DYNASTY (United States official number 951307);

(2) KATIE ANN (United States official number 518441);

(3) AMERICAN TRIUMPH (United States official number 646737);

(4) NORTHERN EAGLE (United States official number 506694);

(5) NORTHERN HAWK (United States official number

643771);

(6) NORTHERN JAEGER (United States official number 521069);

(7) OCEAN ROVER (United States official number 552100);

(8) ALASKA OCEAN (United States official number 637856);

(9) ENDURANCE (United States official number 592206);

(10) AMERICAN ENTERPRISE (United States official number 594803);

(11) ISLAND ENTERPRISE (United States official number 610290);

(12) KODIAK ENTERPRISE (United States official number 579450);

(13) SEATTLE ENTERPRISE (United States official number 904767);

(14) US ENTERPRISE (United States official number 921112);

(15) ARCTIC STORM (United States official number 903511);

(16) ARCTIC FJORD (United States official number 940866);

(17) NORTHERN GLACIER (United States official number 663457);

(18) PACIFIC GLACIER (United States official number 933627);

(19) HIGHLAND LIGHT (United States official number 577044);

(20) STARBOUND (United States official number 944658); and

(21) any catcher/processor not listed in this subsection and determined by the Secretary to have harvested more than 2,000 metric tons of the pollock in the 1997 directed pollock fishery and determined to be eligible to harvest pollock in the directed pollock fishery under the license limitation program recommended by the North Pacific Council and approved by the Secretary, except that catcher/processors eligible under this

paragraph shall be prohibited from harvesting in the aggregate a total of more than one-half (0.5) of a percent of the pollock apportioned for the directed pollock fishery under section 206(b)(2).

Notwithstanding section 213(a), failure to satisfy the requirements of section 4(a) of the Commercial Fishing Industry Vessel Anti-Reflagging Act of 1987 (Public Law 100–239; 46 U.S.C. 12108 note) shall not make a catcher/processor listed under this subsection ineligible for a fishery endorsement.

(f) SHORESIDE PROCESSORS.—(1) Effective January 1, 2000 and except as provided in paragraph (2), the catcher vessels eligible under subsection (a) may deliver pollock harvested from the directed fishing allowance under section 206(b)(1) only to—

(A) shoreside processors (including vessels in a single geographic location in Alaska State waters) determined by the Secretary to have processed more than 2,000 metric tons round-weight of pollock in the inshore component of the directed pollock fishery during each of 1996 and 1997; and

(B) shoreside processors determined by the Secretary to have processed pollock in the inshore component of the directed pollock fishery in 1996 or 1997, but to have processed less than 2,000 metric tons round-weight of such pollock in each year, except that effective January 1, 2000, each such shoreside processor may not process more than 2,000 metric tons round-weight from such directed fishing allowance in any year.

(2) Upon recommendation by the North Pacific Council, the Secretary may approve measures to allow catcher vessels eligible under subsection (a) to deliver pollock harvested from the directed fishing allowance under section 206(b)(1) to shoreside processors not eligible under paragraph (1) if the total allowable catch for pollock in the Bering Sea and Aleutian Islands Management Area increases by more than 10 percent above the total allowable catch in such fishery in 1997, or in the event of the actual total loss or constructive total loss of a shoreside processor eligible under paragraph (1)(A).

(g) VESSEL REBUILDING AND REPLACEMENT.—

(1) IN GENERAL.—

(A) REBUILD OR REPLACE.—Notwithstanding any limitation to the contrary on replacing, rebuilding, or lengthening vessels or transferring permits or licenses to a replacement vessel contained in sections 679.2 and 679.4 of title 50, Code of Federal Regulations, as in effect on the date of enactment of the Coast Guard Authorization Act of 2010 and except as provided in paragraph (4), the owner of a vessel eligible under subsection (a), (b), (c), (d), or (e), in order to improve vessel safety and operational efficiencies (including fuel efficiency), may rebuild or replace that vessel (including fuel efficiency) with a vessel documented with a fishery endorsement under section 12113 of title 46, United States Code.

(B) SAME REQUIREMENTS.—The rebuilt or replacement vessel shall be eligible in the same manner and subject to the same restrictions and limitations under such subsection as the vessel being rebuilt or replaced.

(C) TRANSFER OF PERMITS AND LICENSES.—Each fishing permit and license held by the owner of a vessel or vessels to be rebuilt or replaced under subparagraph (A) shall be transferred to the rebuilt or replacement vessel or its owner, as necessary to permit such rebuilt or replacement vessel to operate in the same manner as the vessel prior to the rebuilding or the vessel it replaced, respectively.

(2) RECOMMENDATIONS OF NORTH PACIFIC FISHERY MANAGEMENT COUNCIL.—The North Pacific Fishery Management Council may recommend for approval by the Secretary such conservation and management measures, including size limits and measures to control fishing capacity, in accordance with the Magnuson-Stevens Act as it considers necessary to ensure that this subsection does not diminish the effectiveness of fishery management plans of the Bering Sea and Aleutian Islands Management Area or the Gulf of Alaska.

(3) SPECIAL RULE FOR REPLACEMENT OF CERTAIN VESSELS.—

(A) IN GENERAL.—Notwithstanding the requirements of subsections (b)(2), (c)(1), and (c)(2) of section 12113 of title 46, United States Code, a vessel that is eligible under subsection (a), (b), (c), or (e) and that qualifies to be documented with a fishery endorsement pursuant to section 213(g) may be replaced with a replacement vessel under paragraph (1) if the vessel that is replaced is validly documented with a fishery endorsement pursuant to section 213(g) before the replacement vessel is documented with a fishery endorsement under section 12113 of title 46, United States Code.

(B) APPLICABILITY.—A replacement vessel under subparagraph (A) and its owner and mortgagee are subject to the same limitations under section 213(g) that are applicable to the vessel that has been replaced and its owner and mortgagee.

(4) SPECIAL RULES FOR CERTAIN CATCHER VESSELS.—

(A) IN GENERAL.—A replacement for a covered vessel described in subparagraph (B) is prohibited from harvesting fish in any fishery (except for the Pacific whiting fishery) managed under the authority of any Regional Fishery Management Council (other than the North Pacific Fishery Management Council) established under section 302(a) of the Magnuson-Stevens Act.

(B) COVERED VESSELS.—A covered vessel referred to in subparagraph (A) is—

(i) a vessel eligible under subsection (a), (b), or (c) that is replaced under paragraph (1); or

(ii) a vessel eligible under subsection (a), (b), or (c) that is rebuilt to increase its registered length, gross tonnage, or shaft horsepower.

(5) LIMITATION ON FISHERY ENDORSEMENTS.—Any vessel that is replaced under this subsection shall thereafter not be eligible for a fishery endorsement under section 12113 of title 46, United States Code, unless that vessel is also a replacement vessel described in paragraph (1).

(6) GULF OF ALASKA LIMITATION.—Notwithstanding paragraph (1), the Secretary shall prohibit from participation in the groundfish fisheries of the Gulf of Alaska any vessel that is rebuilt or replaced under this subsection and that exceeds the maximum length overall specified on the license that authorizes fishing for groundfish pursuant to the license limitation program under part 679 of title 50, Code of Federal Regulations, as in effect on the date of enactment of the Coast Guard Authorization Act of 2010.

(7) AUTHORITY OF PACIFIC COUNCIL.—Nothing in this

section shall be construed to diminish or otherwise affect the authority of the Pacific Council to recommend to the Secretary conservation and management measures to protect fisheries under its jurisdiction (including the Pacific whiting fishery) and participants in such fisheries from adverse impacts caused by this Act.

(h) ELIGIBILITY DURING IMPLEMENTATION.—In the event the Secretary is unable to make a final determination about the eligibility of a vessel under subsection (b)(8) or subsection (e)(21) before January 1, 1999, or a vessel or shoreside processor under subsection (a), subsection (c)(21), or subsection (f) before January 1, 2000, such vessel or shoreside processor, upon the filing of an application for eligibility, shall be eligible to participate in the directed pollock fishery pending final determination by the Secretary with respect to such vessel or shoreside processor.

(i) ELIGIBILITY NOT A RIGHT.—Eligibility under this section shall not be construed—

(1) to confer any right of compensation, monetary or otherwise, to the owner of any catcher vessel, catcher/processor, mothership, or shoreside processor if such eligibility is revoked or limited in any way, including through the revocation or limitation of a fishery endorsement or any federal permit or license;

(2) to create any right, title, or interest in or to any fish in any fishery; or

(3) to waive any provision of law otherwise applicable to such catcher vessel, catcher/processor, mothership, or shoreside processor.

SEC. 209. [16 U.S.C. 1851 note] LIST OF INELIGIBLE VESSELS.

Effective December 31, 1998, the following vessels shall be permanently ineligible for fishery endorsements, and any claims (including relating to catch history) associated with such vessels that could qualify any owners of such vessels for any present or future limited access system permit in any fishery within the exclusive economic zone of the United States (including a vessel moratorium permit or license limitation program permit in fisheries under the authority of the North Pacific Council) are hereby extinguished:

(1) AMERICAN EMPRESS (United States official number 942347);

(2) PACIFIC SCOUT (United States official number 934772);

(3) PACIFIC EXPLORER (United States official number 942592);

(4) PACIFIC NAVIGATOR (United States official number 592204);

(5) VICTORIA ANN (United States official number 592207);

(6) ELIZABETH ANN (United States official number 534721);

(7) CHRISTINA ANN (United States official number 653045);

(8) REBECCA ANN (United States official number 592205); and

(9) BROWNS POINT (United States official number 587440).

SEC. 210. [16 U.S.C. 1851 note] FISHERY COOPERATIVE LIMITATIONS.

(a) PUBLIC NOTICE.—(1) Any contract implementing a fishery cooperative under section 1 of the Act of June 25, 1934 (15 U.S.C. 521) in the directed pollock fishery and any material modifications to any such contract shall be filed not less than 30 days prior to the start of fishing under the contract with the North Pacific Council and with the Secretary, together with a copy of a letter from a party to the contract requesting a business review letter on the fishery cooperative from the Department of Justice and any response to such request. Notwithstanding section 402 of the Magnuson-Stevens Act (16 U.S.C. 1881a) or any other provision of law, but taking into account the interest of parties to any such contract in protecting the confidentiality of proprietary information, the North Pacific Council and Secretary shall—

(A) make available to the public such information about the contract, contract modifications, or fishery cooperative the North Pacific Council and Secretary deem appropriate, which at a minimum shall include a list of the parties to the contract, a list of the vessels involved, and the amount of pollock and other fish to be harvested by each party to such contract; and

(B) make available to the public in such manner as the North Pacific Council and Secretary deem appropriate information about the harvest by vessels under a fishery cooperative of all species (including bycatch) in the directed pollock fishery on a vessel-by-vessel basis.

(b) CATCHER VESSELS ONSHORE.—

(1) CATCHER VESSEL COOPERATIVES.—Effective January 1, 2000, upon the filing of a contract implementing a fishery cooperative under subsection (a) which—

(A) is signed by the owners of 80 percent or more of the qualified catcher vessels that delivered pollock for processing by a shoreside processor in the directed pollock fishery in the year prior to the year in which the fishery cooperative will be in effect; and

(B) specifies, except as provided in paragraph (6), that such catcher vessels will deliver pollock in the directed pollock fishery only to such shoreside processor during the year in which the fishery cooperative will be in effect and that such shoreside processor has agreed to process such pollock,

the Secretary shall allow only such catcher vessels (and catcher vessels whose owners voluntarily participate pursuant to paragraph (2)) to harvest the aggregate percentage of the directed fishing allowance under section 206(b)(1) in the year in which the fishery cooperative will be in effect that is equivalent to the aggregate total amount of pollock harvested by such catcher vessels (and by such catcher vessels whose owners voluntarily participate pursuant to paragraph (2)) in the directed pollock fishery for processing by the inshore component during 1995, 1996, and 1997 relative to the aggregate total amount of pollock harvested in the directed pollock fishery for processing by the inshore component during such years and shall prevent such catcher vessels (and catcher vessels whose owners voluntarily participate pursuant to paragraph (2)) from harvesting in aggregate in excess of such percentage of such directed fishing allowance.

(2) VOLUNTARY PARTICIPATION.—Any contract implementing a fishery cooperative under paragraph (1) must

allow the owners of other qualified catcher vessels to enter into such contract after it is filed and before the calender year in which fishing will begin under the same terms and conditions as the owners of the qualified catcher vessels who entered into such contract upon filing.

(3) QUALIFIED CATCHER VESSEL.—For the purposes of this subsection, a catcher vessel shall be considered a "qualified catcher vessel" if, during the year prior to the year in which the fishery cooperative will be in effect, it delivered more pollock to the shoreside processor to which it will deliver pollock under the fishery cooperative in paragraph (1) than to any other shoreside processor.

(4) CONSIDERATION OF CERTAIN VESSELS.—Any contract implementing a fishery cooperative under paragraph (1) which has been entered into by the owner of a qualified catcher vessel eligible under section 208(a) that harvested pollock for processing by catcher/processors or motherships in the directed pollock fishery during 1995, 1996, and 1997 shall, to the extent practicable, provide fair and equitable terms and conditions for the owner of such qualified catcher vessel.

(5) OPEN ACCESS.—A catcher vessel eligible under section 208(a) the catch history of which has not been attributed to a fishery cooperative under paragraph (1) may be used to deliver pollock harvested by such vessel from the directed fishing allowance under section 206(b)(1) (other than pollock reserved under paragraph (1) for a fishery cooperative) to any of the shoreside processors eligible under section 208(f). A catcher vessel eligible under section 208(a) the catch history of which has been attributed to a fishery cooperative under paragraph (1) during any calendar year may not harvest any pollock apportioned under section 206(b)(1) in such calendar year other than the pollock reserved under paragraph (1) for such fishery cooperative.

(6) TRANSFER OF COOPERATIVE HARVEST.—A contract implementing a fishery cooperative under paragraph (1) may, notwithstanding the other provisions of this subsection, provide for up to 10 percent of the pollock harvested under such cooperative to be processed by a shoreside processor eligible under section 208(f) other than the shoreside processor to which pollock will be delivered under paragraph (1).

(7) FISHERY COOPERATIVE EXIT PROVISIONS.—

(A) FISHING ALLOWANCE DETERMINATION.—For purposes of determining the aggregate percentage of directed fishing allowances under paragraph (1), when a catcher vessel is removed from the directed pollock fishery, the fishery allowance for pollock for the vessel being removed—

(i) shall be based on the catch history determination for the vessel made pursuant to section 679.62 of title 50, Code of Federal Regulations, as in effect on the date of enactment of the Coast Guard Authorization Act of 2010; and

(ii) shall be assigned, for all purposes under this title, in the manner specified by the owner of the vessel being removed to any other catcher vessel or among other catcher vessels participating in the fishery cooperative if such vessel or vessels remain in the fishery cooperative for at least one year after the date on which the vessel being removed leaves the directed pollock fishery.

(B) ELIGIBILITY FOR FISHERY ENDORSEMENT.—Except as provided in subparagraph (C), a vessel that is removed pursuant to this paragraph shall be permanently ineligible for a fishery endorsement, and any claim (including relating to catch history) associated with such vessel that could qualify any owner of such vessel for any permit to participate in any fishery within the exclusive economic zone of the United States shall be extinguished, unless such removed vessel is thereafter designated to replace a vessel to be removed pursuant to this paragraph.

(C) LIMITATIONS ON STATUTORY CONSTRUCTION.—Nothing in this paragraph shall be construed—

(i) to make the vessels AJ (United States official number 905625), DONA MARTITA (United States official number 651751), NORDIC EXPLORER (United States official number 678234), and PROVIDIAN (United States official number 1062183) ineligible for a fishery endorsement or any permit necessary to participate in any fishery under the

authority of the New England Fishery Management
Council or the Mid-Atlantic Fishery Management
Council established, respectively, under
subparagraphs (A) and (B) of section 302(a)(1) of the
Magnuson-Stevens Act; or

(ii) to allow the vessels referred to in clause (i) to
participate in any fishery under the authority of the
Councils referred to in clause (i) in any manner that
is not consistent with the fishery management plan
for the fishery developed by the Councils under section
303 of the Magnuson-Stevens Act.

(c) CATCHER VESSELS TO CATCHER/PROCESSORS.—Effective
January 1, 1999, not less than 8.5 percent of the directed fishing
allowance under section 206(b)(2) shall be available for harvest only
by the catcher vessels eligible under section 208(b). The owners
of such catcher vessels may participate in a fishery cooperative
with the owners of the catcher/processors eligible under paragraphs
(1) through (20) of the section 208(e). The owners of such catcher
vessels may participate in a fishery cooperative that will be in effect
during 1999 only if the contract implementing such cooperative
establishes penalties to prevent such vessels from exceeding in 1999
the traditional levels harvested by such vessels in all other fisheries
in the exclusive economic zone of the United States.

(d) CATCHER VESSELS TO MOTHERSHIPS.—

(1) PROCESSING.—Effective January 1, 2000, the authority
in section 1 of the Act of June 25, 1934 (48 Stat. 1213 and 1214;
15 U.S.C. 521 et seq.) shall extend to processing by motherships
eligible under section 208(d) solely for the purposes of forming
or participating in a fishery cooperative in the directed pollock
fishery upon the filing of a contract to implement a fishery
cooperative under subsection (a) which has been entered into by
the owners of 80 percent or more of the catcher vessels eligible
under section 208(c) for the duration of such contract, provided
that such owners agree to the terms of the fishery cooperative
involving processing by the motherships.

(2) VOLUNTARY PARTICIPATION.—Any contract
implementing a fishery cooperative described in paragraph (1)
must allow the owners of any other catcher vessels eligible
under section 208(c) to enter such contract after it is filed and
before the calendar year in which fishing will begin under the

same terms and conditions as the owners of the catcher vessels who entered into such contract upon filing.

(e) EXCESSIVE SHARES.—

(1) HARVESTING.—No particular individual, corporation, or other entity may harvest, through a fishery cooperative or otherwise, a total of more than 17.5 percent of the pollock available to be harvested in the directed pollock fishery.

(2) PROCESSING.—Under the authority of section 301(a)(4) of the Magnuson-Stevens Act (16 U.S.C. 1851(a)(4)), the North Pacific Council is directed to recommend for approval by the Secretary conservation and management measures to prevent any particular individual or entity from processing an excessive share of the pollock available to be harvested in the directed pollock fishery. In the event the North Pacific Council recommends and the Secretary approves an excessive processing share that is lower than 17.5 percent, any individual or entity that previously processed a percentage greater than such share shall be allowed to continue to process such percentage, except that their percentage may not exceed 17.5 percent (excluding pollock processed by catcher/processors that was harvested in the directed pollock fishery by catcher vessels eligible under 208(b)) and shall be reduced if their percentage decreases, until their percentage is below such share. In recommending the excessive processing share, the North Pacific Council shall consider the need of catcher vessels in the directed pollock fishery to have competitive buyers for the pollock harvested by such vessels.

(3) REVIEW BY MARITIME ADMINISTRATION.—At the request of the North Pacific Council or the Secretary, any individual or entity believed by such Council or the Secretary to have exceeded the percentage in either paragraph (1) or (2) shall submit such information to the Administrator of the Maritime Administration as the Administrator deems appropriate to allow the Administrator to determine whether such individual or entity has exceeded either such percentage. The Administrator shall make a finding as soon as practicable upon such request and shall submit such finding to the North Pacific Council and the Secretary. For the purposes of this subsection, any entity in which 10 percent or more of the interest is owned or controlled by another individual or entity shall be considered

to be the same entity as the other individual or entity.

(f) LANDING TAX JURISDICTION.—Any contract filed under subsection (a) shall include a contract clause under which the parties to the contract agree to make payments to the State of Alaska for any pollock harvested in the directed pollock fishery which is not landed in the State of Alaska, in amounts which would otherwise accrue had the pollock been landed in the State of Alaska subject to any landing taxes established under Alaska law. Failure to include such a contract clause or for such amounts to be paid shall result in a revocation of the authority to form fishery cooperatives under section 1 of the Act of June 25, 1934 (15 U.S.C. 521 et seq.).

(g) PENALTIES.—The violation of any of the requirements of this subtitle or any regulation or permit issued pursuant to this subtitle shall be considered the commission of an act prohibited by section 307 of the Magnuson-Stevens Act (16 U.S.C. 1857), and sections 308, 309, 310, and 311 of such Act (16 U.S.C. 1858, 1859, 1860, and 1861) shall apply to any such violation in the same manner as to the commission of an act prohibited by section 307 of such Act (16 U.S.C. 1857). In addition to the civil penalties and permit sanctions applicable to prohibited acts under section 308 of such Act (16 U.S.C. 1858), any person who is found by the Secretary, after notice and an opportunity for a hearing in accordance with section 554 of title 5, United States Code, to have violated a requirement of this section shall be subject to the forfeiture to the Secretary of Commerce of any fish harvested or processed during the commission of such act.

SEC. 211. [16 U.S.C. 1851 note] PROTECTIONS FOR OTHER FISHERIES; CONSERVATION MEASURES.

(a) GENERAL.—The North Pacific Council shall recommend for approval by the Secretary such conservation and management measures as it determines necessary to protect other fisheries under its jurisdiction and the participants in those fisheries, including processors, from adverse impacts caused by this Act or fishery cooperatives in the directed pollock fishery.

(b) CATCHER/PROCESSOR RESTRICTIONS.—

(1) GENERAL.—The restrictions in this subsection shall take effect on January 1, 1999 and shall remain in effect thereafter except that they may be superceded (with the exception of paragraph (4)) by conservation and management

measures recommended after the date of the enactment of this Act by the North Pacific Council and approved by the Secretary in accordance with the Magnuson-Stevens Act.

(2) BERING SEA FISHING.—The catcher/processors eligible under paragraphs (1) through (20) of section 208(e) are hereby prohibited from, in the aggregate—

(A) exceeding the percentage of the harvest available in the offshore component of any Bering Sea and Aleutian Islands groundfish fishery (other than the pollock fishery) that is equivalent to the total harvest by such catcher/processors and the catcher/processors listed in section 209 in the fishery in 1995, 1996, and 1997 relative to the total amount available to be harvested by the offshore component in the fishery in 1995, 1996, and 1997;

(B) exceeding the percentage of the prohibited species available in the offshore component of any Bering Sea and Aleutian Islands groundfish fishery (other than the pollock fishery) that is equivalent to the total of the prohibited species harvested by such catcher/processors and the catcher/processors listed in section 209 in the fishery in 1995, 1996, and 1997 relative to the total amount of prohibited species available to be harvested by the offshore component in the fishery in 1995, 1996, and 1997; and

(C) fishing for Atka mackerel in the eastern area of the Bering Sea and Aleutian Islands and from exceeding the following percentages of the directed harvest available in the Bering Sea and Aleutian Islands Atka mackerel fishery—

(i) 11.5 percent in the central area; and

(ii) 20 percent in the western area.

(3) BERING SEA PROCESSING.—The catcher/processors eligible under paragraphs (1) through (20) of section 208(e) are hereby prohibited from—

(A) processing any of the directed fishing allowances under paragraphs (1) or (3) of section 206(b); and

(B) processing any species of crab harvested in the Bering Sea and Aleutian Islands Management Area.

(4) GULF OF ALASKA.—The catcher/processors eligible under paragraphs (1) through (20) of section 208(e) are hereby

prohibited from—

(A) harvesting any fish in the Gulf of Alaska;

(B) processing any groundfish harvested from the portion of the exclusive economic zone off Alaska known as area 630 under the fishery management plan for Gulf of Alaska groundfish; or

(C) processing any pollock in the Gulf of Alaska (other than as bycatch in non-pollock groundfish fisheries) or processing, in the aggregate, a total of more than 10 percent of the cod harvested from areas 610, 620, and 640 of the Gulf of Alaska under the fishery management plan for Gulf of Alaska groundfish.

(5) FISHERIES OTHER THAN NORTH PACIFIC.—The catcher/processors eligible under paragraphs (1) through (20) of section 208(e) and motherships eligible under section 208(d) are hereby prohibited from harvesting fish in any fishery under the authority of any regional fishery management council established under section 302(a) of the Magnuson-Stevens Act (16 U.S.C. 1852(a)) other than the North Pacific Council, except for the Pacific whiting fishery, and from processing fish in any fishery under the authority of any such regional fishery management council other than the North Pacific Council, except in the Pacific whiting fishery, unless the catcher/processor or mothership is authorized to harvest or process fish under a fishery management plan recommended by the regional fishery management council of jurisdiction and approved by the Secretary.

(6) OBSERVERS AND SCALES.—The catcher/processors eligible under paragraphs (1) through (20) of section 208(e) shall—

(A) have two observers onboard at all times while groundfish is being harvested, processed, or received from another vessel in any fishery under the authority of the North Pacific Council; and

(B) weigh its catch on a scale onboard approved by the National Marine Fisheries Service while harvesting groundfish in fisheries under the authority of the North Pacific Council.

This paragraph shall take effect on January 1, 1999 for catcher/

processors eligible under paragraphs (1) through (20) of section 208(e) that will harvest pollock allocated under section 206(a) in 1999, and shall take effect on January 1, 2000 for all other catcher/processors eligible under such paragraphs of section 208(e).

(c) CATCHER VESSEL AND SHORESIDE PROCESSOR RESTRICTIONS.—

(1) REQUIRED COUNCIL RECOMMENDATIONS.—By not later than July 1, 1999, the North Pacific Council shall recommend for approval by the Secretary conservation and management measures to—

(A) prevent the catcher vessels eligible under subsections (a), (b), and (c) of section 208 from exceeding in the aggregate the traditional harvest levels of such vessels in other fisheries under the authority of the North Pacific Council as a result of fishery cooperatives in the directed pollock fishery; and

(B) protect processors not eligible to participate in the directed pollock fishery from adverse effects as a result of this Act or fishery cooperatives in the directed pollock fishery.

If the North Pacific Council does not recommend such conservation and management measures by such date, or if the Secretary determines that such conservation and management measures recommended by the North Pacific Council are not adequate to fulfill the purposes of this paragraph, the Secretary may by regulation restrict or change the authority in section 210(b) to the extent the Secretary deems appropriate, including by preventing fishery cooperatives from being formed pursuant to such section and by providing greater flexibility with respect to the shoreside processor or shoreside processors to which catcher vessels in a fishery cooperative under section 210(b) may deliver pollock.

(2) BERING SEA CRAB AND GROUNDFISH.—

(A) Effective January 1, 2000, the owners of the motherships eligible under section 208(d) and the shoreside processors eligible under section 208(f) that receive pollock from the directed pollock fishery under a fishery cooperative are hereby prohibited from processing, in the aggregate for each calendar year, more than the percentage of the total catch of each species of crab in directed fisheries under the jurisdiction of the North Pacific Council than facilities operated by such owners processed of each such species in the aggregate, on average, in 1995, 1996, 1997. For the purposes of this subparagraph, the term "facilities" means any processing plant, catcher/processor, mothership, floating processor, or any other operation that processes fish. Any entity in which 10 percent or more of the interest is owned or controlled by another individual or entity shall be considered to be the same entity as the other individual or entity for the purposes of this subparagraph.

(B) Under the authority of section 301(a)(4) of the Magnuson-Stevens Act (16 U.S.C. 1851(a)(4)), the North Pacific Council is directed to recommend for approval by the Secretary conservation and management measures to prevent any particular individual or entity from harvesting or processing an excessive share of crab or of groundfish in fisheries in the Bering Sea and Aleutian Islands Management Area.

(C) The catcher vessels eligible under section 208(b) are hereby prohibited from participating in a directed fishery for any species of crab in the Bering Sea and Aleutian Islands Management Area unless the catcher vessel harvested crab in the directed fishery for that species of crab in such Area during 1997 and is eligible to harvest such crab in such directed fishery under the license limitation program recommended by the North Pacific Council and approved by the Secretary. The North Pacific Council is directed to recommend measures for approval by the Secretary to eliminate latent licenses under such program, and nothing in this subparagraph shall preclude the Council from recommending measures more restrictive than under this paragraph.

(3) FISHERIES OTHER THAN NORTH PACIFIC.—

(A) By not later than July 1, 2000, the Pacific Fishery Management Council established under section 302(a)(1)(F) of the Magnuson-Stevens Act (16 U.S.C. 1852(a)(1)(F)) shall recommend for approval by the Secretary conservation and management measures to protect fisheries under its jurisdiction and the participants in those fisheries from adverse impacts caused by this Act or by any fishery cooperatives in the directed pollock fishery.

(B) If the Pacific Council does not recommend such conservation and management measures by such date, or if the Secretary determines that such conservation and management measures recommended by the Pacific Council are not adequate to fulfill the purposes of this paragraph, the Secretary may by regulation implement adequate measures including, but not limited to, restrictions on vessels which harvest pollock under a fishery cooperative which will prevent such vessels from harvesting Pacific groundfish, and restrictions on the number of processors eligible to process Pacific groundfish.

(d) BYCATCH INFORMATION.—Notwithstanding section 402 of the Magnuson-Stevens Act (16 U.S.C. 1881a), the North Pacific Council may recommend and the Secretary may approve, under such terms and conditions as the North Pacific Council and Secretary deem appropriate, the public disclosure of any information from the groundfish fisheries under the authority of such Council that would be beneficial in the implementation of section 301(a)(9) or section 303(a)(11) of the Magnuson-Stevens Act (16 U.S.C. 1851(a)(9) and 1853(a)(11)).

(e) COMMUNITY DEVELOPMENT LOAN PROGRAM.—Under the authority of title XI of the Merchant Marine Act, 1936 (46 U.S.C. App. 1271 et seq.), and subject to the availability of appropriations, the Secretary is authorized to provide direct loan obligations to communities eligible to participate in the western Alaska community development quota program established under 304(i) of the Magnuson-Stevens Act (16 U.S.C. 1855(i)) for the purposes of purchasing all or part of an ownership interest in vessels and shoreside processors eligible under subsections (a), (b), (c), (d), (e), or (f) of section 208. Notwithstanding the eligibility criteria in section 208(a) and section 208(c), the LISA MARIE (United States official number 1038717) shall be eligible under such sections in the same manner as other vessels eligible under such sections.

SEC. 212. RESTRICTION ON FEDERAL LOANS. [Made amendments to section 302(b) of the Fisheries Financing Act (46

U.S.C. 1274 note).]

SEC. 213. [16 U.S.C. 1851 note] DURATION.

(a) GENERAL.—Except as otherwise provided in this title, the provisions of this title shall take effect upon the date of the enactment of this Act. There are authorized to be appropriated $6,700,000 per year to carry out the provisions of this Act through fiscal year 2004.

(b) EXISTING AUTHORITY.—Except for the measures required by this subtitle, nothing in this subtitle shall be construed to limit the authority of the North Pacific Council or the Secretary under the Magnuson-Stevens Act.

(c) CHANGES TO FISHERY COOPERATIVE LIMITATIONS AND POLLOCK CDQ ALLOCATION.—The North Pacific Council may recommend and the Secretary may approve conservation and management measures in accordance with the Magnuson-Stevens Act—

(1) that supersede the provisions of this title[5], except for sections 206 and 208, for conservation purposes or to mitigate adverse effects in fisheries or on owners of fewer than three vessels in the directed pollock fishery caused by this title[5] or fishery cooperatives in the directed pollock fishery, provided such measures take into account all factors affecting the fisheries and are imposed fairly and equitably to the extent practicable among and within the sectors in the directed pollock fishery;

---

[5] Paragraph (6) of section 3027(a) of Public Law 106–31 (113 Stat. 101) amends this paragraph by striking "title" and inserting "subtitle". The amendment was not executed, because it did not specify which occurence of the word "title" to strike.

---

(2) that supersede the allocation in section 206(a) for any of the years 2002, 2003, and 2004, upon the finding by such Council that the western Alaska community development quota program for pollock has been adversely affected by the amendments in this subtitle; or

(3) that supersede the criteria required in paragraph (1) of section 210(b) to be used by the Secretary to set the percentage allowed to be harvested by catcher vessels pursuant to a fishery cooperative under such paragraph.

(d) REPORT TO CONGRESS.—Not later than October 1, 2000, the North Pacific Council shall submit a report to the Secretary and to Congress on the implementation and effects of this Act, including the effects on fishery conservation and management, on bycatch levels, on fishing communities, on business and employment practices of participants in any fishery cooperatives, on the western Alaska community development quota program, on any fisheries outside of the authority of the North Pacific Council, and such other matters as the North Pacific Council deems appropriate.

(e) REPORT ON FILLET PRODUCTION.—Not later than June 1, 2000, the General Accounting Office shall submit a report to the North Pacific Council, the Secretary, and the Congress on whether this Act has negatively affected the market for fillets and fillet blocks, including through the reduction in the supply of such fillets and fillet blocks. If the report determines that such market has been negatively affected, the North Pacific Council shall recommend measures for the Secretary's approval to mitigate any negative effects.

(f) SEVERABILITY.—If any provision of this title, an amendment made by this title, or the application of such provision or amendment to any person or circumstance is held to be unconstitutional, the remainder of this title, the amendments made by this title, and the application of the provisions of such to any person or circumstance shall not be affected thereby.

(g) INTERNATIONAL AGREEMENTS.—In the event that any provision of section 12102(c) or section 31322(a) of title 46, United States Code, as amended by this Act, is determined to be inconsistent with an existing international agreement relating to foreign investment to which the United States is a party with respect to the owner or mortgagee on of[6] a vessel with a fishery endorsement, such provision shall not apply to that owner or mortgagee with respect to their ownership or mortgage interest in such vessel on that date to the extent of any such inconsistency. The provisions of section 12102(c) and section 31322(a) of title 46, United States Code, as amended by this Act, shall apply to all subsequent owners and mortgagees of such vessel, and shall apply, notwithstanding the preceding sentence, to the owner on of[6] such vessel if any ownership interest in that owner is transferred to or otherwise acquired by a foreign individual or entity after or if the percentage of foreign ownership in the vessel is increased after the effective date of this subsection.

---

6   So in law. See amendment made by section 2202(e)(1)(A) of Public Law
107–20, 115 Stat. 170.

---

* * * * * * *

TITLE III—DENALI COMMISSION

SEC. 301. [42 U.S.C. 3121 note] SHORT TITLE.

This title may be cited as the "Denali Commission Act of 1998".

SEC. 302. [42 U.S.C. 3121 note] PURPOSES.

The purposes of this title are as follows:

(1) To deliver the services of the Federal Government in the most cost-effective manner practicable by reducing administrative and overhead costs.

(2) To provide job training and other economic development services in rural communities particularly distressed communities (many of which have a rate of unemployment that exceeds 50 percent).

(3) To promote rural development, provide power generation and transmission facilities, modern communication systems, water and sewer systems and other infrastructure needs.

SEC. 303. [42 U.S.C. 3121 note] ESTABLISHMENT OF COMMISSION.

(a) ESTABLISHMENT.—There is established a commission to be known as the Denali Commission (referred to in this title as the "Commission").

(b) MEMBERSHIP.—

(1) COMPOSITION.—The Commission shall be composed of 7 members, who shall be appointed by the Secretary of Commerce (referred to in this title as the "Secretary"), of whom—

(A) one shall be the Governor of the State of Alaska, or an individual selected from nominations submitted by the Governor, who shall serve as the State Cochairperson;

(B) one shall be the President of the University of Alaska, or an individual selected from nominations submitted by the President of the University of Alaska;

(C) one shall be the President of the Alaska Municipal League or an individual selected from nominations submitted by the President of the Alaska Municipal League;

(D) one shall be the President of the Alaska Federation of Natives or an individual selected from nominations submitted by the President of the Alaska Federation of Natives;

(E) one shall be the Executive President of the Alaska State AFL–CIO or an individual selected from nominations submitted by the Executive President;

(F) one shall be the President of the Associated General Contractors of Alaska or an individual selected from nominations submitted by the President of the Associated General Contractors of Alaska; and

(G) one shall be the Federal Cochairperson, who shall be selected in accordance with the requirements of paragraph (2).

(2) FEDERAL COCHAIRPERSON.—

(A) IN GENERAL.—The President pro temporare of the Senate and the Speaker of the House of Representatives shall each submit a list of nominations for the position of the Federal Cochairperson under paragraph (1)(G), including pertinent biographical information, to the Secretary.

(B) APPOINTMENT.—The Secretary shall appoint the Federal Cochairperson from among the list of nominations submitted under subparagraph (A). The Federal Cochairperson shall serve as an employee of the Department of Commerce, and may be removed by the Secretary for cause.

(C) FEDERAL COCHAIRPERSON VOTE.—The Federal Cochairperson appointed under this paragraph shall break any tie in the voting of the Commission.

(4) DATE.—The appointments of the members of the Commission shall be made no later than January 1, 1999.

(c) PERIOD OF APPOINTMENT; VACANCIES.—

(1) TERM OF FEDERAL COCHAIRPERSON.—The Federal Cochairperson shall serve for a term of four years and may be reappointed. shall be appointed for the life of the Commission.

(2) INTERIM FEDERAL COCHAIRPERSON.—In the event of a vacancy for any reason in the position of Federal Cochairperson, the Secretary may appoint an Interim Federal Cochairperson, who shall have all the authority of the Federal Cochairperson, to serve until such time as the vacancy in the position of Federal Cochairperson is filled in accordance with subsection (b)(2)).

(3) TERM OF ALL OTHER MEMBERS.—All other members shall be appointed for the life of the Commission.

(4) VACANCIES.—Except as provided in paragraph (2), any vacancy in the Commission shall not affect its powers, but shall be filled in the same manner as the original appointment.

(d) MEETINGS.—

(1) IN GENERAL.—The Commission shall meet at the call of the Federal Cochairperson not less frequently than 2 times each year, and may, as appropriate, conduct business by telephone or other electronic means.

(2) NOTIFICATION.—Not later than 2 weeks before calling a meeting under this subsection, the Federal Cochairperson shall—

(A) notify each member of the Commission of the time, date and location of that meeting; and

(B) provide each member of the Commission with a written agenda for the meeting, including any proposals for discussion and consideration, and any appropriate background materials.

(e) QUORUM.—A majority of the members of the Commission shall constitute a quorum, but a lesser number of members may hold hearings.

(f) NO FEDERAL EMPLOYEE STATUS.—No member of the Commission, other than the Federal Cochairperson, shall be considered to be a Federal employee for any purpose.

(g) CONFLICTS OF INTEREST.—

(1) IN GENERAL.—Except as provided in paragraphs (2) and (3), no member of the Commission (referred to in this subsection

as a "member") shall participate personally or substantially, through recommendation, the rendering of advice, investigation, or otherwise, in any proceeding, application, request for a ruling or other determination, contract claim, controversy, or other matter in which, to the knowledge of the member, 1 or more of the following has a direct financial interest:

(A) The member.

(B) The spouse, minor child, or partner of the member.

(C) An organization described in subparagraph (B), (C), (D), (E), or (F) of subsection (b)(1) for which the member is serving as an officer, director, trustee, partner, or employee.

(D) Any individual, person, or organization with which the member is negotiating or has any arrangement concerning prospective employment.

(2) DISCLOSURE.—Paragraph (1) shall not apply if the member—

(A) immediately advises the designated agency ethics official for the Commission of the nature and circumstances of the matter presenting a potential conflict of interest;

(B) makes full disclosure of the financial interest; and

(C) before the proceeding concerning the matter presenting the conflict of interest, receives a written determination by the designated agency ethics official for the Commission that the interest is not so substantial as to be likely to affect the integrity of the services that the Commission may expect from the member. The written determination shall specify the rationale and any evidence or support for the decision, identify steps, if any, that should be taken to mitigate any conflict of interest, and be available to the public.

(3) ANNUAL DISCLOSURES.—Once each calendar year, each member shall make full disclosure of financial interests, in a manner to be determined by the designated agency ethics official for the Commission.

(4) TRAINING.—Once each calendar year, each member shall undergo disclosure of financial interests training, as prescribed by the designated agency ethics official for the

Commission.

(5) CLARIFICATION.—A member of the Commission may continue to participate personally or substantially, through decision, approval, or disapproval on the focus of applications to be considered but not on individual applications where a conflict of interest exists.

(6) VIOLATION.—Any person that violates this subsection shall be fined not more than $10,000, imprisoned for not more than 2 years, or both.

SEC. 304. [42 U.S.C. 3121 note] DUTIES OF THE COMMISSION.

(a) WORK PLAN.—

(1) IN GENERAL.—Not later than 1 year after the date of enactment of this Act and annually thereafter, the Commission shall develop a proposed work plan for Alaska that meets the requirements of paragraph (2) and submit that plan to the Federal Cochairperson for review in accordance with the requirements of subsection (b).

(2) WORK PLAN.—In developing the work plan, the Commission shall—

(A) solicit project proposals from local governments and other entities and organizations; and

(B) provide for a comprehensive work plan for rural and infrastructure development and necessary job training in the area covered under the work plan.

(3) REPORT.—Upon completion of a work plan under this subsection, the Commission shall prepare, and submit to the Secretary, the Federal Cochairperson, and the Director of the Office of Management and Budget, a report that outlines the work plan and contains recommendations for funding priorities.

(b) REVIEW BY FEDERAL COCHAIRPERSON.—

(1) IN GENERAL.—Upon receiving a work plan under this section, the Secretary, acting through the Federal Cochairperson, shall publish the work plan in the Federal Register, with notice and an opportunity for public comment. The period for public review and comment shall be the 30-day period beginning on the date of publication of that notice.

(2) CRITERIA FOR REVIEW.—In conducting a review under

paragraph (1), the Secretary, acting through the Federal Cochairperson, shall—

(A) take into consideration the information, views, and comments received from interested parties through the public review and comment process specified in paragraph (1); and

(B) consult with appropriate Federal officials in Alaska including but not limited to Bureau of Indian Affairs, Economic Development Administration, and Rural Development Administration.

(3) APPROVAL.—Not later than 30 days after the end of the period specified in paragraph (1), the Secretary acting through the Federal Cochairperson, shall—

(A) approve, disapprove, or partially approve the work plan that is the subject of the review; and

(B) issue to the Commission a notice of the approval, disapproval, or partial approval that—

(i) specifies the reasons for disapproving any portion of the work plan; and

(ii) if applicable, includes recommendations for revisions to the work plan to make the plan subject to approval.

(4) REVIEW OF DISAPPROVAL OR PARTIAL APPROVAL.—If the Secretary, acting through the Federal Cochairperson, disapproves or partially approves a work plan, the Federal Cochairperson shall submit that work plan to the Commission for review and revision.

SEC. 305. [42 U.S.C. 3121 note] POWERS OF THE COMMISSION.

(a) INFORMATION FROM FEDERAL AGENCIES.—The Commission may secure directly from any Federal department or agency such information as it considers necessary to carry out the provisions of this Act. Upon request of the Federal Cochairperson of the Commission, the head of such department or agency shall furnish such information to the Commission. Agencies must provide the Commission with the requested information in a timely manner. Agencies are not required to provide the Commission any information that is exempt from disclosure by the Freedom of Information Act. Agenices may, upon request by the Commission, make services and personnel available to the Commission to carry out the duties of the Commission. To the maximum extent practicable, the Commission shall contract for completion of necesssary work utilizing local firms and labor to minimize costs.

(b) POSTAL SERVICES.—The Commission may use the United States mails in the same manner and under the same conditions as other departments and agencies of the Federal Government.

(c) GIFTS.—

(1) IN GENERAL.—Except as provided in paragraph (2), the Commission, on behalf of the United States, may accept use, and dispose of gifts or donations of services, property, or money for purposes of carrying out this Act.

(2) CONDITIONAL.—With respect to conditional gifts—

(A)(i) the Commission, on behalf of the United States, may accept conditional gifts for purposes of carrying out this Act, if approved by the Federal Cochairperson; and

(ii) the principal of and income from any such conditional gift shall be held, invested, reinvested, and used in accordance with the condition applicable to the gift; but

(B) no gift shall be accepted that is conditioned on any expenditure not to be funded from the gift or from the income generated by the gift unless the expenditure has been approved by Act of Congress.

(d) The Commission, acting through the Federal Cochairperson, is authorized to enter into contracts and cooperative agreements, award grants, and make payments necessary to carry out the purposes of the Commission. With respect to funds appropriated to the Commission for fiscal year 1999, the Commission, acting through the Federal Cochairperson, is authorized to enter into contracts and cooperative agreements, award grants, and make payments to implement an interim work plan for fiscal year 1999 approved by the Commission.

SEC. 306. [42 U.S.C. 3121 note] COMMISSION PERSONNEL MATTERS.

(a) COMPENSATION OF MEMBERS.—Each member of the Commission who is not an officer or employee of the Federal Government shall be compensated at a rate equal to the daily equivalent of the annual rate of basic pay prescribed for level IV of the Executive Schedule under section 5315 of title 5, United States Code, for each day (including travel time) during the time such member is engaged in the performance of the duties of the Commission. The Federal Cochairperson shall be compensated at the annual rate prescribed for level IV of the Executive Schedule under section 5315 of title 5, United States Code. All members of the Commission who are officers or employees of the United States shall serve without compensation that is in addition to that received for their services as officers or employees of the United States.

(b) TRAVEL EXPENSES.—The members of the Commission shall be allowed travel expenses, including per diem in lieu of subsistence, at rates authorized for employees of agencies under subchapter I of chapter 57 of title 5, United States Code, while away from their homes or regular places of business in the performance of services for the Commission.

(c) STAFF.—

(1) IN GENERAL.—The Federal Cochairperson of the Commission may, without regard to the civil service laws and regulations, appoint such personnel as may be necessary to enable the Commission to perform its duties.

(2) COMPENSATION.—The Federal Cochairperson of the Commission may fix the compensation of personnel without regard to the provisions of chapter 51 and subchapter III of chapter 53 of title 5, United States Code, relating to classification of positions and General Schedule pay rates.

(d) DETAIL OF GOVERNMENT EMPLOYEES.—Any Federal Government employee may be detailed to the Commission without reimbursement, and such detail shall be without interruption or loss of civil service status or privilege.

(e) PROCUREMENT OF TEMPORARY AND INTERMITTENT SERVICES.—The Federal Cochairperson of the Commission may procure temporary and intermittent services under section 3109(b) of title 5, United States Code, at rates for individuals which do not exceed the daily equivalent of the annual rate of basic pay prescribed for level V of the Executive Schedule under section 5316 of such title.

(f) OFFICES.—The principal office of the Commission shall be located in Alaska, at a location that the Commission shall select.

(g) ADMINISTRATIVE EXPENSES AND RECORDS.—The Commission is hereby prohibited from using more than 5 percent of the amounts appropriated under the authority of this Act or transferred pursuant to section 329 of the Department of Transportation and Related Agencies Appropriations Act, 1999 (section 101(g) of division A of this Act) for administrative expenses. The Commission and its grantees shall maintain accurate and complete records which shall be available for audit and examination by the Comptroller General or his or her designee.

(h) INSPECTOR GENERAL.—Section 8G(a)(2) of the Inspector General Act of 1978 (5 U.S.C. App. 3, section 8G(a)(2)) is amended by inserting "the Denali Commission," after "the Corporation for Public Broadcasting,".

SEC. 307. [42 U.S.C. 3121 note] SPECIAL FUNCTIONS.

(a) RURAL UTILITIES.—In carrying out its functions under this title, the Commission shall as appropriate, provide assistance, seek to avoid duplicating services and assistance, and complement the water and sewer wastewater programs under section 306D of the Consolidated Farm and Rural Development Act (7 U.S.C. 1926d) and section 303 of the Safe Drinking Water Act Amendments of 1996 (33 U.S.C. 1263a).

(b) BULK FUELS.—Funds transferred to the Commission pursuant to section 329 of the Department of Transportation and Related Agencies Appropriations Act, 1999 (section 101(g) of division A of this Act) shall be available without further appropriation and until expended. The Commission, in consultation with the Commandant of the Coast Guard, shall develop a plan to provide for the repair or replacement of bulk fuel storage tanks in Alaska that are not in compliance with applicable—

(1) Federal law, including the Oil Pollution Act of 1990 (104 Stat. 484); or

(2) State law.

(c) DEMONSTRATION HEALTH PROJECTS.—In order to demonstrate the value of adequate health facilities and services to the economic development of the region, the Secretary of Health and Human Services is authorized to make interagency transfers to the Denali Commission to plan, construct, and equip demonstration health, nutrition, and child care projects, including hospitals, health care clinics, and mental health facilities (including drug and alcohol treatment centers) in accordance with the Work Plan referred to under section 304 of Title III-Denali Commission of Division C-Other Matters of Public Law 105–277. No grant for construction or equipment of a demonstration project shall exceed 50 percentum of such costs, unless the project is located in a severely economically distressed community, as identified in the Work Plan referred to under section 304 of Title III-Denali Commission of Division C-Other Matters of Public Law 105–277, in which case no grant shall exceed 80 percentum of such costs. To carry out this section, there is authorized to be appropriated such sums as may be necessary.

(d) SOLID WASTE.—The Secretary of Agriculture is authorized to make direct lump sum payments which shall remain available until expended to the Denali Commission to address deficiencies in solid waste disposal sites which threaten to contaminate rural drinking water supplies.

(e) DOCKS, WATERFRONT TRANSPORTATION DEVELOPMENT, AND RELATED INFRASTRUCTURE PROJECTS.—The Secretary of Transportation is authorized to make direct lump sum payments to the Commission to construct docks, waterfront development projects, and related transportation infrastructure, provided the local community provides a ten percent non-Federal match in the form of any necessary land or planning and design funds. To carry out this section, there is authorized to be appropriated such sums as may be necessary.

SEC. 308. [42 U.S.C. 3121 note] EXEMPTION FROM CHAPTER 10 OF TITLE 5, UNITED STATES CODE.

Chapter 10 of title 5, United States Code, shall not apply to the Commission.

SEC. 309. [42 U.S.C. 3121 note] DENALI ACCESS SYSTEM PROGRAM.

(a) ESTABLISHMENT OF THE DENALI ACCESS SYSTEM PROGRAM.—Not later than 3 months after the date of enactment of the SAFETEA-LU, the Secretary of Transportation shall establish a program to pay the costs of planning, designing, engineering, and constructing road and other surface transportation infrastructure identified for the Denali access system program under this section.

(b) DENALI ACCESS SYSTEM PROGRAM ADVISORY COMMITTEE.—

(1) ESTABLISHMENT.—Not later than 3 months after the date of enactment of the SAFETEA-LU, the Denali Commission

shall establish a Denali Access System Program Advisory Committee (referred to in this section as the "advisory committee").

(2) MEMBERSHIP.—The advisory committee shall be composed of nine members to be appointed by the Governor of the State of Alaska as follows:

(A) The chairman of the Denali Commission.

(B) Four members who represent existing regional native corporations, native nonprofit entities, or tribal governments, including one member who is a civil engineer.

(C) Four members who represent rural Alaska regions or villages, including one member who is a civil engineer.

(3) TERMS.—

(A) IN GENERAL.—Except for the chairman of the Commission who shall remain a member of the advisory committee, members shall be appointed to serve a term of 4 years.

(B) INITIAL MEMBERS.—Except for the chairman of the Commission, of the eight initial members appointed to the advisory committee, two shall be appointed for a term of 1 year, two shall be appointed for a term of 2 years, two shall be appointed for a term of 3 years, and two shall be appointed for a term of 4 years. All subsequent appointments shall be for 4 years.

(4) RESPONSIBILITIES.—The advisory committee shall be responsible for the following activities:

(A) Advising the Commission on the surface transportation needs of Alaska Native villages and rural communities, including projects for the construction of essential access routes within remote Alaska Native villages and rural communities and for the construction of roads and facilities necessary to connect isolated rural communities to a road system.

(B) Advising the Commission on considerations for coordinatedtransportation planning among the Alaska Native villages, Alaska rural villages, the State of Alaska, and other government entities.

(C) Establishing a list of transportation priorities for Alaska Native village and rural community transportation projects on an annual basis, including funding recommendations.

(D) Facilitate the Commission's work on transportation projects involving more than one region.

(5) CHAPTER 10 OF TITLE 5, UNITED STATES CODE, EXEMPTION.—The provisions of chapter 10 of title 5, United States Code, shall not apply to the advisory committee.

(c) ALLOCATION OF FUNDS.—

(1) IN GENERAL.—The Secretary shall allocate funding authorized and made available for the Denali access system program to the Commission to carry out this section.

(2) DISTRIBUTION OF FUNDING.—In distributing funds for surface transportation projects funded under the program, the Commission shall consult the list of transportation priorities developed by the advisory committee.

(d) PREFERENCE TO ALASKA MATERIALS AND PRODUCTS.—To construct a project under this section, the Commission shall encourage, to the maximum extent practicable, the use of employees and businesses that are residents of Alaska.

(e) DESIGN STANDARDS.—Each project carried out under this section shall use technology and design standards determined by the Commission to be appropriate given the location and the functionality of the project.

(f) MAINTENANCE.—Funding for a construction project under this section may include an additional amount equal to not more than 10 percent of the total cost of construction, to be retained for future maintenance of the project. All such retained funds shall be dedicated for maintenance of the project and may not be used for other purposes.

(g) LEAD AGENCY DESIGNATION.—For purposes of projects carried out under this section, the Commission shall be designated as the lead agency for purposes of accepting Federal funds and for purposes of carrying out this project.

(h) NON-FEDERAL SHARE.—Notwithstanding any other provision of law, funds made available to carry out this section may be used to meet the non-Federal share of the cost of projects under title 23, United States Code.

(i) SURFACE TRANSPORTATION PROGRAM TRANSFERABILITY.—

(1) TRANSFERABILITY.—In any fiscal year, up to 15 percent of the amounts made available to the State of Alaska for surface transportation by section 133 of title 23, United States Code, may be transferred to the Denali access system program.

(2) NO EFFECT ON SET-ASIDE.—Paragraph (2) of section 133(d), United States Code, shall not apply to funds transferred under paragraph (1).

(j) AUTHORIZATION OF APPROPRIATIONS.—

(1) IN GENERAL.—There is authorized to be appropriated out of the Highway Trust Fund (other than the Mass Transit Account) to carry out this section $15,000,000 for each of fiscal years 2006 through 2009.

(2) APPLICABILITY OF TITLE 23.—Funds made available to carry out this section shall be available for obligation in the same manner as if such funds were apportioned under chapter 1 of title 23, United States Code; except that such funds shall not be transferable and shall remain available until expended, and the Federal share of the cost of any project carried out using such funds shall be determined in accordance with section 120(b).

SEC. 310. [42 U.S.C. 3121 note] (a) The Federal Co-chairman of the Denali Commission shall appoint an economic development committee to be chaired by the president of the Alaska federation of natives which shall include the commissioner of community and economic affairs for the state of Alaska, a representative from the Alaska bankers association, the chairman of the Alaska permanent fund, a representative from the Alaska state chamber of commerce, and a representative from each region. of the regional representatives, at least two each shall be from native regional corporations, native non-profit corporations, tribes, and borough governments

(b) The Economic Development Committee is authorized to consider and approve applications from Regional Advisory Committees for grants and loans to promote economic development and promote private sector investment to reduce poverty in economically distressed rural villages. The Economic Development Committee may make mini-grants to individual applicants and may issue loans under such terms and conditions as it determines.

(c) The State Co-chairman of the Denali Commission shall appoint a Regional Advisory Committee for each region which may include representatives from local, borough, and tribal governments, the Alaska Native non-profit corporation operating in the region, local Chambers of Commerce, and representatives of the private sector. Each Regional Advisory Committee shall develop a regional economic development plan for consideration by the Economic Development Committee.

(d) The Economic Development Committee, in consultation with the First Alaskans Institute, may develop rural development performance measures linking economic growth to poverty reduction to measure the success of its program which may include economic, educational, social, and cultural indicators. The performance measures will be tested in one region for years and evaluated by the University of Alaska before being deployed statewide. Thereafter, performance in each region shall be evaluated using the performance measures, and the Economic Development Committee shall not fund projects which do not demonstrate success.

(e) Within the amounts made available annually to the Denali Commission for training, the Commission may make a grant to the First Alaskans Foundation upon submittal of an acceptable work plan to assist Alaska Natives and other rural residents in acquiring the skills and training necessary to participate fully in private sector business and economic and development opportunities through fellowships, scholarships, internships, public service programs, and other leadership initiatives.

(f) The Committee shall sponsor a statewide economic development summit in consultation with the World Bank to evaluate the best practices for economic development worldwide and how they can be incorporated into regional economic development plans.

(g) There is authorized to be appropriated such sums as may be necessary to the following agencies which shall be transferred to the Denali Commission as a direct lump sum payment to implement this section—

    (1) Department of Commerce, Economic Development Administration,

    (2) Department of Housing and Urban Development,

(3) Department of the Interior, Bureau of Indian Affairs,

(4) Department of Agriculture, Rural Development Administration, and

(5) Small Business Administration.

SEC. 311. [42 U.S.C. 3121 note] TRANSFER OF FUNDS FROM OTHER FEDERAL AGENCIES.

(a) IN GENERAL.—Subject to subsection (c), for purposes of this Act, the Commission may accept transfers of funds from other Federal agencies.

(b) TRANSFERS.—Any Federal agency authorized to carry out an activity that is within the authority of the Commission may transfer to the Commission any appropriated funds for the activity.

(c) TREATMENT.—Any funds transferred to the Commission under this subsection—

(1) shall remain available until expended;

(2) may, to the extent necessary to carry out this Act, be transferred to, and merged with, the amounts made available by appropriations Acts for the Commission by the Federal Cochairperson; and

(3) notwithstanding any other provision of law, shall—

(A) be treated as if directly appropriated to the Commission and subject to applicable provisions of this Act; and

(B) not be subject to any requirements that applied to the funds before the transfer, including a requirement in an appropriations Act or a requirement or regulation of the Federal agency from which the funds are transferred.

SEC. 312.[7] [42 U.S.C. 3121 note] AUTHORIZATION OF APPROPRIATIONS.

(a) IN GENERAL.—There are authorized to be appropriated to the Commission to carry out the duties of the Commission consistent with the purposes of this title and pursuant to the work plan approved under section 304, $15,000,000 for each of fiscal years 2017 through 2021.

---

[7] The placement of section 312 reflects the probable intent of Congress. The amendment made by paragraph (2) of section 5002(b) of Public Law 114–322 did

not include language to transfer section 312 (as so redesignated) to appear after section 311.

(b) AVAILABILITY.—Any sums appropriated under the authorization contained in this section shall remain available until expended.

SEC. 323. [16 U.S.C. 1011a] (a) WATERSHED RESTORATION AND ENHANCEMENT AGREEMENTS.—For fiscal year 2006 and each fiscal year thereafter, to the extent funds are otherwise available, appropriations for the Forest Service may be used by the Secretary of Agriculture for the purpose of entering into cooperative agreements with willing Federal, tribal, State and local governments, private and nonprofit entities and landowners for the protection, restoration and enhancement of fish and wildlife habitat, and other resources on public or private land, the reduction of risk from natural disaster where public safety is threatened, or a combination thereof or both that benefit these resources within the watershed.

(b) DIRECT AND INDIRECT WATERSHED AGREEMENTS.—The Secretary of Agriculture may enter into a watershed restoration and enhancement agreement—

(1) directly with a willing private landowner; or

(2) indirectly through an agreement with a State, local or tribal government or other public entity, educational institution, or private nonprofit organization.

(c) TERMS AND CONDITIONS.—In order for the Secretary to enter into a watershed restoration and enhancement agreement—

(1) the agreement shall—

(A) include such terms and conditions mutually agreed to by the Secretary and the landowner, state[8] or local government, or private or nonprofit entity;

---

[8] The term "state" should be capitalized in subsection (c)(1)(A).

(B) improve the viability of and otherwise benefit the fish, wildlife, and other resources on national forests lands within the watershed;

(C) authorize the provision of technical assistance by the Secretary in the planning of management activities that will further the purposes of the agreement;

(D) provide for the sharing of costs of implementing the agreement among the Federal Government, the landowner(s), and other entities, as mutually agreed on by the affected interests; and

(E) ensure that any expenditure by the Secretary pursuant to the agreement is determined by the Secretary to be in the public interest; and

(2) the Secretary may require such other terms and conditions as are necessary to protect the public investment on non-Federal lands, provided such terms and conditions are mutually agreed to by the Secretary and other landowners, State and local governments or both.

(d) APPLICABLE LAW.—Chapter 63 of title 31, United States Code, shall not apply to—

(1) a watershed restoration and enhancement agreement entered into under this section; or

(2) an agreement entered into under the first section of Public Law 94–148 (16 U.S.C. 565a–1).

(e) REPORTING REQUIREMENTS.—Not later than December 31, 1999, the Secretary shall submit a report to the Committees on Appropriations of the House and Senate, which contains—

(1) A concise description of each project, including the project purpose, location on federal and non-federal land, key activities, and all parties to the agreement.

(2) the[9] funding and/or other contributions provided by each party for each project agreement.

---

[9]   The first letter of subsection (e)(2) should be capitalized.

SEC. 329. [16 U.S.C. 535a] (a) PROHIBITION ON TIMBER PURCHASER ROAD CREDITS.—In financing any forest development road pursuant to section 4 of Public Law 88–657 (16 U.S.C. 535, commonly known as the National Forest Roads and Trails Act), the Secretary of Agriculture may not provide effective credit for road construction to any purchaser of national forest timber or other forest products or for the construction and repair of barge mooring points and barge landing sites to facilitate pumping fuel from fuel transport barges into bulk fuel storage tanks. .

(b)(1) CONSTRUCTION OF ROADS BY TIMBER PURCHASERS.—Whenever the Secretary of Agriculture makes a determination that a forest development road referred to in subsection (a) shall be constructed or paid for, in whole or in part, by a purchaser of national forest timber or other forest products, the Secretary shall include notice of the determination in the notice of sale of the timber or other forest products or for the construction and repair of barge mooring points and barge landing sites to facilitate pumping fuel from fuel transport barges into bulk fuel storage tanks. . The notice of sale shall contain, or announce the availability of, sufficient information related to the road described in the notice to permit a prospective bidder on the sale to calculate the likely cost that would be incurred by the bidder to construct or finance the construction of the road so that the bidder may reflect such cost in the bid.

(2) If there is an increase or decrease in the cost of roads constructed by the timber purchaser, caused by variations in quantities, changes or modifications subsequent to the sale of timber made in accordance with applicable timber sale contract provisions, then an adjustment to the price paid for timber harvested by the purchaser shall be made. The adjustment shall be applied by the Secretary as soon as practicable after any such design change is implemented.

(c) SPECIAL ELECTION BY SMALL BUSINESS CONCERNS.—(1) A notice of sale referred to in subsection (b) containing specified road construction of $50,000 or more, shall give a purchaser of national forest timber or other forest products that qualifies as a "small business concern" under the Small Business Act (15 U.S.C. 631 et seq.), and regulations issued thereunder, the option to elect that the Secretary of Agriculture build the roads described in the notice. The Secretary shall provide the small business concern with an estimate of the cost that would be incurred by the Secretary to construct the roads on behalf of the small business concern. The notice of sale shall also include the date on which the roads described in the notice will be completed by the Secretary if the election is made.

(2) If the election referred to in paragraph (1) is made, the purchaser of the national forest timber or other forest products shall pay to the Secretary of Agriculture, in addition to the price paid for the timber or other forest products, an amount equal to the estimated cost of the roads which otherwise would be

paid by the purchaser as provided in the notice of sale. Pending receipt of such amount, the Secretary may use receipts from the sale of national forest timber or other forest products and such additional sums as may be appropriated for the construction of roads, such funds to be available until expended, to accomplish the requested road construction.

(d) POST CONSTRUCTION HARVESTING.—In each sale of national forest timber or other forest products referred to in this section, the Secretary of Agriculture is encouraged to authorize harvest of the timber or other forest products in a unit included in the sale as soon as road work for that unit is completed and the road work is approved by the Secretary.

(e) CONSTRUCTION STANDARD.—For any forest development road that is to be constructed or paid for by a purchaser of national forest timber or other forest products, the Secretary of Agriculture may not require the purchaser to design, construct, or maintain the road (or pay for the design, construction, or maintenance of the road) to a standard higher than the standard, consistent with applicable environmental laws and regulations, that is sufficient for the harvesting and removal of the timber or other forest products, unless the Secretary bears that part of the cost necessary to meet the higher standard.

(f) TREATMENT OF ROAD VALUE.—For any forest development road that is constructed or paid for by a purchaser of national forest timber or other forest products, the estimated cost of the road construction, including subsequent design changes, shall be considered to be money received for purposes of the payments required to be made under the sixth paragraph under the heading "FOREST SERVICE" in the Act of May 23, 1908 (35 Stat. 260, 16 U.S.C. 500), and section 13 of the Act of March 1, 1911 (35 Stat. 963; commonly known as the Weeks Act; 16 U.S.C. 500). To the extent that the appraised value of road construction determined under this subsection reflects funds contributed by the Secretary of Agriculture to build the road to a higher standard pursuant to subsection (e), the Secretary shall modify the appraisal of the road construction to exclude the effect of the Federal funds.

(g) EFFECTIVE DATE.—(1) This section and the requirements of this section shall take effect (and apply thereafter) upon the earlier of—

(A) April 1, 1999; or

(B) the date that is the later of—

(i) the effective date of regulations issued by the Secretary of Agriculture to implement this section; and

(ii) the date on which new timber sale contract provisions designed to implement this section, that have been published for public comment, are approved by the Secretary.

(2) Notwithstanding paragraph (1), any sale of national forest timber or other forest products for which notice of sale is provided before the effective date of this section, and any effective purchaser road credit earned pursuant to a contract resulting from such a notice of sale or otherwise earned before that effective date shall remain in effect, and shall continue to be subject to section 4 of Public Law 88–657 and section 14(i) of the National Forest Management Act of 1976 (16 U.S.C. 472a(i)), and rules issued thereunder, as in effect on the day before the date of the enactment of this Act.

[Section 347 (relating to Stewardship End Result Contracting Projects) was repealed by section 8205(b) of Public Law 113–79.]

TITLE IV—AMERICAN COMPETITIVENESS AND WORKFORCE IMPROVEMENT ACT

SEC. 401. SHORT TITLE; TABLE OF CONTENTS; AMENDMENTS TO IMMIGRATION AND NATIONALITY ACT.

(a) SHORT TITLE.—This title may be cited as the "American Competitiveness and Workforce Improvement Act of 1998".

* * * * * * *

SEC. 414. COLLECTION AND USE OF H–1B NONIMMIGRANT FEES FOR SCHOLARSHIPS FOR LOW-INCOME MATH, ENGINEERING, AND COMPUTER SCIENCE STUDENTS AND JOB TRAINING OF UNITED STATES WORKERS.

(a)

* * *

* * * * * * *

(c) [29 U.S.C. 3224a] JOB TRAINING GRANTS.—

(1) IN GENERAL.—The Secretary of Labor shall use funds available under section 286(s)(2) of the Immigration and Nationality Act (8 U.S.C. 1356(s)(2)) to award grants to eligible entities to provide job training and related activities for workers to assist them in obtaining or upgrading employment in industries and economic sectors identified pursuant to paragraph (4) that are projected to experience significant growth and ensure that job training and related activities funded by such grants are coordinated with the public workforce investment system.

(2) USE OF FUNDS.—

(A) TRAINING PROVIDED.—Funds under this subsection may be used to provide job training services and related activities that are designed to assist workers (including unemployed and employed workers) in gaining the skills and competencies needed to obtain or upgrade career ladder employment positions in the industries and economic sectors identified pursuant to paragraph (4).

(B) ENHANCED TRAINING PROGRAMS AND INFORMATION.—In order to facilitate the provision of job training services described in subparagraph (A), funds under this subsection may be used to assist in the development and implementation of model activities such as developing appropriate curricula to build core competencies and train workers, identifying and disseminating career and skill information, and increasing the integration of community and technical college activities with activities of businesses and the public workforce investment system to meet the training needs for the industries and economic sectors identified pursuant to paragraph (4).

(3) ELIGIBLE ENTITIES.—Grants under this subsection may be awarded to partnerships of private and public sector entities, which may include—

(A) businesses or business-related nonprofit organizations, such as trade associations;

(B) education and training providers, including

community colleges and other community-based organizations; and

(C) entities involved in administering the workforce development system, as defined in section 3 of the Workforce Innovation and Opportunity Act, and economic development agencies.

(4) HIGH GROWTH INDUSTRIES AND ECONOMIC SECTORS.—For purposes of this subsection, the Secretary of Labor, in consultation with State workforce investment boards, shall identify industries and economic sectors that are projected to experience significant growth, taking into account appropriate factors, such as the industries and sectors that—

(A) are projected to add substantial numbers of new jobs to the economy;

(B) are being transformed by technology and innovation requiring new skill sets for workers;

(C) are new and emerging businesses that are projected to grow; or

(D) have a significant impact on the economy overall or on the growth of other industries and economic sectors.

(5) EQUITABLE DISTRIBUTION.—In awarding grants under this subsection, the Secretary of Labor shall ensure an equitable distribution of such grants across geographically diverse areas.

(6) LEVERAGING OF RESOURCES AND AUTHORITY TO REQUIRE MATCH.—

(A) LEVERAGING OF RESOURCES.—In awarding grants under this subsection, the Secretary of Labor shall take into account, in addition to other factors the Secretary determines are appropriate—

(i) the extent to which resources other than the funds provided under this subsection will be made available by the eligible entities applying for grants to support the activities carried out under this subsection; and

(ii) the ability of such entities to continue to carry out and expand such activities after the expiration of the grants.

(B) AUTHORITY TO REQUIRE MATCH.—The Secretary of Labor may require the provision of specified levels of a matching share of cash or noncash resources from resources other than the funds provided under this subsection for projects funded under this subsection.

(7) PERFORMANCE ACCOUNTABILITY.—The Secretary of Labor shall require grantees to report on the employment outcomes obtained by workers receiving training under this subsection using indicators of performance that are consistent with other indicators used for employment and training programs administered by the Secretary, such as entry into employment, retention in employment, and increases in earnings. The Secretary of Labor may also require grantees to participate in evaluations of projects carried out under this subsection.

(d) [16 U.S.C. 1869c] LOW-INCOME SCHOLARSHIP PROGRAM.—

(1) ESTABLISHMENT.—The Director of the National Science Foundation (referred to in this subsection as the "Director") shall award scholarships to low-income individuals to enable such individuals to pursue associate, undergraduate, or graduate level degrees in mathematics, engineering, computer science, or cybersecurity.

(2) ELIGIBILITY.—

(A) IN GENERAL.—To be eligible to receive a scholarship under this subsection, an individual—

(i) must be a citizen of the United States, a national of the United States (as defined in section 101(a) of the Immigration and Nationality Act), an alien admitted as a refugee under section 207 of the Immigration and Nationality, or an alien lawfully admitted to the United States for permanent residence;

(ii) shall prepare and submit to the Director an application at such time, in such manner, and containing such information as the Director may require; and

(iii) shall certify to the Director that the individual intends to use amounts received under the scholarship to enroll or continue enrollment at an institution of higher education (as defined in section 101(a) of the Higher Education Act of 1965) in order to pursue an associate, undergraduate, or graduate level degree in mathematics, engineering, computer science, cybersecurity, or other technology and science programs designated by the Director.

(B) ABILITY.—Awards of scholarships under this subsection shall be made by the Director solely on the basis of the ability of the applicant, except that in any case in which 2 or more applicants for scholarships are deemed by the Director to be possessed of substantially equal ability, and there are not sufficient scholarships available to grant one to each of such applicants, the available scholarship or scholarships shall be awarded to the applicants in a manner that will tend to result in a geographically wide distribution throughout the United States of recipients' places of permanent residence.

(3) LIMITATION.—The amount of a scholarship awarded under this subsection shall be determined by the Director. The Director may renew scholarships for up to 5 years.

(4) FUNDING.—The Director shall carry out this subsection only with funds made available under section 286(s)(3) of the Immigration and Nationality Act. The Director may use no more than 50 percent of such funds for undergraduate programs for curriculum development, professional and workforce development, and to advance technological education. Funds for these other programs may be used for purposes other than scholarships.

(5) FEDERAL REGISTER.—Not later than 60 days after the date of enactment of the L-1 Visa and H-1B Visa Reform Act, the Director shall publish in the Federal Register a list of eligible programs of study.

(e) [8 U.S.C. 1356 note] REPORTING REQUIREMENT.—The Secretary of Labor and the Director of the National Science Foundation shall—

(1) track and monitor the performance of programs receiving H-1B Nonimmigrant Fee grant money; and

(2) not later than one year after the date of enactment of this subsection, submit a report to the Committees on the

Judiciary of the House of Representatives and the Senate—

(A) the tracking system to monitor the performance of programs receiving H-1B grant funding; and

(B) the number of individuals who have completed training and have entered the high-skill workforce through these programs.

* * * * * * *

TITLE VII—OFFICE OF NATIONAL DRUG CONTROL POLICY REAUTHORIZATION

SEC. 701. [21 U.S.C. 1701 note] SHORT TITLE.

This title may be cited as the "Office of National Drug Control Policy Reauthorization Act of 1998".

SEC. 702. [21 U.S.C. 1701] DEFINITIONS.

In this title:

(1) AGENCY.—The term "agency" has the meaning given the term "executive agency" in section 102 of title 31, United States Code.

(2) APPROPRIATE CONGRESSIONAL COMMITTEES.—

(A) IN GENERAL.—The term "appropriate congressional committees" means—

(i) the Committee on the Judiciary, the Committee on Appropriations, and the Committee on Health, Education, Labor, and Pensions of the Senate; and

(ii) the Committee on Oversight and Government Reform, the Committee on the Judiciary, the Committee on Energy and Commerce, and the Committee on Appropriations of the House of Representatives.

(B) SUBMISSION TO CONGRESS.—Any submission to Congress shall mean submission to the appropriate congressional committees.

(3) DEMAND REDUCTION.—The term "demand reduction" means any activity conducted by a National Drug Control Program agency, other than an enforcement activity, that is

intended to reduce or prevent the use of drugs or support, expand, or provide treatment and recovery efforts, including—

(A) education about the dangers of illicit drug use;

(B) services, programs, or strategies to prevent substance use disorder, including evidence-based education campaigns, community-based prevention programs, collection and disposal of unused prescription drugs, and services to at-risk populations to prevent or delay initial use of an illicit drug;

(C) substance use disorder treatment;

(D) support for long-term recovery from substance use disorders;

(E) drug-free workplace programs;

(F) drug testing, including the testing of employees;

(G) interventions for illicit drug use and dependence;

(H) expanding availability of access to health care services for the treatment of substance use disorders;

(I) international drug control coordination and cooperation with respect to activities described in this paragraph;

(J) pre- and post-arrest criminal justice interventions such as diversion programs, drug courts, and the provision of evidence-based treatment to individuals with substance use disorders who are arrested or under some form of criminal justice supervision, including medication assisted treatment;

(K) other coordinated and joint initiatives among Federal, State, local, and Tribal agencies to promote comprehensive drug control strategies designed to reduce the demand for, and the availability of, illegal drugs;

(L) international illicit drug use education, prevention, treatment, recovery, research, rehabilitation activities, and interventions for illicit drug use and dependence; and

(M) research related to illicit drug use and any of the activities described in this paragraph.

(4) DIRECTOR.—The term "Director" means the Director of National Drug Control Policy.

(5) DRUG.—The term "drug" has the meaning given the term "controlled substance" in section 102(6) of the Controlled Substances Act (21 U.S.C. 802(6)).

(6) DRUG CONTROL.—The term "drug control" means any activity conducted by a National Drug Control Program agency involving supply reduction or demand reduction.

(7) EMERGING DRUG THREAT.—The term "emerging drug threat" means the occurrence of a new and growing trend in the use of an illicit drug or class of drugs, including rapid expansion in the supply of or demand for such drug.

(8) ILLICIT DRUG USE; ILLICIT DRUGS; ILLEGAL DRUGS.—The terms "illicit drug use", "illicit drugs", and "illegal drugs" include the illegal or illicit use of prescription drugs.

(9) LAW ENFORCEMENT.—The term "law enforcement" or "drug law enforcement" means all efforts by a Federal, State, local, or Tribal government agency to enforce the drug laws of the United States or any State, including investigation, arrest, prosecution, and incarceration or other punishments or penalties.

(10) NATIONAL DRUG CONTROL PROGRAM.—The term "National Drug Control Program" means programs, policies, and activities undertaken by National Drug Control Program agencies pursuant to the responsibilities of such agencies under the National Drug Control Strategy, including any activities involving supply reduction, demand reduction, or State, local, and tribal affairs.

(11) NATIONAL DRUG CONTROL PROGRAM AGENCY.—The term "National Drug Control Program agency" means any agency (or bureau, office, independent agency, board, division, commission, subdivision, unit, or other component thereof) that is responsible for implementing any aspect of the National Drug Control Strategy, including any agency that receives Federal funds to implement any aspect of the National Drug Control Strategy, but does not include any agency that receives funds for drug control activity solely under the National Intelligence Program or the Joint Military Intelligence Program.

(12) NATIONAL DRUG CONTROL STRATEGY.—The term "National Drug Control Strategy"or "Strategy" means the strategy developed and submitted to Congress under section

706, including any report, plan, or strategy required to be incorporated into or issued concurrently with such strategy.

(13) NONPROFIT ORGANIZATION.—The term "nonprofit organization" means an organization that is described in section 501(c)(3) of the Internal Revenue Code of 1986 and exempt from tax under section 501(a) of such Code.

(14) OFFICE.—The term "Office" means the Office of National Drug Control Policy established under section 703(a).

(15) STATE, LOCAL, AND TRIBAL AFFAIRS.—The term "State, local, and Tribal affairs" means domestic activities conducted by a National Drug Control Program agency that are intended to reduce the availability and use of illegal drugs, including—

(A) coordination and enhancement of Federal, State, local, and Tribal law enforcement drug control efforts;

(B) coordination and enhancement of efforts among National Drug Control Program agencies and State, local, and Tribal demand reduction and supply reduction agencies;

(C) coordination and enhancement of Federal, State, local, and Tribal law enforcement initiatives to gather, analyze, and disseminate information and law enforcement intelligence relating to drug control among domestic law enforcement agencies; and

(D) other coordinated and joint initiatives among Federal, State, local, and Tribal agencies to promote comprehensive drug control strategies designed to reduce the demand for, and the availability of, illegal drugs.

(16) SUBSTANCE USE DISORDER TREATMENT.—The term "substance use disorder treatment" means an evidence-based, professionally directed, deliberate, and planned regimen including evaluation, observation, medical monitoring, and rehabilitative services and interventions such as pharmacotherapy, behavioral therapy, and individual and group counseling, on an inpatient or outpatient basis, to help patients with substance use disorder reach recovery.

(17) SUPPLY REDUCTION.—The term "supply reduction" means any activity or program conducted by a National Drug Control Program agency that is intended to reduce the availability or use of illegal drugs in the United States or

abroad, including—

(A) law enforcement outside the United States;

(B) domestic law enforcement;

(C) source country programs, including economic development programs primarily intended to reduce the production or trafficking of illicit drugs;

(D) activities to control international trafficking in, and availability of, illegal drugs, including—

(i) accurate assessment and monitoring of international drug production and interdiction programs and policies; and

(ii) coordination and promotion of compliance with international treaties relating to the production, transportation, or interdiction of illegal drugs;

(E) activities to conduct and promote international law enforcement programs and policies to reduce the supply of drugs;

(F) activities to facilitate and enhance the sharing of domestic and foreign intelligence information among National Drug Control Program agencies, relating to the production and trafficking of drugs in the United States and in foreign countries;

(G) activities to prevent the diversion of drugs for their illicit use; and

(H) research related to any of the activities described in this paragraph.

SEC. 703. [21 U.S.C. 1702] OFFICE OF NATIONAL DRUG CONTROL POLICY.

(a) ESTABLISHMENT OF OFFICE.—There is established in the Executive Office of the President an Office of National Drug Control Policy, which shall—

(1) lead the national drug control effort, including coordinating with the National Drug Control Program agencies;

(2) coordinate and oversee the implementation of the national drug control policy, including the National Drug Control Strategy;

(3) assess and certify the adequacy of National Drug

Control Programs and the budget for those programs;

(4) evaluate the effectiveness of national drug control policy efforts, including the National Drug Control Program Agencies'[10]programs, by developing and applying specific goals and performance measurements and monitoring the agencies' program-level spending;

---

[10] Probably should read "agencies'".

---

(5) identify and respond to emerging drug threats related to illicit drug use;

(6) administer the Drug-Free Communities Program, the High Intensity Drug Trafficking Areas Program, and other grant programs directly authorized to be administered by the Office in furtherance of the National Drug Control Strategy; and

(7) facilitate broad-scale information sharing and data standardization among Federal, State, and local entities to support the national drug control efforts.

[Subsection (b) was repealed by section 8222(1) of Public Law 115–271.]

(c) ACCESS BY CONGRESS.—The location of the Office in the Executive Office of the President shall not be construed as affecting access by Congress, or any committee of the House of Representatives or the Senate, to any—

(1) information, document, or study in the possession of, or conducted by or at the direction of the Director; or

(2) personnel of the Office.

(d) OFFICE OF NATIONAL DRUG CONTROL POLICY GIFT FUND.—

(1) ESTABLISHMENT.—There is established in the Treasury of the United States a fund for the receipt of gifts, both real and personal, for the purpose of aiding or facilitating the work of the Office under section 704(c).

(2) CONTRIBUTIONS.—The Office may accept, hold, and administer contributions to the Fund.

(3) USE OF AMOUNTS DEPOSITED.—Amounts deposited in the Fund are authorized to be appropriated, to remain available until expended for authorized purposes at the discretion of the Director.

(4) ETHICS GUIDELINES.—The Director shall establish written guidelines setting forth the criteria to be used in determining whether a gift or donation should be declined under this subsection because the acceptance of the gift or donation would—

(A) reflect unfavorably upon the ability of the Director or the Office, or any employee of the Office, to carry out responsibilities or official duties under this title in a fair and objective manner; or

(B) compromise the integrity or the appearance of integrity of programs or services provided under this title or of any official involved in those programs or services.

(5) REGISTRY OF GIFTS.—The Director shall maintain a list of—

(A) the source and amount of each gift or donation accepted by the Office; and

(B) the source and amount of each gift or donation accepted by a contractor to be used in its performance of a contract for the Office.

(6) REPORT TO CONGRESS.—The Director shall include in the annual assessment under section 706(g) a copy of the registry maintained under paragraph (5).

SEC. 704. [21 U.S.C. 1703] APPOINTMENT AND DUTIES OF DIRECTOR AND DEPUTY DIRECTORS.

(a) APPOINTMENT.—

(1) IN GENERAL.—

(A) DIRECTOR.—

(i) IN GENERAL.—There shall be at the head of the Office a Director who shall hold the same rank and status as the head of an executive department listed in section 101 of title 5, United States Code.

(ii) APPOINTMENT.—The Director shall be appointed by the President, by and with the advice and consent of the Senate, and shall serve at the pleasure of the President.

(B) DEPUTY DIRECTOR.—There shall be a Deputy Director who shall report directly to the Director, and who shall be appointed by the President, and shall serve at the pleasure of the President.

(C) COORDINATORS.—The following coordinators shall be appointed by the Director:

(i) Performance Budget Coordinator, as described in subsection (c)(5).

(ii) Interdiction Coordinator, as described in section 711.

(iii) Emerging and Continuing Threats Coordinator, as described in section 709.

(iv) State, Local, and Tribal Affairs Coordinator, to carry out the activities described in subsection (j).

(v) Demand Reduction Coordinator, as described in subparagraph (D).

(D) DEMAND REDUCTION COORDINATOR.—The Director shall designate or appoint a United States Demand Reduction Coordinator to be responsible for the activities described in section 702(3). For purposes of carrying out the previous sentence, the Director shall designate or appoint an appointee in the Senior Executive Service or an appointee in a position at level 15 of the General Schedule (or equivalent).

(2) DUTIES OF DEPUTY DIRECTOR OF NATIONAL DRUG CONTROL POLICY.—The Deputy Director of National Drug Control Policy shall—

(A) carry out the duties and powers prescribed by the Director; and

(B) serve as the Director in the absence of the Director or during any period in which the office of the Director is vacant.

(3) ACTING DIRECTOR.—If the Director dies, resigns, or is otherwise unable to perform the functions and duties of the office, the Deputy Director shall perform the functions and duties of the Director temporarily in an acting capacity pursuant to subchapter III of chapter 33 of title 5, United States Code.

(4) PROHIBITION.—No person shall serve as Director or a Deputy Director while serving in any other position in the

Federal Government.

(5) PROHIBITION ON POLITICAL CAMPAIGNING.—Any officer or employee of the Office who is appointed to that position by the President, by and with the advice and consent of the Senate, may not participate in Federal election campaign activities, except that such officer or employee is not prohibited by this paragraph from making contributions to individual candidates.

(6) PROHIBITION ON THE USE OF FUNDS FOR BALLOT INITIATIVES.—No funds authorized under this title may be obligated for the purpose of expressly advocating the passage or defeat of a State or local ballot initiative.

(b) RESPONSIBILITIES.—The Director—

(1) shall assist the President in the establishment of policies, goals, objectives, and priorities for the National Drug Control Program;

(2) shall promulgate the National Drug Control Strategy under section 706(a) and each report under section 706(b) in accordance with section 706;

(3) shall coordinate and oversee the implementation by the National Drug Control Program agencies of the policies, goals, objectives, and priorities established under paragraph (1) and the fulfillment of the responsibilities of such agencies under the National Drug Control Strategy and make recommendations to National Drug Control Program agency heads with respect to implementation of Federal counter-drug programs;

(4) shall make such recommendations to the President as the Director determines are appropriate regarding changes in the organization, management, and budgets of National Drug Control Program agencies, and changes in the allocation of personnel to and within those departments and agencies, to implement the policies, goals, priorities, and objectives established under paragraph (1) and the National Drug Control Strategy;

(5) shall consult with and assist State and local governments with respect to the formulation and implementation of National Drug Control Policy and their relations with the National Drug Control Program agencies;

(6) shall appear before duly constituted committees and subcommittees of the House of Representatives and of the

Senate to represent the drug policies of the executive branch;

(7) shall notify any National Drug Control Program agency if its policies are not in compliance with the responsibilities of the agency under the National Drug Control Strategy, transmit a copy of each such notification to the President and the appropriate congressional committees, and maintain a copy of each such notification;

(8) shall provide, by July 1 of each year, budget recommendations, including requests for specific initiatives that are consistent with the priorities of the President under the National Drug Control Strategy, to the heads of departments and agencies with responsibilities under the National Drug Control Program, which recommendations shall—

(A) apply to the next budget year scheduled for formulation under the Budget and Accounting Act of 1921, and each of the 4 subsequent fiscal years; and

(B) address funding priorities developed in the National Drug Control Strategy;

(9) may serve as representative of the President in appearing before Congress on all issues relating to the National Drug Control Program;

(10) shall, in any matter affecting national security interests, work in conjunction with the Assistant to the President for National Security Affairs;

(11) may serve as spokesperson of the Administration on drug issues;

(12) shall ensure that no Federal funds appropriated to the Office of National Drug Control Policy shall be expended for any study or contract relating to the legalization (for a medical use or any other use) of a substance listed in schedule I of section 202 of the Controlled Substances Act (21 U.S.C. 812) and take such actions as necessary to oppose any attempt to legalize the use of a substance (in any form) that—

(A) is listed in schedule I of section 202 of the Controlled Substances Act (21 U.S.C. 812); and

(B) has not been approved for use for medical purposes by the Food and Drug Administration;

[Paragraph (13) was repealed by seciton 8221(b)(1)(A) of Public Law 115–271.]

(14) shall submit to the appropriate congressional committees on an annual basis, not later than 60 days after the date of the last day of the applicable period, a summary of—

(A) each of the evaluations received by the Director under section 706(g)(2); and

(B) the progress of each National Drug Control Program agency toward the drug control program goals of the agency using the performance measures for the agency developed under section 706(c);

(15) shall ensure that drug prevention and drug treatment research and information is effectively disseminated by National Drug Control Program agencies to State and local governments and nongovernmental entities involved in demand reduction by—

(A) encouraging formal consultation between any such agency that conducts or sponsors research, and any such agency that disseminates information in developing research and information product development agendas;

(B) encouraging such agencies (as appropriate) to develop and implement dissemination plans that specifically target State and local governments and nongovernmental entities involved in demand reduction; and

(C) supporting the substance abuse information clearinghouse administered by the Administrator of the Substance Abuse and Mental Health Services Administration and established in section 501(d)(16) of the Public Health Service Act by—

(i) encouraging all National Drug Control Program agencies to provide all appropriate and relevant information; and

(ii) supporting the dissemination of information to all interested entities;

(16) shall coordinate with the private sector to promote private research and development of medications to treat addiction;[Paragraph (17) was repealed by seciton 8221(b)(1)(A) of Public Law 115–271.]

(18) shall monitor and evaluate the allocation of resources among Federal law enforcement agencies in response to significant local and regional drug trafficking and production threats;

(19) shall submit an annual report to Congress detailing how the Office of National Drug Control Policy has consulted with and assisted State, local, and tribal governments with respect to the formulation and implementation of the National Drug Control Strategy and other relevant issues;

(20) shall, within 1 year after the date of the enactment of the Office of National Drug Control Policy Reauthorization Act of 2006, report to Congress on the impact of each Federal drug reduction strategy upon the availability, addiction rate, use rate, and other harms of illegal drugs; and

(21) in order to formulate the national drug control policies, goals, objectives, and priorities—

(A) shall consult with and assist—

(i) State and local governments;

(ii) National Drug Control Program agencies;

(iii) each committee, working group, council, or other entity established under this title, as appropriate;

(iv) the public;

(v) appropriate congressional committees; and

(vi) any other person in the discretion of the Director; and

(B) may—

(i) establish advisory councils;

(ii) acquire data from agencies; and

(iii) request data from any other entity.

(c) NATIONAL DRUG CONTROL PROGRAM BUDGET.—

(1) RESPONSIBILITIES OF NATIONAL DRUG CONTROL PROGRAM AGENCIES.—

(A) IN GENERAL.—For each fiscal year, the head of each department, agency, or program of the Federal Government with responsibilities under the National Drug Control Program Strategy shall transmit to the Director a copy of the proposed drug control budget request of the department, agency, or program at the same time as that budget request is submitted to their superiors (and before submission to the Office of Management and Budget) in the preparation of the budget of the President submitted to Congress under section 1105(a) of title 31, United States Code.

(B) SUBMISSION OF DRUG CONTROL BUDGET REQUESTS.—The head of each National Drug Control Program agency shall ensure timely development and submission to the Director of each proposed drug control budget request transmitted pursuant to this paragraph, in such format as may be designated by the Director with the concurrence of the Director of the Office of Management and Budget.

(C) CONTENT OF DRUG CONTROL BUDGET REQUESTS.—A drug control budget request submitted by a department, agency, or program under this paragraph shall include all requests for funds for any drug control activity undertaken by that department, agency, or program, including demand reduction, supply reduction, and State, local, and tribal affairs, including any drug law enforcement activities. If an activity has both drug control and nondrug control purposes or applications, the department, agency, or program shall estimate by a documented calculation the total funds requested for that activity that would be used for drug control, and shall set forth in its request the basis and method for making the estimate.

(2) NATIONAL DRUG CONTROL PROGRAM BUDGET PROPOSAL.—For each fiscal year, following the transmission of proposed drug control budget requests to the Director under paragraph (1), the Director shall, in consultation with the head of each National Drug Control Program agency and the head of each major national organization that represents law enforcement officers, agencies, or associations—

(A) develop a consolidated National Drug Control Program budget proposal designed to implement the National Drug Control Strategy and to inform Congress and the public about the total amount proposed to be spent on all supply reduction, demand reduction, State, local, and tribal affairs, including any drug law enforcement, and other drug control activities by the Federal Government, which shall conform to the content requirements set forth in paragraph (1)(C) and include—

(i) the funding level for each National Drug Control Program agency; and

(ii) alternative funding structures that could improve progress on achieving the goals of the National Drug Control Strategy; and

(B) submit the consolidated budget proposal to the President and Congress.

(3) REVIEW AND CERTIFICATION OF BUDGET REQUESTS AND BUDGET SUBMISSIONS OF NATIONAL DRUG CONTROL PROGRAM AGENCIES.—

(A) IN GENERAL.—The Director shall review each drug control budget request submitted to the Director under paragraph (1).

(B) REVIEW OF BUDGET REQUESTS.—

(i) INADEQUATE REQUESTS.—If the Director concludes that a budget request submitted under paragraph (1) is inadequate, in whole or in part, to implement the objectives of the National Drug Control Strategy with respect to the department, agency, or program at issue for the year for which the request is submitted, the Director shall submit to the head of the applicable National Drug Control Program agency a written description of funding levels and specific initiatives that would, in the determination of the Director, make the request adequate to implement those objectives.

(ii) ADEQUATE REQUESTS.—If the Director concludes that a budget request submitted under paragraph (1) is adequate to implement the objectives of the National Drug Control Strategy with respect to the department, agency, or program at issue for the year for which the request is submitted, the Director shall submit to the head of the applicable National Drug Control Program agency a written statement confirming the adequacy of the request.

(iii) RECORD.—The Director shall maintain a record of each description submitted under clause (i) and each statement submitted under clause (ii).

(C) SPECIFIC REQUESTS.—The Director shall not confirm the adequacy of any budget request that requests a level of funding that will not enable achievement of the goals of the National Drug Control Strategy, including—

(i) requests funding for Federal law enforcement activities that do not adequately compensate for transfers of drug enforcement resources and personnel to law enforcement and investigation activities;

(ii) requests funding for law enforcement activities on the borders of the United States that do not adequately direct resources to drug interdiction and enforcement;

(iii) requests funding for substance use disorder prevention and treatment activities that do not provide adequate results and accountability measures; and

(iv) requests funding for drug treatment activities that do not adequately support and enhance Federal drug treatment programs and capacity.

(D) AGENCY RESPONSE.—

(i) IN GENERAL.—The head of a National Drug Control Program agency that receives a description under subparagraph (B)(i) shall include the funding levels and initiatives described by the Director in the budget submission for that agency to the Office of Management and Budget.

(ii) IMPACT STATEMENT.—The head of a National Drug Control Program agency that has altered its budget submission under this subparagraph shall include as an appendix to the budget submission for that agency to the Office of Management and Budget an impact statement that summarizes—

(I) the changes made to the budget under this subparagraph; and

(II) the impact of those changes on the ability of that agency to perform its other responsibilities, including any impact on specific missions or programs of the agency.

(iii) CONGRESSIONAL NOTIFICATION.—The head of a National Drug Control Program agency shall submit a copy of any impact statement under clause (ii) to the Senate and the House of Representatives and the appropriate congressional committees,[11] at the time the budget for that agency is submitted to Congress under section 1105(a) of title 31, United States Code.

---

[11] Sections 103(c)(1) and 105(c)(3) of Public Law 109–469 (120 Stat. 3507, 3513) amend clause (iii) by inserting "and the appropriate congressional committees" after "House of Representatives". The amendment made by section 105(c)(3) of such Public Law was not carried out.

(E) CERTIFICATION OF BUDGET SUBMISSIONS.—

(i) IN GENERAL.—At the time a National Drug Control Program agency submits its budget request to the Office of Management and Budget, the head of the National Drug Control Program agency shall submit a copy of the budget request to the Director.

(ii) CERTIFICATION.—The Director shall—

(I) review each budget submission submitted under clause (i);

(II) based on the review under subclause (I), make a determination as to whether the budget submission of a National Drug Control Program agency includes the funding levels and initiatives described in subparagraph (B); and

(III) submit to the appropriate congressional committees—

(aa) a written statement that either—

(AA) certifies that the budget submission includes sufficient funding; or

(BB) decertifies the budget submission as not including sufficient funding;

(bb) a copy of the description made under subparagraph (B); and (cc) the budget recommendations made under subsection (b)(8).

(4) REPROGRAMMING AND TRANSFER REQUESTS.—

(A) IN GENERAL.—No National Drug Control Program agency shall submit to Congress a reprogramming or transfer request with respect to any amount of appropriated funds in an amount exceeding $5,000,000 or 10 percent of a specific program or account that is included in the National Drug Control Program budget unless the request has been approved by the Director. If the Director has not responded to a request for reprogramming subject to this subparagraph within 30 days after receiving notice of the request having been made, the request shall be deemed approved by the Director under this subparagraph and forwarded to Congress.

(B) APPEAL.—The head of any National Drug Control Program agency may appeal to the President any disapproval by the Director of a reprogramming or transfer request under this paragraph.

(5) PERFORMANCE-BUDGET COORDINATOR.—

(A) DESIGNATION.—The Director shall designate or appoint a United States Performance-Budget Coordinator to—

(i) ensure the Director has sufficient information necessary to analyze the performance of each National Drug Control Program agency, the impact Federal funding has had on the goals in the Strategy, and the likely contributions to the goals of the Strategy based on funding levels of each National Drug Control Program agency, to make an independent assessment of the budget request of each agency under this subsection;

(ii) advise the Director on agency budgets, performance measures and targets, and additional data and research needed to make informed policy decisions under this section and section 706; and

(iii) other duties as may be determined by the Director with respect to measuring or assessing performance or agency budgets.

(B) DETERMINATION OF POSITION.—For purposes of carrying out subparagraph (A), the Director shall designate or appoint an appointee in the Senior Executive Service or an appointee in a position at level 15 of the General Schedule (or equivalent).

(6) BUDGET ESTIMATE OR REQUEST SUBMISSION TO CONGRESS.—Whenever the Director submits any budget estimate or request to the President or the Office of Management and Budget, the Director shall concurrently transmit to the appropriate congressional committees a detailed statement of the budgetary needs of the Office to execute its mission based on the good-faith assessment of the Director.

(d) POWERS OF THE DIRECTOR.—In carrying out subsection (b), the Director may—

(1) select, appoint, employ, and fix compensation of such officers and employees of the Office as may be necessary to carry out the functions of the Office under this title;

(2) subject to subsection (e)(3), request the head of a department or agency, or program of the Federal Government to place department, agency, or program personnel who are engaged in drug control activities on temporary detail to another department, agency, or program in order to implement the National Drug Control Strategy, and the head of the department or agency shall comply with such a request;

(3) use for administrative purposes, on a reimbursable basis, the available services, equipment, personnel, and facilities of Federal, State, and local agencies;

(4) procure the services of experts and consultants in accordance with section 3109 of title 5, United States Code, relating to appointments in the Federal Service, at rates of compensation for individuals not to exceed the daily equivalent of the rate of pay payable under level IV of the Executive Schedule under section 5311 of title 5, United States Code;

(5) accept and use gifts and donations of property from Federal, State, and local government agencies, and from the private sector, as authorized in section 703(d);

(6) use the mails in the same manner as any other department or agency of the executive branch;

(7) monitor implementation of the National Drug Control Program, including—

(A) conducting program and performance audits and evaluations; and

(B) requesting assistance from the Inspector General of the relevant agency in such audits and evaluations;

(8) transfer funds made available to a National Drug Control Program agency for National Drug Control Strategy programs and activities to another account within such agency or to another National Drug Control Program agency for National Drug Control Strategy programs and activities, except that—

(A) the authority under this paragraph may be limited in an annual appropriations Act or other provision of Federal law;

(B) the Director may exercise the authority under this paragraph only with the concurrence of the head of each affected agency;

(C) in the case of an interagency transfer, the total amount of transfers under this paragraph may not exceed 3 percent of the total amount of funds made available for National Drug Control Strategy programs and activities to the agency from which those funds are to be transferred;

(D) funds transferred to an agency under this paragraph may only be used to increase the funding for programs or activities authorized by law;

(E) the Director shall—

(i) submit to the appropriate congressional committees and any other applicable committees of jurisdiction, a reprogramming or transfer request in advance of any transfer under this paragraph in accordance with the regulations of the affected agency ; and

(ii) annually submit to the appropriate congressional committees a report describing the effect of all transfers of funds made pursuant to this paragraph or subsection (c)(4) during the 12-month period preceding the date on which the report is submitted; and

(F) funds may only be used for—

(i) expansion of demand reduction activities;

(ii) interdiction of illicit drugs on the high seas, in United States territorial waters, and at United States ports of entry by officers and employees of National Drug Control Program agencies and domestic and foreign law enforcement officers;

(iii) accurate assessment and monitoring of international drug production and interdiction programs and policies;

(iv) activities to facilitate and enhance the sharing of domestic and foreign intelligence information among National Drug Control Program agencies related to the production and trafficking of drugs in the United States and foreign countries; and

(v) research related to any of these activities;

(9) issue to the head of a National Drug Control Program agency a fund control notice described in subsection (f) to ensure compliance with the National Drug Control Program Strategy and notify the appropriate congressional committees of any fund control notice issued in accordance with subsection (f)(5); and[12]

(10) participate in the drug certification process pursuant to section 490 of the Foreign Assistance Act of 1961 (22 U.S.C. 2291j) and section 706 of the Department of State Authorization Act for Fiscal Year 2003 (22 U.S.C. 229j–1).[13]

---

[12] Sections 103(d)(1) and 105(e)(2) of Public Law 109–469 (120 Stat. 3507, 3513) both provide for amendments to paragraph (9). The amendment made by section 105(e)(2) of such Public Law could not be executed. Paragraph (2) of section 105(e) provides as follows:
  (2) in paragraph (9), by striking "Strategy; and" and inserting "Strategy and notify the appropriate congressional committees of any fund control notice issued; and"; and

---

[13] Sections 103(d)(2) and 105(e)(3) of Public Law 109–469 (120 Stat. 3507, 3513) both provide for amendments to paragraph (10). The amendment made by section 105(e)(3) of such Public Law could not be executed. Paragraph (3) of section 105(e) provides as follows:
  (3) in paragraph (10), by striking "(22 U.S.C. 2291j)." and inserting "(22 U.S.C. 2291j) and section 706 of the Foreign Relations Authorization Act, Fiscal Year 2003 (22 U.S.C. 2291j–1).".

(e) PERSONNEL DETAILED TO OFFICE.—

(1) EVALUATIONS.—Notwithstanding any provision of chapter 43 of title 5, United States Code, the Director shall perform the evaluation of the performance of any employee detailed to the Office for purposes of the applicable performance appraisal system established under such chapter for any rating period, or part thereof, that such employee is detailed to such office.

(2) COMPENSATION.—

(A) BONUS PAYMENTS.—Subject to the availability of appropriations, the Director may provide periodic bonus payments to any employee detailed to the Office.

(B) RESTRICTIONS.—An amount paid under this paragraph to an employee for any period—

(i) shall not be greater than 20 percent of the basic pay paid or payable to such employee for such period; and

(ii) shall be in addition to the basic pay of such employee.

(C) AGGREGATE AMOUNT.—The aggregate amount paid during any fiscal year to an employee detailed to the Office as basic pay, awards, bonuses, and other compensation shall not exceed the annual rate payable at the end of such fiscal year for positions at level III of the Executive Schedule.

(3) MAXIMUM NUMBER OF DETAILEES.—The maximum number of personnel who may be detailed to another department or agency (including the Office) under subsection (d)(2) during any fiscal year is—

(A) for the Department of Defense, 50; and

(B) for any other department or agency, 10.

(f) FUND CONTROL NOTICES.—

(1) IN GENERAL.—A fund control notice may direct that all or part of an amount appropriated to the National Drug Control Program agency account be obligated by—

(A) months, fiscal year quarters, or other time periods; and

(B) activities, functions, projects, or object classes.

(2) UNAUTHORIZED OBLIGATION OR EXPENDITURE PROHIBITED.—An officer or employee of a National Drug Control Program agency shall not make or authorize an expenditure or obligation contrary to a fund control notice issued by the Director.

(3) DISCIPLINARY ACTION FOR VIOLATION.—In the case of a violation of paragraph (2) by an officer or employee of a National Drug Control Program agency, the head of the agency, upon the request of and in consultation with the Director, may subject the officer or employee to appropriate administrative discipline, including, when circumstances warrant, suspension from duty without pay or removal from office.

(4) CONGRESSIONAL NOTICE.—A copy of each fund control notice shall be transmitted to the appropriate congressional committees.

(5) RESTRICTIONS.—The Director shall not issue a fund control notice to direct that all or part of an amount appropriated to the National Drug Control Program agency account be obligated, modified, or altered in any manner contrary, in whole or in part, to a specific appropriation or statute.

(g) INAPPLICABILITY TO CERTAIN PROGRAMS.—The provisions of this section shall not apply to the National Intelligence Program, the Joint Military Intelligence Program, and Tactical and Related Activities, unless such program or an element of such program is designated as a National Drug Control Program—

(1) by the President; or

(2) jointly by—

(A) in the case of the National Intelligence Program, the Director and the Director of National Intelligence; or

(B) in the case of the Joint Military Intelligence Program and Tactical and Related Activities, the Director, the Director of National Intelligence, and the Secretary of Defense.

(h) CONSTRUCTION.—Nothing in this Act shall be construed as derogating the authorities and responsibilities of the Director of National Intelligence or the Director of the Central Intelligence Agency contained in the National Security Act of 1947 (50 U.S.C. 401 et seq.), the Central Intelligence Agency Act of 1949 (50 U.S.C.

403a et seq.), or any other law.

(i) MODEL ACTS PROGRAM.—

(1) IN GENERAL.—The Director shall provide for or shall enter into an agreement with a nonprofit organization to—

(A) advise States on establishing laws and policies to address illicit drug use issues; and

(B) revise such model State drug laws and draft supplementary model State laws to take into consideration changes in illicit drug use issues in the State involved.

(2) AUTHORIZATION OF APPROPRIATIONS.—There is authorized to be appropriated to carry out this subsection $1,250,000 for each of fiscal years 2018 through 2023.

(j) STATE, LOCAL, AND TRIBAL AFFAIRS COORDINATOR.—The Director shall designate or appoint a United States State, Local, and Tribal Affairs Coordinator to perform the duties of the Office outlined in this section and section 706 and such other duties as may be determined by the Director with respect to coordination of drug control efforts between agencies and State, local, and Tribal governments. For purposes of carrying out the previous sentence, the Director shall designate or appoint an appointee in the Senior Executive Service or an appointee in a position at level 15 of the General Schedule (or equivalent).

(k) HARM REDUCTION PROGRAMS.—When developing the national drug control policy, any policy of the Director, including policies relating to syringe exchange programs for intravenous drug users, shall be based on the best available medical and scientific evidence regarding the effectiveness of such policy in promoting individual health and preventing the spread of infectious disease and the impact of such policy on drug addiction and use. In making any policy relating to harm reduction programs, the Director shall consult with the National Institutes of Health and the National Academy of Sciences.

SEC. 705. [21 U.S.C. 1704] COORDINATION WITH NATIONAL DRUG CONTROL PROGRAM AGENCIES IN DEMAND REDUCTION, SUPPLY REDUCTION, AND STATE AND LOCAL AFFAIRS.

(a) ACCESS TO INFORMATION.—

(1) IN GENERAL.—Upon the request of the Director, the head of any National Drug Control Program agency shall

cooperate with and provide to the Director any statistics, studies, reports, and other information prepared or collected by the agency concerning the responsibilities of the agency under the National Drug Control Strategy that relate to—

(A) drug control; or

(B) the manner in which amounts made available to that agency for drug control are being used by that agency.

(2) PROTECTION OF INTELLIGENCE INFORMATION.—

(A) IN GENERAL.—The authorities conferred on the Office and the Director by this title shall be exercised in a manner consistent with provisions of the National Security Act of 1947 (50 U.S.C. 401 et seq.). The Director of National Intelligence shall prescribe such regulations as may be necessary to protect information provided pursuant to this title regarding intelligence sources and methods.

(B) DUTIES OF DIRECTOR.—The Director of National Intelligence and the Director of the Central Intelligence Agency shall, to the maximum extent practicable in accordance with subparagraph (A), render full assistance and support to the Office and the Director.

(3) REQUIRED REPORTS.—

(A) SECRETARIES OF THE INTERIOR AND AGRICULTURE.—Not later than July 1 of each year, the Secretaries of Agriculture and the Interior shall jointly submit to the Director and the appropriate congressional committees an assessment of the quantity of illegal drug cultivation and manufacturing in the United States on lands owned or under the jurisdiction of the Federal Government for the preceding year.

(B) SECRETARY OF HOMELAND SECURITY.—Not later than July 1 of each year, the Secretary of Homeland Security shall submit to the Director and the appropriate congressional committees information for the preceding year regarding—

(i) the number and type of seizures of drugs by each component of the Department of Homeland Security seizing drugs, as well as statistical information on the geographic areas of such seizures; and

(ii) the number of air and maritime patrol hours primarily dedicated to drug supply reduction missions undertaken by each component of the Department of Homeland Security.

(C) SECRETARY OF DEFENSE.—The Secretary of Defense shall, by July 1 of each year, submit to the Director and the appropriate congressional committees information for the preceding year regarding the number of air and maritime patrol hours primarily dedicated to drug supply reduction missions undertaken by each component of the Department of Defense.

(D) ATTORNEY GENERAL.—The Attorney General shall, by July 1 of each year, submit to the Director and the appropriate congressional committees information for the preceding year regarding the number and type of—

(i) arrests for drug violations;

(ii) prosecutions for drug violations by United States Attorneys; and

(iii) seizures of drugs by each component of the Department of Justice seizing drugs, as well as statistical information on the geographic areas of such seizures.

(b) CERTIFICATION OF POLICY CHANGES TO DIRECTOR.—

(1) IN GENERAL.—Subject to paragraph (2), the head of a National Drug Control Program agency shall, unless exigent circumstances require otherwise, notify the Director in writing regarding any proposed change in policies relating to the activities of that agency under the National Drug Control Program prior to implementation of such change. The Director shall promptly review such proposed change and certify to the head of that agency in writing whether such change is consistent with the National Drug Control Strategy.

(2) EXCEPTION.—If prior notice of a proposed change under paragraph (1) is not practicable—

(A) the head of the National Drug Control Program agency shall notify the Director of the proposed change as soon as practicable; and

(B) upon such notification, the Director shall review the change and certify to the head of that agency in writing whether the change is consistent with the National Drug Control Strategy.

(c) GENERAL SERVICES ADMINISTRATION.—The Administrator of General Services shall provide to the Director, on a reimbursable basis, such administrative support services as the Director may request.

(d) ACCOUNTING OF FUNDS EXPENDED.—

(1) IN GENERAL.—Not later than February 1 of each year, in accordance with guidance issued by the Director, the head of each National Drug Control Program agency shall submit to the Director a detailed accounting of all funds expended by the agency for National Drug Control Program activities during the previous fiscal year and shall ensure such detailed accounting is authenticated for the previous fiscal year by the Inspector General for such agency prior to the submission to the Director as frequently as determined by the Inspector General but not less frequently than every 3 years.

(2) SUBMISSION TO CONGRESS.—The Director shall submit to Congress not later than April 1 of each year the information submitted to the Director under paragraph (1).

(e) DRUG COURT TRAINING AND TECHNICAL ASSISTANCE PROGRAM.—

(1) GRANTS AUTHORIZED.—The Director may make a grant to a nonprofit organization for the purpose of providing training and technical assistance to drug courts.

(2) AUTHORIZATION OF APPROPRIATIONS.—There is authorized to be appropriated to carry out this subsection $2,000,000 for each of fiscal years 2018 through 2023.

(f) TRACKING SYSTEM FOR FEDERALLY FUNDED GRANT PROGRAMS.—

(1) ESTABLISHMENT.—The Director, or the head of an agency designated by the Director, in coordination with the Secretary of Health and Human Services, shall track federally-funded grant programs to—

(A) ensure the public has electronic access to information identifying:

(i) all drug control grants and pertinent identifying information for each grant; and

(ii) any available performance metrics, evaluations, or other information indicating the effectiveness of such programs;

(B) facilitate efforts to identify duplication, overlap, or gaps in funding to provide increased accountability of Federally-funded grants for substance use disorder treatment, prevention, and enforcement; and

(C) identify barriers that may impede applicants in the grant application process .

(2) NATIONAL DRUG CONTROL PROGRAM AGENCIES.—The head of each National Drug Control Program agency shall provide to the Director a complete list of all drug control program grant programs and any other relevant information for inclusion in the system developed under paragraph (1) and annually update such list.

(3) UPDATING EXISTING SYSTEMS.—The Director may meet the requirements of this subsection by utilizing, updating, or improving existing Federal information systems to ensure they meet the requirements of this subsection.

(4) REPORT.—Not later than 3 years after the date of enactment of this subsection, the Comptroller General of the United States shall submit to Congress a report examining implementation of this subsection.

SEC. 706. [21 U.S.C. 1705] DEVELOPMENT, SUBMISSION, IMPLEMENTATION, AND ASSESSMENT OF NATIONAL DRUG CONTROL STRATEGY.

(a) IN GENERAL.—

(1) STATEMENT OF DRUG POLICY PRIORITIES.—The Director shall release a statement of drug control policy priorities in the calendar year of a Presidential inauguration following the inauguration, but not later than April 1.

(2) NATIONAL DRUG CONTROL STRATEGY SUBMITTED BY THE PRESIDENT.—Not later than the first Monday in February following the year in which the term of the President commences, and every 2 years thereafter, the President shall submit to Congress a National Drug Control Strategy.

(b) DEVELOPMENT OF THE NATIONAL DRUG CONTROL STRATEGY.—

(1) PROMULGATION.—The Director shall promulgate the National Drug Control Strategy, which shall set forth a comprehensive plan to reduce illicit drug use and the consequences of such illicit drug use in the United States by limiting the availability of and reducing the demand for illegal drugs and promoting prevention, early intervention, treatment, and recovery support for individuals with substance use disorders.

(2) STATE AND LOCAL COMMITMENT.—The Director shall seek the support and commitment of State, local, and Tribal officials in the formulation and implementation of the National Drug Control Strategy.

(3) STRATEGY BASED ON EVIDENCE.—The Director shall ensure the National Drug Control Strategy is based on the best available evidence regarding the policies that are most effective in reducing the demand for and supply of illegal drugs.

(4) PROCESS FOR DEVELOPMENT AND SUBMISSION OF NATIONAL DRUG CONTROL STRATEGY.—In developing and effectively implementing the National Drug Control Strategy, the Director—

(A) shall consult with—

(i) the heads of the National Drug Control Program agencies;

(ii) each Coordinator listed in section 704;

(iii) the Interdiction Committee and the Emerging Threats Committee;

(iv) the appropriate congressional committees and any other committee of jurisdiction;

(v) State, local, and Tribal officials;

(vi) private citizens and organizations, including community and faith-based organizations, with experience and expertise in demand reduction;

(vii) private citizens and organizations with experience and expertise in supply reduction; and

(viii) appropriate representatives of foreign governments; and

(B) in satisfying the requirements of subparagraph (A), shall ensure, to the maximum extent possible, that State, local, and Tribal officials and relevant private organizations commit to support and take steps to achieve the goals and objectives of the National Drug Control Strategy.

(c) CONTENTS OF THE NATIONAL DRUG CONTROL STRATEGY.—

(1) IN GENERAL.—The National Drug Control Strategy submitted under subsection (a)(2) shall include the following:

(A) A mission statement detailing the major functions of the National Drug Control Program.

(B) Comprehensive, research-based, long-range, quantifiable goals for reducing illicit drug use, and the consequences of illicit drug use in the United States.

(C) Annual quantifiable and measurable objectives and specific targets to accomplish long-term quantifiable goals that the Director determines may be achieved during each year beginning on the date on which the National Drug Control Strategy is submitted.

(D) A 5-year projection for the National Drug Control Program and budget priorities.

(E) A review of international, State, local, and private sector drug control activities to ensure that the United States pursues coordinated and effective drug control at all levels of government.

(F) A description of how each goal established under subparagraph (B) will be achieved, including for each goal—

(i) a list of each relevant National Drug Control Program agency and each such agency's related programs, activities, and available assets and the role of each such program, activity, and asset in achieving such goal;

(ii) a list of relevant stakeholders and each such stakeholder's role in achieving such goal;

(iii) an estimate of Federal funding and other resources needed to achieve such goal;

(iv) a list of each existing or new coordinating mechanism needed to achieve such goal; and

(v) a description of the Office's role in facilitating

the achievement of such goal.

(G) For each year covered by the Strategy, a performance evaluation plan for each goal established under subparagraph (B) for each National Drug Control Program agency, including—

(i) specific performance measures for each National Drug Control Program agency;

(ii) annual and, to the extent practicable, quarterly objectives and targets for each performance measure; and

(iii) an estimate of Federal funding and other resources needed to achieve each performance objective and target.

(H) A list identifying existing data sources or a description of data collection needed to evaluate performance, including a description of how the Director will obtain such data.

(I) A list of any anticipated challenges to achieving the National Drug Control Strategy goals and planned actions to address such challenges.

(J) A description of how each goal established under subparagraph (B) was determined, including—

(i) a description of each required consultation and a description of how such consultation was incorporated; and

(ii) data, research, or other information used to inform the determination to establish the goal.

(K) A description of the current prevalence of illicit drug use in the United States, including both the availability of illicit drugs and the prevalence of substance use disorders.

(L) Such other statistical data and information as the Director considers appropriate to demonstrate and assess trends relating to illicit drug use, the effects and consequences of illicit drug use (including the effects on children), supply reduction, demand reduction, drug-related law enforcement, and the implementation of the National Drug Control Strategy.

(M) A systematic plan for increasing data collection to enable real time surveillance of drug control threats, developing analysis and monitoring capabilities, and identifying and addressing policy questions related to the National Drug Control Strategy and Program, which shall include—

(i) a list of policy-relevant questions for which the Director and each National Drug Control Program agency intends to develop evidence to support the National Drug Control Program and Strategy;

(ii) a list of data the Director and each National Drug Control Program agency intends to collect, use, or acquire to facilitate the use of evidence in drug control policymaking and monitoring;

(iii) a list of methods and analytical approaches that may be used to develop evidence to support the National Drug Control Program and Strategy and related policy;

(iv) a list of any challenges to developing evidence to support policymaking, including any barriers to accessing, collecting, or using relevant data;

(v) a description of the steps the Director and the head of each National Drug Control Program agency will take to effectuate the plan; and

(vi) any other relevant information as determined by the Director.

(N) A plan to expand treatment of substance use disorders, which shall—

(i) identify unmet needs for treatment for substance use disorders and a strategy for closing the gap between available and needed treatment;

(ii) describe the specific roles and responsibilities of the relevant National Drug Control Program agencies for implementing the plan;

(iii) identify the specific resources required to enable the relevant National Drug Control Program agencies to implement that strategy; and

(iv) identify the resources, including private

sources, required to eliminate the unmet need for evidence-based substance use disorder treatment.

(2) CONSULTATION.—In developing the plan required under paragraph (1)(M), the Director shall consult with the following:

(A) The public.

(B) Any evaluation or analysis units and personnel of the Office.

(C) Office officials responsible for implementing privacy policy.

(D) Office officials responsible for data governance.

(E) The appropriate congressional committees.

(F) Any other individual or entity as determined by the Director.

(3) ADDITIONAL STRATEGIES.—

(A) IN GENERAL.—The Director shall include in the National Drug Control Strategy the additional strategies described under this paragraph and shall comply with the following:

(i) Provide a copy of the additional strategies to the appropriate congressional committees and to the Committee on Armed Services and the Committee on Homeland Security of the House of Representatives, and the Committee on Homeland Security and Governmental Affairs and the Committee on Armed Services of the Senate.

(ii) Issue the additional strategies in consultation with the head of each relevant National Drug Control Program agency, any relevant official of a State, local, or Tribal government, and the government of other relevant countries.

(iii) Not change any existing agency authority or construe any strategy described under this paragraph to amend or modify any law governing interagency relationship but may include recommendations about changes to such authority or law.

(iv) Present separately from the rest of any strategy described under this paragraph any information classified under criteria established by an

Executive order, or whose public disclosure, as determined by the Director or the head of any relevant National Drug Control Program agency, would be detrimental to the law enforcement or national security activities of any Federal, State, local, or Tribal agency.

(B) REQUIREMENT FOR SOUTHWEST BORDER COUNTERNARCOTICS STRATEGY.—

(i) PURPOSES.—The Southwest Border Counternarcotics Strategy shall—

(I) set forth the Government's strategy for preventing the illegal trafficking of drugs across the international border between the United States and Mexico, including through ports of entry and between ports of entry on that border;

(II) state the specific roles and responsibilities of the relevant National Drug Control Program agencies for implementing that strategy; and

(III) identify the specific resources required to enable the relevant National Drug Control Program agencies to implement that strategy.

(ii) SPECIFIC CONTENT RELATED TO DRUG TUNNELS BETWEEN THE UNITED STATES AND MEXICO.—The Southwest Border Counternarcotics Strategy shall include—

(I) a strategy to end the construction and use of tunnels and subterranean passages that cross the international border between the United States and Mexico for the purpose of illegal trafficking of drugs across such border; and

(II) recommendations for criminal penalties for persons who construct or use such a tunnel or subterranean passage for such a purpose.

(C) REQUIREMENT FOR NORTHERN BORDER COUNTERNARCOTICS STRATEGY.—

(i) PURPOSES.—The Northern Border Counternarcotics Strategy shall—

(I) set forth the strategy of the Federal

Government for preventing the illegal trafficking of drugs across the international border between the United States and Canada, including through ports of entry and between ports of entry on the border;

(II) state the specific roles and responsibilities of each relevant National Drug Control Program agency for implementing the strategy;

(III) identify the specific resources required to enable the relevant National Drug Control Program agencies to implement the strategy;

(IV) be designed to promote, and not hinder, legitimate trade and travel; and

(V) reflect the unique nature of small communities along the international border between the United States and Canada, ongoing cooperation and coordination with Canadian law, enforcement authorities, and variations in the volumes of vehicles and pedestrians crossing through ports of entry along the international border between the United States and Canada.

(ii) SPECIFIC CONTENT RELATED TO CROSS-BORDER INDIAN RESERVATIONS.—The Northern Border Counternarcotics Strategy shall include—

(I) a strategy to end the illegal trafficking of drugs to or through Indian reservations on or near the international border between the United States and Canada; and

(II) recommendations for additional assistance, if any, needed by Tribal law enforcement agencies relating to the strategy, including an evaluation of Federal technical and financial assistance, infrastructure capacity building, and interoperability deficiencies.

(4) CLASSIFIED INFORMATION.—Any contents of the National Drug Control Strategy that involve information properly classified under criteria established by an Executive order shall be presented to Congress separately from the rest of the National Drug Control Strategy.

(5) SELECTION OF DATA AND INFORMATION.—In selecting data and information for inclusion in the Strategy, the Director shall ensure—

(A) the inclusion of data and information that will permit analysis of current trends against previously compiled data and information where the Director believes such analysis enhances long-term assessment of the National Drug Control Strategy; and

(B) the inclusion of data and information to permit a standardized and uniform assessment of the effectiveness of drug treatment programs in the United States.

(d) SUBMISSION OF REVISED STRATEGY.—The President may submit to Congress a revised National Drug Control Strategy that meets the requirements of this section—

(1) at any time, upon a determination of the President, in consultation with the Director, that the National Drug Control Strategy in effect is not sufficiently effective; or

(2) if a new President or Director takes office.

(e) FAILURE OF DIRECTOR TO SUBMIT NATIONAL DRUG CONTROL STRATEGY.—If the Director does not submit a National Drug Control Strategy to Congress in accordance with subsection (a)(2), not later than five days after the first Monday in February following the year in which the term of the President commences, the Director shall send a notification to the appropriate congressional committees—

(1) explaining why the Strategy was not submitted; and

(2) specifying the date by which the Strategy will be submitted.

(f) DRUG CONTROL DATA DASHBOARD.—

(1) IN GENERAL.—The Director shall collect and disseminate, as appropriate, such information as the Director determines is appropriate, but not less than the information described in this subsection. The data shall be publicly available in a machine-readable format on the online portal of the Office, and to the extent practicable on the Drug Control Data Dashboard.

(2) ESTABLISHMENT.—The Director shall publish to the online portal of the Office in a machine-readable, sortable, and

searchable format, or to the extent practicable, establish and maintain a data dashboard on the online portal of the Office to be known as the "Drug Control Data Dashboard". To the extent practicable, when establishing the Drug Control Dashboard, the Director shall ensure the user interface of the dashboard is constructed with modern design standards. To the extent practicable, the data made available on the dashboard shall be publicly available in a machine-readable format and searchable by year, agency, drug, and location.

(3) DATA.—The data included in the Drug Control Data Dashboard shall be updated quarterly to the extent practicable, but not less frequently than annually and shall include, at a minimum, the following:

(A) For each substance identified by the Director as having a significant impact on the prevalence of illicit drug use—

(i) data sufficient to show the quantities of such substance available in the United States, including—

(I) the total amount seized and disrupted in the calendar year and each of the previous 3 calendar years, including to the extent practicable the amount seized by State, local, and Tribal governments;

(II) the known and estimated flows into the United States from all sources in the calendar year and each of the previous 3 calendar years;

(III) the total amount of known flows that could not be interdicted or disrupted in the calendar year and each of the previous 3 calendar years;

(IV) the known and estimated levels of domestic production in the calendar year and each of the previous three calendar years, including the levels of domestic production if the drug is a prescription drug, as determined under the Federal Food, Drug, and Cosmetic Act, for which a listing is in effect under section 202 of the Controlled Substances Act (21 U.S.C. 812);

(V) the average street price for the calendar

year and the highest known street price during the preceding 10-year period; and

(VI) to the extent practicable, related prosecutions by State, local, and Tribal governments;

(ii) data sufficient to show the frequency of use of such substance, including—

(I) use of such substance in the workplace and productivity lost by such use;

(II) use of such substance by arrestees, probationers, and parolees;

(III) crime and criminal activity related to such substance; and

(IV) to the extent practicable, related prosecutions by State, local, and Tribal governments.

(B) For the calendar year and each of the previous three years data sufficient to show, disaggregated by State and, to the extent feasible, by region within a State, county, or city, the following:

(i) The number of fatal and non-fatal overdoses caused by each drug identified under subparagraph (A)(i).

(ii) The prevalence of substance use disorders.

(iii) The number of individuals who have received substance use disorder treatment, including medication assisted treatment, for a substance use disorder, including treatment provided through publicly-financed health care programs.

(iv) The extent of the unmet need for substance use disorder treatment, including the unmet need for medication-assisted treatment.

(C) Data sufficient to show the extent of prescription drug diversion, trafficking, and misuse in the calendar year and each of the previous 3 calendar years.

(D) Any quantifiable measures the Director determines to be appropriate to detail progress toward the achievement of the goals of the National Drug Control

Strategy.

(g) DEVELOPMENT OF AN ANNUAL NATIONAL DRUG CONTROL ASSESSMENT.—

(1) TIMING.—Not later than the first Monday in February of each year, the Director shall submit to the President, Congress, and the appropriate congressional committees, a report assessing the progress of each National Drug Control Program agency toward achieving each goal, objective, and target contained in the National Drug Control Strategy applicable to the prior fiscal year.

(2) PROCESS FOR DEVELOPMENT OF THE ANNUAL ASSESSMENT.—Not later than November 1 of each year, the head of each National Drug Control Program agency shall submit, in accordance with guidance issued by the Director, to the Director an evaluation of progress by the agency with respect to the National Drug Control Strategy goals using the performance measures for the agency developed under this title, including progress with respect to—

(A) success in achieving the goals of the National Drug Control Strategy;

(B) success in reducing domestic and foreign sources of illegal drugs;

(C) success in expanding access to and increasing the effectiveness of substance use disorder treatment;

(D) success in protecting the borders of the United States (and in particular the Southwestern border of the United States) from penetration by illegal narcotics;

(E) success in reducing crime associated with drug use in the United States;

(F) success in reducing the negative health and social consequences of drug use in the United States;

(G) implementation of evidence-based substance use disorder treatment and prevention programs in the United States and improvements in the adequacy and effectiveness of such programs; and

(H) success in increasing the prevention of illicit drug use.

(3) CONTENTS OF THE ANNUAL ASSESSMENT.—The Director

shall include in the annual assessment required under paragraph (1)—

(A) a summary of each evaluation received by the Director under paragraph (2);

(B) a summary of the progress of each National Drug Control Program agency toward the National Drug Control Strategy goals of the agency using the performance measures for the agency developed under this title;

(C) an assessment of the effectiveness of each National Drug Control Program agency and program in achieving the National Drug Control Strategy for the previous year, including a specific evaluation of whether the applicable goals, measures, objectives, and targets for the previous year were met; and

(D) the assessments required under this subsection shall be based on the Performance Measurement System.

(h) PERFORMANCE MEASUREMENT SYSTEM.—Not later than February 1 of each year, the Director shall submit to Congress as part of the National Drug Control Strategy, a description of a national drug control performance measurement system, that—

(1) develops 2-year and 5-year performance measures and targets for each National Drug Control Strategy goal and objective established for reducing drug use, availability, and the consequences of drug use;

(2) describes the sources of information and data that will be used for each performance measure incorporated into the performance measurement system;

(3) identifies major programs and activities of the National Drug Control Program agencies that support the goals and annual objectives of the National Drug Control Strategy;

(4) evaluates the contribution of demand reduction and supply reduction activities as defined in section 702 implemented by each National Drug Control Program agency in support of the National Drug Control Strategy;

(5) monitors consistency between the drug-related goals and objectives of the National Drug Control Program agencies and ensures that each agency's goals and budgets support and are fully consistent with the National Drug Control Strategy;

(6) coordinates the development and implementation of national drug control data collection and reporting systems to support policy formulation and performance measurement, including an assessment of—

(A) the quality of current drug use measurement instruments and techniques to measure supply reduction and demand reduction activities;

(B) the adequacy of the coverage of existing national drug use measurement instruments and techniques to measure the illicit drug user population, and groups that are at risk for illicit drug use;

(C) the adequacy of the coverage of existing national treatment outcome monitoring systems to measure the effectiveness of drug abuse treatment in reducing illicit drug use and criminal behavior during and after the completion of substance abuse treatment; and

(D) the actions the Director shall take to correct any deficiencies and limitations identified pursuant to subparagraphs (A) and (B) of this subsection; and

(7) develops performance measures and targets for the National Drug Control Strategy for supplemental strategies (the Southwest Border, Northern Border, and Caribbean Border Counternarcotics Strategies) to effectively evaluate region- specific goals, to the extent the performance measurement system does not adequately measure the effectiveness of the strategies, as determined by the Director, such strategies may evaluate interdiction efforts at and between ports of entry, interdiction technology, intelligence sharing, diplomacy, and other appropriate metrics, specific to each supplemental strategies region, as determined by the Director.

(i) MODIFICATIONS.—A description of any modifications made during the preceding year to the national drug performance measurement system described in subsection (c) shall be included in each report submitted under subsection (b).

SEC. 707. [21 U.S.C. 1706] HIGH INTENSITY DRUG TRAFFICKING AREAS PROGRAM.

(a) ESTABLISHMENT.—

(1) IN GENERAL.—There is established in the Office a program to be known as the High Intensity Drug Trafficking Areas Program (in this section referred to as the "Program").

(2) PURPOSE.—The purpose of the Program is to reduce drug trafficking and drug production in the United States by—

(A) facilitating cooperation among Federal, State, local, and tribal law enforcement agencies to share information and implement coordinated enforcement activities;

(B) enhancing law enforcement intelligence sharing among Federal, State, local, and tribal law enforcement agencies;

(C) providing reliable law enforcement intelligence to law enforcement agencies needed to design effective enforcement strategies and operations; and

(D) supporting coordinated law enforcement strategies which maximize use of available resources to reduce the supply of illegal drugs in designated areas and in the United States as a whole.

(b) DESIGNATION.—

(1) IN GENERAL.—The Director, in consultation with the Attorney General, the Secretary of the Treasury, the Secretary of Homeland Security, heads of the National Drug Control Program agencies, and the Governor of each applicable State, may designate any specified area of the United States as a high intensity drug trafficking area.

(2) ACTIVITIES.—After making a designation under paragraph (1) and in order to provide Federal assistance to the area so designated, the Director may—

(A) obligate such sums as are appropriated for the Program;

(B) direct the temporary reassignment of Federal personnel to such area, subject to the approval of the head of the department or agency that employs such personnel;

(C) take any other action authorized under section 704 to provide increased Federal assistance to those areas; and

(D) coordinate activities under this section (specifically administrative, recordkeeping, and funds management activities) with State, local, and tribal officials.

(c) PETITIONS FOR DESIGNATION.—The Director shall establish regulations under which a coalition of interested law enforcement agencies from an area may petition for designation as a high intensity drug trafficking area. Such regulations shall provide for a regular review by the Director of the petition, including a recommendation regarding the merit of the petition to the Director by a panel of qualified, independent experts.

(d) FACTORS FOR CONSIDERATION.—In considering whether to designate an area under this section as a high intensity drug trafficking area, the Director shall consider, in addition to such other criteria as the Director considers to be appropriate, the extent to which—

(1) the area is a significant center of illegal drug production, manufacturing, importation, or distribution;

(2) State, local, and tribal law enforcement agencies have committed resources to respond to the drug trafficking problem in the area, thereby indicating a determination to respond aggressively to the problem;

(3) drug-related activities in the area are having a significant harmful impact in the area, and in other areas of the country; and

(4) a significant increase in allocation of Federal resources is necessary to respond adequately to drug-related activities in the area.

(e) ORGANIZATION OF HIGH INTENSITY DRUG TRAFFICKING AREAS.—

(1) EXECUTIVE BOARD AND OFFICERS.—To be eligible for funds appropriated under this section, each high intensity drug trafficking area shall be governed by an Executive Board. The Executive Board shall designate a chairman, vice chairman, and any other officers to the Executive Board that it determines are necessary.

(2) RESPONSIBILITIES.—The Executive Board of a high intensity drug trafficking area shall be responsible for—

(A) providing direction and oversight in establishing and achieving the goals of the high intensity drug trafficking area;

(B) managing the funds of the high intensity drug trafficking area;

(C) reviewing and approving all funding proposals consistent with the overall objective of the high intensity drug trafficking area; and

(D) reviewing and approving all reports to the Director on the activities of the high intensity drug trafficking area.

(3) BOARD REPRESENTATION.—None of the funds appropriated under this section may be expended for any high intensity drug trafficking area, or for a partnership or region of a high intensity drug trafficking area, if the Executive Board for such area, region, or partnership, does not apportion an equal number of votes between representatives of participating Federal agencies and representatives of participating State, local, and tribal agencies. Where it is impractical for an equal number of representatives of Federal agencies and State, local, and tribal agencies to attend a meeting of an Executive Board in person, the Executive Board may use a system of proxy votes or weighted votes to achieve the voting balance required by this paragraph.

(4) NO AGENCY RELATIONSHIP.—The eligibility requirements of this section are intended to ensure the responsible use of Federal funds. Nothing in this section is intended to create an agency relationship between individual high intensity drug trafficking areas and the Federal Government.

(f) USE OF FUNDS.—The Director shall ensure that not more than a total of 5 percent of Federal funds appropriated for the Program are expended for substance use disorder treatment programs and drug prevention programs.

(g) COUNTERTERRORISM ACTIVITIES.—

(1) ASSISTANCE AUTHORIZED.—The Director may authorize use of resources available for the Program to assist Federal, State, local, and tribal law enforcement agencies in investigations and activities related to terrorism and prevention of terrorism, especially but not exclusively with respect to such investigations and activities that are also related to drug trafficking.

(2) LIMITATION.—The Director shall ensure—

(A) that assistance provided under paragraph (1) remains incidental to the purpose of the Program to reduce drug availability and carry out drug-related law enforcement activities; and

(B) that significant resources of the Program are not redirected to activities exclusively related to terrorism, except on a temporary basis under extraordinary circumstances, as determined by the Director.

(h) ROLE OF DRUG ENFORCEMENT ADMINISTRATION.—The Director, in consultation with the Attorney General, shall ensure that a representative of the Drug Enforcement Administration is included in the Intelligence Support Center for each high intensity drug trafficking area.

(i) ANNUAL HIDTA PROGRAM BUDGET SUBMISSIONS.—As part of the documentation that supports the President's annual budget request for the Office, the Director shall submit to Congress a budget justification that includes—

(1) the amount proposed for each high intensity drug trafficking area, conditional upon a review by the Office of the request submitted by the HIDTA and the performance of the HIDTA, with supporting narrative descriptions and rationale for each request;

(2) a detailed justification that explains—

(A) the reasons for the proposed funding level; how such funding level was determined based on a current assessment of the drug trafficking threat in each high intensity drug trafficking area;

(B) how such funding will ensure that the goals and objectives of each such area will be achieved; and

(C) how such funding supports the National Drug Control Strategy; and

(3) the amount of HIDTA funds used to investigate and prosecute organizations and individuals trafficking in methamphetamine in the prior calendar year, and a description of how those funds were used.

(j) EMERGING THREAT RESPONSE FUND.—

(1) IN GENERAL.—Subject to the availability of appropriations, the Director may expend up to 10 percent of

the amounts appropriated under this section on a discretionary basis, to respond to any emerging drug trafficking threat in an existing high intensity drug trafficking area, or to establish a new high intensity drug trafficking area or expand an existing high intensity drug trafficking area, in accordance with the criteria established under paragraph (2).

(2) CONSIDERATION OF IMPACT.—In allocating funds under this subsection, the Director shall consider—

(A) the impact of activities funded on reducing overall drug traffic in the United States, or minimizing the probability that an emerging drug trafficking threat will spread to other areas of the United States; and

(B) such other criteria as the Director considers appropriate.

(k) EVALUATION.—

(1) INITIAL REPORT.—Not later than 90 days after the date of the enactment of this section, the Director shall, after consulting with the Executive Boards of each designated high intensity drug trafficking area, submit a report to Congress that describes, for each designated high intensity drug trafficking area—

(A) the specific purposes for the high intensity drug trafficking area;

(B) the specific long-term and short-term goals and objectives for the high intensity drug trafficking area;

(C) the measurements that will be used to evaluate the performance of the high intensity drug trafficking area in achieving the long-term and short-term goals; and

(D) the reporting requirements needed to evaluate the performance of the high intensity drug trafficking area in achieving the long-term and short-term goals.

(2) EVALUATION OF HIDTA PROGRAM AS PART OF NATIONAL DRUG CONTROL STRATEGY.—For each designated high intensity drug trafficking area, the Director shall submit, as part of the annual National Drug Control Strategy report, a report that—

(A) describes—

(i) the specific purposes for the high intensity drug trafficking area; and

(ii) the specific long-term and short-term goals and objectives for the high intensity drug trafficking area; and

(B) includes an evaluation of the performance of the high intensity drug trafficking area in accomplishing the specific long-term and short-term goals and objectives identified under paragraph (1)(B).

(l) ASSESSMENT OF DRUG ENFORCEMENT TASK FORCES IN HIGH INTENSITY DRUG TRAFFICKING AREAS.—Not later than 1 year after the date of enactment of this subsection, and as part of each subsequent annual National Drug Control Strategy report, the Director shall submit to Congress a report—

(1) assessing the number and operation of all federally funded drug enforcement task forces within each high intensity drug trafficking area; and

(2) describing—

(A) each Federal, State, local, and tribal drug enforcement task force operating in the high intensity drug trafficking area;

(B) how such task forces coordinate with each other, with any high intensity drug trafficking area task force, and with investigations receiving funds from the Organized Crime and Drug Enforcement Task Force;

(C) what steps, if any, each such task force takes to share information regarding drug trafficking and drug production with other federally funded drug enforcement task forces in the high intensity drug trafficking area;

(D) the role of the high intensity drug trafficking area in coordinating the sharing of such information among task forces;

(E) the nature and extent of cooperation by each Federal, State, local, and tribal participant in ensuring that such information is shared among law enforcement agencies and with the high intensity drug trafficking area;

(F) the nature and extent to which information sharing and enforcement activities are coordinated with joint terrorism task forces in the high intensity drug trafficking area; and

(G) any recommendations for measures needed to ensure that task force resources are utilized efficiently and effectively to reduce the availability of illegal drugs in the high intensity drug trafficking areas.

(m) ASSESSMENT OF LAW ENFORCEMENT INTELLIGENCE SHARING IN HIGH INTENSITY DRUG TRAFFICKING AREAS PROGRAM.—Not later than 180 days after the date of the enactment of this section, and as part of each subsequent annual National Drug Control Strategy report, the Director, in consultation with the Director of National Intelligence, shall submit to Congress a report—

(1) evaluating existing and planned law enforcement intelligence systems supported by each high intensity drug trafficking area, or utilized by task forces receiving any funding under the Program, including the extent to which such systems ensure access and availability of law enforcement intelligence to Federal, State, local, and tribal law enforcement agencies within the high intensity drug trafficking area and outside of it;

(2) the extent to which Federal, State, local, and tribal law enforcement agencies participating in each high intensity drug trafficking area are sharing law enforcement intelligence information to assess current drug trafficking threats and design appropriate enforcement strategies; and

(3) the measures needed to improve effective sharing of information and law enforcement intelligence regarding drug trafficking and drug production among Federal, State, local, and tribal law enforcement participating in a high intensity drug trafficking area, and between such agencies and similar agencies outside the high intensity drug trafficking area.

(n) COORDINATION OF LAW ENFORCEMENT INTELLIGENCE SHARING WITH ORGANIZED CRIME DRUG ENFORCEMENT TASK FORCE PROGRAM.—The Director, in consultation with the Attorney General, shall ensure that any drug enforcement intelligence obtained by the Intelligence Support Center for each high intensity drug trafficking area is shared, on a timely basis, with the drug intelligence fusion center operated by the Organized Crime Drug Enforcement Task Force of the Department of Justice.

(o) USE OF FUNDS TO COMBAT METHAMPHETAMINE TRAFFICKING.—

(1) REQUIREMENT.—As part of the documentation that supports the President's annual budget request for the Office, the Director shall submit to Congress a report describing the use of HIDTA funds to investigate and prosecute organizations and individuals trafficking in methamphetamine in the prior calendar year.

(2) CONTENTS.—The report shall include—

(A) the number of methamphetamine manufacturing facilities discovered through HIDTA-funded initiatives in the previous fiscal year;

(B) the amounts of methamphetamine or listed chemicals (as that term is defined in section 102(33) of the Controlled Substances Act (21 U.S.C. 802(33))) seized by HIDTA-funded initiatives in the area during the previous year; and

(C) law enforcement intelligence and predictive data from the Drug Enforcement Administration showing patterns and trends in abuse, trafficking, and transportation in methamphetamine and listed chemicals.

(3) CERTIFICATION.—Before the Director awards any funds to a high intensity drug trafficking area, the Director shall certify that the law enforcement entities participating in that HIDTA are providing laboratory seizure data to the national clandestine laboratory database at the El Paso Intelligence Center.

(p) AUTHORIZATION OF APPROPRIATIONS.—There is authorized to be appropriated to the Office of National Drug Control Policy to carry out this section—

(1) $240,000,000 for fiscal year 2007;

(2) $250,000,000 for fiscal year 2008;

(3) $260,000,000 for fiscal year 2009;

(4) $270,000,000 for fiscal year 2010;

(5) $280,000,000 for each of fiscal year 2011; and

(6) $280,000,000 for each of fiscal years 2018 through 2023.

(q) SPECIFIC PURPOSES.—

(1) IN GENERAL.—The Director shall ensure that, of the amounts appropriated for a fiscal year for the Program, at least $7,000,000 is used in high intensity drug trafficking areas

with severe neighborhood safety and illegal drug distribution problems.

(2) REQUIRED USES.—The funds used under paragraph (1) shall be used to ensure the safety of neighborhoods and the protection of communities, including the prevention of the intimidation of witnesses of illegal drug distribution and related activities and the establishment of, or support for, programs that provide protection or assistance to witnesses in court proceedings.

(3) BEST PRACTICE MODELS.—The Director shall work with HIDTAs to develop and maintain best practice models to assist State, local, and Tribal governments in addressing witness safety, relocation, financial and housing assistance, or any other services related to witness protection or assistance in cases of illegal drug distribution and related activities. The Director shall ensure dissemination of the best practice models to each HIDTA.

(r) DRUG OVERDOSE RESPONSE STRATEGY IMPLEMENTATION.—The Director may use funds appropriated to carry out this section to implement a drug overdose response strategy in high intensity drug trafficking areas on a nationwide basis by—

(1) coordinating multi-disciplinary efforts to prevent, reduce, and respond to drug overdoses, including the uniform reporting of fatal and non-fatal overdoses to public health and safety officials;

(2) increasing data sharing among public safety and public health officials concerning drug-related abuse trends, including new psychoactive substances, and related crime; and

(3) enabling collaborative deployment of prevention, intervention, and enforcement resources to address substance use addiction and narcotics trafficking.

(s) SUPPLEMENTAL GRANTS.—The Director is authorized to use not more than $10,000,000 of the amounts otherwise appropriated to carry out this section to provide supplemental competitive grants to high intensity drug trafficking areas that have experienced high seizures of fentanyl and new psychoactive substances for the purposes of—

(1) purchasing portable equipment to test for fentanyl and

other substances;

(2) training law enforcement officers and other first responders on best practices for handling fentanyl and other substances; and

(3) purchasing protective equipment, including overdose reversal drugs.

[Section 708 was repealed by section 8222(3) of Public Law 115–271.]

SEC. 709. [21 U.S.C. 1708] EMERGING THREATS COMMITTEE, PLAN, AND MEDIA CAMPAIGN.

(a) EMERGING AND CONTINUING THREATS COORDINATOR.—The Director shall designate or appoint a United States Emerging and Continuing Threats Coordinator to perform the duties of that position described in this section and such other duties as may be determined by the Director. For purposes of carrying out the previous sentence, the Director shall designate or appoint an appointee in the Senior Executive Service or an appointee in a position at level 15 of the General Schedule (or equivalent).

(b) EMERGING THREATS COMMITTEE.—

(1) IN GENERAL.—The Emerging Threats Committee shall—

(A) monitor evolving and emerging drug threats in the United States;

(B) identify and discuss evolving and emerging drug trends in the United States using the criteria required to be established under paragraph (6);

(C) assist in the formulation of and oversee implementation of any plan described in subsection (d);

(D) provide such other advice to the Coordinator and Director concerning strategy and policies for emerging drug threats and trends as the Committee determines to be appropriate; and

(E) disseminate and facilitate the sharing with Federal, State, local, and Tribal officials and other entities as determined by the Director of pertinent information and data relating to—

(i) recent trends in drug supply and demand;

(ii) fatal and nonfatal overdoses;

(iii) demand for and availability of evidence-based substance use disorder treatment, including the extent of the unmet treatment need, and treatment admission trends;

(iv) recent trends in drug interdiction, supply, and demand from State, local, and Tribal law enforcement agencies; and

(v) other subject matter as determined necessary by the Director.

(2) CHAIRPERSON.—The Director shall designate one of the members of the Emerging Threats Committee to serve as Chairperson.

(3) MEMBERS.—The Director shall appoint other members of the Committee, which shall include—

(A) representatives from National Drug Control Program agencies or other agencies;

(B) representatives from State, local, and Tribal governments; and

(C) representatives from other entities as designated by the Director.

(4) MEETINGS.—The members of the Emerging Threats Committee shall meet, in person and not through any delegate or representative, not less frequently than once per calendar year, before June 1. At the call of the Director or the Chairperson, the Emerging Threats Committee may hold additional meetings as the members may choose.

(5) CONTRACT, AGREEMENT, AND OTHER AUTHORITY.—The Director may award contracts, enter into interagency agreements, manage individual projects, and conduct other activities in support of the identification of emerging drug threats and in support of the development, implementation, and assessment of any Emerging Threat Response Plan.

(6) CRITERIA TO IDENTIFY EMERGING DRUG THREATS.—Not later than 180 days after the date on which the Committee first meets, the Committee shall develop and recommend to the Director criteria to be used to identify an emerging drug threat or the termination of an emerging drug threat designation

based on information gathered by the Committee, statistical data, and other evidence.

(c) DESIGNATION.—

(1) IN GENERAL.—The Director, in consultation with the Coordinator, the Committee, and the head of each National Drug Control Program agency, may designate an emerging drug threat in the United States.

(2) STANDARDS FOR DESIGNATION.—The Director, in consultation with the Coordinator, shall promulgate and make publicly available standards by which a designation under paragraph (1) and the termination of such designation may be made. In developing such standards, the Director shall consider the recommendations of the committee and other criteria the Director considers to be appropriate.

(3) PUBLIC STATEMENT REQUIRED.—The Director shall publish a public written statement on the portal of the Office explaining the designation of an emerging drug threat or the termination of such designation and shall notify the appropriate congressional committees of the availability of such statement when a designation or termination of such designation has been made.

(d) PLAN.—

(1) PUBLIC AVAILABILITY OF PLAN.—Not later than 90 days after making a designation under subsection (c), the Director shall publish and make publicly available an Emerging Threat Response Plan and notify the President and the appropriate congressional committees of such plan's availability.

(2) TIMING.—Concurrently with the annual submissions under section 706(g), the Director shall update the plan and report on implementation of the plan, until the Director issues the public statement required under subsection (c)(3) to terminate the emerging drug threat designation.

(3) CONTENTS OF AN EMERGING THREAT RESPONSE PLAN.—The Director shall include in the plan required under this subsection—

(A) a comprehensive strategic assessment of the emerging drug threat, including the current availability of, demand for, and effectiveness of evidence-based prevention, treatment, and enforcement programs and efforts to respond to the emerging drug threat;

(B) comprehensive, research-based, short- and long-term, quantifiable goals for addressing the emerging drug threat, including for reducing the supply of the drug designated as the emerging drug threat and for expanding the availability and effectiveness of evidence-based substance use disorder treatment and prevention programs to reduce the demand for the emerging drug threat;

(C) performance measures pertaining to the plan's goals, including quantifiable and measurable objectives and specific targets;

(D) the level of funding needed to implement the plan, including whether funding is available to be reprogrammed or transferred to support implementation of the plan or whether additional appropriations are necessary to implement the plan;

(E) an implementation strategy for the media campaign under subsection (f), including goals as described under subparagraph (B) of this paragraph and performance measures, objectives, and targets, as described under subparagraph (C) of this paragraph; and

(F) any other information necessary to inform the public of the status, progress, or response to an emerging drug threat.

(4) IMPLEMENTATION.—

(A) IN GENERAL.—Not later than 120 days after the date on which a designation is made under subsection (c), the Director, in consultation with the President, the appropriate congressional committees, and the head of each National Drug Control Program agency, shall issue guidance on implementation of the plan described in this subsection to the National Drug Control Program agencies and any other relevant agency determined to be necessary by the Director.

(B) COORDINATOR'S RESPONSIBILITIES.—The Coordinator shall—

(i) direct the implementation of the plan among the agencies identified in the plan, State, local, and Tribal governments, and other relevant entities;

(ii) facilitate information-sharing between agencies identified in the plan, State, local, and Tribal governments, and other relevant entities; and

(iii) monitor implementation of the plan by coordinating the development and implementation of collection and reporting systems to support performance measurement and adherence to the plan by agencies identified in the plan, where appropriate.

(C) REPORTING.—Not later than 180 days after the date on which a designation is made under subsection (c) and in accordance with subparagraph (A), the head of each agency identified in the plan shall submit to the Coordinator a report on implementation of the plan.

(e) EVALUATION OF MEDIA CAMPAIGN.—Upon designation of an emerging drug threat, the Director shall evaluate whether a media campaign would be appropriate to address that threat.

(f) NATIONAL ANTI-DRUG MEDIA CAMPAIGN.—

(1) IN GENERAL.—The Director shall, to the extent feasible and appropriate, conduct a national anti-drug media campaign (referred to in this subsection as the "national media campaign") in accordance with this subsection for the purposes of—

(A) preventing substance abuse among people in the United States;

(B) educating the public about the dangers and negative consequences of substance use and abuse, including patient and family education about the characteristics and hazards of substance abuse and methods to safeguard against substance use, to include the safe disposal of prescription medications;

(C) supporting evidence-based prevention programs targeting the attitudes, perception, and beliefs of persons concerning substance use and intentions to initiate or continue such use;

(D) encouraging individuals affected by substance use disorders to seek treatment and providing such individuals with information on—

(i) how to recognize addiction issues;

(ii) what forms of evidence-based treatment options are available; and

(iii) how to access such treatment;

(E) combating the stigma of addiction and substance use disorders, including the stigma of treating such disorders with medication-assisted treatment therapies; and

(F) informing the public about the dangers of any drug identified by the Director as an emerging drug threat as appropriate.

(2) USE OF FUNDS.—

(A) IN GENERAL.—Amounts made available to carry out this subsection for the national media campaign may only be used for the following:

(i) The purchase of media time and space, including the strategic planning for, tracking, and accounting of, such purchases.

(ii) Creative and talent costs, consistent with subparagraph (B)(i).

(iii) Advertising production costs, which may include television, radio, internet, social media, and other commercial marketing venues.

(iv) Testing and evaluation of advertising.

(v) Evaluation of the effectiveness of the national media campaign.

(vi) Costs of contracts to carry out activities authorized by this subsection.

(vii) Partnerships with professional and civic groups, community-based organizations, including faith-based organizations, and government organizations related to the national media campaign.

(viii) Entertainment industry outreach, interactive outreach, media projects and activities, public information, news media outreach, and corporate sponsorship and participation.

(ix) Operational and management expenses.

(B) SPECIFIC REQUIREMENTS.—

(i) CREATIVE SERVICES.—In using amounts for creative and talent costs under subparagraph (A)(ii), the Director shall use creative services donated at no cost to the Government wherever feasible and may only procure creative services for advertising—

(I) responding to high-priority or emergent campaign needs that cannot timely be obtained at no cost; or

(II) intended to reach a minority, ethnic, or other special audience that cannot reasonably be obtained at no cost.

(ii) TESTING AND EVALUATION OF ADVERTISING.—In using amounts for testing and evaluation of advertising under subparagraph (A)(iv), the Director shall test all advertisements prior to use in the national media campaign to ensure that the advertisements are effective with the target audience and meet industry-accepted standards. The Director may waive this requirement for advertisements using no more than 10 percent of the purchase of advertising time purchased under this subsection in a fiscal year and no more than 10 percent of the advertising space purchased under this subsection in a fiscal year, if the advertisements respond to emergent and time-sensitive campaign needs or the advertisements will not be widely utilized in the national media campaign.

(iii) CONSULTATION. For the planning of the campaign under paragraph (1), the Director may consult with—

(I) the head of any appropriate National Drug Control Program agency;

(II) experts on the designated drug;

(III) State, local, and Tribal government officials and relevant agencies;

(IV) communications professionals;

(V) the public; and

(VI) appropriate congressional committees.

(iv) EVALUATION OF EFFECTIVENESS OF NATIONAL

MEDIA CAMPAIGN.—In using amounts for the evaluation of the effectiveness of the national media campaign under subparagraph (A)(v), the Director shall—

> (I) designate an independent entity to evaluate by April 20 of each year the effectiveness of the national media campaign based on data from—

>> (aa) the Monitoring the Future Study published by the Department of Health and Human Services;

>> (bb) the National Survey on Drug Use and Health; and

>> (cc) other relevant studies or publications, as determined by the Director, including tracking and evaluation data collected according to marketing and advertising industry standards; and

> (II) ensure that the effectiveness of the national media campaign is evaluated in a manner that enables consideration of whether the national media campaign has contributed to changes in attitude or behaviors among the target audience with respect to substance use and such other measures of evaluation as the Director determines are appropriate.

(3) ADVERTISING.—In carrying out this subsection, the Director shall ensure that sufficient funds are allocated to meet the stated goals of the national media campaign.

(4) RESPONSIBILITIES AND FUNCTIONS UNDER THE PROGRAM.—

(A) IN GENERAL.—The Director shall determine the overall purposes and strategy of the national media campaign.

(B) DIRECTOR.—

(i) IN GENERAL.—The Director shall approve—

> (I) the strategy of the national media campaign;

(II) all advertising and promotional material used in the national media campaign; and

(III) the plan for the purchase of advertising time and space for the national media campaign.

(ii) IMPLEMENTATION.—The Director shall be responsible for implementing a focused national media campaign to meet the purposes set forth in paragraph (1) and shall ensure—

(I) information disseminated through the campaign is accurate and scientifically valid; and

(II) the campaign is designed using strategies demonstrated to be the most effective at achieving the goals and requirements of paragraph (1), which may include—

(aa) a media campaign, as described in paragraph (2);

(bb) local, regional, or population specific messaging;

(cc) the development of websites to publicize and disseminate information;

(dd) conducting outreach and providing educational resources for parents;

(ee) collaborating with law enforcement agencies; and

(ff) providing support for school-based public health education classes to improve teen knowledge about the effects of substance use.

(5) PROHIBITIONS.—None of the amounts made available under paragraph (2) may be obligated or expended for any of the following:

(A) To supplant current anti-drug community-based coalitions.

(B) To supplant pro bono public service time donated by national and local broadcasting networks for other public service campaigns.

(C) For partisan political purposes, or to express advocacy in support of or to defeat any clearly identified candidate, clearly identified ballot initiative, or clearly identified legislative or regulatory proposal.

(D) To fund advertising that features any elected officials, persons seeking elected office, cabinet level officials, or other Federal officials employed pursuant to section 213 of Schedule C of title 5, Code of Federal Regulations.

(E) To fund advertising that does not contain a primary message intended to reduce or prevent substance use.

(F) To fund advertising containing a primary message intended to promote support for the national media campaign or private sector contributions to the national media campaign.

(6) MATCHING REQUIREMENT.—

(A) IN GENERAL.—Amounts made available under paragraph (2) for media time and space shall be matched by an equal amount of non-Federal funds for the national media campaign, or be matched with in-kind contributions of the same value.

(B) NO-COST MATCH ADVERTISING DIRECT RELATIONSHIP REQUIREMENT.—The Director shall ensure that not less than 85 percent of no-cost match advertising directly relates to substance abuse prevention consistent with the specific purposes of the national media campaign.

(C) NO-COST MATCH ADVERTISING NOT DIRECTLY RELATED.—The Director shall ensure that no-cost match advertising that does not directly relate to substance abuse prevention consistent with the purposes of the national media campaign includes a clear anti-drug message. Such message is not required to be the primary message of the match advertising.

(7) FINANCIAL AND PERFORMANCE ACCOUNTABILITY.—The Director shall cause to be performed—

(A) audits and reviews of costs of the national media campaign pursuant to section 4706 of title 41, United States Code; and

(B) an audit to determine whether the costs of the national media campaign are allowable under chapter 43 of title 41, United States Code.

(8) REPORT TO CONGRESS.—The Director shall submit on an annual basis a report to Congress that describes—

(A) the strategy of the national media campaign and whether specific objectives of the national media campaign were accomplished;

(B) steps taken to ensure that the national media campaign operates in an effective and efficient manner consistent with the overall strategy and focus of the national media campaign;

(C) plans to purchase advertising time and space;

(D) policies and practices implemented to ensure that Federal funds are used responsibly to purchase advertising time and space and eliminate the potential for waste, fraud, and abuse;

(E) all contracts entered into with a corporation, partnership, or individual working on behalf of the national media campaign;

(F) the results of any financial audit of the national media campaign;

(G) a description of any evidence used to develop the national media campaign;

(H) specific policies and steps implemented to ensure compliance with this section;

(I) a detailed accounting of the amount of funds obligated during the previous fiscal year for carrying out the national media campaign, including each recipient of funds, the purpose of each expenditure, the amount of each expenditure, any available outcome information, and any other information necessary to provide a complete accounting of the funds expended; and

(J) a review and evaluation of the effectiveness of the national media campaign strategy for the past year.

(9) REQUIRED NOTICE FOR COMMUNICATION FROM THE OFFICE.—Any communication, including an advertisement, paid for or otherwise disseminated by the Office directly or through a contract awarded by the Office shall include a prominent notice informing the audience that the communication was paid for by the Office.

(g) AUTHORIZATION OF APPROPRIATIONS.—There is authorized to be appropriated to the Office to carry out this section, $25,000,000 for each of fiscal years 2018 through 2023.

SEC. 710. Repealed by section 1101(a) of Public Law 109–469

SEC. 711. [21 U.S.C. 1710] DRUG INTERDICTION COORDINATOR AND COMMITTEE.

(a) UNITED STATES INTERDICTION COORDINATOR.—

(1) IN GENERAL.—The Director shall designate or appoint an appointee in the Senior Executive Service or an appointee in a position at level 15 of the General Schedule (or equivalent) as the United States Interdiction Coordinator to perform the duties of that position described in paragraph (2) and such other duties as may be determined by the Director with respect to coordination of efforts to interdict illicit drugs from entering the United States.

(2) RESPONSIBILITIES.—The United States Interdiction Coordinator shall be responsible to the Director for—

(A) coordinating the interdiction activities of the National Drug Control Program agencies to ensure consistency with the National Drug Control Strategy;

(B) on behalf of the Director, developing and issuing, on or before September 1 of each year and in accordance with paragraph (4), a National Interdiction Command and Control Plan to ensure the coordination and consistency described in subparagraph (A);

(C) assessing the sufficiency of assets committed to illicit drug interdiction by the relevant National Drug Control Program agencies; and

(D) advising the Director on the efforts of each National Drug Control Program agency to implement the National Interdiction Command and Control Plan.

(3) STAFF.—The Director shall assign such permanent staff of the Office as he considers appropriate to assist the United States Interdiction Coordinator to carry out the responsibilities described in paragraph (2), and may request that appropriate National Drug Control Program agencies detail or assign staff to assist in carrying out such responsibilities.

(4) NATIONAL INTERDICTION COMMAND AND CONTROL PLAN.—

(A) PURPOSES.—The National Interdiction Command and Control Plan shall—

(i) set forth the Government's strategy for drug interdiction;

(ii) state the specific roles and responsibilities of the relevant National Drug Control Program agencies for implementing that strategy; and

(iii) identify the specific resources required to enable the relevant National Drug Control Program agencies to implement that strategy.

(B) CONSULTATION WITH OTHER AGENCIES.—Before submission of the National Drug Control Strategy or annual assessment required under section 706, as applicable, the United States Interdiction Coordinator shall issue the National Interdiction Command and Control Plan in consultation with the other members of the Interdiction Committee described in subsection (b).

(C) REPORT TO CONGRESS.—On or before September 1 of each year, the Director, acting through the United States Interdiction Coordinator, shall provide to the appropriate congressional committees, to the Committee on Armed Services and the Committee on Homeland Security of the House of Representatives, and to the Committee on Homeland Security and Governmental Affairs and the Committee on Armed Services of the Senate a report that—

(i) includes—

(I) a copy of that year's National Interdiction Command and Control Plan, including information about how each National Drug Control Program agency conducting drug interdiction activities is engaging with relevant international partners;

(II) information for the previous 10 years regarding the number and type of seizures of drugs by each National Drug Control Program agency conducting drug interdiction activities and statistical information on the geographic areas of such seizures; and

(III) information for the previous 10 years regarding the number of air and maritime patrol hours undertaken by each National Drug Control Program agency conducting drug interdiction activities and statistical information on the geographic areas in which such patrol hours took place; and

(ii) may include recommendations for changes to existing agency authorities or laws governing interagency relationships.

(D) CLASSIFIED ANNEX.—Each report required to be submitted under subparagraph (C) shall be in unclassified form, but may include a classified annex.

(b) INTERDICTION COMMITTEE.—

(1) IN GENERAL.—The Interdiction Committee shall meet to—

(A) discuss and resolve issues related to the coordination, oversight and integration of international, border, and domestic drug interdiction efforts in support of the National Drug Control Strategy;

(B) review the annual National Interdiction Command and Control Plan, and provide advice to the Director and the United States Interdiction Coordinator concerning that plan and how to strengthen international partnerships to better achieve the goals of that plan; and

(C) provide such other advice to the Director concerning drug interdiction strategy and policies as the committee determines is appropriate.

(2) CHAIRPERSON.—The Director shall designate one of the members of the Interdiction Committee to serve as Chairperson.

(3) MEETINGS.—The members of the Interdiction Committee shall meet, in person and not through any delegate or representative, at least once per calendar year, before June 1. At the call of the Director or the Chairperson, the Interdiction Committee may hold additional meetings, which shall be attended by the members in person, or through such delegates or representatives as the members may choose.

(4) REPORT.—Not later than September 30 of each year, the Chairperson of the Interdiction Committee shall submit to the Director and to the appropriate congressional committees a report describing the results of the meetings and any significant findings of the Committee during the previous 12 months. The report required under this paragraph shall be in unclassified form, but may include a classified annex.

(c) INTERNATIONAL COORDINATION.—The Director may facilitate international drug control coordination efforts.

SEC. 712. [21 U.S.C. 1710a] REQUIREMENT FOR DISCLOSURE OF FEDERAL SPONSORSHIP OF ALL FEDERAL ADVERTISING OR OTHER COMMUNICATION MATERIALS.

(a) REQUIREMENT.—Each advertisement or other communication paid for by the Office, either directly or through a contract awarded by the Office, shall include a prominent notice informing the target audience that the advertisement or other communication is paid for by the Office.

(b) ADVERTISEMENT OR OTHER COMMUNICATION.—In this section, the term "advertisement or other communication" includes—

(1) an advertisement disseminated in any form, including print or by any electronic means; and

(2) a communication by an individual in any form, including speech, print, or by any electronic means.

SEC. 713. TECHNICAL AND CONFORMING AMENDMENTS. [Made technical amendments to several laws.]

SEC. 714. [21 U.S.C. 1711] AUTHORIZATION OF APPROPRIATIONS.
There are authorized to be appropriated to carry out this title except activities otherwise specified, to remain available until expended, $18,400,000 for each of fiscal years 2018 through 2023. [Section 715 was repealed by section 8202(b)(2) of Public Law 115–271.]

SEC. 716. [21 U.S.C. 1714] AWARDS FOR DEMONSTRATION PROGRAMS BY LOCAL PARTNERSHIPS TO COERCE ABSTINENCE IN CHRONIC HARD-DRUG USERS UNDER COMMUNITY SUPERVISION THROUGH THE USE OF DRUG TESTING AND SANCTIONS.

(a) AWARDS REQUIRED.—The Director shall make competitive awards to fund demonstration programs by eligible partnerships for the purpose of reducing the use of illicit drugs by chronic hard-drug users living in the community while under the supervision of the criminal justice system.

(b) USE OF AWARD AMOUNTS.—Award amounts received under this section shall be used—

(1) to support the efforts of the agencies, organizations, and researchers included in the eligible partnership;

(2) to develop and field a drug testing and graduated sanctions program for chronic hard-drug users living in the community under criminal justice supervision; and

(3) to assist individuals described in subsection (a) by strengthening rehabilitation efforts through such means as job training, drug treatment, or other services.

(c) ELIGIBLE PARTNERSHIP DEFINED.—In this section, the term "eligible partnership" means a working group whose application to the Director—

(1) identifies the roles played, and certifies the involvement of, two or more agencies or organizations, which may include—

(A) State, local, or tribal agencies (such as those carrying out police, probation, prosecution, courts, corrections, parole, or treatment functions);

(B) Federal agencies (such as the Drug Enforcement Agency, the Bureau of Alcohol, Tobacco, Firearms, and Explosives, and United States Attorney offices); and

(C) community-based organizations;

(2) includes a qualified researcher;

(3) includes a plan for using judicial or other criminal justice authority to administer drug tests to individuals described in subsection (a) at least twice a week, and to swiftly and certainly impose a known set of graduated sanctions for non-compliance with community-release provisions relating to drug abstinence (whether imposed as a pre-trial, probation, or parole condition or otherwise);

(4) includes a strategy for responding to a range of substance use and abuse problems and a range of criminal histories;

(5) includes a plan for integrating data infrastructure among the agencies and organizations included in the eligible partnership to enable seamless, real-time tracking of individuals described in subsection (a);

(6) includes a plan to monitor and measure the progress toward reducing the percentage of the population of individuals described in subsection (a) who, upon being summoned for a drug test, either fail to show up or who test positive for drugs.

(d) REPORTS TO CONGRESS.—

(1) INTERIM REPORT.—Not later than June 1, 2009, the Director shall submit to Congress a report that identifies the best practices in reducing the use of illicit drugs by chronic hard-drug users, including the best practices identified through the activities funded under this section.

(2) FINAL REPORT.—Not later than June 1, 2010, the Director shall submit to Congress a report on the demonstration programs funded under this section, including on the matters specified in paragraph (1).

(e) AUTHORIZATION OF APPROPRIATIONS.—There is authorized to be appropriated to carry out this section $4,900,000 for each of fiscal years 2007 through 2009.

* * * * * * *

TITLE XI—MORATORIUM ON CERTAIN TAXES

SEC. 1100. [47 U.S.C. 151 note] SHORT TITLE.
This title may be cited as the "Internet Tax Freedom Act".

SEC. 1101. [47 U.S.C. 151 note] MORATORIUM.

(a) MORATORIUM.—No State or political subdivision thereof may impose any of the following taxes:

(1) Taxes on Internet access.

(2) Multiple or discriminatory taxes on electronic commerce.

(b) PRESERVATION OF STATE AND LOCAL TAXING AUTHORITY.—Except as provided in this section, nothing in this title shall be construed to modify, impair, or supersede, or authorize the modification, impairment, or superseding of, any State or local law pertaining to taxation that is otherwise permissible by or under the Constitution of the United States or other Federal law and in effect on the date of enactment of this Act.

(c) LIABILITIES AND PENDING CASES.—Nothing in this title affects liability for taxes accrued and enforced before the date of enactment of this Act, nor does this title affect ongoing litigation relating to such taxes.

(d) EXCEPTION TO MORATORIUM.—

(1) IN GENERAL.—Subsection (a) shall also not apply in the case of any person or entity who knowingly and with knowledge of the character of the material, in interstate or foreign commerce by means of the World Wide Web, makes any communication for commercial purposes that is available to any minor and that includes any material that is harmful to minors unless such person or entity has restricted access by minors to material that is harmful to minors—

(A) by requiring use of a credit card, debit account, adult access code, or adult personal identification number;

(B) by accepting a digital certificate that verifies age; or

(C) by any other reasonable measures that are feasible under available technology.

(2) SCOPE OF EXCEPTION.—For purposes of paragraph (1), a person shall not be considered to making a communication for commercial purposes of material to the extent that the person is—

(A) a telecommunications carrier engaged in the provision of a telecommunications service;

(B) a person engaged in the business of providing an Internet access service;

(C) a person engaged in the business of providing an Internet information location tool; or

(D) similarly engaged in the transmission, storage, retrieval, hosting, formatting, or translation (or any combination thereof) of a communication made by another person, without selection or alteration of the communication.

(3) DEFINITIONS.—In this subsection:

(A) BY MEANS OF THE WORLD WIDE WEB.—The term "by means of the World Wide Web" means by placement of material in a computer server-based file archive so that it is publicly accessible, over the Internet, using hypertext transfer protocol, file transfer protocol, or other similar protocols.

(B) COMMERCIAL PURPOSES; ENGAGED IN THE BUSINESS.—

(i) COMMERCIAL PURPOSES.—A person shall be considered to make a communication for commercial purposes only if such person is engaged in the business of making such communications.

(ii) ENGAGED IN THE BUSINESS.—The term "engaged in the business" means that the person who makes a communication, or offers to make a communication, by means of the World Wide Web, that includes any material that is harmful to minors, devotes time, attention, or labor to such activities, as a regular course of such person's trade or business, with the objective of earning a profit as a result of such activities (although it is not necessary that the person make a profit or that the making or offering to make such communications be the person's sole or principal business or source of income). A person may be considered to be engaged in the business of making, by means of the World Wide Web, communications for commercial purposes that include material that is harmful to minors, only if the person knowingly causes the material that is harmful to minors to be posted on the World Wide Web or knowingly solicits such material to be posted on the World Wide Web.

(C) INTERNET.—The term "Internet" means collectively the myriad of computer and telecommunications facilities, including equipment and operating software, which comprise the interconnected world-wide network of networks that employ the Transmission Control Protocol/Internet Protocol, or any predecessor or successor protocols to such protocol, to communicate information of all kinds by wire or radio.

(D) INTERNET ACCESS SERVICE.—The term "Internet access service" means a service that enables users to access content, information, electronic mail, or other services offered over the Internet and may also include access to proprietary content, information, and other services as part of a package of services offered to consumers. The term "Internet access service" does not include telecommunications services, except to the extent such services are purchased, used, or sold by a provider of Internet access to provide Internet access.

(E) INTERNET INFORMATION LOCATION TOOL.—The term "Internet information location tool" means a service that refers or links users to an online location on the World Wide Web. Such term includes directories, indices, references, pointers, and hypertext links.

(F) MATERIAL THAT IS HARMFUL TO MINORS.—The term "material that is harmful to minors" means any communication, picture, image, graphic image file, article, recording, writing, or other matter of any kind that is obscene or that—

(i) the average person, applying contemporary community standards, would find, taking the material as a whole and with respect to minors, is designed to appeal to, or is designed to pander to, the prurient interest;

(ii) depicts, describes, or represents, in a manner patently offensive with respect to minors, an actual or simulated sexual act or sexual contact, an actual or simulated normal or perverted sexual act, or a lewd exhibition of the genitals or post-pubescent female breast; and

(iii) taken as a whole, lacks serious literary, artistic, political, or scientific value for minors.

(G) MINOR.—The term "minor" means any person under 17 years of age.

(H) TELECOMMUNICATIONS CARRIER; TELECOMMUNICATIONS SERVICE.—The terms "telecommunications carrier" and "telecommunications service" have the meanings given such terms in section 3 of the Communications Act of 1934 (47 U.S.C. 153).

(e) ADDITIONAL EXCEPTION TO MORATORIUM.—

(1) IN GENERAL.—Subsection (a) shall also not apply with respect to an Internet access provider, unless, at the time of entering into an agreement with a customer for the provision of Internet access services, such provider offers such customer (either for a fee or at no charge) screening software that is designed to permit the customer to limit access to material on the Internet that is harmful to minors.

(2) DEFINITIONS.—In this subsection:

(A) INTERNET ACCESS PROVIDER.—The term "Internet access provider" means a person engaged in the business of providing a computer and communications facility through which a customer may obtain access to the Internet, but does not include a common carrier to the extent that it provides only telecommunications services.

(B) INTERNET ACCESS SERVICES.—The term "Internet access services" means the provision of computer and communications services through which a customer using a computer and a modem or other communications device may obtain access to the Internet, but does not include telecommunications services provided by a common carrier.

(C) SCREENING SOFTWARE.—The term "screening software" means software that is designed to permit a person to limit access to material on the Internet that is harmful to minors.

(3) APPLICABILITY.—Paragraph (1) shall apply to agreements for the provision of Internet access services entered into on or after the date that is 6 months after the date of enactment of this Act.

SEC. 1102. [47 U.S.C. 151 note] ADVISORY COMMISSION ON ELECTRONIC COMMERCE.

(a) ESTABLISHMENT OF COMMISSION.—There is established a commission to be known as the Advisory Commission on Electronic Commerce (in this title referred to as the "Commission"). The Commission shall—

(1) be composed of 19 members appointed in accordance with subsection (b), including the chairperson who shall be

selected by the members of the Commission from among themselves; and

(2) conduct its business in accordance with the provisions of this title.

(b) MEMBERSHIP.—

(1) IN GENERAL.—The Commissioners shall serve for the life of the Commission. The membership of the Commission shall be as follows:

(A) 3 representatives from the Federal Government, comprised of the Secretary of Commerce, the Secretary of the Treasury, and the United States Trade Representative (or their respective delegates).

(B) 8 representatives from State and local governments (one such representative shall be from a State or local government that does not impose a sales tax and one representative shall be from a State that does not impose an income tax).

(C) 8 representatives of the electronic commerce industry (including small business), telecommunications carriers, local retail businesses, and consumer groups, comprised of—

(i) 5 individuals appointed by the Majority Leader of the Senate;

(ii) 3 individuals appointed by the Minority Leader of the Senate;

(iii) 5 individuals appointed by the Speaker of the House of Representatives; and

(iv) 3 individuals appointed by the Minority Leader of the House of Representatives.

(2) APPOINTMENTS.—Appointments to the Commission shall be made not later than 45 days after the date of the enactment of this Act. The chairperson shall be selected not later than 60 days after the date of the enactment of this Act.

(3) VACANCIES.—Any vacancy in the Commission shall not affect its powers, but shall be filled in the same manner as the original appointment.

(c) ACCEPTANCE OF GIFTS AND GRANTS.—The Commission may accept, use, and dispose of gifts or grants of services or property, both real and personal, for purposes of aiding or facilitating the work of the Commission. Gifts or grants not used at the expiration of the Commission shall be returned to the donor or grantor.

(d) OTHER RESOURCES.—The Commission shall have reasonable access to materials, resources, data, and other information from the Department of Justice, the Department of Commerce, the Department of State, the Department of the Treasury, and the Office of the United States Trade Representative. The Commission shall also have reasonable access to use the facilities of any such Department or Office for purposes of conducting meetings.

(e) SUNSET.—The Commission shall terminate 18 months after the date of the enactment of this Act.

(f) RULES OF THE COMMISSION.—

(1) QUORUM.—Nine members of the Commission shall constitute a quorum for conducting the business of the Commission.

(2) MEETINGS.—Any meetings held by the Commission shall be duly noticed at least 14 days in advance and shall be open to the public.

(3) OPPORTUNITIES TO TESTIFY.—The Commission shall provide opportunities for representatives of the general public, taxpayer groups, consumer groups, and State and local government officials to testify.

(4) ADDITIONAL RULES.—The Commission may adopt other rules as needed.

(g) DUTIES OF THE COMMISSION.—

(1) IN GENERAL.—The Commission shall conduct a thorough study of Federal, State and local, and international taxation and tariff treatment of transactions using the Internet and Internet access and other comparable intrastate, interstate or international sales activities.

(2) ISSUES TO BE STUDIED.—The Commission may include in the study under subsection (a)—

(A) an examination of—

(i) barriers imposed in foreign markets on United States providers of property, goods, services, or information engaged in electronic commerce and on

501

United States providers of telecommunications services; and

(ii) how the imposition of such barriers will affect United States consumers, the competitiveness of United States citizens providing property, goods, services, or information in foreign markets, and the growth and maturing of the Internet;

(B) an examination of the collection and administration of consumption taxes on electronic commerce in other countries and the United States, and the impact of such collection on the global economy, including an examination of the relationship between the collection and administration of such taxes when the transaction uses the Internet and when it does not;

(C) an examination of the impact of the Internet and Internet access (particularly voice transmission) on the revenue base for taxes imposed under section 4251 of the Internal Revenue Code of 1986;

(D) an examination of model State legislation that—

(i) would provide uniform definitions of categories of property, goods, service, or information subject to or exempt from sales and use taxes; and

(ii) would ensure that Internet access services, online services, and communications and transactions using the Internet, Internet access service, or online services would be treated in a tax and technologically neutral manner relative to other forms of remote sales;

(E) an examination of the effects of taxation, including the absence of taxation, on all interstate sales transactions, including transactions using the Internet, on retail businesses and on State and local governments, which examination may include a review of the efforts of State and local governments to collect sales and use taxes owed on in-State purchases from out-of-State sellers; and

(F) the examination of ways to simplify Federal and State and local taxes imposed on the provision of telecommunications services.

(3) EFFECT ON THE COMMUNICATIONS ACT OF 1934.—Nothing in this section shall include an examination of

any fees or charges imposed by the Federal Communications Commission or States related to—

(A) obligations under the Communications Act of 1934 (47 U.S.C. 151 et seq.); or

(B) the implementation of the Telecommunications Act of 1996 (or of amendments made by that Act).

(h) NATIONAL TAX ASSOCIATION COMMUNICATIONS AND ELECTRONIC COMMERCE TAX PROJECT.—The Commission shall, to the extent possible, ensure that its work does not undermine the efforts of the National Tax Association Communications and Electronic Commerce Tax Project.

SEC. 1103. [47 U.S.C. 151 note] REPORT.

Not later than 18 months after the date of the enactment of this Act, the Commission shall transmit to Congress for its consideration a report reflecting the results, including such legislative recommendations as required to address the findings of the Commission's study under this title. Any recommendation agreed to by the Commission shall be tax and technologically neutral and apply to all forms of remote commerce. No finding or recommendation shall be included in the report unless agreed to by at least two-thirds of the members of the Commission serving at the time the finding or recommendation is made.

SEC. 1104. [47 U.S.C. 151 note] GRANDFATHERING OF STATES THAT TAX INTERNET ACCESS.

(a) PRE-OCTOBER 1998 TAXES.—

(1) IN GENERAL.—Section 1101(a) does not apply to a tax on Internet access that was generally imposed and actually enforced prior to October 1, 1998, if, before that date—

(A) the tax was authorized by statute; and

(B) either—

(i) a provider of Internet access services had a reasonable opportunity to know, by virtue of a rule or other public proclamation made by the appropriate administrative agency of the State or political subdivision thereof, that such agency has interpreted and applied such tax to Internet access services; or

(ii) a State or political subdivision thereof

generally collected such tax on charges for Internet access.

(2) TERMINATION.—

(A) IN GENERAL.—Except as provided in subparagraph (B), this subsection shall not apply after June 30, 2020.

(B) STATE TELECOMMUNICATIONS SERVICE TAX.—

(i) DATE FOR TERMINATION.—This subsection shall not apply after November 1, 2006, with respect to a State telecommunications service tax described in clause (ii).

(ii) DESCRIPTION OF TAX.—A State telecommunications service tax referred to in subclause (i) is a State tax—

(I) enacted by State law on or after October 1, 1991, and imposing a tax on telecommunications service; and

(II) applied to Internet access through administrative code or regulation issued on or after December 1, 2002.

(3) EXCEPTION.—Paragraphs (1) and (2) shall not apply to any State that has, more than 24 months prior to the date of enactment of this paragraph, enacted legislation to repeal the State's taxes on Internet access or issued a rule or other proclamation made by the appropriate agency of the State that such State agency has decided to no longer apply such tax to Internet access.

(b) PRE-NOVEMBER 2003 TAXES.—

(1) IN GENERAL.—Section 1101(a) does not apply to a tax on Internet access that was generally imposed and actually enforced as of November 1, 2003, if, as of that date, the tax was authorized by statute and—

(A) a provider of Internet access services had a reasonable opportunity to know by virtue of a public rule or other public proclamation made by the appropriate administrative agency of the State or political subdivision thereof, that such agency has interpreted and applied such tax to Internet access services; and

(B) a State or political subdivision thereof generally

collected such tax on charges for Internet access.

(2) TERMINATION.—This subsection shall not apply after November 1, 2005.

(c) APPLICATION OF DEFINITION.—

(1) IN GENERAL.—Effective as of November 1, 2003—

(A) for purposes of subsection (a), the term "Internet access" shall have the meaning given such term by section 1104(5) of this Act, as enacted on October 21, 1998; and

(B) for purposes of subsection (b), the term "Internet access" shall have the meaning given such term by section 1104(5) of this Act as enacted on October 21, 1998, and amended by section 2(c) of the Internet Tax Nondiscrimination Act (Public Law 108–435).

(2) EXCEPTIONS.—Paragraph (1) shall not apply until June 30, 2008, to a tax on Internet access that is—

(A) generally imposed and actually enforced on telecommunications service purchased, used, or sold by a provider of Internet access, but only if the appropriate administrative agency of a State or political subdivision thereof issued a public ruling prior to July 1, 2007, that applied such tax to such service in a manner that is inconsistent with paragraph (1); or

(B) the subject of litigation instituted in a judicial court of competent jurisdiction prior to July 1, 2007, in which a State or political subdivision is seeking to enforce, in a manner that is inconsistent with paragraph (1), such tax on telecommunications service purchased, used, or sold by a provider of Internet access.

(3) NO INFERENCE.—No inference of legislative construction shall be drawn from this subsection or the amendments to section 1105(5) made by the Internet Tax Freedom Act Amendments Act of 2007 for any period prior to June 30, 2008, with respect to any tax subject to the exceptions described in subparagraphs (A) and (B) of paragraph (2).

SEC. 1105. [47 U.S.C. 151 note] DEFINITIONS.

For the purposes of this title:

(1) BIT TAX.—The term "bit tax" means any tax on

electronic commerce expressly imposed on or measured by the volume of digital information transmitted electronically, or the volume of digital information per unit of time transmitted electronically, but does not include taxes imposed on the provision of telecommunications.

(2) DISCRIMINATORY TAX.—The term "discriminatory tax" means—

(A) any tax imposed by a State or political subdivision thereof on electronic commerce that—

(i) is not generally imposed and legally collectible by such State or such political subdivision on transactions involving similar property, goods, services, or information accomplished through other means;

(ii) is not generally imposed and legally collectible at the same rate by such State or such political subdivision on transactions involving similar property, goods, services, or information accomplished through other means, unless the rate is lower as part of a phase-out of the tax over not more than a 5-year period;

(iii) imposes an obligation to collect or pay the tax on a different person or entity than in the case of transactions involving similar property, goods, services, or information accomplished through other means;

(iv) establishes a classification of Internet access service providers or online service providers for purposes of establishing a higher tax rate to be imposed on such providers than the tax rate generally applied to providers of similar information services delivered through other means; or

(B) any tax imposed by a State or political subdivision thereof, if—

(i) the sole ability to access a site on a remote seller's out-of-State computer server is considered a factor in determining a remote seller's tax collection obligation; or

(ii) a provider of Internet access service or online

services is deemed to be the agent of a remote seller for determining tax collection obligations solely as a result of—

(I) the display of a remote seller's information or content on the out-of-State computer server of a provider of Internet access service or online services; or

(II) the processing of orders through the out-of-State computer server of a provider of Internet access service or online services.

(3) ELECTRONIC COMMERCE.—The term "electronic commerce" means any transaction conducted over the Internet or through Internet access, comprising the sale, lease, license, offer, or delivery of property, goods, services, or information, whether or not for consideration, and includes the provision of Internet access.

(4) INTERNET.—The term "Internet" means collectively the myriad of computer and telecommunications facilities, including equipment and operating software, which comprise the interconnected world-wide network of networks that employ the Transmission Control Protocol/Internet Protocol, or any predecessor or successor protocols to such protocol, to communicate information of all kinds by wire or radio.

(5) INTERNET ACCESS.—The term "Internet access"—

(A) means a service that enables users to connect to the Internet to access content, information, or other services offered over the Internet;

(B) includes the purchase, use or sale of telecommunications by a provider of a service described in subparagraph (A) to the extent such telecommunications are purchased, used or sold—

(i) to provide such service; or

(ii) to otherwise enable users to access content, information or other services offered over the Internet;

(C) includes services that are incidental to the provision of the service described in subparagraph (A) when furnished to users as part of such service, such as a home page, electronic mail and instant messaging (including voice- and video-capable electronic mail and instant messaging), video clips, and personal electronic storage capacity;

(D) does not include voice, audio or video programming, or other products and services (except services described in subparagraph (A), (B), (C), or (E)) that utilize Internet protocol or any successor protocol and for which there is a charge, regardless of whether such charge is separately stated or aggregated with the charge for services described in subparagraph (A), (B), (C), or (E); and

(E) includes a homepage, electronic mail and instant messaging (including voice- and video-capable electronic mail and instant messaging), video clips, and personal electronic storage capacity, that are provided independently or not packaged with Internet access.

(6) MULTIPLE TAX.—

(A) IN GENERAL.—The term "multiple tax" means any tax that is imposed by one State or political subdivision thereof on the same or essentially the same electronic commerce that is also subject to another tax imposed by another State or political subdivision thereof (whether or not at the same rate or on the same basis), without a credit (for example, a resale exemption certificate) for taxes paid in other jurisdictions.

(B) EXCEPTION.—Such term shall not include a sales or use tax imposed by a State and 1 or more political subdivisions thereof on the same electronic commerce or a tax on persons engaged in electronic commerce which also may have been subject to a sales or use tax thereon.

(C) SALES OR USE TAX.—For purposes of subparagraph (B), the term "sales or use tax" means a tax that is imposed on or incident to the sale, purchase, storage, consumption, distribution, or other use of tangible personal property or services as may be defined by laws imposing such tax and which is measured by the amount of the sales price or other charge for such property or service.

(7) STATE.—The term "State" means any of the several States, the District of Columbia, or any commonwealth, territory, or possession of the United States.

(8) TAX.—

(A) IN GENERAL.—The term "tax" means—

(i) any charge imposed by any governmental entity for the purpose of generating revenues for governmental purposes, and is not a fee imposed for a specific privilege, service, or benefit conferred; or

(ii) the imposition on a seller of an obligation to collect and to remit to a governmental entity any sales or use tax imposed on a buyer by a governmental entity.

(B) EXCEPTION.—Such term does not include any franchise fee or similar fee imposed by a State or local franchising authority, pursuant to section 622 or 653 of the Communications Act of 1934 (47 U.S.C. 542, 573), or any other fee related to obligations or telecommunications carriers under the Communications Act of 1934 (47 U.S.C. 151 et seq.).

(9) TELECOMMUNICATIONS.—The term "telecommunications" means "telecommunications" as such term is defined in section 3(43) of the Communications Act of 1934 (47 U.S.C. 153(43)) and "telecommunications service" as such term is defined in section 3(46) of such Act (47 U.S.C. 153(46)), and includes communications services (as defined in section 4251 of the Internal Revenue Code of 1986 (26 U.S.C. 4251)).

(10) TAX ON INTERNET ACCESS.—

(A) IN GENERAL.—The term "tax on Internet access" means a tax on Internet access, regardless of whether such tax is imposed on a provider of Internet access or a buyer of Internet access and regardless of the terminology used to describe the tax.

(B) GENERAL EXCEPTION.—The term "tax on Internet access" does not include a tax levied upon or measured by net income, capital stock, net worth, or property value.

(C) SPECIFIC EXCEPTION.—

(i) SPECIFIED TAXES.—Effective November 1, 2007, the term "tax on Internet access" also does not include a State tax expressly levied on commercial activity, modified gross receipts, taxable margin, or gross income of the business, by a State law specifically using one of the foregoing terms, that—

(I) was enacted after June 20, 2005, and before November 1, 2007 (or, in the case of a State business and occupation tax, was enacted after January 1, 1932, and before January 1, 1936);

(II) replaced, in whole or in part, a modified value-added tax or a tax levied upon or measured by net income, capital stock, or net worth (or, is a State business and occupation tax that was enacted after January 1, 1932 and before January 1, 1936);

(III) is imposed on a broad range of business activity; and

(IV) is not discriminatory in its application to providers of communication services, Internet access, or telecommunications.

(ii)   MODIFICATIONS.—Nothing   in   this subparagraph shall be construed as a limitation on a State's ability to make modifications to a tax covered by clause (i) of this subparagraph after November 1, 2007, as long as the modifications do not substantially narrow the range of business activities on which the tax is imposed or otherwise disqualify the tax under clause (i).

(iii) NO INFERENCE.—No inference of legislative construction shall be drawn from this subparagraph regarding the application of subparagraph (A) or (B) to any tax described in clause (i) for periods prior to November 1, 2007.

SEC. 1106. [47 U.S.C. 151 note] ACCOUNTING RULE.

(a) IN GENERAL.—If charges for Internet access are aggregated with and not separately stated from charges for telecommunications or other charges that are subject to taxation, then the charges for Internet access may be subject to taxation unless the Internet access provider can reasonably identify the charges for Internet access from its books and records kept in the regular course of business.

(b) DEFINITIONS.—In this section:

(1) CHARGES FOR INTERNET ACCESS.—The term "charges for Internet access" means all charges for Internet access as defined in section 1105(5).

(2) CHARGES FOR TELECOMMUNICATIONS.—The term "charges for telecommunications" means all charges for telecommunications, except to the extent such telecommunications are purchased, used, or sold by a provider of Internet access to provide Internet access or to otherwise enable users to access content, information or other services offered over the Internet.

SEC. 1107. [47 U.S.C. 151 note] EFFECT ON OTHER LAWS.

(a) UNIVERSAL SERVICE.—Nothing in this Act shall prevent the imposition or collection of any fees or charges used to preserve and advance Federal universal service or similar State programs—

(1) authorized by section 254 of the Communications Act of 1934 (47 U.S.C. 254); or

(2) in effect on February 8, 1996.

(b) 911 AND E–911 SERVICES.—Nothing in this Act shall prevent the imposition or collection, on a service used for access to 911 or E–911 services, of any fee or charge specifically designated or presented as dedicated by a State or political subdivision thereof for the support of 911 or E–911 services if no portion of the revenue derived from such fee or charge is obligated or expended for any purpose other than support of 911 or E–911 services.

(c) NON-TAX REGULATORY PROCEEDINGS.—Nothing in this Act shall be construed to affect any Federal or State regulatory proceeding that is not related to taxation.

SEC. 1108. Repealed.

SEC. 1109. [47 U.S.C. 151 note] EXCEPTION FOR TEXAS MUNICIPAL ACCESS LINE FEE.

Nothing in this Act shall prohibit Texas or a political subdivision thereof from imposing or collecting the Texas municipal access line fee pursuant to Texas Local Govt. Code Ann. ch. 283 (Vernon 2005) and the definition of access line as determined by the Public Utility Commission of Texas in its "Order Adopting Amendments to Section 26.465 As Approved At The February 13,

2003 Public Hearing", issued March 5, 2003, in Project No. 26412.

TITLE XII—OTHER PROVISIONS

SEC. 1201. DECLARATION THAT INTERNET SHOULD BE FREE OF NEW FEDERAL TAXES.

It is the sense of Congress that no new Federal taxes similar to the taxes described in section 1101(a) should be enacted with respect to the Internet and Internet access during the moratorium provided in such section.

SEC. 1202. NATIONAL TRADE ESTIMATE.

Section 181 of the Trade Act of 1974 (19 U.S.C. 2241) is amended—

(1) in subsection (a)(1)—

(A) in subparagraph (A)—

(i) by striking "and" at the end of clause (i);

(ii) by inserting "and" at the end of clause (ii); and

(iii) by inserting after clause (ii) the following new clause:

"(iii) United States electronic commerce,"

; and

(B) in subparagraph (C)—

(i) by striking "and" at the end of clause (i);

(ii) by inserting "and" at the end of clause (ii);

(iii) by inserting after clause (ii) the following new clause:

"(iii) the value of additional United States electronic commerce,"

; and

(iv) by inserting "or transacted with," after "or invested in";

(2) in subsection (a)(2)(E)—

(A) by striking "and" at the end of clause (i);

(B) by inserting "and" at the end of clause (ii); and

(C) by inserting after clause (ii) the following new

clause:

"(iii) the value of electronic commerce transacted with,"

; and

(3) by adding at the end the following new subsection:

"(d) ELECTRONIC COMMERCE.—For purposes of this section, the term "'electronic commerce'" has the meaning given that term in section 1104(3) of the Internet Tax Freedom Act."

SEC. 1203. [19 U.S.C. 2241 note] DECLARATION THAT THE INTERNET SHOULD BE FREE OF FOREIGN TARIFFS, TRADE BARRIERS, AND OTHER RESTRICTIONS.

(a) IN GENERAL.—It is the sense of Congress that the President should seek bilateral, regional, and multilateral agreements to remove barriers to global electronic commerce through the World Trade Organization, the Organization for Economic Cooperation and Development, the Trans-Atlantic Economic Partnership, the Asia Pacific Economic Cooperation forum, the Free Trade Area of the America, the North American Free Trade Agreement, and other appropriate venues.

(b) NEGOTIATING OBJECTIVES.—The negotiating objectives of the United States shall be—

(1) to assure that electronic commerce is free from—

(A) tariff and nontariff barriers;

(B) burdensome and discriminatory regulation and standards; and

(C) discriminatory taxation; and

(2) to accelerate the growth of electronic commerce by expanding market access opportunities for—

(A) the development of telecommunications infrastructure;

(B) the procurement of telecommunications equipment;

(C) the provision of Internet access and telecommunications services; and

(D) the exchange of goods, services, and digitalized information.

(c) ELECTRONIC COMMERCE.—For purposes of this section, the term "electronic commerce" has the meaning given that term in section 1104(3).

SEC. 1204. [19 U.S.C. 2241 note] NO EXPANSION OF TAX AUTHORITY.

Nothing in this title shall be construed to expand the duty of any person to collect or pay taxes beyond that which existed immediately before the date of the enactment of this Act.

SEC. 1205. [19 U.S.C. 2241 note] PRESERVATION OF AUTHORITY.

Nothing in this title shall limit or otherwise affect the implementation of the Telecommunications Act of 1996 (Public Law 104–104) or the amendments made by such Act.

SEC. 1206. [19 U.S.C. 2241 note] SEVERABILITY.

If any provision of this title, or any amendment made by this title, or the application of that provision to any person or circumstance, is held by a court of competent jurisdiction to violate any provision of the Constitution of the United States, then the other provisions of that title, and the application of that provision to other persons and circumstances, shall not be affected.

TITLE XIII—CHILDREN'S ONLINE PRIVACY PROTECTION

SEC. 1301. [15 U.S.C. 6501 note] SHORT TITLE.

This title may be cited as the "Children's Online Privacy Protection Act of 1998".

SEC. 1302. [15 U.S.C. 6501] DEFINITIONS.

In this title:

(1) CHILD.—The term "child" means an individual under the age of 13.

(2) OPERATOR.—The term "operator"—

(A) means any person who operates a website located on the Internet or an online service and who collects or maintains personal information from or about the users of or visitors to such website or online service, or on whose behalf such information is collected or maintained, where such website or online service is operated for commercial purposes, including any person offering products or services for sale through that website or online service, involving commerce—

(i) among the several States or with 1 or more foreign nations;

(ii) in any territory of the United States or in the District of Columbia, or between any such territory and—

(I) another such territory; or

(II) any State or foreign nation; or

(iii) between the District of Columbia and any State, territory, or foreign nation; but

(B) does not include any nonprofit entity that would otherwise be exempt from coverage under section 5 of the Federal Trade Commission Act (15 U.S.C. 45).

(3) COMMISSION.—The term "Commission" means the Federal Trade Commission.

(4) DISCLOSURE.—The term "disclosure" means, with respect to personal information—

(A) the release of personal information collected from a child in identifiable form by an operator for any purpose, except where such information is provided to a person other than the operator who provides support for the internal operations of the website and does not disclose or use that information for any other purpose; and

(B) making personal information collected from a child by a website or online service directed to children or with actual knowledge that such information was collected from a child, publicly available in identifiable form, by any means including by a public posting, through the Internet, or through—

(i) a home page of a website;

(ii) a pen pal service;

(iii) an electronic mail service;

(iv) a message board; or

(v) a chat room.

(5) FEDERAL AGENCY.—The term "Federal agency" means an agency, as that term is defined in section 551(1) of title 5, United States Code.

(6) INTERNET.—The term "Internet" means collectively the myriad of computer and telecommunications facilities, including equipment and operating software, which comprise the interconnected world-wide network of networks that employ the Transmission Control Protocol/Internet Protocol, or any predecessor or successor protocols to such protocol, to communicate information of all kinds by wire or radio.

(7) PARENT.—The term "parent" includes a legal guardian.

(8) PERSONAL INFORMATION.—The term "personal information" means individually identifiable information about an individual collected online, including—

(A) a first and last name;

(B) a home or other physical address including street name and name of a city or town;

(C) an e-mail address;

(D) a telephone number;

(E) a Social Security number;

(F) any other identifier that the Commission determines permits the physical or online contacting of a specific individual; or

(G) information concerning the child or the parents of that child that the website collects online from the child and combines with an identifier described in this paragraph.

(9) VERIFIABLE PARENTAL CONSENT.—The term "verifiable parental consent" means any reasonable effort (taking into consideration available technology), including a request for authorization for future collection, use, and disclosure described in the notice, to ensure that a parent of a child receives notice of the operator's personal information collection, use, and disclosure practices, and authorizes the collection, use, and disclosure, as applicable, of personal information and the subsequent use of that information before that information is collected from that child.

(10) WEBSITE OR ONLINE SERVICE DIRECTED TO CHILDREN.—

(A) IN GENERAL.—The term "website or online service directed to children" means—

(i) a commercial website or online service that is targeted to children; or

(ii) that portion of a commercial website or online service that is targeted to children.

(B) LIMITATION.—A commercial website or online service, or a portion of a commercial website or online service, shall not be deemed directed to children solely for referring or linking to a commercial website or online service directed to children by using information location tools, including a directory, index, reference, pointer, or hypertext link.

(11) PERSON.—The term "person" means any individual, partnership, corporation, trust, estate, cooperative, association, or other entity.

(12) ONLINE CONTACT INFORMATION.—The term "online contact information" means an e-mail address or another substantially similar identifier that permits direct contact with a person online.

SEC. 1303. [15 U.S.C. 6502] REGULATION OF UNFAIR AND DECEPTIVE ACTS AND PRACTICES IN CONNECTION WITH THE COLLECTION AND USE OF PERSONAL INFORMATION FROM AND ABOUT CHILDREN ON THE INTERNET.

(a) ACTS PROHIBITED.—

(1) IN GENERAL.—It is unlawful for an operator of a website or online service directed to children, or any operator that has actual knowledge that it is collecting personal information from a child, to collect personal information from a child in a manner that violates the regulations prescribed under subsection (b).

(2) DISCLOSURE TO PARENT PROTECTED.—Notwithstanding paragraph (1), neither an operator of such a website or online service nor the operator's agent shall be held to be liable under any Federal or State law for any disclosure made in good faith and following reasonable procedures in responding to a request for disclosure of personal information under subsection (b)(1)(B)(iii) to the parent of a child.

(b) REGULATIONS.—

(1) IN GENERAL.—Not later than 1 year after the date of the enactment of this Act, the Commission shall promulgate under section 553 of title 5, United States Code, regulations that—

(A) require the operator of any website or online service directed to children that collects personal information from children or the operator of a website or online service that has actual knowledge that it is collecting personal information from a child—

(i) to provide notice on the website of what information is collected from children by the operator, how the operator uses such information, and the operator's disclosure practices for such information; and

(ii) to obtain verifiable parental consent for the collection, use, or disclosure of personal information from children;

(B) require the operator to provide, upon request of a parent under this subparagraph whose child has provided personal information to that website or online service, upon proper identification of that parent, to such parent—

(i) a description of the specific types of personal information collected from the child by that operator;

(ii) the opportunity at any time to refuse to permit the operator's further use or maintenance in retrievable form, or future online collection, of personal information from that child; and

(iii) notwithstanding any other provision of law, a means that is reasonable under the circumstances for the parent to obtain any personal information collected from that child;

(C) prohibit conditioning a child's participation in a game, the offering of a prize, or another activity on the child disclosing more personal information than is reasonably necessary to participate in such activity; and

(D) require the operator of such a website or online service to establish and maintain reasonable procedures to protect the confidentiality, security, and integrity of personal information collected from children.

(2) WHEN CONSENT NOT REQUIRED.—The regulations shall

provide that verifiable parental consent under paragraph (1)(A)(ii) is not required in the case of—

(A) online contact information collected from a child that is used only to respond directly on a one-time basis to a specific request from the child and is not used to recontact the child and is not maintained in retrievable form by the operator;

(B) a request for the name or online contact information of a parent or child that is used for the sole purpose of obtaining parental consent or providing notice under this section and where such information is not maintained in retrievable form by the operator if parental consent is not obtained after a reasonable time;

(C) online contact information collected from a child that is used only to respond more than once directly to a specific request from the child and is not used to recontact the child beyond the scope of that request—

(i) if, before any additional response after the initial response to the child, the operator uses reasonable efforts to provide a parent notice of the online contact information collected from the child, the purposes for which it is to be used, and an opportunity for the parent to request that the operator make no further use of the information and that it not be maintained in retrievable form; or

(ii) without notice to the parent in such circumstances as the Commission may determine are appropriate, taking into consideration the benefits to the child of access to information and services, and risks to the security and privacy of the child, in regulations promulgated under this subsection;

(D) the name of the child and online contact information (to the extent reasonably necessary to protect the safety of a child participant on the site)—

(i) used only for the purpose of protecting such safety;

(ii) not used to recontact the child or for any other purpose; and

(iii) not disclosed on the site,

if the operator uses reasonable efforts to provide a parent notice of the name and online contact information collected from the child, the purposes for which it is to be used, and an opportunity for the parent to request that the operator make no further use of the information and that it not be maintained in retrievable form; or

(E) the collection, use, or dissemination of such information by the operator of such a website or online service necessary—

(i) to protect the security or integrity of its website;

(ii) to take precautions against liability;

(iii) to respond to judicial process; or

(iv) to the extent permitted under other provisions of law, to provide information to law enforcement agencies or for an investigation on a matter related to public safety.

(3) TERMINATION OF SERVICE.—The regulations shall permit the operator of a website or an online service to terminate service provided to a child whose parent has refused, under the regulations prescribed under paragraph (1)(B)(ii), to permit the operator's further use or maintenance in retrievable form, or future online collection, of personal information from that child.

(c) ENFORCEMENT.—Subject to sections 1304 and 1306, a violation of a regulation prescribed under subsection (a) shall be treated as a violation of a rule defining an unfair or deceptive act or practice prescribed under section 18(a)(1)(B) of the Federal Trade Commission Act (15 U.S.C. 57a(a)(1)(B)).

(d) INCONSISTENT STATE LAW.—No State or local government may impose any liability for commercial activities or actions by operators in interstate or foreign commerce in connection with an activity or action described in this title that is inconsistent with the treatment of those activities or actions under this section.

SEC. 1304. [15 U.S.C. 6503] SAFE HARBORS.

(a) GUIDELINES.—An operator may satisfy the requirements of regulations issued under section 1303(b) by following a set of self-regulatory guidelines, issued by representatives of the marketing or online industries, or by other persons, approved under subsection (b).

(b) INCENTIVES.—

(1) SELF-REGULATORY INCENTIVES.—In prescribing regulations under section 1303, the Commission shall provide incentives for self-regulation by operators to implement the protections afforded children under the regulatory requirements described in subsection (b) of that section.

(2) DEEMED COMPLIANCE.—Such incentives shall include provisions for ensuring that a person will be deemed to be in compliance with the requirements of the regulations under section 1303 if that person complies with guidelines that, after notice and comment, are approved by the Commission upon making a determination that the guidelines meet the requirements of the regulations issued under section 1303.

(3) EXPEDITED RESPONSE TO REQUESTS.—The Commission shall act upon requests for safe harbor treatment within 180 days of the filing of the request, and shall set forth in writing its conclusions with regard to such requests.

(c) APPEALS.—Final action by the Commission on a request for approval of guidelines, or the failure to act within 180 days on a request for approval of guidelines, submitted under subsection (b) may be appealed to a district court of the United States of appropriate jurisdiction as provided for in section 706 of title 5, United States Code.

SEC. 1305. [15 U.S.C. 6504] ACTIONS BY STATES.

(a) IN GENERAL.—

(1) CIVIL ACTIONS.—In any case in which the attorney general of a State has reason to believe that an interest of the residents of that State has been or is threatened or adversely affected by the engagement of any person in a practice that violates any regulation of the Commission prescribed under section 1303(b), the State, as parens patriae, may bring a civil action on behalf of the residents of the State in a district court of the United States of appropriate jurisdiction to—

(A) enjoin that practice;

(B) enforce compliance with the regulation;

(C) obtain damage, restitution, or other compensation on behalf of residents of the State; or

(D) obtain such other relief as the court may consider to be appropriate.

(2) NOTICE.—

(A) IN GENERAL.—Before filing an action under paragraph (1), the attorney general of the State involved shall provide to the Commission—

(i) written notice of that action; and

(ii) a copy of the complaint for that action.

(B) EXEMPTION.—

(i) IN GENERAL.—Subparagraph (A) shall not apply with respect to the filing of an action by an attorney general of a State under this subsection, if the attorney general determines that it is not feasible to provide the notice described in that subparagraph before the filing of the action.

(ii) NOTIFICATION.—In an action described in clause (i), the attorney general of a State shall provide notice and a copy of the complaint to the Commission at the same time as the attorney general files the action.

(b) INTERVENTION.—

(1) IN GENERAL.—On receiving notice under subsection (a)(2), the Commission shall have the right to intervene in the action that is the subject of the notice.

(2) EFFECT OF INTERVENTION.—If the Commission intervenes in an action under subsection (a), it shall have the right—

(A) to be heard with respect to any matter that arises in that action; and

(B) to file a petition for appeal.

(3) AMICUS CURIAE.—Upon application to the court, a person whose self-regulatory guidelines have been approved by the Commission and are relied upon as a defense by any defendant to a proceeding under this section may file amicus curiae in that proceeding.

(c) CONSTRUCTION.—For purposes of bringing any civil action under subsection (a), nothing in this title shall be construed to prevent an attorney general of a State from exercising the powers conferred on the attorney general by the laws of that State to—

(1) conduct investigations;

(2) administer oaths or affirmations; or

(3) compel the attendance of witnesses or the production of documentary and other evidence.

(d) ACTIONS BY THE COMMISSION.—In any case in which an action is instituted by or on behalf of the Commission for violation of any regulation prescribed under section 1303, no State may, during the pendency of that action, institute an action under subsection (a) against any defendant named in the complaint in that action for violation of that regulation.

(e) VENUE; SERVICE OF PROCESS.—

(1) VENUE.—Any action brought under subsection (a) may be brought in the district court of the United States that meets applicable requirements relating to venue under section 1391 of title 28, United States Code.

(2) SERVICE OF PROCESS.—In an action brought under subsection (a), process may be served in any district in which the defendant—

(A) is an inhabitant; or

(B) may be found.

SEC. 1306. [15 U.S.C. 6505] ADMINISTRATION AND APPLICABILITY OF ACT.

(a) IN GENERAL.—Except as otherwise provided, this title shall be enforced by the Commission under the Federal Trade Commission Act (15 U.S.C. 41 et seq.).

(b) PROVISIONS.—Compliance with the requirements imposed under this title shall be enforced under—

(1) section 8 of the Federal Deposit Insurance Act (12 U.S.C. 1818), in the case of—

(A) national banks, and Federal branches and Federal agencies of foreign banks, by the Office of the Comptroller of the Currency;

(B) member banks of the Federal Reserve System (other than national banks), branches and agencies of foreign banks (other than Federal branches, Federal agencies, and insured State branches of foreign banks), commercial lending companies owned or controlled by foreign banks, and organizations operating under section 25 or 25(a) of the Federal Reserve Act (12 U.S.C. 601 et seq. and 611 et seq.), by the Board; and

(C) banks insured by the Federal Deposit Insurance Corporation (other than members of the Federal Reserve System) and insured State branches of foreign banks, by the Board of Directors of the Federal Deposit Insurance Corporation;

(2) section 8 of the Federal Deposit Insurance Act (12 U.S.C. 1818), by the Director of the Office of Thrift Supervision, in the case of a savings association the deposits of which are insured by the Federal Deposit Insurance Corporation;

(3) the Federal Credit Union Act (12 U.S.C. 1751 et seq.) by the National Credit Union Administration Board with respect to any Federal credit union;

(4) part A of subtitle VII of title 49, United States Code, by the Secretary of Transportation with respect to any air carrier or foreign air carrier subject to that part;

(5) the Packers and Stockyards Act, 1921 (7 U.S.C. 181 et seq.) (except as provided in section 406 of that Act (7 U.S.C. 226, 227)), by the Secretary of Agriculture with respect to any activities subject to that Act; and

(6) the Farm Credit Act of 1971 (12 U.S.C. 2001 et seq.) by the Farm Credit Administration with respect to any Federal land bank, Federal land bank association, Federal intermediate credit bank, or production credit association.

(c) EXERCISE OF CERTAIN POWERS.—For the purpose of the exercise by any agency referred to in subsection (a) of its powers under any Act referred to in that subsection, a violation of any requirement imposed under this title shall be deemed to be a violation of a requirement imposed under that Act. In addition to its powers under any provision of law specifically referred to in subsection (a), each of the agencies referred to in that subsection may exercise, for the purpose of enforcing compliance with any requirement imposed under this title, any other authority conferred on it by law.

(d) ACTIONS BY THE COMMISSION.—The Commission shall prevent any person from violating a rule of the Commission under section 1303 in the same manner, by the same means, and with the same jurisdiction, powers, and duties as though all applicable terms and provisions of the Federal Trade Commission Act (15 U.S.C. 41 et seq.) were incorporated into and made a part of this title. Any entity that violates such rule shall be subject to the penalties and entitled to the privileges and immunities provided in the Federal Trade Commission Act in the same manner, by the same means, and with the same jurisdiction, power, and duties as though all applicable terms and provisions of the Federal Trade Commission Act were incorporated into and made a part of this title.

(e) EFFECT ON OTHER LAWS.—Nothing contained in the Act shall be construed to limit the authority of the Commission under any other provisions of law.

SEC. 1307. [15 U.S.C. 6506] REVIEW.

Not later than 5 years after the effective date of the regulations initially issued under section 1303, the Commission shall—

(1) review the implementation of this title, including the effect of the implementation of this title on practices relating to the collection and disclosure of information relating to children, children's ability to obtain access to information of their choice online, and on the availability of websites directed to children; and

(2) prepare and submit to Congress a report on the results of the review under paragraph (1).

SEC. 1308. [15 U.S.C. 6501 note] EFFECTIVE DATE.

Sections 1303(a), 1305, and 1306 of this title take effect on the later of—

(1) the date that is 18 months after the date of enactment of this Act; or

(2) the date on which the Commission rules on the first application filed for safe harbor treatment under section 1304 if the Commission does not rule on the first such application within one year after the date of enactment of this Act, but in no case later than the date that is 30 months after the date of enactment of this Act.

* * * * * * *

TITLE XVII—GOVERNMENT PAPERWORK ELIMINATION ACT

SEC. 1701. SHORT TITLE.

This title may be cited as the "Government Paperwork Elimination Act".

SEC. 1702. AUTHORITY OF OMB TO PROVIDE FOR ACQUISITION AND USE OF ALTERNATIVE INFORMATION TECHNOLOGIES BY EXECUTIVE AGENCIES.

Section 3504(a)(1)(B)(vi) of title 44, United States Code, is amended to read as follows:

SEC. 1703. PROCEDURES FOR USE AND ACCEPTANCE OF ELECTRONIC SIGNATURES BY EXECUTIVE AGENCIES.

(a) IN GENERAL.—In order to fulfill the responsibility to administer the functions assigned under chapter 35 of title 44, United States Code, the provisions of the Clinger-Cohen Act of 1996 (divisions D and E of Public Law 104–106) and the amendments made by that Act, and the provisions of this title, the Director of the Office of Management and Budget shall, in consultation with the National Telecommunications and Information Administration and not later than 18 months after the date of enactment of this Act, develop procedures for the use and acceptance of electronic signatures by Executive agencies.

(b) REQUIREMENTS FOR PROCEDURES.—(1) The procedures developed under subsection (a)—

(A) shall be compatible with standards and technology for electronic signatures that are generally used in commerce and industry and by State governments;

(B) may not inappropriately favor one industry or technology;

(C) shall ensure that electronic signatures are as reliable as is appropriate for the purpose in question and keep intact the information submitted;

(D) shall provide for the electronic acknowledgment of electronic forms that are successfully submitted; and

(E) shall, to the extent feasible and appropriate, require an Executive agency that anticipates receipt by electronic means of 50,000 or more submittals of a particular form to take all steps necessary to ensure that multiple methods of electronic signatures are available for the submittal of such form.

(2) The Director shall ensure the compatibility of the procedures under paragraph (1)(A) in consultation with appropriate private bodies and State government entities that set standards for the use and acceptance of electronic signatures.

SEC. 1704. DEADLINE FOR IMPLEMENTATION BY EXECUTIVE AGENCIES OF PROCEDURES FOR USE AND ACCEPTANCE OF ELECTRONIC SIGNATURES.

In order to fulfill the responsibility to administer the functions assigned under chapter 35 of title 44, United States Code, the provisions of the Clinger-Cohen Act of 1996 (divisions D and E of Public Law 104–106) and the amendments made by that Act, and the provisions of this title, the Director of the Office of Management and Budget shall ensure that, commencing not later than five years after the date of enactment of this Act, Executive agencies provide—

(1) for the option of the electronic maintenance, submission, or disclosure of information, when practicable as a substitute for paper; and

(2) for the use and acceptance of electronic signatures, when practicable.

SEC. 1705. ELECTRONIC STORAGE AND FILING OF EMPLOYMENT FORMS.

In order to fulfill the responsibility to administer the functions assigned under chapter 35 of title 44, United States Code, the provisions of the Clinger-Cohen Act of 1996 (divisions D and E of Public Law 104–106) and the amendments made by that Act, and the provisions of this title, the Director of the Office of Management and Budget shall, not later than 18 months after the date of enactment of this Act, develop procedures to permit private employers to store and file electronically with Executive agencies forms containing information pertaining to the employees of such employers.

SEC. 1706. STUDY ON USE OF ELECTRONIC SIGNATURES.

(a) ONGOING STUDY REQUIRED.—In order to fulfill the

responsibility to administer the functions assigned under chapter 35 of title 44, United States Code, the provisions of the Clinger-Cohen Act of 1996 (divisions D and E of Public Law 104–106) and the amendments made by that Act, and the provisions of this title, the Director of the Office of Management and Budget shall, in cooperation with the National Telecommunications and Information Administration, conduct an ongoing study of the use of electronic signatures under this title on—

(1) paperwork reduction and electronic commerce;

(2) individual privacy; and

(3) the security and authenticity of transactions.

(b) REPORTS.—The Director shall submit to Congress on a periodic basis a report describing the results of the study carried out under subsection (a).

SEC. 1707. ENFORCEABILITY AND LEGAL EFFECT OF ELECTRONIC RECORDS.

Electronic records submitted or maintained in accordance with procedures developed under this title, or electronic signatures or other forms of electronic authentication used in accordance with such procedures, shall not be denied legal effect, validity, or enforceability because such records are in electronic form.

SEC. 1708. DISCLOSURE OF INFORMATION.

Except as provided by law, information collected in the provision of electronic signature services for communications with an executive agency, as provided by this title, shall only be used or disclosed by persons who obtain, collect, or maintain such information as a business or government practice, for the purpose of facilitating such communications, or with the prior affirmative consent of the person about whom the information pertains.

SEC. 1709. APPLICATION WITH INTERNAL REVENUE LAWS.

No provision of this title shall apply to the Department of the Treasury or the Internal Revenue Service to the extent that such provision—

(1) involves the administration of the internal revenue laws; or

(2) conflicts with any provision of the Internal Revenue Service Restructuring and Reform Act of 1998 or the Internal

Revenue Code of 1986.

SEC. 1710. DEFINITIONS.

For purposes of this title:

(1) ELECTRONIC SIGNATURE.—The term "electronic signature" means a method of signing an electronic message that—

(A) identifies and authenticates a particular person as the source of the electronic message; and

(B) indicates such person's approval of the information contained in the electronic message.

(2) EXECUTIVE AGENCY.—The term "Executive agency" has the meaning given that term in section 105 of title 5, United States Code.

* * * * * * *

49 U.S.C. - SECTIONS 109 AND 1131

TITLE 49—TRANSPORTATION

This title was enacted by Pub. L. 95–473, §1, Oct. 17, 1978, 92 Stat. 1337; Pub. L. 97–449, §1, Jan. 12, 1983, 96 Stat. 2413; Pub. L. 103–272, July 5, 1994, 108 Stat. 745

* * * * * * *

SUBTITLE I—DEPARTMENT OF TRANSPORTATION

* * * * * * *

CHAPTER 1—ORGANIZATION

* * * * * * *

§109. MARITIME ADMINISTRATION

(a) ORGANIZATION AND MISSION.—The Maritime Administration is an administration in the Department of Transportation. The mission of the Maritime Administration is to foster, promote, and develop the merchant maritime industry of the United States.

(b) MARITIME ADMINISTRATOR.—The head of the Maritime Administration is the Maritime Administrator, who is appointed by the President by and with the advice and consent of the Senate. The Administrator shall report directly to the Secretary of Transportation and carry out the duties prescribed by the Secretary.

(c) DEPUTY MARITIME ADMINISTRATOR.—The Maritime Administration shall have a

Deputy Maritime Administrator, who is appointed in the competitive service by the Secretary, after consultation with the Administrator. The Deputy Administrator shall carry out the duties prescribed by the Administrator. The Deputy Administrator shall be Acting Administrator during the absence or disability of the Administrator and, unless the Secretary designates another individual, during a vacancy in the office of Administrator.

(d) DUTIES AND POWERS VESTED IN SECRETARY.—All duties and powers of the Maritime Administration are vested in the Secretary.

(e) REGIONAL OFFICES.—The Maritime Administration shall have regional offices for the Atlantic, Gulf, Great Lakes, and Pacific port ranges, and may have other regional offices as necessary. The Secretary shall appoint a qualified individual as Director of each regional office. The Secretary shall carry out appropriate activities and programs of the Maritime Administration through the regional offices.

(f) INTERAGENCY AND INDUSTRY RELATIONS.—The Secretary shall establish and maintain liaison with other agencies, and with representative trade organizations throughout the United States, concerned with the transportation of commodities by water in the export and import foreign commerce of the United States, for the purpose of securing preference to vessels of the United States for the transportation of those commodities.

(g) DETAILING OFFICERS FROM ARMED FORCES.—To assist the Secretary in carrying out duties and powers relating to the Maritime Administration, not more than five officers of the armed forces may be detailed to the Secretary at any one time, in addition to details authorized by any other law. During the period of a detail, the Secretary shall pay the officer an amount that, when added to the officer's pay and allowances as an officer in the armed forces, makes the officer's total pay and allowances equal to the amount that would be paid to an individual performing work the Secretary considers to be of similar importance, difficulty, and responsibility as that performed by the officer during the detail.

(h) CONTRACTS, COOPERATIVE AGREEMENTS, AND AUDITS.—

(1) CONTRACTS AND COOPERATIVE AGREEMENTS.—In the same manner that a private corporation may make a contract within the scope of its authority under its charter, the Secretary may make contracts and cooperative agreements for the United States Government and disburse amounts to—

(A) carry out the Secretary's duties and powers under this section, subtitle V of title 46, and all other Maritime Administration programs; and

(B) protect, preserve, and improve collateral held by the Secretary to secure indebtedness.

(2) AUDITS.—The financial transactions of the Secretary under paragraph (1) shall be audited by the Comptroller General. The Comptroller General shall allow credit for an expenditure shown to be necessary because of the nature of the business activities authorized by this section or subtitle V of title 46. At least once a year, the Comptroller General shall report to Congress any departure by the Secretary from this section or subtitle V of title 46.

(i) GRANT ADMINISTRATIVE EXPENSES.—Except as otherwise provided by law, the administrative and related expenses for the administration of any grant programs by the Maritime Administrator may not exceed 3 percent.

(j) AUTHORIZATION OF APPROPRIATIONS.—

(1) IN GENERAL.—Except as otherwise provided in this subsection, there are authorized to be appropriated such amounts as may be necessary to carry out the duties and powers of the Secretary relating to the Maritime Administration.

(2) LIMITATIONS.—Only those amounts specifically authorized by law may be appropriated for the use of the Maritime Administration for—

(A) acquisition, construction, or reconstruction of vessels;

(B) construction-differential subsidies incident to the construction, reconstruction, or reconditioning of vessels;

(C) costs of national defense features;

(D) payments of obligations incurred for operating-differential subsidies;

(E) expenses necessary for research and development activities, including reimbursement of the Vessel Operations Revolving Fund for losses resulting from expenses of experimental vessel operations;

(F) the Vessel Operations Revolving Fund;

(G) National Defense Reserve Fleet expenses;

(H) expenses necessary to carry out part B of subtitle V of title 46; and

(I) other operations and training expenses related to the development of waterborne transportation systems, the use of waterborne transportation systems, and general administration.

(Pub. L. 97–449, §1(b), Jan. 12, 1983, 96 Stat. 2417; Pub. L. 103–272, §5(m)(5), July 5, 1994, 108 Stat. 1375; Pub. L. 109–304, §12, Oct. 6, 2006, 120 Stat. 1698; Pub. L. 111–84, div. C, title XXXV, §3508, Oct. 28, 2009, 123 Stat. 2721; Pub. L. 111–383, div. A, title X, §1075(d)(26), Jan. 7, 2011, 124 Stat. 4374; Pub. L. 112–213, title IV, §409, Dec. 20, 2012, 126 Stat. 1572; Pub. L. 114–328, div. C, title XXXV, §3505(g), Dec. 23, 2016, 130 Stat. 2776.)

* * * * * * *

SUBTITLE II—OTHER GOVERNMENT AGENCIES

Chapter	Sec.
11. National Transportation Safety Board	1101

* * * * * * *

CHAPTER 11—NATIONAL TRANSPORTATION SAFETY BOARD

* * * * * * *

SUBCHAPTER III—AUTHORITY

1131.   General authority.

* * * * * * *

535

SUBCHAPTER III—AUTHORITY

§1131. GENERAL AUTHORITY

(a) GENERAL.—(1) The National Transportation Safety Board shall investigate or have investigated (in detail the Board prescribes) and establish the facts, circumstances, and cause or probable cause of—

(A) an aircraft accident the Board has authority to investigate under section 1132 of this title or an aircraft accident involving a public aircraft as defined by section 40102(a) of this title other than an aircraft operated by the Armed Forces or by an intelligence agency of the United States;

(B) a highway accident, including a railroad grade crossing accident, the Board selects, concurrent with any State investigation, in which case the Board and the relevant State agencies shall coordinate to ensure both the Board and State agencies have timely access to the information needed to conduct each such investigation, including any criminal and enforcement activities conducted by the relevant State agency;

(C) a railroad—

(i) accident in which there is a fatality or substantial property damage, except—

(I) a grade crossing accident or incident, unless selected by the Board; or

(II) an accident or incident involving a trespasser, unless selected by the Board; or

(ii) accident or incident that involves a passenger train, except in any case in which such accident or incident resulted in no fatalities or serious injuries to the passengers or crewmembers of such train, and—

(I) was a grade crossing accident or incident, unless selected by the Board; or

(II) such accident or incident involved a trespasser, unless selected by the Board;

(D) a pipeline accident in which there is a fatality, substantial property damage, or significant injury to the environment;

(E) a major marine casualty (except a casualty involving only public vessels) occurring on or under the navigable waters, internal waters, or the territorial sea of the United States as described in Presidential Proclamation No. 5928 of December 27, 1988, or involving a vessel of the United States (as defined in section 116 of title 46), under regulations prescribed jointly by the Board and the head of the department in which the Coast Guard is operating; and

(F) any other accident related to the transportation of individuals or property when the Board decides—

(i) the accident is catastrophic;

(ii) the accident involves problems of a recurring character; or

(iii) the investigation of the accident would carry out this chapter.

(2)(A) Subject to the requirements of this paragraph, an investigation by the Board under paragraph (1)(A)–(D) or (F) of this subsection has priority over any investigation by another department, agency, or instrumentality of the United States Government. The Board shall provide for appropriate participation by other departments, agencies, or instrumentalities in the investigation. However, those departments, agencies, or instrumentalities may not participate in the decision of the Board about the probable cause of the accident.

(B) If the Attorney General, in consultation with the Chairman of the Board, determines and notifies the Board that circumstances reasonably indicate that the accident may have been caused by an intentional criminal act, the Board shall relinquish investigative priority to the Federal Bureau of Investigation. The relinquishment of investigative priority by the Board shall not otherwise affect the authority of the Board to continue its investigation under this section.

(C) If a Federal law enforcement agency suspects and notifies the Board that an accident being investigated by the Board under subparagraph (A), (B), (C), or (D) of paragraph (1) may have been caused by an intentional criminal act, the Board, in consultation with the law enforcement agency, shall take necessary actions to ensure that evidence of the criminal act is preserved.

(3) This section and sections 1113, 1116(b), 1133, and 1134(a) and (c)–(e) of this title do not affect the authority of another department, agency, or instrumentality of the Government to investigate an accident under applicable law or to obtain information directly from the parties involved in, and witnesses to, the accident. The Board and other departments, agencies, and instrumentalities shall ensure that appropriate information developed about the accident is exchanged in a timely manner.

(b) ACCIDENTS INVOLVING PUBLIC VESSELS.—(1) The Board or the head of the department in which the Coast Guard is operating shall investigate and establish the facts, circumstances, and cause or probable cause of a marine accident involving a public vessel and any other vessel. The results of the investigation shall be made available to the public.

(2) Paragraph (1) of this subsection and subsection (a)(1)(E) of this section do not affect the responsibility, under another law of the United States, of the head of the department in which the Coast Guard is operating.

(c) ACCIDENTS NOT INVOLVING GOVERNMENT MISFEASANCE OR NONFEASANCE.—(1) When asked by the Board, the Secretary of Transportation or the Secretary of the department in which the Coast Guard is operating may—

(A) investigate an accident described under subsection (a) or (b) of this section in which misfeasance or nonfeasance by the Government has not been alleged; and

(B) report the facts and circumstances of the accident to the Board.

(2) The Board shall use the report in establishing cause or probable cause of an accident described under subsection (a) or (b) of this section.

(d) ACCIDENTS INVOLVING PUBLIC AIRCRAFT.—The Board, in furtherance of its investigative duties with respect to public aircraft accidents under subsection (a)(1)(A) of this section, shall have the same duties and powers as are specified for civil aircraft accidents under sections 1132(a), 1132(b), and 1134(a), (b), (d), and (f) of this title.

(e) ACCIDENT REPORTS.—The Board shall report on the facts and circumstances of each accident investigated by it under subsection (a) or (b) of this section. The Board shall make each report available to the public—

(1) in electronic form at no cost in a publicly accessible database on a website of the Board; and

(2) if the electronic form required in paragraph (1) is not printable, in printed form upon a reasonable request at a reasonable cost.

(f) TIMELINESS OF REPORTS.—If any accident report under subsection (e) is not completed within 2 years from the date of the accident, the Board shall submit to the Committee on Transportation and Infrastructure of the House of Representatives and the Committee on Commerce, Science, and Transportation of the Senate a report identifying such accident report and the reasons for which such report has not been completed. The Board shall report progress toward completion of the accident report to each such Committees every 90 days thereafter, until such time as the accident report is completed.

(Pub. L. 103–272, §1(d), July 5, 1994, 108 Stat. 752; Pub. L. 103–411, §3(c), Oct. 25, 1994, 108 Stat. 4237; Pub. L. 106–424, §§6(a), 7, Nov. 1, 2000, 114 Stat. 1885, 1886; Pub. L. 108–168, §7, Dec. 6, 2003, 117 Stat. 2034; Pub. L. 109–443, §9(b), (c), Dec. 21, 2006, 120 Stat. 3301; Pub. L. 115–254, div. C, §1113(b), Oct. 5, 2018, 132 Stat. 3438; Pub. L. 117–263, div. K, title CXVI, §11601(c)(3), Dec. 23, 2022, 136 Stat. 4146; Pub. L. 118–63, title XII, §§1210–1212, May 16, 2024, 138 Stat. 1425, 1426.)